THE NECESSARY DREAM

A STUDY OF THE NOVELS OF MANUEL PUIG

The Necessary Dream

A Study of the Novels of Manuel Puig

PAMELA BACARISSE

BARNES & NOBLE BOOKS
TOTOWA, NEW JERSEY

Published in Great Britain by
The University of Wales Press, 1988

First published in the USA 1988 by
BARNES & NOBLE BOOKS
81 ADAMS DRIVE
TOTOWA, NEW JERSEY, 07512

Library of Congress Cataloging-in-Publication Data

Bacarisse, Pamela.
    The necessary dream: a study of the novels of Manuel Puig / by
Pamela Bacarisse.
      p. cm.
    Includes index.
    ISBN 0-389-20809-4
    1. Puig, Manuel – Criticism and interpretation. I. Title.
PQ7798.26.U4Z6 1988
863 – dc19
                                      88 – 23243
                                         CIP

Set by Quality Phototypesetting Ltd, Bristol
Printed in Great Britain at The Bath Press, Avon

FOR CLAIRE AND BENJAMIN

Contents

Acknowledgements

My warmest gratitude goes to all thse who in so many different ways have made the preparation of this book a pleasure: the Marcondes de Souza family of Rio de Janeiro, whose friendship, hospitality and help can never be repaid; Sr Ítalo Manzi, of Paris, to whose limitless knowledge of the cinema I am greatly indebted; Professor Keith McDuffie, of the University of Pittsburgh; Dr Peter Evans of the University of Newcastle upon Tyne; my aunts, Ángeles and Carmen Cuadrado, of Madrid, without whose help I should still be writing the book; the Joint Committee of the University of Aberdeen Travel Fund for a subvention towards a visit to South America; my colleagues Dr John Cummins and Dr Ian Macdonald, for their unfailing support and the extra work they undertook during my period of study leave; and Mrs Doreen Davidson, secretary to the University of Aberdeen Department of Spanish, who produced the various versions of the typescript with patience and skill. I should also like to express my most sincere thanks to Manuel Puig himself, a helpful and encouraging friend, a generous host and a wonderful correspondent.

CHAPTER I

Introduction

> Hay escritores que tienen sólo críticos y escritores que tienen sólo
> público. Otros, pocos y afortunados, poseen ambas cosas a la vez.
> Puig pertenece a esta última categoría . . .
>
> There are writers who have only critics and writers who have only
> readers. Others, the fortunate few, have both at the same time.
> Puig belongs to this latter group . . .
>
> Nora Catelli, 'El caso Puig'

IT was in 1968 that the Argentine novelist Manuel Puig published his
first book,[1] and though his work met with a fairly cool reception at the
time, both from the public and from critics, he is now, of course, one of
Latin America's best-known writers. He has produced five more very
successful novels, some of them best sellers,[2] the most recent being
Sangre de amor correspondido.[3] He has also turned his hand to plays and
film scripts to no small effect. For many years Puig might have been
judged unique. On the one hand his work impressed academic critics,
who saw it as original, significant and seminal, while on the other he
was a *popular* author, and his fame was, and still is, by no means
restricted to Argentina or the Spanish-speaking world. Some of the
translations of his books have broken records in their own right:[4] for
instance, in Brazil the Portuguese version of *El beso de la mujer araña*
(1976) was in the top-ten list for an unprecedented number of months.[5]

There is an apparently simple explanation for his proven ability to
please both literary critics and the ordinary reader: Manuel Puig
managed to achieve a balance between what we might call literature of

consensus — something similar to the pulp fiction that appeals to the masses — and, for want of a better term, High Art. But this explanation actually explains little. After all, these two cultural areas, with their respective styles, are usually mutually incompatible. Few lovers of Shakespeare are avid readers of sentimental novels, and it is equally unlikely that soap-opera devotees will have much time for Robbe-Grillet. To claim that Puig achieved a balance between pulp fiction and High Art is merely to describe what happened; it does not help us to understand how he did it. It would probably be going too far to classify the earlier books as pure Camp (though this aspect of his work will come under discussion later), but at least it can be claimed that, among other things, he shared with this approach[6] a capacity for belonging simultaneously to two different worlds: the world of that fiction which is directed towards the ingenuous consumer and the world of literature for the sophisticate. Some years ago the Cuban novelist Severo Sarduy pointed out that a genre that turns and looks at itself manages to go on existing while at the same time becoming a copy, perhaps even a parody of itself. 'El artificio termina señalándose a sí mismo' ('the device finishes up by pointing at itself') is how he phrased it, and he illustrates this by claiming that Puig's second book, *Boquitas pintadas,* is not only a 'folletín casi perfecto' ('an almost perfect novelette') but also 'el doble irrisorio de folletín' ('the ludicrous carbon copy of a novelette').[7] Where the general public is concerned, the formats — the detective-story structure used in *The Buenos Aires Affair,* the science-fiction passages in *Pubis angelical,* the film melodramas recounted in *El beso de la mujer araña* — combined with the element of universal pathos that is invariably found in Puig's novels, provided the same kind of pleasure as pulp fiction, photo-novels and televised soap operas do, a pleasure that a large number of ordinary readers and viewers in so many countries relish and even consider an essential part of their lives. Even so, it is tempting to ask what there was in the first four or five books that was appealing for the 'serious' critic.

When Sarduy classified *Boquitas pintadas* as an *almost* perfect novelette, he gave us a clue towards a possible answer. It was this very 'imperfection' in the genre imitation that made Puig's writing so special. The imperfection, paradoxically, consisted of what was *added* to the model; if the copy had been flawless it would have been impossible to classify it as High Art. So it was that the knowing reader had a chance of enjoying two different experiences and sensations. It seems that whatever the reason may be, some examples of mass culture possess something that is immediately attractive, almost instinctively so, and the critic is human enough to be able to enjoy this. But, unlike the uninitiated reader, he stands back, analyses his own reactions and cheerfully has things both ways.

Even the 'serious' reader finds an inordinate amount of pleasure in the earlier works of Puig. He is encouraged and consoled some of the time by facile values and received truths, but is still able to see himself as intellectually superior to those to whom it would never occur to dispute these. He can wallow in soothing security and emotional comfort yet dissociate himself from the experience, as he is perfectly well aware of what he is doing and why. No doubt words such as 'sentimental', 'false' and 'romantic' will come into his considered judgements, but since he will see himself as an uninvolved observer, he can go on enjoying himself.

The situation raises some fairly tricky questions. Why, for example, are his illusions not totally destroyed when he recognizes them for what they are? And we might add that this is a problem of fundamental importance, since dreams and illusion are so vital a part of Puig's writing, and at least some of his characters — frequently looking to the most incongruous, even bizarre, models — survive by means of them. When 'serious' critics enjoy these sentimental, false and romantic illusions, does this mean that there is no difference between them and the pitiful, deceived fictional characters? And since, when we study them more carefully, we find that by no means all these fictional characters truly believe in whatever it is that keeps them going, and some even reject it, could it be that the dichotomy between the ingenuous and the sophisticated reader does not actually exist?

As I hope to demonstrate in the course of this book, the answer to these questions is a complex one. My considered opinion is one based on my conviction that a dichotomy does actually exist, but that it is of a different nature from that implied in the questions. It is not, of course, that the cultured reader is not susceptible to the consolatory elements in pulp fiction or that he is uninterested in the all too easily recognizable formats that it employs. (The universal popularity of the detective story proves this point.) Neither is it true that he is a stranger to false illusions, even if he is basically aware of their lack of foundation. Dreams are necessary for everyone, and ill-founded optimism and the hope of comfort and security are not confined to the unthinking or the uneducated. With *La traición de Rita Hayworth, Boquitas pintadas, The Buenos Aires Affair, El beso de la mujer araña* and, perhaps to a lesser extent, with *Pubis angelical,* Manuel Puig attracted an enormous audience by weaving into his narratives the artistic 'sub-products' of mass culture, as they have so often been called, and these attract virtually everybody, provided that their presentation is technically skilful. This it undoubtedly was and, furthermore, what was added to these — perceptiveness and even profundity — provided a fruitful experience for the 'serious' reader.

The more appropriate question is not why two areas of the reading public who usually have mutually incompatible values and tastes should have been seduced by these novels, but why the later works have lost their popular appeal, for this is unquestionably what has happened. I shall consider this problem in more detail during the course of the book, but the simple answer seems to be that as Puig has matured as a writer, his novels have demonstrated more and more clearly that essential complexity which, in my view, they have always contained. A depressing, even unpalatable, vision of life, no longer even superficially sweetened by palliatives as the mass-media elements are left behind, is increasingly evident. When this world-view is presented in a difficult style, for Puig insists on experimenting with a totally new format for every narrative, this can be taxing, making demands on the reader that may seem unwarranted to those who recognized only the surface elements of *Boquitas pintadas,* for example, and perhaps even misunderstood those. Though it may be somewhat simplistic arbitrarily to divide the reading public into two polarized categories, I would maintain that there is a dichotomy between ingenuous and what I have chosen to call 'sophisticated' readers, though I use the word 'sophisticated' without any of its pejorative connotations, thinking only of those whose experience and knowledge of literature is such that they are disposed and able to contribute to a work what a serious author asks them to; in this way they play a part in the actual creation of a work of art. In his later books, Puig has lost his mass audience because of the fact that he has purged his texts of comforting elements and has taken even greater steps in the direction of novelty in form. So it is that he is no longer unique as a writer, but I would claim that this does not necessarily indicate a decline in quality.

All the novels demand a psychological approach, and even in *Maldición eterna a quien lea estas páginas* and *Sangre de amor correspondido* (1980 and 1982 respectively), the question of the efficacy of dreams and illusion is a major one. However, people are as they are for a multitude of reasons. Given the wide-ranging background of the texts, it is inevitable that in addition to reference to Freudian and Lacanian theory, to which the author often alludes, and some elaboration on my own assertion in the chapter on *Sangre de amor correspondido* that the views of Otto Rank are the most relevant for any interpretation of Puig's characters, our attention will necessarily be drawn to other areas that influence the condition of the human psyche and man's capacity for living in the world. These are often connected with psychology, of course, and include the relationship between the sexes, the role of women, machismo, homosexuality and bisexuality, sadism and masochism, sexuality as a pivot of power, family relationships, the consciousness of death, the sources and function of emotion, attitudes towards religion and the causes of alienation. Then there are those areas in which society and the individual clash: the conflict between a conditioned sense of duty and personal drives, desires and affections, for example; gender roles and their problems; Marxism and its relationship with psychology; myth versus practicality and the common good. Politics are not without their importance in Puig either, and the anomalous position of the first-generation Argentine immigrant and Peronism are subjects that will be dealt with under this heading. Perhaps most striking, if not most important of all, there is the question of indoctrination by means of culture, whether home-grown or imported; I shall consider, for example, the influence of the bogus values of Hollywood and their connection with the therapeutic elements of fairy-tales, as well as popular culture — the photo-novel, the tango, the detective story and the novelette. Finally there is the writing itself, and I shall touch on irony, pointing out how Puig has managed to vary the usual ironic mode, Camp literature, parody, and the language employed.

The purpose behind this book is not just the traditional one of attempting to interpret the various texts in a way that might be helpful and illuminating to other readers, though I would be delighted if that were to prove the case. In addition to that presumptuous ambition, I should very much like to persuade others that there has been no waning of Manuel Puig's powers with the last two or three novels, but that on the contrary, they constitute a rewarding literary experience if read with a mind not coloured by the assumptions created by the enjoyment of the first works, which in any case were also fundamentally serious and provocative.

CHAPTER II

'La Vie est ailleurs':
La traición de Rita Hayworth (1968)

> . . . the movies characteristically offer us packs of lies, but we
> would not consume these lies avidly unless we needed them.
>
> Michael Wood, *America in the Movies*

THERE is little doubt that contemporary Latin-American authors suffer more than most from their critics' inability to reach a consensus of opinion about the orientation of their writings. With seemingly endless and insoluble political, social and cultural problems so much to the fore in their countries, there is no shortage of people who believe that all authors are involved in a constant explicit struggle for social justice, equality and the betterment of their environment, even if so many of them do now live in either voluntary or forced exile. These critics are shocked that there could still be artists who indulge in the luxury of concerning themselves as much with the individual as with society and its effect on him. They would probably go as far as to say that it is, at the very least, reprehensible to play down the question of social revolt. Since the Cuban Revolution, there have been many widely-reported disputes on the subject of the artist's role, and some writers such as Gabriel García Márquez have declared themselves unequivocally committed as far as both politics and society are concerned; others have reserved for themselves the right to be what the Chilean novelist José Donoso once described as 'socialmente inútiles' ('socially useless') in order to be 'culturalmente útiles' ('culturally useful').[1] Many people cannot bring themselves to accept that the aim of 'cultural usefulness' is a valid one, especially when the environment and lack of culture in the life-styles of fictional characters are obviously vital elements, and it is tempting to assign social causes to virtually all problems. It is not without irony that Donoso himself is sometimes seen as basically a socially-committed writer.

When *La traición de Rita Hayworth* came out in 1968, several critics were lured into seeing it merely as a kind of neo-naturalist panorama, with the almost sociological aim of describing how the inhabitants of a small Argentine town live, without culture, with little opportunity for education of any value and, indeed, with few opportunities for anything at all. It seemed to them undeniable that the focus, the essential core, of the novel was the small-town setting. And, of course, it would be absurd to deny that this plays an important part. Puig himself, when recounting his early efforts to write what he originally planned as a film script, admits that he determined to talk about people he knew.[2] About his home town, that is to say. But this does not alter the fact that this is not just a socially-orientated book: there is no explicit authorial concern at this stage about the economic or political causes of conditions and, in writing about 'people he knew' Puig found himself involved in an infinitely more complex activity than could possibly have been foreseen. In the same way that what was supposed to be a film script turned itself into a novel, a view of provincial Argentine society became imbued with insight into the human condition that far transcends its theoretical limitations.

Nevertheless, as we have said, the setting of the novel — which was to be the same for the next book, *Boquitas pintadas* (1969) — is important in the representation of those human truths that pervade all Puig's works, aspects of what the American critic, Alfred J. MacAdam, has called 'human underdevelopment'.[3] It might even be claimed that a small town is where this is most likely to be found, for it is where the abyss that, it seems, always exists between the difficult, tedious and limited reality of everyday life and the paradise dreamt of by the pathetic human beings condemned to live it out, is most apparent. Reflecting the student graffiti that were seen during the so-called *événements* of 1968 in Paris, for Puig's characters 'la vie est ailleurs' — real life is somewhere else. MacAdam has this to say on the subject:

> Reality must be 'somewhere else' for Puig's characters because Coronel Vallejos, the setting of both books, is merely a satellite of Buenos Aires, itself a copy of larger worlds, the world created by Hollywood, the world of cheap literature, with its wars and romances, and the world of popular music, where male and female relationships are expressed as grand archetypes.[4]

The 'Coronel Vallejos' of the first two books is General Villegas, a town on the Pampa more than 250 miles from Buenos Aires, where Manuel Puig was born in 1932. There, 'la vida era muy dura, muy difícil, diría casi de *Far West*' ('life was very hard, very difficult — almost like the Far West, you might say'), the author reveals,[5] and even today, he says, there has been little improvement.[6] In an interview with a Brazilian journalist Puig described the town as he remembers it:

> . . . um lugar sem nada, longe, muito longe do mar, da montanha, de Buenos Aires. Lá não tinha paisagem, era tudo plano. Só o céu era muito claro e o ar muito seco. A cidade também era feia. *Era praticamente um exílio.* Quem nasce lá e não sai de lá, não sabe o que é a vida, nem o que o mundo tem. Por isso quando a minha mãe me levou pela primeira vez ao cinema — eu tinha quatro anos — *achei que a vida estava ali,* aquilo tudo me parecia muito real.[7]

> . . . a place that had nothing, far away, very far away from the sea and the mountains and from Buenos Aires. There was no landscape there, everything was flat. Only the sky was very bright and the air very dry. The town was ugly too. *To all intents and purposes it was like living in exile.* Anyone born there who never goes away has no idea what life is or of what there is in the world. That's why, when my mother took me to the cinema for the first time — I was four — *I thought that was where life was,* it all seemed so real to me.

The facts and events — or, at least, quite a few of them — of the life of the young protagonist, José Luis Casals, known to everyone as Toto, are also authentic. This is what Puig has said about the gestation of the book:

> Toto soy yo. La historia que pensaba escribir para el cine era sobre los amores de mi primo, pero, poco a poco, el personaje mío se fue haciendo cada vez más importante y el libro terminó siendo la historia de mi infancia con un quince por ciento de invención para redondear las cosas.[8]

> I am Toto. The story I intended to write for the screen was about my cousin's love life, but bit by bit my own character acquired more importance and the book finished up as the story of my childhood, with about fifteen per cent of it invented to round things off.

The result is that in a place that exemplifies life's incompleteness, we find a character who by virtue of being a child underlines and emphasizes this condition. Many adults feel inadequate and ignorant and are conscious of the deficiencies in their immediate surroundings, but a sensitive and intelligent child is even more aware of what he does not yet know, what he cannot do and what he is still to experience. The autobiographical nature of the book is an aid to our understanding of

Puig's attitude towards his own 'underdeveloped' characters, unquestionably victims of their circumstances but, far more important, victims of the general human condition. The characters' problems are exacerbated by the limitations of provincial Argentine life in the thirties and forties, not created by them.

The story is set in a region beset by drought (p.10),[9] where nothing will grow (p.18) and where there is nobody interesting to talk to, according to Choli, who is to all intents and purposes the only friend Mita (Ema, Toto's mother) has (p.51). The more immediate setting is a large old rented house, and it is here that Toto spends the formative period of his life. The obvious question to ask about the fifteen years that pass between his birth in 1933 and 1948, the date of the *cuaderno de pensamientos* (a kind of diary or notebook) written by his piano teacher, Herminia, is, 'What happens?' And the answer, perhaps surprisingly, is, 'Nothing'. MacAdam is one of several critics who have pointed this out: he quotes Aristotle's dictum that plot is an imitation of action and then claims that 'from an Aristotelian point of view, *La traición* has no plot because it has no action'.[10] Ricado Piglia is another who has made virtually the same observation. In a stimulating article called 'Clase media: cuerpo y destino' ('The Middle Class: Flesh and Fate'), he says categorically that the novel is no more than 'una toma de conciencia' (perhaps 'a voyage of discovery') on the part of Toto. He adds that it really has no story-line other than a description of 'las consecuencias del choque entre esas conciencias [of family, friends and acquaintances] y ese objeto decorado, "lindo" ' ('The consequences of the confrontation between the avid collective consciousness [of family, friends and acquaintances] and the decorated, "pretty" object') that is Toto.[11] Puig has said that, for him, the book constitutes a kind of inquiry into Argentine *cursilería,* or pretentious vulgarity,[12] and this suggests little preoccupation on his part with either action or plot. Furthermore, it could not even be said that the story of Toto's childhood discoveries constitutes a South-American *Bildungsroman*: there is so little sense of development and no moment of self-knowledge. As MacAdam rightly says, there is no 'coming-to-awareness'. Nevertheless, by the time we reach the end of the book we do suspect that this may one day be achieved.[13]

Instead of action we are presented with a conglomeration of short episodes, stream-of-consciousness monologues, passages of almost choral conversation, diaries, the text of a school essay, an anonymous letter, conventional dialogues and also dialogues in which only one of the voices is recorded. All this represents Toto's life and environment, using an approach that manages to avoid completely the usual third-person narrative form; instead, we judge and know by means of how people express themselves. The narrative begins and ends in the same year: 1933. Although the penultimate chapter (Herminia's *cuaderno*) dates from 1948, the novel actually finishes with the text of a letter written in 1933 by Berto (Roberto Casals, Toto's father) to his brother Jaime (father of Toto's cousin, Héctor). This circularity is an ironic variation on the usual technique; normally a return to the beginning serves as a clarification, the basis for reconsideration and analysis based on what has now been discovered. In this case, the final chapter adds relatively little, and could not be considered the key to the hotchpotch of thoughts, attitudes and minor action that has preceded it in more or less chronological order.[14] It may well be that there *is* no key: life, Puig may be saying, is formless and, perhaps, pointless. Toto and his friends certainly do not understand it, neither do his parents and their neighbours and neither, indeed, do the reader and critic. It is not, though, a question of melodramatic tragedy, even if there are tragic elements, but of something eminently sad. It deals with what ought to be beautiful and is not. There is a kind of double vision: of what life is, and of the universal human tendency to dream of what might be, even if it becomes necessary to dissimulate or lie. And of course, any dream of 'what might be' is very likely to take exotic models as its inspiration.

This is why the ambiance is important. It is not difficult to see that the inhabitants of Coronel Vallejos suffer more than most. In addition to economic and climatic problems — the droughts and basic sterility of the area are to blame for the failure of Berto's business enterprise with young bulls, for example — the characters' personal frustration is in constant evidence. Mita works as a pharmaceutical dispenser in the local hospital, but it was not what she had wanted to do with her life (p.19): her ambition had actually been to study literature at university. Furthermore, she has to live with Berto's constant failures. It is she who suggests that they go to La Plata for him to study law: he sees himself as far too old to take up a new career. Of her three children, one dies a few days after birth, but even before this tragedy we learn that she often cries, although she takes care to keep her tears for when Berto is out. Significantly, Berto's life is not without its quota of frustration either. He is clearly ambitious: he has a car, he disapproves of his wife's working, and he tries to make his way in the business world, even selling his house so as to pay for the bulls that will theoretically make his fortune. But the bulls die, Mita has to go on in her job, and in the 1933 letter that he never in fact sends he spells out all his resentment and bitterness towards Jaime, the brother who years earlier had forced him to give up school, but who was so inefficient and uncaring that he caused both of them to lose a great deal of money. Jaime is apparently enjoying life in Spain, and has left his son, Héctor, with Berto and Mita. His behaviour is disgraceful, to Berto's mind, womanizing in spite of being married, and this would appear to constitute the last straw, since Berto himself gave up a not inconsiderable career as a provincial Don Juan when he married Mita. The letter is a litany of painful memories and present fury, and Berto fails to post it simply because he is too rancorous to waste any money on the stamp. Committing words to paper is merely therapeutic for Berto, handsome, macho, highly-strung and even violent, a man who promised much but achieved little.

There is a sense of communal frustration too: everyone has similar problems. That these characters are vitally important in the book is clearly demonstrated by the amount of space taken up by the expression of their thoughts and obsessions. With the possible exception of Héctor, not one of them is happy, and they are all — even Héctor — conscious of the gap that exists between what they have and are and what they would like to have and be; if Héctor is happy it is because he is the only one who truly believes that this gap can and will be bridged. Though Toto hopes for it too, he is more intelligent and aware and therefore less confident. Since he cannot be sure about what life can provide, he acquires, for at least part of the time, the voluntary blindness that is the common feature of the adults. Héctor is older and stronger and more masculine than his cousin — he is everything Toto is not — but he is less mature. He is a boy with a great awareness of immediate reality, in one sense of the word — of his body, of his sexuality, of what is going on in the circles that he moves in — but ironically, his blindness is absolutely authentic and involuntary, since his own strength and the 'reality' he sees around him are both far less dependable than he thinks. If the mainstay of all children is hope for the future, Héctor possesses this hope in its most unadulterated, ignorant, even fatuous, form. Nevertheless, for many adults life is a school in which they have learned that optimism and enthusiasm invariably lead to cruel deception and disappointment. It is in between these two extremes that we find Toto. Though he does entertain hopes for the future like any normal child, fear and insecurity occasionally show him that life is hard, and he joins the adults in escapist stratagems.

All of them see their problems as the result of externally-imposed limitations. Perhaps the most striking example of this is Herminia, an embittered, asthmatic spinster, with few possibilities for the future. She lives with her mother in squalid conditions and makes something approaching a living by giving piano lessons. As we have seen, her *cuaderno de pensamientos* is found at a key point in the novel: it is almost the last text that we read. It is a document full of the consciousness of the world's injustice, written by someone who detests what she does for a living (p.274) and who is convinced that she will die without ever finding out what life is all about (p.289). Her own existence, she says, is like a blank page on which nothing will ever be written (p.291), but she considers herself too perspicacious to join those who look at life through rose-coloured spectacles, like Héctor. Her hopes and dreams have been destroyed, and she is temperamentally incapable of emulating Choli, a character who manages to ignore all the contradictions, absurdities and illogicalities of her outlook. If happiness does exist, Herminia has never known it, and she appears to have no way of making up for this loss — even, it seems, the capacity for self-deception. In a good example of her mannered, self-conscious style, she refers to other people's ability to store away what they want to forget in blackened cerebral whirls and furrows (p.271); but for her this kind of repression involves cowardice, and she sees herself as superior in her ability to face up to things. This is actually another form of self-deception, for she indulges in an extremely sophisticated kind of escape mechanism all the time, as will soon become clear. With at least some justification she claims that life is unfair: she is a woman; she lives in a sterile, isolated and underdeveloped place surrounded by philistines; she has no money and she is far from well. She knows that all women risk ending up as she has: a boring, ordinary old maid (p.268) whose hopes fade with her youth. The blame lies with Coronel Vallejos. She had to leave Buenos Aires because of her health, and in Vallejos, 'ni siquiera la radio se puede escuchar, fuera de las estaciones tangueras que pueden pagarse antenas fuertes para que el pueblo se eduque escuchando como el compadrito le dio una puñalada a la negra de al lado' ('you can't even listen to the radio, except for the tango stations which can afford strong signals so that people can be educated by hearing how some tough guy has stabbed the woman next door') (p.270). She wishes she could go to Buenos Aires to hear a good opera performance or see a worthwhile play just once a year — she would be more than content (p.299); or if she could revisit the mountains where she had a short holiday with her parents when she was seventeen; if she could go to Mar del Plata, since she has never seen the sea; if she had friends or, at the very least, someone to write to; if she had some money. But perhaps the most unbearable limitation is that she is in poor health. Why this should be so she cannot tell, since she has never harmed anyone (p.291).

Herminia is not the only one for whom life has neither form nor beauty. Another is Esther, an intelligent but poor and vulgar girl, a Peronist, very conscious of socio-political issues. Yet another is Choli, Mita's friend, but she has achieved a *modus vivendi* and an outlook that more or less protect her from the truth. A third example is Toto, who sometimes shares this attitude.

We have here a group of people who find themselves at various stages in the process of acquiring the knack of closing their eyes to reality. They are all aware of life's imperfections but no one admits that at least some of them come from within; instead, they combat boredom and frustration and dissatisfaction by dreaming of external improvements in their lives. The alternative would imply the acceptance of what is totally unacceptable. The tragedy lies in the fact that it is life itself that is like this, not just the provincial version of it.

The exotic models chosen by the inhabitants of Coronel Vallejos are taken from Hollywood films of the thirties and forties in the majority of cases. This is in evidence all the time, even with those who are not obviously obsessed by the cinema. For example, when Herminia recounts the story of her decision to abandon Buenos Aires, it is difficult not to recall the scene from Charles Vidor's *A Song to Remember* (1945) in which Cornel Wilde, an obviously tubercular Chopin, plays the piano and drops of blood fall on to the keys. 'Yo seguía encorvada sobre el piano,' says Herminia in her version of this scene, 'y de repente al toser me cayó saliva con sangre sobre las teclas . . .' ('I went on bent over the piano, and suddenly when I coughed saliva flecked with blood fell onto the keyboard . . .') (p.270). It is unlikely that this connection exists only in the mind of the reader. There are countless more explicit references: from the beginning of the novel to the end, the characters' criteria are imported from this incongruously alien environment, a classic example of the 'underdeveloped mentality', so often analysed and commented upon. If this were only a socio-economic problem, it would be slightly less grave, since there would be hope of a cure. But 'underdevelopment' is a fundamental human condition.

Every moment in the life of the people of Coronel Vallejos is dedicated to comparison, self-evaluation and to classifying others. Berto looks exactly like an (invented) Argentine actor called Carlos Palau (p.11); he is therefore no more than a copy of someone who could hardly be considered 'authentic' himself, since he reflects so many Hollywood heroes. It is not without pathos, either, that the only real life contact anyone has ever had with the famous, the exotic or the glamorous is that years earlier, long before he became a success, Mita had actually gone out with Carlos Palau (p.11). Then we find that when Toto is set on being a good boy, he determines to emulate Shirley Temple (p.46): an incongruous model indeed. He judges his friend Raúl García in cinematic terms: Raúl has the sort of face that goes with the good character who is killed in the war, he thinks (p.85), but later he changes his mind and sees it as the face of a film thief (p.92). He dreams about his friend Alicita's uncle marrying Luise Rainer (Alicita's uncle is already married), because the actress had impressed him so much in Robert Z. Leonard's *The Great Ziegfeld* (1936); indeed, he was so taken with the whole film that when he tells the story of it in a school essay, he includes himself in the recounted action (p.77). It is hardly surprising that Toto should be so involved in the cinema for he is very close to his mother, and Mita is described as being passionately fond of it (p.20); she has even been accused of marrying Berto merely because he looked like a film star (p.20). Mita and Toto go to see a film every afternoon, and it is not long before she has inspired the child with her standards and tastes. It may be that for her the cinema is a form of consolation for having lost the opportunity of studying literature and indulging her love for reading novels, but in any case Toto discovers this world of fantasy when he is very young indeed. He goes for the first time in 1939, when he is six, and immediately falls in love with Hollywood. Mita encourages him to think about films too: so that he is not bored when she and Berto take a siesta, she suggests that he think about a film they have seen together. 'Voy a pensar en la cinta que más me gustó' ('I'm going to think about the film I enjoyed most'), he says on one occasion, and he is already beginning to proffer critical judgments: 'Norma Shearer es una artista que nunca es mala' ('Norma Shearer is a star who is never bad'), for example (p.37). It is natural that at six years of age his mind should deal in polarizations, but it is also clear that this facile comment must have originated with the adults. Toto is young and ignorant and soaks up and repeats other people's prefabricated views. But so do the adults, and that is much more disturbing.

Everything in everyday life can be compared to something seen on the screen. When Mita throws a paper streamer, Toto remembers Ginger Rogers twirling around in a musical (p.39). The picture of a saint on a printed card that he caught a glimpse of at Héctor's first communion is very like his beloved Norma Shearer (p.37). He himself identifies with everything and everyone, even with the fish in an underwater documentary that he has seen. 'Qué mal se porta ese pescadito,' he says about himself and his lack of interest and emotion when his uncle dies, 'no quiere a nadie, que se murió el tío y el pescadito no lloró, se volvió a jugar' ('What a naughty little fishy that was, he doesn't love anybody, his uncle died and the little fishy didn't cry and went back to his games') (p.45). It is always a question of imitation: even when he is drawing he must have something to copy (p.69). Yet again, this is an attitude typical of the lives of all around him, and the act of copying will almost invariably involve self-deception.

Where does the blame lie? Indeed, should it be seen as a question of blame? The fault is certainly not that of the model — in this instance, the cinema. As Emir Rodríguez Monegal points out, the cinema is but a symptom of alienation, not its cause. As far as Toto is concerned, he adds, he is not alienated because he goes to the cinema every evening; rather, going to the cinema is a sign of his alienation.[15] Hollywood, or more accurately, the fantasy world that the critic Michael Wood has called 'America in the movies',[16] is his *ailleurs*. As Wood says, this was 'an independent universe, self-created, self-perpetuating, a licensed zone of unreality', 'a system of assumptions and beliefs and preoccupations', 'a country of familiar faces, a mythology made up of a limited number of stories'. And he goes on, as we have already seen in the epigraph to this chapter, that although the result is a pack of lies, they are essential lies.[17] Like Mita's tears when her baby dies (p.144), they make life bearable.

Toto, of course, is not yet what he and life between them are going to produce. If *La traición de Rita Hayworth* has even the slightest hint of the *Bildungsroman* about it, it goes without saying that the focal point of the development and realization process is Toto. Nevertheless, several critics have claimed that Toto is *not* the protagonist of the book, and certainly not a 'hero'.[18] It seems to me that this view, largely based on the attention paid by the author to the other characters, is quite mistaken. There is no denying that Toto is at the very least the centre of our attention and the most interesting and vital character, not merely because he is more intelligent and sensitive than anyone else, but also because he embodies everybody else's problems in an intensified form.

If we think about the gulf between reality and Toto's dreams, we should better understand the circumstances and the psychology of the adult characters who are not all that different from him. And if we look at how he adapts to his personal reality, we see that the adults' 'therapy' varies little in kind. They may choose different models, and they are likely to have more experience and to be more practised and subtle in the game they are playing, but that is all.

Puig's sympathies appear to be directed towards his female characters in this novel. Although we hear about Berto, his brother, Héctor, Toto's enemy Cobito Umansky, Raúl García and Alicita's uncle, the author's interest lies elsewhere, and even the most passing of references to the female condition is revealing. Furthermore, since Toto is not in a position to understand Héctor's machismo, behaves differently from the other boys, and is a timid, somewhat withdrawn and effeminate child, we can, and should, include him among the female rather than the male characters, those who are exploited or possibly even ill-treated. A child who is powerless in face of the world is the ideal character to demonstrate the female condition, especially here, since it is invariably the women who console themselves by escaping into what has to be called art, even if it is inferior art (a point we shall return to later). 'Quando a realidade se torna intolerável,' Puig has said, 'o homem trata de modificá-la, nem que seja na sua imaginação' ('When real life becomes unbearable, people will try to modify it, if only in their imaginations').[19]

So it is that one reason for seeing Toto as the protagonist of the novel is that his is a representative role. If we consider the layout of the sixteen chapters or sections we find another, and this is that Toto appears in every one of them. Indeed, he is the only character that belongs to the individual worlds of all the other people. The book begins with a kind of Greek chorus of women's voices, and in the course of this conversation we learn of the child's existence. As we read on, we are given information about his family background: Toto has still to utter his first word, but he is already a key figure. From scattered references to him, we reach a visual close-up stage and finally we arrive at the thoughts, voice and, therefore, personality of the child himself. From now on he is ever present, and our picture of him becomes more and more detailed, irrespective of the source of the voice in any given section. We move, too, from the spoken word to the child's own written word when a school essay of his is reproduced. Our last glimpse of him is as a disenchanted schoolboy of fifteen; the year is 1948 and, apart from

Berto's unposted letter (in which, needless to say, he mentions his baby son), the novel is over. Toto is not only the protagonist but, I would say, the hero. Although he does not arrive at a point of maturity, he is the only character that changes and develops, and he has some hope for a future. It is he, of course, who is most strikingly betrayed by Rita Hayworth, even if, as Ricardo Piglia claims, there is more than one 'traición' ('betrayal').[20] His belief in a magical fantasy world becomes increasingly difficult to sustain as he gets older. False assumptions lie behind the irresistible attractions embodied in Rita Hayworth, 'una artista linda' who 'hace traiciones' ('a beautiful star' who 'betrays you') (p.82). For Berto the flesh and dramatic adventures are exciting, but experience has taught him that there is no salvation there; for Toto, the glamour of the same screen image represents the answer to spiritual, aesthetic and emotional needs, and here too its promise is false and misleading. We meet the other characters at moments in their lives when they appear to have reached a kind of limit and become fossilized in their ways of coping. They have no future; this is true even for the young Paquita, who is about to be married.

Thus the gulf between dreams and reality, always more visible where children are concerned, is underlined by Toto's outlook as he grows up. He suspects the unpalatable truth from time to time, but there are enough moments of hope to make a continuing struggle possible and, for some years at least, Hollywood presents Toto with a kind of wonderland that helps him to make progress. Traditionally it is fairy stories that fulfil this function, acting as an aid to young minds and providing escapist relief. Bruno Bettelheim's book *The Uses of Enchantment*[21] sheds considerable light on why this should be so, and even if there are obvious differences between the composition and function of fairy stories, as defined by Bettelheim, and the formats employed by Hollywood in its heyday, what he says is relevant to the Coronel Vallejos situation. It would be wrong to deny that some of these differences are important: the fact, for example, that fairy stories make no claim to present the world as it is, whereas the majority of Hollywood films did; or that, according to Bettelheim, 'the fairy tale is therapeutic because the patient finds his *own* solutions', which is perhaps not true where the cinema is concerned. Nevertheless, the fundamental link lies in the important and relevant messages that people find in the genres, a relevance to the *inner* life of the human being. Bettelheim maintains that 'whatever our age, only a story conforming to the principles underlying our thought processes carries

conviction for us' (p.45). However 'unreal' they are, fairy stories
reflect basic truths for each reader, and although Hollywood films
appear to solve all problems, with fate taking a benevolent hand and
tying up all the loose ends, even here there is individual appeal. The
film-goer invariably indulges in a process of distortion, mentally
changing not only his own circumstances but also, in many cases, his
memory of what he has just seen and heard on the screen, and this
restructuring process takes various forms. There are three basic
reactions. First, the spectator may copy what is clearly admirable and
what can, if only imperfectly, be imitated; or he will long for and dream
about what is equally desirable but which is patently, though perhaps
only temporarily, inaccessible; and third — and this is found mainly in
children or people of great immaturity — he may actually change what
he has seen, so that he himself can become part of it, a kind of
'secondary revision'; or he will apply its circumstances to a fantasized
version of his own life, with not only himself but characters from his
everyday existence as protagonists.

The most normal spectator reaction is admiration: to look up to what
Freud called the *Ichideal* is an unexceptionable phase in the maturing
process of the individual. As Freud himself said, as a child develops he
projects an ideal that will replace his own lost infant narcissism, for he
was once his own ideal.[22] There can be collective ideals too: many of
them will be common to other people in the various groups to which we
belong.[23] In *La traición de Rita Hayworth* there is no shortage of models,
both individual and collective: these are the romantic, simplified
inhabitants of the Hollywood-created world. Berto is said to be as
handsome as a film star (p.29); for Choli, 'interesting' women are those
(obviously fictitious) characters who do something outrageous for the
sake of a man, 'se complican en un robo, se han hecho ladronas de
joyas, de las fronteras, las contrabandistas ¿y las espías? no creo que sea
todo por dinero . . .' ('they become involved in a robbery, have
become jewel-thieves, working the frontiers, they're smugglers. And
what about women spies? I can't believe it's just the money that attracts
them . . .') (p.51). She wears a lot of eye-shadow so as to look like this
kind of woman and she advises Mita to do the same. It makes you more
attractive, she tells her, it looks as though you've had a past (p.68).
Then there is Delia, who very nearly convinces herself that the only
thing that matters when her lover abandons her is that he is not *really* in
love with the other woman: in her imagination she sees him dying of
grief without her (p.134). Everything that happens or can be observed

in the lives of those who turn to this kind of comfort demonstrates the falseness of this vision. It goes without saying, for example, that eternal platonic devotion is not a notable feature among the young men who, like Delia's former lover, come to Coronel Vallejos and make a play for the available females. But it is essential, it seems, to make a great effort and to emulate not only the appearance of admired models but also their attitudes, and this applies to everyone, even Berto, who is one of the few characters in the novel who are not obsessed by the cinema.[24]

When we leave the area of open admiration, the problem becomes more complicated. Where the manifestations of an inaccessible world that is not susceptible to imitation are concerned, Toto once again represents a kind of exacerbated version of the attitude of almost everyone else, though at the same time he is more optimistic than they are, not yet bitter, and not so heavily protected by the emotional armour they have long since adopted. When he was very young indeed, he — like everyone else — had dreamed of happiness, love and excitement in his life. These are likely to be mutually exclusive, and he is beginning to show signs of disillusionment: his view, for example, of a sadistic God (p.288), his scorn for the Romantics, and his conviction that he is superior to the strong and brutish because he is able to think (p.282). His new-found clear-sightedness is accompanied by evidence of intellectual and cultural progress — he reads almost a book a day (p.274) — and we have arrived at the point which, as much as any, constitutes his moment of maturity and awareness. He is no longer a small child trying to re-order the world or changing the plot of a film so that it includes him and the outcome can be happy. Nevertheless, not all the avenues leading to fulfilment have been closed to him. Although he does not share Héctor's fool's paradise, he has a long way to go before he arrives at Herminia's hopeless disgust with life.

As a small child Toto indulged in the third possible reaction to Hollywood models: an attitude that results in taking a real-life situation and changing it in the imagination. It is natural and normal for children to do this, but here again, the adults are equally guilty. If we consider just two cases of this kind of distortion on the part of Toto, it should become clear why it is so frequently indulged in by those who, theoretically, should know better.

In Chapter Five, Toto talks about the film biography *The Great Ziegfeld*. In it, Ziegfeld's dying wife calls him on the telephone, but claims that she is well in order not to upset him (p.76). This scene, in fact, constitutes the last appearance on the screen of the actress

Luise Rainer, and since Toto dislikes Myrna Loy, who plays her successor to Ziegfeld's affections, he invents a continuation of the story that suits his tastes. Not only does it include Luise Rainer, but also a real-life model from Coronel Vallejos, someone who represents everything he would have wished his father to be, had he not 'betrayed' him. This is his friend Alicita's uncle, 'con cara de las cintas' ('who looks like a film star') (p.75), like Berto. In Toto's version, his hero suddenly appears on the scene and nurses Luise Rainer back to health. This *deus ex machina* is helped in the task by a little messenger boy who evidently feels the need for the same dramatic and exciting actions and sacrifices in his life as those that appeal to Choli, for just like her 'interesting' amoral heroines, he actually steals food for Ziegfeld's wife. Toto's identification with the messenger boy is so complete that he writes 'I' at one point instead of 'he'. We discover, too, that the young messenger is fatherless and that he is ill-treated by his stepfather (p.76). When he sees that Luise Rainer is on the road to recovery, he assumes that the protagonists will marry and take him away with them. (An identical happy ending to that reserved for one of his models, Shirley Temple, in the film *Stowaway.*). '¡No voy más con mi padrastro!' ('I shan't live with my stepfather any more!') he says, exultantly; all three are going to live happily ever after in a log cabin in the snowy forest (p.78). The already obvious similarity between Berto and the fictional messenger boy's stepfather becomes even clearer when this plan falls through: in his disappointment the boy cries bitter tears every night, but 'bien despacito para que el padrastro *nervioso* no se despierte *y le grite*' ('very quietly so that his *highly-strung* stepfather doesn't wake up *and shout at him*') (p.78). We have already been told that Berto is eternally 'nervioso' and irascible, especially when Toto cries, and that if there is the slightest noise in the house at siesta time he wakes up furious and shouting.

The other example of this kind of revision is found in the same chapter. Here Toto projects his admiration onto another strong and superficially admirable real-life model: his friend Raúl García. He again thinks about going to live in a cabin in the snowy forest (pp.85 – 86), but this time he himself takes the part previously played by Luise Rainer. In the first version, when she fainted it was Alicita's uncle who nursed her back to health, but here it is Toto who faints: 'si yo me quedo en el trineo desmayado en la nieve viene [Raúl] y me salva' ('if I am unconscious in the sledge in the snow, Raúl will come along and rescue me'). It is only too easy to see the link between Raúl and

Berto in Toto's subconscious: he is eager to do with Raúl everything that he and his father might have done together.

In all this there is a great deal that is usual in a child's growing-up process. First of all we are struck by the apparent arbitrariness of children's judgements, as represented by Toto. They are in no way based on good and evil, but are the result of many diverse contributory factors. It is question of what appeals to the child, and things or people can appeal for all sorts of strange reasons. In fact, though, children's likes and dislikes are not quite as arbitrary as they look, and conditioning and pressures are all-important, especially those that emanate from family and friends. For example, when Berto says that he likes Rita Hayworth more than any other film star, Toto's immediate comment is that he is beginning to like her more than anyone else too (p.82), although the actress's attraction for Berto is something that Toto cannot begin to understand. This represents another aspect of Toto's 'betrayal': he is slowly discovering that he cannot become the copy of his father that Berto wants him to be, and this is the first significant example in Toto's life of the incompatibility revealed by the confrontation of Piglia's 'cuerpo' and 'destino'.

It is usual for children to identify completely with one of the characters in a film or a fairy-tale, and often, if there is no weak and incomplete character, they will invent one. In fairy stories there may be a youngest son, or one who is the laughing-stock in a family of strong men — sometimes he is even looked on as an idiot; but at the end we find that he is cleverer and more astute than the others, that he humiliates giants and kills monsters, that he can and does defeat evil, and that eventually he marries the most beautiful girl in the world, who is also the richest, the purest and the most aristocratic. In other narrative contexts, particularly in films, the weak character may well be a woman, sometimes abandoned or ill-treated, but invariably deprived of love. This is how Toto sees himself at this point in his development, identifying with a helpless character who finds happiness under the wing of a good, virile and well-groomed man. There is nothing abnormal about changing a narrative line. 'Children,' says Bettelheim, 'have their own ways of dealing with story elements that run counter to their emotional needs'.[25]

Toto's version of *The Great Ziegfeld* contains another well-known characteristic of a child's growing-up process, and this is what Freud called the 'Family Romance' (*Familienroman*):[26] fantasies through which the subject invents a family for himself and creates a kind of novel.[27] For Toto, as for so many other children, salvation is actually twice removed. There is, first, the move away from his disappointing real father to an invented stepfather. From here it is easy to leave the stepfather and take refuge with a 'saviour'. In other words, a stepfather has to be conjured up out of the air in order to achieve happiness. This is no more than a subtle and diplomatic means on the part of the child of refusing to face up to his anger and resentment where his real father is concerned. For obvious reasons, he puts himself in a position where he can reject someone other than his father, but the similarity between father and stepfather is clear. The difference between the situation in *La traición de Rita Hayworth* and that more frequently found is that it is usually a question of a child's relationship to his stepmother, a cruel and unpleasant usurper who replaced the real mother who has refused him something. When, in children's tales, there is a good fairy who defends the child and guards him against the wicked stepmother, this has been judged a manifestation of the child's wish to separate the mother's good and bad features. The result is that he can be indignant, angry and resentful towards the usurper without any of the concomitant feelings of guilt that would be unavoidable if he reacted to his real mother in that way. The extension is for the child to imagine that the couple that are bringing him up are not really his parents at all, that he is the son of aristocrats, and that one day they will arrive to save him and elevate him to his true station in life. They will, of course, go off to some other region or country — *ailleurs,* or at least to a cabin in the snowy woods — and there they will live happily ever after. Toto reveals his inner tensions in his fantasizing, but what is important is that he does not really believe in any of it. He knows that it is a combination of two variations on the truth, one of which is his own invention, the other the film which constitutes the first stage in the distortion. He is not really deceived. 'Mucho mejor *sería* . . . ' ('It would be much nicer *if* . . . ') he begins (p. 76), and he goes on; '*sería* lindo que siguiera la cinta con el que . . . ' ('it would be nice *if* the film went on . . . ') (p. 77). He admits that there is no chance of going to live in a log cabin: Alicita's aunt has just given birth to a baby and her husband can no longer visit Luise Rainer (p. 78). Life and inconvenient facts intervene in the plot and interfere with the possibility of dreams coming true. Even at the invented level the story has to stop, but this mental excursion has achieved something. If we substitute the word 'father' for 'mother' in Bettelheim's summing-up, it is clear what this is:

> The fantasy of the wicked stepmother not only preserves the good mother intact, it also prevents having to feel guilty about one's angry thoughts and wishes about her — a guilt which would seriously interfere with the good relation to Mother.[28]

Children know that it is fantasy and do not lose themselves in it, since this would jeopardize their security and their comfort. It is merely a question of a momentary projection of their resentment. The child cannot avoid being afraid that his parents will abandon him. The only safe way to express fury (in Toto's case a fury provoked by the fact that his mother leaves him alone to take a siesta with his father)[29] is to indulge in therapeutic fictions.

One more quotation from Bettelheim contributes towards an understanding of the motives of the adults who abandon themselves to the same practice:

> The fairy tale's extravagant promise of a happy ending would . . . lead to disenchantment with the child's real life if it were part of a realistic story, or projected as something that will happen where the real child lives. But the fairy story's happy ending occurs in fairyland, a country that we can visit only in our minds.[30]

Toto recognizes the frontier between real life and the imagination, but the voluntary blindness that is so much a part of the adults' make-up demonstrates their refusal to do so.

Choli is both ludicrous and touching, and represents an advanced, exaggerated stage in that process of remoulding real life so that it becomes tolerable. It is she who embodies all three possible reactions: she admires and emulates models, she escapes into fantasy dreams and she distorts what she cannot avoid. She is the classic example of someone who is conscious of the difference between what is and what ought to be, and her models come from outside her normal environment. It is, though, worth repeating that alienation is not brought about by an interest in Hollywood, but is the result of many different factors. Despite her protests to the contrary, Choli's therapy lies in hope for a personal happy ending. This kind of aim is seen as somewhat pernicious in children, since it is so likely to cause dissatisfaction with their immediate surroundings, but with an adult who is already irremediably disillusioned it may be the only answer. Even in the classic fairy story there is often some kind of miraculous transformation scene, and audience dissatisfaction is avoided by setting this in a far-distant realm. There may not be any real grounds for optimism as far as the frustrated adult is concerned, but there is a

short-term chance of sublimating depression even if it cannot be
defeated. There is even a possibility of exciting a certain amount of
admiration, misplaced though it may be, in others. This is exactly how
Choli deals with her life. She is actually an unremarkable woman who
has lived through an unsatisfying marriage to an uninteresting man.
Now that she is a widow, she gives herself up to the sentimental and
dramatic values that she so much admires, though, significantly, she
shows no sentiment at all on the subject of her husband's death. She is a
sad copy of the glamorous heroines of Hollywood — she even works for
a company called Hollywood Cosmetics — and she convinces herself
that she could easily be mistaken for a North American. This ill-
founded belief is seen to be absurd when she deliberately talks little in
order to copy the style of an inspector from the United States who, in
fact, keeps silent because she knows no Spanish. Part of Choli's way of
life consists of taking her looks very seriously: she wears her hair loose
(in the unlikely event of having to see someone off at an airport it would
stream out in the breeze and look thrilling) (p.54). She stays in the best
hotels as she travels around the country and spends every free minute
trying on her clothes and inspecting the results in the hotel-room
mirror. It is a shame, she says, that there is never a photographer there
(p.67). She imitates as many of the external manifestations of
Hollywood as possible in the course of a life of the utmost joylessness, all
the while dreaming of what might still happen one day in a perfumed
room with a well-spoken gentleman who is the possessor of a silk
dressing-gown (p.61). She dreams of travel, too, both to the United
States and to London (which she had once thought was in America),
and she even thinks about cultural improvement for herself since,
presumably, this would make her more 'interesting'. Like pre-pubertal
children, she twists things around, taking refuge in daydreams that in
her case are in total and preposterous conflict with everything she
actually knows and has experienced.

   Her attitude to love provides striking evidence of this. If we consider
what she says about her late husband and about men in general, the
incongruity of her outlook becomes very clear: she is enchanted by
Toto's delicate features because, as she points out, he could have got
uglier as he got older, acquiring a 'cara tosca de hombre' ('a coarse,
masculine face') (p.49). She is almost distraught when she thinks about
all the years she spent with her odious husband: 'doce años tirados a la
calle' ('twelve years down the drain') she calls them (p.50). He had
hardly ever listened to her. He had spent all his time ogling other

women, but he mocked her when she dressed attractively. He had scarcely spoken a word of any sort to her before their marriage, and then had subjected her to the profoundest ignominy of all — that of having to take all her clothes off to make love. It was not long before he stopped coming home for supper, and she claims that he was a beast. But she does not admire Berto either, and the men she meets on her sales trips are no improvement: it is not just a question of an unfortunate and atypical experience where her marriage was concerned. In fact, she is repelled by all those characteristics traditionally considered to be masculine. She is even critical of the fact that her son enjoys dismantling car engines. She is conditioned to disapprove of sex and has never admitted to desire: 'es tan feo estar desnuda' ('nakedness is so ugly'), she says (p.56). Indeed, it is at the very moment when a new admirer looks as if he might be about to make an indelicate proposition that he begins to disgust her (p.59). Nevertheless, all her hopes are pinned on finding the Great Love of her Life. And it goes without saying that, like the world created by Hollywood, this vision of love is pure invention. 'The movies did not describe or explore America,' says Michael Wood, 'they invented it, dreamed up an America all their own',[31] and included in this is the Hollywood vision of the relationship between the sexes. What Choli is looking for is mystery, drama, dedication, beauty, culture, education and elegance. It is invariably having clean hair, an unfathomable look in the eyes and the constant desire to die for a man. It is to be eternally young and admirably well dressed. It has very little to do with love.

But, as Wood also says, 'even thin and calculated dreams have secrets to give away', and this particular dream reveals that again we are in the presence of an immature character: Choli is as incomplete as a child. And children, like primitive man, see themselves as the centre of everything, judging life in relationship to their own individual needs. They fill the world with images from their own unconscious minds.[32] Choli is as much in search of independence and personal integrity as children are, and she is also narcissistic and lacking in self-sufficiency, for though she dreams of great sacrifices, her attitude towards love is self-serving. There *is* no world of grand, asexual passion, with perfumed and well-dressed protagonists, and Choli knows this perfectly well; but she must repress this knowledge. Hollywood, reflected in the Argentine film industry, helps her to do this: in the latter it is no coincidence that the favourite of both Choli and Puig (whose real-life affection was largely based on the unreality of the character she invariably portrayed) was the actress Mecha Ortiz. She was always the Fatal Woman, Puig has said, the woman with a past, superior and confident, with great experience of life, *and she resembled no one at all.* [33] Mecha Ortiz is a bizarre model for Choli, but she feels a sense of affinity with her, especially as in real life the actress was wrongly thought to be a widow. It is this capacity for providing escape that Hollywood and its imitators share with the fairy-tale. The subtitle of one of the best-known and seminal works on the cinema, Siegfried Kracauer's *Theory of Film,* is *The Redemption of Physical Reality.* [34] Choli looks back to that period of her life when she was totally innocent, and makes a calculated decision to go on in that state, but converts what has happened in between into what it obviously was not: a 'past'. A paradox indeed, as incongruous as the asexual passion which forms the basis of her dreams, and which we shall return to in later chapters. In contrast to Toto, who shows more maturity than she does, she believes — or she has decided to believe — wholeheartedly in the stratagem she has adopted. The film critic Parker Tyler's view of 'the unhappier aspects of the myth of Pygamalion' in the cinema as 'a simulacrum so ''real'' that we fall in love with it *at the expense of our own reality*' is an appropriate one here. [35] Choli's behaviour is disingenuous.

As we saw, Herminia's reaction to frustration is different. She is weighed down by the clarity of her understanding of her situation, and appears to eschew the self-delusion of hoping for a Hollywood-style denouement to the plot of her life. She goes to the other extreme, showing an almost obsessive awareness of her lack of charm, her defects and her lack of talent. With the combination of a reasonable level of education, relatively speaking, and her natural perspicacity, she almost persuades us that life is as she claims it is. One of the first hints that her acuity is not all that it seems can be detected in her signal failure to interpret her own recurring nightmare of being crushed by a weightless train falling from the roof, even though she has heard of Freud and remembers that she first experienced this dream on hearing the news of seventeen-year-old Paquita's engagement. She is not even helped in her incomprehension by the fact that she admits to sexual curiosity as well as social envy: when writing of the film *Lujuria (Lust),* for example, [36] she comments drily that for her it might just as well be called *Atlántida (Atlantis)* or *El Dorado* — something that sounds promising but is entirely unknown. And she makes no attempt to hide the desire she feels to be married, though all she wants is someone ordinary who would work uncomplainingly 'para mis hijos' ('for my children') (p.291). The key to her attitude is that her capacity for distinguishing between the real and a fantasy world is less developed than it seems, for she is actually an able creator of scenarios. For example, 'para mis hijos' on Herminia's lips is not all that far removed from Toto's 'y yo desde la cocina del hotel le tiro una moneda' ('and I toss him a coin from the hotel kitchen') in his version of *The Great Ziegfeld* (p.77). Her discourse is full of expressions such as, 'tal vez yo esté idealizando demasiado' ('perhaps I'm being too idealistic') (p.289) and 'estaré . . . yo pidiendo lo imposible' ('I'm probably asking the impossible') (p.290), but this is not clear-sightedness, only suitable lines of dialogue for the part she is playing. She and Choli are very different: Choli so concerned with her looks and Herminia unkempt, even dirty; Choli forever on the move, Herminia trapped and seldom leaving the house; Choli consoling herself with the hope of meeting a man of distinction and irresistible charm, Herminia refusing to entertain such a thought; Choli ignorant of the location of London, Herminia comparatively well-read and knowledgeable. Nevertheless, Herminia is just as involved in escape tactics. The variation lies only in the choice of a Hollywood model. Herminia's relief is achieved by means of almost total passivity, conforming to everything. The irony of her favourite maxim, 'No hay mal que por bien no venga' ('It's an ill wind that blows no good') is seen at its most striking when she congratulates herself on being a chronic asthma sufferer and in that way avoiding death on the Titanic, but there are countless less obtrusive moments when she protects herself with its consolatory powers. She escapes into therapeutic pessimism and inertia, misery, and a sense of impotence; paradoxically, it is the resulting cynicism that makes life tolerable, and it conceals some optimism. It is the most insecure kind of salvation, and she escapes by the skin of her teeth, but she does escape. Her role models are far removed from mysterious *femmes fatales*: she is, instead, a reflection of all those figures of feminine impotence and abnegation often shown on the screen as deformed or crippled or even ugly. Weakness is symbolized by physical infirmity or extreme plainness (in theory, at least). Herminia's asthma could be seen as falling into the same category as Dorothy McGuire's vulnerable deafness in *The Spiral Staircase* (1945), Loretta Young's deafness in *And Now Tomorrow* (1944), Dorothy McGuire's supposed lack of beauty in *The Enchanted Cottage* (1945), and the fact that Jane Wyman is both deaf and dumb in *Johnny Belinda* (1948). The part played by Jane Wyman in the film version of Tennessee Williams's *The Glass Menagerie* — that of a lame girl embittered by the squalid and tawdry nature of her surroundings — is typical of this stereotype. Herminia too indulges in voluntary blindness: Choli is optimistic, Herminia pessimistic. The more usual position is found between the two extremes, and again it could be claimed that this normality is represented by Toto, living as he does partly in a world of make-believe, but not entirely believing in it. As Puig has said, Toto is a boy who does not belong to his immediate environment.[37] The only hope for Herminia is that she does not quite believe in her world of make-believe either. In the gloom of her view of the future there is a tiny pinpoint of light, for she too must have seen Garbo in *Camille* (1936) and she knows that although a woman may be alone, terminally ill, shunned by society, unapproachable and even discourteous towards the opposite sex, she may still win the undying love of someone as handsome and appealing as Robert Taylor.

The word 'normal' has sexual connotations too, and although homosexuality as a theme and as a device will be discussed in more detail in connection with later novels, we cannot fail to notice that in *La traición de Rita Hayworth* it is already hinted at: Toto is explicitly referred to as lacking in conventional masculine characteristics. He does not enjoy traditional male pastimes and games and he is interested in clothes and love stories; he is often afraid and he has few friends (the boys are rough and uncouth, the girls have no wish to play with him); he refuses to learn the facts of life; he is highly-strung. Everything, in fact, seems to point to a homosexual future for him. Ironically enough, though, it is his alienation from the society that surrounds him as a child that demonstrates his normality; when he reaches maturity, the opposite will be the case. When he is young, it is society that is 'abnormal', but later he may be the one that this same society classifies in that way.

The absurdity of people's role models makes it hard to avoid the suspicion that there is an element of perversity in their refusal to emulate at least some of the people that they actually know, but there is a notable lack of adequate local models. In Coronel Vallejos, it is almost impossible to find a suitable combination of the fantastic and the real to act as ideals, and the fantastic will always predominate. But even in Buenos Aires, first-generation Argentine immigrants had no one to imitate. This is what Puig said on one occasion:

> En mis novelas me he ocupado principalmente de una primera generación de argentinos, los hijos de los inmigrantes españoles e

italianos que llegaron al país a fines del siglo. Se trataba en general de campesinos que venían aquí a hacer fortuna, a cambiar de *status*. Las tradiciones que podían aportar no valían, eran tradiciones de campesinos, una identidad que convenía olvidar. En el caso de los inmigrantes italianos era peor: ni siquiera pudieron aportar un idioma a sus hijos . . . Y los hijos no eran ni italianos ni españoles, eran argentinos, pero no sabían cómo era ser argentino. Entonces esa primera generación que no pudo hallar en casa los modelos de conducta adecuados — por el contrario, rechazaba lo que oía en casa — los encontraba donde podía . . . se proponían modelos dudosos — irreales más que nada.[38]

In my novels I have concerned myself principally with first-generation Argentines, the children of the Spanish and Italian immigrants who arrived in the country at the turn of the century. Generally speaking, they were land-workers who came here to make their fortune and to try to go up in the world. The traditions they could bring with them were irrelevant, they were the traditions of country-folk, and that was an identity it would be better to forget. It was even worse for the Italian immigrants: they couldn't even give their children a language. . . . And the children were neither Italians nor Spanish, they were Argentines, but they didn't know what being an Argentine consisted of. So it was that this first generation, unable to find suitable models of behaviour at home — on the contrary, they rejected everything they heard at home — found them wherever they could . . . they adopted models that were dubious — or 'unreal' would be a better word.

There are many examples of this. In the second chapter, Amparo, who is just twelve years of age, works with a servant girl, apparently somewhat older, called Felisa. The most accessible real-life models for Amparo would be Felisa and her own elder sister. It is not long, however, before we discover that her unmarried sister has had a baby and been evicted by their father (p.22), and Felisa is no more than a servant. With a coarseness of expression not entirely admirable in a twelve-year-old, Amparo swears that she will never be like her (p.22). There is only one real person who merits some admiration, and that is one Mora Menéndez, who has achieved a little luxury in her life as a nursemaid; Amparo's avowed wish to emulate her constitutes a rare moment of clear-sightedness. Perhaps the most ironic example of unthinking emulation of models is that her sister's child, who never had a father and who does not know her mother, can now say 'mamá' and 'papá' (p.23). Amparo has pretensions; though she lives in abject poverty, she is careful about her appearance, she always wears a clean apron and she is the proud possessor of a dress given to her by nuns. She refuses to consider becoming a nurse since, according to her, all nurses are good-for-nothing idlers who don't take care of their uniforms (p.26).[39] It is not, perhaps, surprising that the milkman finds this amazing: 'Who do you think you are?' he asks, little realizing what a vital question this is. At twelve she is still nobody and is theoretically capable of becoming whatever and whoever she chooses to be. Unlike Toto, she is almost certainly going to turn out like all the other girls of her class and background.

Esther also fights desperately to avoid following her immediate models with her faith in the promises of Peronism, 'el primer peronismo' ('first-wave Peronism') as Puig calls it, a movement that he himself was caught up with.[40] (As Juan Goytisolo has pointed out,[41] Puig is partly a political writer and his subtle commentaries on Peronism in particular are perceptive and effective. This aspect of his work will be discussed later.) Esther is yet another deceived victim. Disillusioned by the inequality between her life-style and that of her classmates, she has come to believe that she can change her life with education. In one of the 'written' as opposed to 'spoken' chapters, she reveals her sense of oppression at having to study relentlessly so as to ensure that her annual scholarship is renewed, and her feeling of guilt when she fails to do so. She is conscious of her parents' sacrifices and determines to go on fighting. But she is only fourteen, and political theory holds little attraction for her. What she would really like is for Fate to present her with a life of glamour and romance, luxury and happiness, something that only the rich can possibly know. She is resentful, like so many others, and she refers to 'the consolations of the poor' with bitter sarcasm. She is shocked by her classmates' extravagance; she already has a sense of potential collective power; she is scornful of the spoiled and protected 'niños inconscientes' ('blind children') (p.221) who have no idea of what is going on in the world, and infuriated by the fact that there are people in her own deprived circles (her sister in particular) who are not even aware of these anomalies (p.226). Yet she is romantically inclined, with the same desires as other girls of her age — desires expressed with the utmost Peronist pretentiousness and *cursilería*. We discover that her one wish is not for good health or better social conditions or even money, but for love. Her aim — like Choli's — is an unreal paradise. Everyone looks to unknown and perhaps unknowable areas.

These are not always the dreams created by Hollywood, or literature, or even the promises of a political movement. Toto's cousin Teté has no illusions about a better life on this earth and finds some consolation in religion. This is given a boost by the satisfaction she feels in her superiority to Toto, who never goes to Mass, never says his prayers, and is naughty and effeminate. She is also comforted by her scorn for those among her contemporaries who are beginning to be aware of their own sexuality, and she is obsessed by the thought of sin and the attribution of blame. She is not unlike Herminia, who wonders what she has done to merit the life that has been wished upon her, since she too equates 'good' behaviour with immediate good results; she is convinced that she must placate God so as to be spared the horrors of the end of the world, and the struggle, laced with cunning, includes blackmailing pacts with her maker. Nevertheless, Teté is like all the characters in the novel in that she is not totally unjustified in her fears and beliefs. She is terrified of suffocating because she once saw a tubercular relative die in this way. She is fearful of causing distress and hurt to her sick mother because she has seen the effect a major shock had on her grandfather. People *are* victims and do need consolation. For Teté, life is a constant fight against Evil, and religion and 'good behaviour' are her weapons. It is not hard to find parallels between this escape route and all the others.

Teté's sense of inadequacy is not based on underdevelopment in society. Neither is that of Berto, who first took refuge in womanizing, then in commercial ambitions and, ultimately, in bad temper. The same could be said for Paquita, who opts for an unappealing marriage, Herminia, who survives through self-pity and, indeed, all the other characters. This is why, in one way, the *vie est ailleurs* syndrome could be seen as less important than might at first have been supposed, since 'underdevelopment' is a symptom common to all social classes and nations. But of course, herein lies the real tragedy: life itself — difficult family relationships, shattered ambitions, the incompatibility between the sexes, illness, natural disasters and death, social injustice, the fear of divine retribution — is made tolerable only by means of dreams. Popular art, the subculture of Hollywood, sentimental novels, radio melodramas, constitute some of the more enjoyable and effective of these, and their value and appeal are greater for the female protagonists than politics or religion since they actually do offer hope for the one efficacious defence against life's difficulties, a hope that women instinctively seem more aware of. According to Bettelheim, happy endings may not deceive anyone, but they do demonstrate that there is just one solution in life, and that is to establish a satisfactory union with another person.[42] This union will compensate for the child's dread of separation from his parents as well as the fear of death in adults, who recognise that it exists but live as if it did not. 'There are no escapes,' Michael Wood claims, 'even in the most escapist movie,'[43] but, again, we live as if there were. In the vast majority of the case histories presented to us by Puig, love shows itself as unexciting and unsatisfactory, but the search and the need for it continue in the female characters, and the manifestations of mass art promise that it does exist. It is a question of human impulses in action. 'The happy ending is justly scorned as a misrepresentation,' writes Joseph Campbell,[44] 'for the world as we know it, as we have seen it, yields but one ending: death, disintegration, dismemberment, and the crucifixion of our heart with the passing of the forms that we have loved.' But he adds, consolingly: 'The happy ending of the fairy tale, the myth, and the divine comedy of the soul, is to be read, not as a contradiction, but as a transcendence of the universal tragedy of man.'[45]

CHAPTER III

'The Rules of the Game': *Boquitas pintadas* (1969)

> . . . en *Boquitas pintadas* más que las piezas de ajedrez en sí mismas, su descripción, interesan las tensiones que se producen entre ellas durante sus desplazamientos por el tablero.
>
> . . . in *Boquitas pintadas* it is not so much the chess-pieces themselves or their make-up that is important, but rather the tensions that are created as they move across the board.
>
> Manuel Puig, 'El folletin rescatado'

WHEN Puig's second novel was published in 1969, only a year after the first,[1] the similarities between them made it seem that authorial patterns had already been established. In fact, subsequent books were to show that many of these patterns existed only in the minds of those critics who had rushed rather too hastily to judgement.[2] The author's early preoccupation with the thirties and the forties, for instance, so evident in the first two novels, was not actually destined to become a common denominator in his writing, and until *Sangre de amor correspondido* (1982) even the element of nostalgia, which many had thought would surely be repeated, was discarded. (In the 1982 book, when the past is considered and recounted, the purpose is new and very different.) Sentimentality in the characters is not frequently found after *Boquitas pintadas* either, and in most cases the geographical setting, the theme of *cursilería* (pretentious vulgarity), and even the concern with the sterility of provincial Argentine life are also left behind.

It is worth pointing out, though, that in addition to those features that the first two novels obviously do have in common, there is one that is less striking, and that is that neither of them is what it appears to be at first glance. As we saw, *La traición de Rita Hayworth* gives the impression of being a neo-naturalist, almost sociological, novel but this is certainly not the case. *Boquitas pintadas,* on the other hand, seems to make a very strong claim for consideration as a psychological work. This, too, would be an inaccurate classification, unless we redefine the term, for in spite of Puig's gift of making his characters sympathetic, even pathetic, this is a book about a group, perhaps a generation; and furthermore, the group consists of two-dimensional characters. Puig once accounted for his choice of the format of the cheap novelette — the *género folletinesco* — for this book by pointing out that it is only too appropriate for a writer whose intention it is to portray schematic characters, and he added that his interest in this kind of person actually stems from their having so little mystery about them, from there being no inner life behind their actions. They are uncomplicated, but quite capable of crushing their innermost needs so as to follow 'the rules of the game' that have been dictated to them. That they are *chatos,* or 'flat', is obvious; the majority of people in General Villegas were actually like the fictional characters in *Boquitas pintadas,* as far as he could judge — boring and colourless. In *La traición de Rita Hayworth,* Toto had been attracted by the other kind of person, by individuals with a certain neurotic tension about them who were therefore 'different'. The grown-up 'Toto', now recalling the scenes of his childhood, thought to recapture the rest of the people he had known — those entirely weighed down and controlled by the conventions of their environment — and he sees what he calls their 'trajectory' as the element that should most interest the reader.[3] Puig later expanded on this view of his dramatis personae:

> Volví a Buenos Aires después de once años de ausencia y fue el reencuentro con ciertos personajes de mi infancia en el pueblo que me inspiró esta historia [*Boquitas pintadas*]. Noté un enorme desencanto en quienes habían vivido de acuerdo al sistema social de su momento, sin la menor rebeldía. Habían aceptado todo ese mundo de represión sexual, habían aceptado sus reglas, la hipocresía del mito de la virginidad femenina, y, claro, habían aceptado la autoridad. Los noté decepcionados en su madurez . . . No era un descencanto consciente, destilaban simplemente frustración, tristeza . . . esta gente había creído en la retórica del gran amor, de la gran pasión, pero no habían actuado de acuerdo a ella.

> I went back to Buenos Aires after an absence of eleven years and met up again with some of the characters from my childhood in the town that

inspired the story [*Boquitas pintadas*]. I was struck by an overwhelming disenchantment in those whose lives had fitted into the social system of the period and who had never made any attempt to rebel. They had accepted all that world of sexual repression, had accepted its rules, the hypocrisy of the myth of female virginity and, needless to say, they had accepted authority. They struck me as disillusioned, now that they were growing older . . . It wasn't that they were conscious of being let down, just that they gave off an air of frustration and unhappiness . . . these people had believed in the rhetoric of irresistible love, irresistible passion, but their lives had not reflected this in any way.

Critics have used expressions such as 'soap-opera characters' and 'characters without human qualities' when referring to these people,[5] and one has claimed that there is no tragic dimension to them.[6] Why, then, does this *appear* to be a psychological novel, and can this view be compatible with the fact that so many other readers (and not a few critics) have seen it as extremely touching? One is Emir Rodríguez Monegal, who tells us that though his first reaction was hostile, he finished up by feeling moved. He shed, he says, 'a metaphorical tear' over the fate of the heroine, Nené, and when he reached the end of the book he no longer saw her as a vulgar stereotype, but as a complete human being.[7] Many others have shed tears that were not just metaphorical, responding, perhaps, to a representation of group, rather than individual, psychology. The characters are brainwashed, conditioned by contemporary and partly local ideologies and mores, conforming, obeying and suffering: those who believed in the standards of the epoch, Puig calls them.[8] They are without spontaneity and they are dull, but they are real. The point is that their psychology is only too familiar to many readers. Indeed, Margery A. Safir's assertion that here the role played by the reader is of unusual importance is undeniable. She sees the work as consisting of two different mythic systems plus a pre-textual myth and, in her opinion, the reader has to judge events and values subjectively, thus becoming a kind of Borgesian 'reader-author'.[9] And of course this subjective judgement will be based on recognition and identification. Juan Manuel García Ramos is also right when he maintains that both here and in *La traición de Rita Hayworth* Puig has elaborated a great depersonalization metaphor:[10] a familiar syndrome. Our understanding of this group is enhanced, rather than diminished, by the blurring of their individual features and by their search for security in anonymous and depersonalized conformity.

There is little need to elaborate on the features that the first two books do have in common — the period, the town of Coronel Vallejos (though, of course, with new characters), a limited story-line (virtually everything has taken place before the narrative begins) and the ever-present element of self-deception. In any case, these similarities are overshadowed by an important initial point of divergence, and the reader's impressions are immediately affected by this. Since the second novel opens with the death notice of a young man (an older, tubercular version of Toto's cousin Héctor in *La traición*), it is straight away apparent that the narrative will look in a backwards direction. There is, indeed, no hope for the future in *Boquitas pintadas* and, as Alicia Borinsky has pointed out, the whole work is constructed from the tension of remembering, of recapturing something belonging to the past.[11] Those who have been foolish — or calculating — enough to believe what they were told have seen their hopes gradually fade, as disillusion and death reveal themselves as the only prospect. The first two Puig books explicitly portray hopeless human desires and longings, but in the second the romance is tarnished from the very beginning. Curiously enough, though, in virtually every case even total disillusion fails to bring about any kind of revolt: with the exception of Nené's brief and fruitless sojourn away from her husband, the reaction to the realization that conformity is futile is more conformity.

Because *La traición de Rita Hayworth* contains a certain amount of optimism, because it has a child as its protagonist and is without immediate melodramatic or sensational events based on the misapprehensions of the characters, it is occasionally touched with humour: Toto's childish wilfulness and ignorance and other people's ludicrous pretensions are cases in point. There is, however, no humour at all in *Boquitas pintadas*. The tone set by the opening epigraph is confirmed and reinforced by the first few lines of the first of the novel's sixteen *entregas*, or instalments. The epigraph, 'Era . . . para mí la vida entera' ('He was my whole life'), taken from an Alfredo Le Pera tango lyric,[12] makes it clear that we have by no means abandoned the world of bizarre models and inaccessible dreams. The sentiments of these lyrics, used to set the emotional scene of each chapter, are one aspect of it. Even the novel's title comes from a Le Pera song — this time not a tango, but nevertheless part of the process by means of which the characters 'se trasvisten continuamente' (perhaps 'adopt other personalities'), as García Ramos puts it.[13] The tango, as one of the different objective correlatives for the world-view (if it can be called that) of the characters in the second book, could hardly be more appropriate. If *La traición de Rita Hayworth* portrayed people dependent on Hollywood palliatives with their essential basic optimism, it is apt that here the attitude models should be taken from the sad, even sardonic, world of the tango, a world that reflects what Ernesto Sábato has seen as two of the principal attributes of the immigrants to the Argentine since the turn of the century: 'el resentimiento y la tristeza' ('resentment and sadness').[14] And it was Enrique Santos Discépolo, probably the genre's greatest composer and lyricist, who defined the tango as 'un pensamiento triste que se baila' ('a sad thought that is danced').[15] A further justification for the presence of these lyrics in what is again a largely female-orientated novel is that the 'pensamiento triste' of the original, and indeed later, tango writers and performers is so often connected with the absence of love in a man's life and his longing for one particular woman. The lonely immigrant, part of the enormous throng of solitary men that constituted Buenos Aires in the early years of the century, dreamt not of sex, which was obtainable at a price, but of love.[16] And this is precisely the attitude that the female characters project on to their ideal lovers. The fact that nostalgia and the desire to either recapture or, if that is impossible, erase painful memories of past happiness, are also key elements in the tango makes it all the more apposite. When a woman can believe that a man's life has been blighted by the loss of the only person he could ever love — and it is not difficult to do so, given the frequency of this theme — it helps to make her own unfulfilled existence more tolerable. Furthermore, in spite of the pain, there is always a glimmer of hope when men can suffer too:

> Cuántas noches voy vagando, angustiado, silencioso,
> recordando mi pasado con mi amiga la ilusión.
> Voy en curda, no lo niego que será muy vergonzoso,
> pero llevo más en curda a mi pobre corazón.
>
> (*Trago amargo*)[17]

> How many nights do I wander around, in silent agony
> Recalling past days with my mistress, hope.
> Drunk I may be, and the shame of it I can't deny,
> But my poor heart is more drunk than I.
>
> (*The Bitter Draught*)

The past illusion that has been lost is almost always one either implicitly or explicitly based on love, and there is always the chance — even though common sense denies this — of going back and regaining what has vanished. One of the best-known — and most appealing — tangos, which was made famous by Carlos Gardel, is *Volver* (*Going Back*):

> Sentir,
> que es un soplo la vida,
> que veinte años no es nada,
> que febril la mirada
> errante en la sombra
> te busca y te nombra.[18]

> Feeling,
> that life is but a brief instant,
> that twenty years are nothing,
> and my feverish gaze,
> roaming in the shadows,
> searches for you and calls your name.

and it is significant that these six lines form the epigraph to the last chapter of *Boquitas pintadas* (p.250), immediately preceding the announcement of Nené's death at the early, but undeniably unromantic, age of fifty-two. There was no going back for her and there never could have been.

It is obvious from the beginning that the characters have been doomed to failure from birth, and the reader's reactions are heightened by the fact that it is so easy to know these characters through and through. When *La traición de Rita Hayworth* comes to an end, even Toto is little more than a sketch, though one that promises a complex future. When we put down *Boquitas pintadas*, on the other hand, we know all there is to know about Juan Carlos, Nené, la Raba, Pancho and all the other characters. Their trajectory holds our interest and we recognize their collective suffering and bewilderment, for they hold no mystery for us.

Clearly, the plot of a novel of this sort will have to be skilfully presented: if characterization stops short of individual delineation, what actually happens will, of necessity, be unusually important. And equally clearly, the fact that almost all the action lies in the past is also bound to increase the author's problems in creating a telling narrative. Nevertheless, the result is incontrovertibly successful, and this success is due both to the accomplished disposition of vital information and to the great variety of stylistic approaches.

The narrative layout has several key points. The opening announcement of the death of Juan Carlos Etchepare at the age of twenty-nine is, of course, one of them. This has two potential effects on the reader: it creates a certain mystery, but its impact could also be seen as negative, since it precludes any possibility of *Boquitas pintadas* being a 'winning through' tale with a happy ending — the *sine qua non* of the *folletín*, or novelette. In the event, it seems to be the reader's desire to find out why and in what circumstances this ideal example of young manhood came to die that prevails, and this curiosity is stimulated even further by what follows: a series of nostalgic letters written to Juan Carlos's widowed mother by a former sweetheart of his. This is Nené, or Nélida Fernández de Massa, now married to someone else, the mother of two children and living unhappily in Buenos Aires. Then, in the third *entrega*, our interest is rekindled as we learn more about Juan Carlos himself. He had, so it seems, been 'la vida entera' ('life itself'), as the epigraph puts it, to more women than one. One of his conquests had been Mabel, a friend of Nené's (though from a higher social bracket); indeed, Mabel had preceded Nené in his affections. Another was an older woman, always referred to as 'la viuda Di Carlo' ('widow Di Carlo'). This gives added impetus to the narration: Nené's feverish desire to capture something lost for ever — or at the very least, to have her love letters returned to her as symbols of this period and the relationship — is given a new dimension with our realization that what she has lost never, in fact, existed. Nené's present existence is devoid of either pleasure or fulfilment, and in this she is one of many. There are two possible consolatory outlets: anticipation and nostalgia, and she has no option but to resort to the latter. Her life is unsatisfying from an emotional and a material point of view. Marriage and motherhood have failed her, as of course they were bound to, given her hopes, and Buenos Aires (the only spatial *ailleurs* in the second novel) is a bitter disappointment to someone who thought that the sophistication of a big city would solve all problems. Anticipation, it goes without saying, is pointless for the *Boquitas pintadas* characters. Conversely, this is one of the keys to the author's manipulation of the reader, whose interest is maintained by providing the denouement of component stories or episodes *before* their narration and explanation. The death of Juan Carlos, just one example of this technique, could perhaps be seen as the most important instance of it, since it is with this piece of information that we are led into the novel in the first place.

In the following chapters, this method of presentation is interspersed with the occasional narrative surprise, which constitutes another means of winning over the reader. Not the least of these minor climaxes, as MacAdam has called them,[19] is the discovery in the fifteenth *entrega* that the recipient of Nené's confessional letters and the author of the encouraging replies she has been receiving is Celina, Juan Carlos's hostile and antipathetic sister, and not his elderly mother. But before this revelation, we find out about Mabel's brief engagement to an Englishman whose only attraction is his social standing and his money, and the successful pursuit of la Raba by Juan Carlos's great friend, Pancho. When Juan Carlos has to enter a sanatorium at Cosquín, and his love letters to two different girls are reproduced, this is little more than a narrative elaboration, since his wide-ranging interest in the opposite sex has already been indicated, but another 'minor climax' is brought about when the potentially happy relationship between Pancho and la Raba comes to an abrupt end: she finds that she is pregnant, and he leaves for a police training course in Buenos Aires. If the reader has entertained any hopes for their future together, this optimism suddenly and irrevocably evaporates, and it is not long before la Raba faces up to the truth. As everyone's situation becomes more and more difficult and disappointing, there is yet another narrative surprise. This time it consists of the revelation of a clandestine sexual relationship between Mabel and — although there is a wide social gulf between them — Pancho. Mabel's engagement has ended, her family has lost its money and gone down in the world, and her father has become involved in litigation with her ex-fiancé, once his partner. But Pancho (somewhat ironically, since la Raba has by this time gone to work in Buenos Aires), is back in Coronel Vallejos, and a new episode begins.

Although it comes as no surprise to the reader, given the reverse layout of the plot, Nené's marriage could also be judged a key point in the novel's narrative, together with the attempts made by la Raba to visit her in her new home in Buenos Aires, attempts doomed to failure because of Nené's sense of shame that her surroundings are far less impressive than she might have hoped. It is when la Raba herself returns to Coronel Vallejos and goes to work for Mabel's family that the tragic melodramatic climax of the narrative, second only in importance to the death of Juan Carlos, but greater in its impact, is recounted. 'La sorpresa que le espera' ('What a surprise it will be for him') (p. 169) thinks la Raba, as she anticipates an 'accidental' meeting with Pancho in the street and his first sight of the son who will inspire him with love, compassion and remorse. Her pathetic desire to impress Pancho in any way she can results in a more sensational event than she could have anticipated, for when they do actually meet, she knifes him. He is furtively leaving Mabel's bedroom, and the scene bears no relation to how she had imagined it. The sentimental tango lyrics that run through her mind form ironic objective correlatives to her action, for these emphasize the horror and pain of her situation.

Further minor surprises are in store: that Juan Carlos's sister, Celina, should approve of the widow Di Carlo's moving to the mountains to look after Juan Carlos is not entirely to be expected, given the version of her character and views presented by Nené. Can this unfriendly creature, who ruined Nené's life, possibly have her brother's happiness and wellbeing in mind, and be sensible enough to countenance such a liaison? The conversation between Mabel and Nené that follows this *entrega* is revelatory too. Mabel is to be married, but there is none of the excitement that there ought to be in the circumstances. Things, it seems, are turning sour. But in fact they have never been otherwise, and Mabel's confession of her involvement in Pancho's death, her regrets on the subject of her relationship with Juan Carlos, followed immediately by the recounting of the day of Juan Carlos's burial from the point of view of those who loved him, all confirm this impression. We hear of poverty (in the case of the widow Di Carlo who supported him until he died), bitterness, vows of vengeance (from Celina, convinced of Nené's guilt in causing her brother's illness) and unhappiness all round.

There is narrative movement again as the situation becomes ever clearer. Now the key action is the anonymous letter sent to Nené's husband by the furious Celina, denouncing his wife's fantasized unfaithfulness and revealing her avowed regrets at having married him. Once Nené herself finds out about his, she goes away, apparently definitively, to Cosquín, where Juan Carlos had lived with the widow Di Carlo. This could have been the sentimental end of the story, with Nené, realizing her mistake in marrying a dull, pedestrian husband, at last having the courage to leave him and to return, if only in her imagination, to one who represented romance and beauty and joy. But this is not a sentimental story, and that is not the end of it. The sixteenth and last *entrega* presents us with the most significant moment of all: Nené's death notice, and the details of the final conversation between her and her husband. She revokes the instructions for her burial that she had once put in a sealed envelope and deposited with their lawyer; they had stipulated that a bundle of old letters, also deposited with him, should be put in her coffin with her. Now what she wants, she says, is a lock of her granddaughter's hair, the watch she gave to her younger son when he made his first communion and her husband's wedding ring. The letters, she adds, can be destroyed.

The layout of the narration and the extremely carefully-calculated distribution of information are probably enough in themselves to hold the reader's interest, but there is an added bonus in the text's linguistic variety. It was Josefina Ludmer who first analysed this, and García Ramos reproduces her findings.[20] There are, as Josefina Ludmer points out, two rhetorical techniques in the novel: one based on internal discourse and one on narrative communication with the reader. The first technique is, of course, indirect; the second, direct. Within the second we find four kinds of *relator* (narrator): the transcriber, who presents something already written by someone else (newspaper items, for example); the objective narrator, describing, for instance, the décor of Mabel's bedroom (in the third *entrega*); the objective classifier, who gives ordered, official-sounding information from a position of omniscience (this is not a rhetorical device, of course), and the subjective narrator, found in the eleventh *entrega*, where the tragic outcome of la Raba and Pancho's relationship is played out. There is much of interest in this breakdown of the text, but for the present argument what is important is the absence of monotony for the reader, who goes from letters to the contents of a diary, from lists to timetables, and from dialogue to the traditional techniques of presentation of an *histoire*.

There is consummate authorial skill behind the revelation that life is far from satisfactory, to say nothing of containing actual happiness. Nevertheless, the characters do not, on the whole, go in search of a spatial *ailleurs*, at least not in the direct way that those obsessed by Hollywood films did in the previous novel. In *Boquitas pintadas*, the sentimental words of the tangos recall the past, that different country that is beyond the reach of everyone, and which is here as bogus as any Hollywood scenario.

Like *La traición de Rita Hayworth*, the second book is predominantly about women, notwithstanding the fact that its most attractive and desirable emblem figure is Juan Carlos. It might even be argued that it has a feminist viewpoint. No female character finds happiness or fulfilment, and the centre of life's attraction in every case is a feckless man (this is true even of Celina). Could it be that Juan Carlos, embodying as he does masculine beauty and macho qualities, is destroyed because of the author's vengeful anger? Is the reader being led to a greater consciousness of the social injustice of most women's lives? The film of *Boquitas pintadas* made by the late Leopoldo Torre Nilsson was judged an exposé of this kind by several critics, one labelling it 'a fierce piece of social criticism'.[21] However, the film is not the book, and Puig has admitted that he always knew that it would be a Torre Nilsson product, not his own, thus implying recognition of shifts of emphasis.[22] In any case, some audiences, apparently, did not react as the director presumably hoped they would. When the novelist V. S. Naipaul saw the film in Buenos Aires, he was saddened, even exasperated it seems, by what he saw as a misplaced emotional response on the part of the other spectators. What amazed him was to find that cinema-goers were weeping for the wrong reasons, lamenting 'the foreseeable death of the macho, the poor boy of humble family who made his conquests the hard way, by his beauty'.[23] And if this is so patently *not* what the film was meant to be about, we must add that this is not what the novel is about either. Could it be about the evils of machismo, as Naipaul implies? This is his definition of that much-discussed phenomenon (he is talking about men who live in what he calls 'colonial mimicry'):

> For men so diminished there remains only machismo . . . which is really about the conquest and humiliation of women. In the sterile society it is the victimization by the simple of the simpler. Women in Argentina are uneducated and have few rights; they are reared either for early marriage or for domestic service. Very few have money or the means of earning money. *They are meant to be victims; and they accept their victim role.*[24]

The 'colonial mimicry' of Coronel Vallejos is, as we have already noted, even further removed than usual from its model: it is not even Buenos Aires, itself a simulacrum. Here women are victims — often willing, even eager, to be so, it seems — and men are only too ready to play their part as exploiters and oppressors. This pattern, so often considered typically Latin, is something that Puig has commented on in the past and of which he is very conscious. For him the woman of today, emancipated and clear-thinking, by and large, is totally incapable of believing in the fallacy of the all-powerful male, the 'macho superior', but in the epoch and setting of *Boquitas pintadas* this state of affairs still lay in the future, and neither sex thought to question its stereotyped role. It is not only in Coronel Vallejos that women have striven to conform to the images that men have thought up for them, in the name of love. Furthermore — and this is of great relevance where Puig's first two novels are concerned — for the last sixty years or so, the way to discover exactly what the current acceptable image was has been to consult the mass media, particularly and in the first place the cinema. Recent studies of female role-playing have drawn our attention to the way that the dominating male has dictated feminine fashion, and to the

frequent anomalies between what he wanted (and what was therefore
aimed for by the subservient sex) and the actual conditions of life that
women endured. Until recently, any change in society's attitude
towards women has come about exclusively as the result of masculine
caprice; there has been little self-recognition or awareness on the part of
the victims. The cinema reflects this: in its early days, for example, it
presented audiences with the child-woman and the fragile, spiritual
virgin, and then emphasized sexual freedom, embodied in the female
stereotype of the twenties. What Hollywood's unquestioned models
had in common was that they diminished women and, as Marjorie
Rosen has put it, made them 'smaller than life'.[25] Female expectations
of the reward, a great love, were usually thwarted: the observations of
one of the characters in the 1955 Argentine novel *Rosaura a las diez*, by
Marco Denevi, are apt as far as this subject is concerned. Rosaura, the
story's heroine, is seen as:

> . . . una de esas espléndidas mujeres sensitivas, las grandes amadoras de
> Goethe, a las que la educación burguesa . . . malogra en parte. No
> gozan de libertad anímica, tienen que pasarse la vida encerradas en sus
> casas, entre personas mediocres, sin horizontes espirituales, sin
> satisfacciones, sin expansiones, hasta que se unen a un hombre que ellas
> no han elegido, que no las comprende, y que ellas no aman, o que, si lo
> amaban, pronto las defrauda . . . estas mujeres por lo general, como
> viven espiritualmente frustradas, esperan que el amor les compense de
> todo. Se hacen del amor una idea fantástica, hipertrofiada, y cuando se
> casan, y el hombre no las entiende, o es un grosero que no está a la altura
> de su sensibilidad, sufren horriblemente. Y entonces, claro, se produce
> la escisión dentro de su estructura espiritual. La realidad les es
> aborrecible, y para evadirse de ella se fabrican otro mundo, un mundo
> imaginario, el de la fantasía y de los sueños.[26]

> . . . one of those splendid, sensitive women who adore Goethe and whose
> middle-class upbringing . . . could not be judged entirely successful.
> They enjoy no freedom of mind, they have no option but to spend their
> lives shut up at home surrounded by mediocre people, without spiritual
> horizons, without ever achieving satisfaction, without any possibility of
> expansion, until they marry a man not of their own choice, who doesn't
> understand them, that they are not in love with; if they ever did love him,
> he soon proves a disappointment to them . . . Generally speaking,
> because they live in a state of spiritual frustration, these women expect
> love to make up for everything. They turn love into something fantastic
> and overblown, and when they marry and acquire a husband who
> doesn't understand them, or who turns out to be a brute with much less
> sensibility than they themselves possess, they suffer horribly. And then,
> of course, there comes a split in their spiritual make-up. Reality is hateful

to them, and they run away from it by inventing another world, an imaginary world, a world of fantasy and dreams.

La traición de Rita Hayworth is a straightforward example of the invention of this kind of fantasy world, but in *Boquitas pintadas* there is a variation. The female characters, at the moment of narration, yearn less for another world than for that period in their lives when they could still believe that it existed. Nené sadly looks back on her far-from-ideal relationship with Juan Carlos; Mabel indulges in regrets and remorse too, and la Raba's efforts and daydreams revolve around the possibility of regaining the affections of the worthless Pancho. The reader is saddened by the realization that not only are the conditions of the past clearly impossible to recapture in any circumstances, but also that the original relationships in no way resembled the idyllic view the female characters now have of them. Life is unsatisfactory and unjust for these women as it was for those in *La traición de Rita Hayworth* and, as García Ramos points out, basically they are aware of this: it is typical and significant that when Nené meets up with her old friend and rival, Mabel, in Buenos Aires, they prefer to listen to the romantic serial on the radio than to tell each other what has actually happened to them.[27]

It would be only too easy to assume that *Boquitas pintadas* is about social injustice and, in particular, about the role of women in an unfair situation, where they are misled, misinformed, uneducated and unaware. This would entail a certain moralizing — even proselytizing — aim on the part of the author, and would justify the use of the word 'satire' by critics of Puig's early works. The essential characteristic of any satirist is the confident knowledge that what he sees before him is wrong, and the belief that there is a remedy, if only people can be made to recognize this. Yet it seems to me that there is too much *general* unhappiness and frustration for this one-sided viewpoint to be judged the *raison d'être* of the first two Puig books and, furthermore, the author manifests far too much sympathy for his characters and too little clear-cut condemnation for any one of them for us to classify his work as satire.

Women are exploited and dominated, but the fate of the men is not altogether enviable either. Their lives, though considerably easier, could not be judged happy or fulfilled in contrast to those of their female counterparts. Berto, in *La traición de Rita Hayworth*, is no more contented than Mita; La Paqui's fiancé, in the same novel, has no real reason to be happy; in *Boquitas pintadas*, even Juan Carlos cannot be said

to have enjoyed an easy life, in spite of his good looks and his
charismatic powers: he is bitter because he has been cheated of an estate
that he judged himself entitled to, he is unable to live up to the rhetoric
of love and he is mortally ill. Life is not paradise for men in the field of
sexual relations either. The romantic, other-worldly attitude of the
women towards love often involves a certain distaste for, or at least
disapproval of, sex. As a consequence, marriage is often as much of a
disappointment to the husband as it is to the wife. La Choli, in *La
traición*, was more than disenchanted with her boorish husband, but
there is little doubt that he was severely disappointed in her too: her
attitude towards sex, either with him or with another lover when she
covers up an affair she has later, is scarcely normal, to say nothing of
being joyful or spontaneous. Society's many anomalies include the
possibility of lateral sexual activity for the man, and this is rightly seen
as yet another insult to women. But it is also, of course, a sad indication
of the unsatisfied condition of the rejected husbands. Nevertheless, it is
not that the women are totally devoid of sexual urges, or that they are
totally innocent. In *Boquitas pintadas*, Nené has had an affair with her
employer, Dr Aschero, and Mabel has been involved with Pancho and
Juan Carlos; there does not seem to have been any pressure put on them
in these cases. Even where the most unjustly used woman is concerned,
la Raba, it was not a question of force or obligation. Yet, in the end, the
female viewpoint is different: there is a (conditioned) sense of shame
about them, a fear that these lapses will be discovered and, in the worst
cases, broken marriages, hatred, even social ostracism can be the
outcome. Society has misled both sexes. The men know that they want
sex, but love is, perhaps, less easily defined for them; conversely,
women aim only for love — or, at least, what they consider to be love —
and are thrown off balance and made to feel ashamed by their sexuality.
For Puig, sexuality is 'total innocence', but for his female characters it
is at odds with social laws and falsely-imposed ideals.[28] Women have
been made to feel guilty and are inhibited and confused; for men, sex
becomes a question of conquest and deceit.

If — as I maintain — Puig is grieved by the sufferings of these
admittedly unappealing Lotharios as well as by the unhappy
circumstances of the women they exploit, then it is surely what lies
behind all this that he is highlighting. Though machismo has so often
been seen as an almost codified series of indignities directed at women,
it has taken a Manuel Puig to show how any society that follows this
doctrine will also be made up of disenchanted men, with ever more

bizarre goals in life and disappointment around every corner. Though in interviews he has made no bones about asserting that women *are* oppressed in his native Argentina, he also makes it clear that the whole of Argentine life suffers as the result of a national attitude that extends into the world of culture and the arts. Until the country is able to shake off machismo, he said at the time of the election of President Alfonsín, it has no hope of getting rid of all the other forms of oppression.[29] For him, sexual and political oppression are virtually interchangeable, as the later novels illustrate.

In the first book it was the Hollywood dream that provided the objective correlative to the hopes and ambitions of the female characters. In the second, as we have seen, the temporal *ailleurs* is signified by a variation of this world, with nostalgic radio soap operas and tango lyrics. Inarticulate, two-dimensional people say what they need to say by means of the platitudes of these mass art forms, while all the while remaining fundamentally aware of the hopelessness of their situation. This juxtaposition of a popular art form and overwhelming but inexpressible emotions was highly original when *Boquitas pintadas* was published. Since then it has been repeated, and it might be interesting to consider just one later example of the technique that was particularly successful: the Dennis Potter television serial *Pennies from Heaven,* which was turned into a film in the United States by Herbert Ross (1981). Although the film version involved very many changes, it still retained the basic device of incongruity and pathos, and succeeded in impressing many critics, including Pauline Kael. The idea, she claimed, was obvious yet strange, and had a certain pungency. She points out how in this particular vehicle for it (which in the film version was 'a stylized mythology of the Depression'), the popular songs of the period constitute expressions of people's deepest longings. 'When the characters can't say how they feel,' she says, 'they open their mouths, and the voices on hit records of the thirties come out of them . . . Their souls are in those voices . . .' Her claim that the film does not allow the spectator to distance himself could equally well be applied to *Boquitas pintadas,* and furthermore, her conclusion that 'the emotions of the songs can't be realized in life' is just as appropriate where the novel is concerned.[30]

If it is what is *added* to the original novelettish pulp fiction genre that turns it into a successful work of art, then there is no doubt that *Boquitas pintadas* cannot be judged a mere *folletín,* or novelette. Unlike the authentic *folletín,* the mythic background indicated in *Boquitas pintadas* is one of vital importance, and its evocation serves as an aid to self-understanding on the part of the reader; the cheapness, even worthlessness (though this is debatable in this case), of a signifier is not necessarily an indication of frivolity, inaccuracy or irrelevance in what is signified. However, the fact that the author draws our attention to the appreciable distance between real life and dreams does not necessarily mean that he has any parodic intention. Like the satirist, the modern parodist maintains himself aloof from what he is portraying, and his tone is almost invariably self-righteous and contemptuous. Puig, though clearly not totally identifying with the inhibited and misguided victims of the *Boquitas pintadas* society, is still too close to them to be anything but sympathetic, even distressed. Indeed, it is this that might be seen as the *raison d'être* of the book. There is no scorn or amusement in his approach, and Sarduy's claim that the novel is not just a *folletín* but also the 'doble irrisorio del folletín ('the ludicrous carbon copy of a novelette') merits much closer examination. It may be that, as I suggested in Chapter I, neither of these assertions can be accepted, at least not without major reservations.

Let us consider the claim that the novel actually *is* a *folletín*. If it is true that its mythic background is one that is fundamental, and is on a universal level, this claim could not be made for the novelette. On the other hand, Puig himself has said that that is indeed what *Boquitas pintadas* is, and it is true that he originally intended to publish it in instalments: only problems of a practical and commercial nature prevented this. Nevertheless, I contend that it is impossible to classify the book in this way, and for many reasons. In the first place, although Puig has enjoyed an unusual amount of popular success for a serious novelist, no one could suppose that this book is directed at the usual *folletín* reader. Andrés Amorós, who has made a study of the phenomenon known in Spanish as *subliteratura* and in French as *paralittérature* and which includes the *folletín*, has given us a clear picture of its typical reader: naïve and uncomplicated, totally lacking in any sense of modernity, a traditionalist who is sentimental and almost certainly female. She will not be a great reader, since she enjoys the most hackneyed conventions and clichés, and she will be impecunious enough to want to avoid the expense of buying books. Research, as well as common sense, indicates that she may well live in a rural area where bookshops are few and far between. The vast majority of Puig's readers do not fall into this category, even if some of his characters do. Then it is evident that there is a commercially and politically manipulative aim on the part of the (often anonymous) author of this kind of literature, an aim based on his knowledge of the precise nature of his audience. Since a best seller will necessarily reproduce many of the beliefs society has conditioned in the reader (the rules of the game, in fact), he would be foolish not to incorporate and emphasize these in an approving fashion. The resultant work will both reflect and influence its readers.[31] This is not true either where Puig is concerned. If he does highlight the standards of the society he is describing, it is in order to question them, not so as to find any profit in them. In fact, very few of the usual features of the classic novelette are in evidence in *Boquitas pintadas*, other than at one remove in the stories so admired by its female characters. The narrative itself is not sentimental, even if it is moving. There is nothing really implausible in it, unless we see Celina's extended rancour as unlikely. Although there are typically enticing chapter titles, made up from touching lines taken from tango lyrics, there is little else that is typical. There are no incredible coincidences — the element so beloved of Romantic narrators — and dishonour and social inequality are not unduly emphasized; the author makes no attempt to avoid specific spatial and temporal settings and there are few fairy-tale elements. Moreover there is no way of claiming that the morality of the work is guaranteed, as invariably happens in the *folletín*. And though it is difficult to sympathize with the male protagonists, it is also true that at first it is not all that easy to feel for the females either. There is no respect for great institutions in the book, either explicit or implicit, no cheap homespun philosophy (again, other than at one remove), virtually no facial determinism, no highly moral role models, no maudlin patriotism, no religiosity, no anti-female assumptions (the opposite is nearer the truth), no insidious approval of traditionalism, no idyllic vision of the countryside, no lack of ambiguity and certainly no happy ending. There are, in fact, countless areas of divergence between *Boquitas pintadas* and the usual manifestations of 'subliterature', and though it true that in order to merit consideration for inclusion in a genre, novels do not have to reflect every one of its observed features, at least a reasonable number of them should be in evidence. Perhaps the most obvious variation, where *Boquitas pintadas* is concerned, lies in the style. Amorós has noted the plethora of exclamations, the use of archaic, or at least anachronistic, language, the frequency of purple passages and 'poetic' phrases, the incidence of extended similes and prolonged comparisons, the over-use of adjectives, the intercalation of philosophical reflections, the repetition of bathetic oxymorons and,

perhaps most obtrusive of all, abnormal syntax, in the *folletín*. Not one
of these features is discernible in Puig's mode of writing, though the
female characters sometimes clothe the expression of their emotions
and descriptions of their situations in a not dissimilar style. The most
striking example is Mabel, who at one point resorts to writing to a
magazine advice column as she tries to understand and come to a
decision about her feelings for Juan Carlos. There is here a fascinating
juxtaposition of model and imitator as we read the editorial answers to
her letters. In the same way that the authentic *folletín* both reproduces
and influences the values of its readers, so the advice columns of the
magazine *Mundo femenino (Woman's World)* reproduce and influence
popular style and, therefore, attitudes. 'Me ama un muchacho bueno
pero de incierto porvenir,' confesses Mabel in standard fashion ('I am
loved by a fine young man, but his future is not assured'); 'al principio
yo estaba segura de quererlo con toda el alma' ('at first I was sure that I
loved him with all my heart'), and, again typically, but unnecessarily,
she refers to his 'apuesta figura' ('his handsome looks'). She signs
herself, 'Espíritu confuso' ('Confused soul'). The printed reply reflects
not only the style of cheap literature — 'Eres muy joven y puedes
esperar la llegada de un príncipe azul . . .' ('You are still very young
and can afford to wait for your fairy prince to come along . . .'), for
example — but also its priorities. The fact that Mabel consults an older,
'wiser' person in the first place is another instance of the influence of the
folletín: this move is tacitly, or even sometimes explicitly, recommended
in many of them. The insistence in the journalist's answer on
maintaining family harmony and waiting for someone respectable and
rich (though this latter condition is only implied), together with her
consolatory optimism — 'confío en que saldrás adelante' ('I'm sure
you'll win through') — based on doing what is socially the right thing, is
also standard.[32] In the end, the *folletín* has a strong influence on Mabel
and Nené, but not on Manuel Puig.

If *Boquitas pintadas* is not really a *folletín*, in spite of Puig's claim that he
made use of the format in order to reach a wider public, to avoid
hermeticism and to encourage a special, different kind of reaction in his
readers and critics,[33] could it be seen as a 'hilarious' or 'ludicrous'
carbon copy of one, as Sarduy claims? The use of the word 'irrisorio' in
the original affirmation suggests parody, with the theories of Mikhail
Bakhtin on the subject as the basis for assessment. Bakhtin's seminal
study of Rabelais has frequently been invoked and elaborated on by
critics of contemporary Latin-American fiction, but it may be that this

is a misguided approach where Manuel Puig is concerned.[34]

That the use of the parodic format 'discrowns' its counterpart, as the English translation of Bakhtin puts it,[35] tempts us to consider *Boquitas pintadas* in this way. Certainly, whenever and wherever the reader of Puig's novel is aware of the literary model it is to the disadvantage of that model, and each reference constitutes a step in the process of demythification, if indeed such a genre could be said to be susceptible to this. It is this point, though, that leads us to the main problem where the concept of parody is concerned. Parody, in the terms used by Bakhtin, mimicked and mocked serious rituals, and the key to the process was laughter; institutions and people were both glorified and derided. It may be argued, of course, that the modern use of parody is different. Bakhtin himself points out how the mediaeval carnival was 'far distant from the negative and formal parody of modern times', since 'bare negation is completely alien to folk culture'.[36] In the old sense of the word, then, glorification and derision; in the modern, bare negation. It seems to me surprising that Puig has ever been thought a parodist: there is no point in either *Boquitas pintadas* or *La traición de Rita Hayworth* where the author could be thought to be laughing at his characters, mocking their mindlessness, or distorting them and exaggerating their characteristics so as to reveal their weaknesses. On the contrary, Puig recognizes and identifies with his characters; this is clear enough from a reading of both novels, but it is also a point that he himself has made on several occasions. When actually discussing the question of parody, he admitted looking up the word and finding the definition: 'imitación burlesca' ('burlesque imitation'). 'Yo te aseguro,' he said to his interviewer, 'que nunca mi intención es la de burlarme de mis personajes' ('I assure you that it is never my intention to mock my characters'). He went on to talk about the extent of his identification with them: when I write a letter signed by Nené, I am Nené, he claimed, and what he calls the 'density' of the result depends on the level of identification that he can achieve. 'Yo no condeno la cursilería' he added ('I do not condemn pretentious vulgarity'), 'al contrario, me enternece' ('on the contrary, I find it touching'). For him *cursilería* comes about because people want to be better, to improve life, and if the result is incongruous this arouses pity in him, rather than scorn: 'No creo que mis personajes sean caricaturas, yo me propongo hacer retratos' ('I don't see my characters as caricatures. My intention is to portray real people').[37] Furthermore, there is no question of 'bare negation' in either of the first two books. To begin with, Puig does not see the novelette as an inferior genre, so that ridicule is not his intention, even as far as the format is concerned.[38] The people he writes about are victims, both women *and* men, since it is not really a question of the strong exploiting the weak, but of the weak exploiting the even weaker. The culprit, to a certain extent at least, is society, with rules and conventions that are far removed from the needs and conditon of human beings. Puig has said that he does not try to judge or make pronouncements: the reader can draw his own conclusions.[39] Although it is clear that by following the rules of the game, many of his characters in *Boquitas pintadas* are denying fundamental desires and convictions and are motivated by self interest — Mabel is a good example — it is also true that it is the system that they live in that convinces them that this is what they have to do. They deceive themselves because they have been deceived, and society must assume part of the blame. In the first novel life was made tolerable by dreams. In the second, 'the necessary dream' is not really a solution. But in a way, the characters have no choice, for to rebel would denote individualism, and we are dealing with a collectivity.

There is a certain amount of negation here but there is also an ambivalence in the author that invalidates the label 'parody'. Perhaps the answer is that Puig uses the format for precisely the reason he gave in the first place — so as to reach a wider public and attempt to provoke a special type of reaction. *Boquitas pintadas* is not parodic, any more than *The Buenos Aires Affair*, his third novel, really parodies the detective story. These structures are attractive showcases for the author's investigations and research. The judgements are the reader's.

Because of a seemingly irresistible desire to place everything into neatly-labelled categories, critics have also seen the first two Puig novels as Camp literature. In this case they may be justified. The temptation to classify them thus comes about in the first place because of the element of awareness in the writing — that is, of using a genre while at the same time being eminently conscious of the process. This is not to denigrate, or even to see as Camp figures, the many famous artists who have made use of mass art forms to create works of undoubted excellence. As Richard Collins has pointed out, no one can deny the debt of Shakespeare, Jonson and Webster to popular Tudor and Jacobean theatre, of Mozart to café entertainments, of many an early British novel to eighteenth-century journalism, or of Dickens to nineteenth-century melodrama. Furthermore, as Collins claims (and Puig would surely agree with him on this point), it is dishonest to maintain a categorical differentiation between 'culture' and 'popular culture' by annexing all the important artists for 'culture'.[40] Nevertheless, the question of frequency is important and should not be ignored: it is not open to doubt that standards of excellence are often lower, and great and illuminating works less often encountered, in the mass art forms. Contemporary writers in particular are well aware of this, particularly those whose heritage, so to speak, is almost entirely made up by those mass art forms. This is frequently the case in Latin-American countries and the Caribbean, where the source of cultural diffusion is elsewhere, where illiteracy and poverty are rife, and where the colonizing power, whether overt or insidious — like Hollywood models in Argentina — creates attitudes by means of entertainment. It is often a question of manipulation. An instance of cultural dependence on exotic commercial and political interests is amusingly recalled by the Puerto Rican novelist, Luis Rafael Sánchez, who sees what he now describes as 'the invention of another reality' in his childhood as something he could not then recognize.[41] Later, knowingly, the mass media and the pop world are pilloried and twisted, indeed brilliantly used, in his novel *La guaracha del macho Camacho* (1976). Nothing could be more artful than this book, and yet a good deal of its appeal for the reader lies in the joy of recognition of the original sources of language and attitudes taken from popular culture and commercial communication. Both Sánchez and the reader enjoy riding two horses at once. Is *Boquitas pintadas*, though, really Camp writing?

If we consult Puig himself, we find that he more or less admits that it is. When talking about his genuine affection for popular art forms, he once added his own definition of the essence of Camp: 'ridiculizar, tratar de destruir algo que se ama, para demostrar que es indestructible' ('ridiculing and trying to destroy something one loves in order to prove that it is indestructible'). On the same occasion he went on to confess that he had never read the Susan Sontag article 'Notes on Camp' (1964) because he was afraid to do so, afraid that too much awareness of his own techniques could be pernicious: he preferred to depend on intuition or inspiration.[42] At that time, at least, he could not know if his work corresponded to Sontag's criteria, and those critics who have written on the subject since the sixties are unlikely to have attracted his interest.

In effect, the second novel contains all the best qualities that Sontag attributes to Camp writing, while avoiding the less appealing features of it. On the positive side, even the author's avowed innocence is something that the American critic recognizes and sees as a virtue. 'Pure Camp is always naïve', she claims. 'Camp which knows itself to be Camp (camping) is usually less satisfying'. Furthermore, its essential element is seriousness.[43] Camp is generous, it wants to enjoy, it finds success in certain passionate failures (this can certainly be applied to Puig), and its knowingness is an aspect of intelligence, for the Camp sensibility is 'alive to a double sense in which some things can be taken'.[44] In his more recent book, Mark Booth presents a view of the phenomenon in which he denies the word 'sensibility', seeing Camp as 'primarily a matter of self presentation',[45] and justifying this assertion by pointing out that secret or private activities have no purpose and no effect:

> If you . . . try to amuse yourself by watching an awful old film, you are not being camp. You only become so if you subsequently proclaim to others that you thought Victor Mature was divine in *Samson and Delilah*. China ducks on the wall are a serious matter to 'straights', but the individual who displays them in a house of otherwise modernist and modish furniture is being camp.[46]

His whole approach to Camp is less sympathetic than Sontag's and he is often dismissive, claiming that the mode of behaviour in question is sometimes no more than a matter of natural preferences disguised as condescension, and referring to scandal, luxury and self-decoration, to commitment to the unworthy and to the fact that Camp people have created very little themselves: what Camp prose there is, he says (contradicting Sontag), is 'unserious'.[47] He is not persuaded. Even Susan Sontag confesses to having mixed feelings on the subject, and she lists characteristics that could in no way be seen as admirable: Camp taste, for example, is connected to snobbish taste, and style is everything. The areas that she condemns and which Booth sees as repellent are mostly irrelevant to Puig's approach. Camp's defects are not usually his defects, though we shall discuss the conflict between what is aesthetically acceptable and what is immoral, though stylish, in a later chapter.

Puig's Camp writing is indeed the *manifestation* of a sensibility, and does constitute what Booth would call a mode of behaviour. He makes no secret of his tastes and fondness for what he might have pilloried, and his real commitment to what some might see as marginal is evident. There is, however, a major difference between his pure approach and that referred to by Booth with a certain amount of disapproval, and that is the motivation that lies behind the glorification, if that is what it is, of something that is less than High Art. Puig is dealing with the tragedy of life and his sympathy with his characters is deeply felt. Sontag has claimed that tragedy and Camp are incompatible bedfellows, and that Camp represents the victory of irony over tragedy. Puig proves conclusively that this is not the only way to see the issue: he is not disdainful and he does not distance himself. What I shall call 'non-distanced irony' is another point that will be referred to later. If it can be said that this work is not really parodic, it should also be added that it is not ironic either, or at least not in the way we normally understand irony; both parody and irony start from a point of view almost unknown to this author at this moment in his career. In this his closest counterpart could again be seen as the British dramatist Dennis Potter, whose play *Sufficient Carbohydrate* was based on the soap-opera format. Potter himself asserted that despite what people thought, this format could not be seen as completely redundant, since 'it allows the release of emotional truths that you couldn't get at in any other way'. And a critic who interviewed him on the subject of this play pointed out that 'instead of ironic distance, the form offers an unusually direct contact with the energies behind the play'.[48] Potter is like Puig in that his intentions could not be more serious. Susan Sontag's assessment of Camp as 'a kind of love, love for human nature',[49] is an appropriate comment as far as *Boquitas pintadas* is concerned, but it is only a beginning, for from this we must move on to the ultimate view that the author's awareness of his characters' socially-induced wrong-headedness, poor taste, naïveté and their doomed aspirations is a way of revealing his frustration in the face of the fate of mankind. There is no censoriousness here and no self-righteousness. Observing the rules of the game, whether they be moral, political or aesthetic, brings people no fulfilment, but the fault lies in the game.

CHAPTER IV

'The Divided Self':
The Buenos Aires Affair (1973)

> People are not sadistic *or* masochistic, but there is a constant
> oscillation between the active and the passive side of the symbiotic
> complex, so that it is often difficult to determine which side of it is
> operating at a given moment.
>
> Erich Fromm, *The Fear of Freedom*

THE Buenos Aires Affair may well be Puig's most misunderstood novel.
He himself once said this, but that was in 1981, and *Sangre de amor
correspondido* had yet to be launched on an audience that, by and large,
received it with puzzlement and disappointment. Nevertheless, it
cannot be denied that Puig's third book has met with more than its fair
share of incomprehension.

Perhaps its most immediately misleading characteristic is the
detective-story format for, like the novelette framework of *Boquitas
pintadas*, this really is a red herring. It should always be borne in mind
that part of this author's strategy to arouse and maintain the reader's
interest (he himself has admitted to a low boredom threshold) consists of
trying out new formats. As Michael Wood has claimed, much
contemporary Latin-American fiction is 'constantly in search of new
stances, angles, tones, twists and modes of narrative,' adding,
however, that 'it asks these discoveries to lead it back to a shared world,
not off into a region of pure play or dream'. Puig's formal variety,
Wood says, is itself 'a fidelity to the shifting relations between
experience and its representation'.[1] In this way, too, the reader's
reaction to the novels will be more spontaneous, and it will perhaps

contain a glimpse of something that might otherwise be inaccessible. Popular art, as Richard Collins claims, offers forms which may be annexed by great artists; this is common currency,[2] but Puig's novelty lies in his unusual use of *certain* elements, no more, that make up these forms, and ultimately in the way that incongruously serious, even tragic, truths are held up for our inspection by means of them. As Rodríguez Monegal said as long ago as 1974, every new novel by Manuel Puig discards the format of its predecessor and explores a new kind of narrative; he goes on to say, incontrovertibly, that Puig uses the detective story more as an emotional archetype than a rhetorical prototype.[3] For the principal, indeed the vital, characteristic of the detective-story genre is actually not present in *The Buenos Aires Affair*, as we shall see. Others disagree on this. García Ramos, for example, believes that the novel *can* be classified in this way, and he refers to those features that are usually considered essential to the genre and which are evident in it (the conflict between rationality and irrationality, together with mystery, individualism, good versus evil, and adventure leading to a final victorious outcome).[4]

Clearly, though, this is not enough: if all these elements are put together, they do not necessarily make up a detective story — and *The Buenos Aires Affair* could hardly be said to have a triumphant ending. The important divergences are that there is no investigation in the Puig novel, no real detective, virtually no police involvement, no hunt for a criminal, and there is even a certain ambivalence about which of the two crimes contained in the narrative is crucial to it — the killing of a young homosexual prostitute by the male protagonist, Leopoldo Druscovich, or the abduction of the heroine, Gladys Hebe D'Onofrio, from her holiday home. The police show no interest in the former, since they are given the wrong information about it, and the latter is never even reported to them. This is, basically, a psychological, or more accurately a psychoanalytic, novel, and though it is undeniable that there have been writers of suspense stories whose principal interest lay in psychology and motivation rather than what Puig has denied an interest in, 'problemas ajedrecísticos' ('chess problems')[5] — Georges Simenon and Patricia Highsmith immediately spring to mind — these authors always make use of some kind of investigation in order to provide a backbone to their narratives. Rodríguez Monegal is surely right when he maintains that the paramount variation where *The Buenos Aires Affair* is concerned is that the emotional focus of the novel lies not in an investigation of a crime but in the fantasies, dreams and delusions of the protagonists.[6].

It is the discovery by her mother of Gladys's disappearance that acts as a kind of detonator, to use García Ramos's word,[7] to the story, somewhat after the fashion of Juan Carlos's death notice in *Boquitas pintadas*. In this third novel, though, we have left behind the limiting provincial sterility of Coronel Vallejos, with its pathetic and often two-dimensional characters. We are no longer concerned with emblems of *subdesarrollo* (underdevelopment), but rather with knowledgeable and cultured people, products of a big city, who are travelled, cosmopolitan and talented, since Gladys is a prize-winning sculptor and Leo has become a powerful and respected art critic.

In the invented holiday resort of Playa Blanca, Gladys, a neurotic thirty-four-year-old spinster, is trying to regain her health, cared for by her resentful widowed mother, Clara Evelia. As the book progresses, Gladys's background and personality, her life story, and ultimately the cause of her disappearance, are revealed to us. We learn about her depressing childhood, her contempt for her mother's vulgarity, her unsatisfactory relationship with her father, and her later dreams and obsessions. We are also told of her sexual problems and her attitude towards her own sexuality. On a narrative level, we hear about the years she spent working in the United States, about her initial success as a sculptor — an interest she gave up when she went abroad — her unproductive love affairs and, above all, about the traumatic loss of an eye in an assault in Washington DC in 1962, when she was twenty-seven years of age (the attacker was a demented exhibitionist who exposed himself to her before striking her with a cudgel). To return to Argentina seems the only solution four years later, when her nervous condition becomes suicidal. It is there that she takes up sculpture again, attracting the attention of Leo, the art editor responsible for the choice of a national representative for an Inter-American Art Fair shortly to be held in Brazil. The lives of these two become closely entwined, but not before Leo's background and upbringing are catalogued too.

Like Gladys, he is neurotic and unhappy. Brought up by his sisters after his mother's death (when he was only three months old), he had virtually no contact with his father. Highly-sexed, but apparently incapable of love, he is obsessed by a general sense of guilt, which was implanted in him in his childhood, and by remorse for two specific actions from his later life: the first, the death at his hands of a homosexual prostitute, and the second — and this time his guilt is entirely without justification — his choice of Gladys as the Argentine

representative in Brazil. He regrets this decision bitterly, attributing it
to favouritism on his part: he misremembers his original professional
enthusiasm and now sees himself as biased in her favour because of the
relationship between them.

Leo's sexual prowess is entirely dependent on violence and is fired by
resistance on the part of the woman, a fact he discovers fairly early in his
adult life. His sadism is obviously an extension of the machismo of the
male characters in the previous two novels. Both Leo and Gladys are, in
fact, exaggerations, perhaps even caricatures, but they are not really
'sexual outsiders' as was once claimed for them,[8] and Puig's stated
intention of demythifying with this book all that is murky and taboo in
human sexuality[9] is well served by the way in which they are portrayed.
It contributes towards the reader's increased self-understanding if the
novel is interpreted in the way I think that it should be. It is, of course,
Leo who has kidnapped Gladys in order to further a complex plan
designed to persuade his middle-aged confidante and surrogate mother
figure, María Esther Vila, who is afraid and suspicious of him, that he
could not possibly be the author of the violence perpetrated all those
years ago on the homosexual, a crime he half confessed to her in an
unguarded moment. She is the candidate he now supports for the São
Paulo Fair furthermore, transferring his affections to his substitute
mother. He drugs Gladys, ties her up, and forces her to submit to him
sexually in front of María Esther; then misinterpreting the extent of the
danger he is in, with almost Borgesian logic[10] (he is actually not
suspected of anything) he drives too fast, and is killed. Gladys is at the
lowest possible point of her affective and professional life, and is saved
from suicide only by the friendly interest of a well-meaning and
outgoing neighbour of Leo's, a young married woman with a baby; her
husband, who works for an airline, has just gone off to work and left her
alone in the house. As García Ramos rightly says, an 'auténtico
anticlímax' ('authentic anticlimax') indeed.[11]

This is not a detective story, and certainly not a light-hearted parody
of one: we are not conquering fear with laughter, and we are not re-
creating something solemn; nor are we aiming for 'a lighter tone', as
Bakhtin's interpretation of the genre supposes.[12] Though the author's
objective might be seen as having something in common with parody's
aim of degradation, and the obvious emphasis on the excesses of the
flesh echoes parody's insistence on earthy detail, that is not enough to
invalidate our assertion that the choice of the detective-story format is
based only on the artist's wish to experiment and to pave the way for a

new, and therefore different, critical reaction. In each of Puig's novels the sixteen chapters act as a kind of skeleton for his construction, the materials of which are taken from all sorts of known and admired literary genres and sub-genres, and from diverse areas of language.[13] It was Héctor Libertella who originally claimed that Puig belongs to the group of Latin-American writers who can be seen as creators of the *novela del lenguaje* ('language novel'),[14] and he is right in the sense that Puig constantly experiments, and has turned what he once saw as his incapacity to deal with Spanish (as opposed to the English of the Hollywood paradigm that was ever before him), into an eminently effective hotchpotch of what is often referred to as 'non-literary' language. García Ramos has pointed out that after the first two books, Puig is no longer a chronicler but a novelist, with the concomitant danger that 'se arriesga más al conocer menos' ('he risks more through knowing less').[15] But happily, he sails through these risks with consummate skill. In this book we have fourteen chapters of conventional third-person narrative, and a move away from characters who speak for and explain themselves, as in *La traición de Rita Hayworth*. This is not to say that we are no longer dealing, to a certain extent at least, with 'voices', the spoken rather than the literary word, but these are now mixed up with all kinds of other styles — jotted-down telephone conversations, a caricature of the elegant glossy magazine interview of the epoch, a chapter (Chapter One) that is pure cinema, then, later, a scene described from the point of view of more than one participant in it (partly influenced by Faulkner, partly a repetition of camera takes, from — literally — different angles), excerpts from newspapers used as objective correlatives, and the so-called 'sensations' of Leo, Gladys and María Esther, which are a kind of stream of unconsciousness.

What is new, too, is the function of the mass art form that the author uses. This time it is again the Hollywood and, in one case, the Argentine cinema of the thirties and forties: each chapter of the book is preceded by a still and some dialogue. The dialogue has in many cases been taken from the Spanish versions of the scripts, which were adaptations rather than translations of the original, specially created for the South-American market; the distortions serve to make what Rodríguez Monegal has called the 'diálogo intertextual' ('intertextual dialogue') between the epigraphs and the chapters all the more comprehensible and accessible. There is no literal correspondence between them, but they create an emotional climate — again, Rodríguez Monegal's words — that clarifies everything.[16] What is remarkable about Puig's style, especially evident in *The Buenos Aires Affair*, is the way in which he manages to achieve two aims at once. He is a devotee of narrative, he says, and this cannot be denied. He wants to tell stories that will entertain people (and like the *nouveau roman* authors, this he does with a *soi-disant* detective story), but at the same time there is something more, and this something is a series of reflecting metaphorical points that create an atmosphere and send out waves, so that it might almost be possible to deny the importance of the narrative. This is something more than a story, it is a psychological study, and surprisingly, it is universal psychology that is being investigated. The subjects may be exaggerated, but their extremes are only an extension of what we all know and recognize and are. They may be *superdesarrollados* (overdeveloped), but the grotesque nature of this intensification does not remove them from our sphere of acquaintance and, ultimately, we shall see that like the rest of their fictional counterparts in Puig, they are in fact *subdesarrollados* (underdeveloped). We have already discovered that this epithet could be applied to those characters who could not be called individualistic; now, in the third novel, we find that it is true of those who apparently are.

One more or less obvious truth that we have noted in Puig's first two books is that although women are markedly worse off than men in this patriarchal, indeed *machista*, society, neither sex is truly happy. This is not to say that nothing should be done, nor that a change in our approach to the relationship between the sexes is not essential, but it does suggest that there is no heaven on this earth. In order to survive it may be necessary to believe that there is, but there is no evidence to support this belief. Ironically, if both sexes endured the same degree of suffering it would be something worth aiming for, marking a dramatic step forward in social development. The fact that neither Leo nor Gladys finds happiness in life can be considered in the light of its social significance. Both of them transcend the limitations imposed on them by their backgrounds and family circumstances, both of them leave home and live in countries noted for an advanced social system (in the case of Leo) and for the power and importance of women (in the case of Gladys). Yet this does not seem to provide a solution. Many of the characters in *La traición de Rita Hayworth* were conscious of the lack of culture in their lives. Gladys and Leo are no strangers to culture and are able to appreciate some of the good things that, for example, Herminia, in the first novel, was longing for. However, longed-for social improvements are insufficient where deep-rooted human ills are concerned. Indeed, they may well be totally irrelevant to them. Coronel Vallejos did not cause the characters' unhappiness in the first two novels, and neither New York nor Scandinavia will cure it here.

If Puig is not primarily concerned with formal originality in his novels, and if, with *Boquitas pintadas*, it became clear that he was less concerned with social injustice than might at first have seemed likely, it is *The Buenos Aires Affair* that confirms what might always have been suspected: that his passion is for people, what makes them function and, particularly, what makes their lives unhappy to the point of being intolerable. Gladys and Leo are indeed exaggerations. They are exaggerations of the complementary sides of each human being, an enlargement of what makes up each one of us, and the picture is in almost unbearably clear focus.

It is easy to see that the two characters have a great deal in common. In the first place, both Gladys and Leo 'lose' their mother and their father. Gladys rejects her mother at an early age, even if she does not actually die. She is ashamed of her *cursi* cultural pretensions, as evidenced in her reciting poetry (p.13), her social style in general (pp.31-32), her ignorance, and even her use of mascara and her long, painted nails (p.31);[17] it is not long before the child has transferred her affections to a neighbour. (We are reminded of Toto's preferring Alicita's uncle to his own father in *La traición de Rita Hayworth*.) There is no clear gender model here. Conversely, Clara Evelia resents her daughter and has, to say the least, an ambivalent reaction to her disappearance at the beginning of the book. (This is a point we shall return to later.) Even Gladys's father is not over-affectionate, and does not think very highly of her feminine charms (p.35); in any case, he later dies. As for Leo, he is deprived of both parents throughout his childhood. After his mother's death, his father abandons his three children and no relationship at all develops between them before he, in his turn, dies. Neither child has felt, or inspired, love in its formative years.

Then, both of them are oppressed by their sexuality: it actually makes them ill and they are undeserving victims. Furthermore there is no cure, for ironically enough, 'satisfaction' is equated with further suffering, usually in the form of a headache. It is not without significance that Leo's ambition is to be middle-aged, as he says to María Esther, so as to be rid of sexual problems and 'calmar los nervios' ('have calm nerves') (p.236), and that towards the end of the novel, Gladys sees the only possibility for her future survival as a quiet life, a *vita minima*, looked after by her mother and then, on her mother's inevitable death, 'permanecería quieta en su cama; si se quedaba quieta en su cama, allí moriría porque nadie le llevaría nada de comer' ('she would lie quietly in her bed; if she stayed quietly in her bed, she would die there because no one would bring her anything to eat') (p.236). Earlier on, though, the only consolation for Gladys is masturbatory fantasizing, after which she invariably feels worse (p.75). In parallel fashion, Leo desperately tries to control the frequency of his adolescent masturbation, since 'a la mañana siguiente le atacaban indefectiblemente dolor de cabeza y depresión anímica' ('the following morning he would unfailingly suffer from a headache and depression') (pp.106–7). He is better off than Gladys, of course: life is always easier for men. He can at least find some sexual release — either with prostitutes, eager girl-friends or, ultimately, in marriage. Leo is not much better off, however, since he finds that success is invariably linked with violence: for him there is never any unadulterated pleasure. Without sadism he is impotent, a fact that his wife discovers in due course.

In spite of Leo's countless sexual experiences and the almost desperate avidity with which Gladys acquires lovers when she is in the United States, neither of them finds love. This is what Gladys wants, but not one of the six lovers catalogued in the novel is the answer to her prayers. When she meets Leo, it seems to be her last chance, but this relationship is doomed to failure too. Puig himself describes his characters and their love affair like this: 'Mi protagonista lo que busca es un ser superior y lo que encuentra es un sádico que se interesa por su condición de masoquista; por su condición de mujer ávida de mal trato, pero ella no es una "verdadera" masoquista' ('My protagonist is in search of a superior being, and what she actually finds is a sadist, interested in her condition as a masochist, a woman who is longing to be ill-treated; but she is not an "authentic" masochist').[18] It is true to say, however, that although Leo is an 'authentic' sadist, his condition is explicable. He would have wanted love, like everyone else, but uncontrollable physical and psychological pressures stand in his way. Even his surname connotes friendliness.

It is not only Leo who associates sex with violence. Gladys is consumed by fear of intercourse from childhood onwards, never advancing from the view of sex as aggression, which Freud tells us is by no means uncommon in children. When she first sees a totally naked man, she thinks about 'el terrible dolor que significaría ser poseída por un hombre' ('the terrible pain that being possessed by a man would entail') (p.39); male genitals are equated with hell in her mind (p.63); in an imagined interview with *Harper's Bazaar*, she describes her sexual encounter with Leo in terms of torture and bestiality (p.128). This goes back to when she was still very young: her reaction to a friend who had slept with her boy-friend was to see in her mind's eye 'la profunda herida de la carne de Fanny' ('the deep wound in Fanny's flesh') (p.39). Sex is the cause of physical as well as nervous anguish. Gladys is afraid of men, and indeed her fears are justified when she is assaulted by a sex maniac with the kind of club that suggests both phallic power and the brutality of the cave-man. And, of course, Leo's sadistic tendencies make her fearful attitude seem less abnormal. For him, relief comes from thinking that a woman sees a phallus as 'un arma del diablo' ('a weapon of the devil') (p.99); then he frequently imagines 'una sangrienta desfloración ('a bloody deflowering') and this helps him to achieve orgasm (p.96). He shares Gladys's view of intercourse as an 'ataque' (an 'assault').[19] He is unable to function sexually if there is tenderness in his partner's reaction or even a minimal amount of friendly affection. He feels revulsion and contempt towards his first girl-friend as soon a she is actually willing to have intercourse with him, and he becomes impotent when she reveals her dependency on him (p.99). Even when he has recourse to prostitutes, he avoids establishing any kind of relationship with them. He prefers the suspicious hesitation of the initial encounter to the enthusiastic acceptance which they might display if he met up with them again (p.106). When he realizes that Gladys is in love with him, he begins to find her repellent. He rationalizes this by claiming that she is trying to control him: 'In her own timid way,' he says to his psychoanalyst, 'she's trying to take me over. She disgusts me now . . .' (p.142).

It is interesting, too, that both Leo and Gladys have guilt *and* inferiority complexes. Where Gladys is concerned, she feels inferior because she is not a real, fulfilled woman. No one has ever loved her. Even her father had warned her against letting her appearance go: 'Tenés que hacer caso a mami,' he had said when Gladys's mother complained about her posture, 'porque papi no quiere tener una hija loro' ('You must pay attention to what your mother says, because Daddy doesn't want an ugly daughter') (p.35). She is plain, and she knows it. And, of course, when she loses an eye this makes things even worse. She describes herself as 'depresiva, tuerta y carente de talento real' ('depressive, one-eyed and without any real talent') (p.231), she is a 'ser inferior' ('an inferior being') who is not even worthy to use luxury materials for her sculpture (p.119) and who therefore resorts to scavenging on the beach for odds and ends that the tide washes up. She is ever-conscious of how humiliating her condition is. When she is in Washington, for example, her concern is with her 'compañeros triunfantes y casados' ('her all-conquering, married colleagues') (p.48). Love — or her desire for it — even dictates her attitude in the field in which she does have talent, for when she wins a sculpture competition as a young girl, the pleasure is spoiled for her because of the *machista* disapproval of a boy rival that she is attracted to, and later in life she equates Leo's indifference with rejection of her work, and determines that she will never show it to anyone again (p.230). Her fantasized magazine interview makes what she really wants quite clear: although long after the articulation of her novelettish ambition to acquire a mysterious and attractive image as a foreigner living abroad, and to become involved in a thrilling 'eternal triangle' (p.42), little has changed. Her 'necessary dream' is revealed in her combining a certain titillating and exciting vision of sex with the admission that her greatest ambition in life is 'to fulfil herself in love' (p.117). She sees herself as successful — 'a luminary in the plastic arts' (p.117), 'the woman of the year' (p.117) — but shy; confident but reticent; cultured but simple; discerning but at the same time spontaneous. She may be different from her provincial predecessors in Puig's writings in many ways, but she has a lot in common with them too. Through all her fantasizing can be perceived her fears and neuroses, in spite of the gloss of sophistication. She is conscious all the time of what she is not, but in her case she is sure that it is her own fault.

Leo's guilt and sense of inferiority are, of course, not without justification, since he is frequently uncontrollably violent and in all probability a murderer.[20] Yet he too is a victim. As a small child he was made to feel shame at the pleasure he derived when his sister touched his genitals; when he was jokingly encouraged by the maid to do the same to her, he was punished (pp.93–94). He cannot really be blamed for his uncaring attitude when his father is dying either — he is too young and too much a stranger to his father to feel what the adult world thinks he should feel — just like Toto, in *La traición*, who refused to cry at the death of his uncle. Even the murder he committed was unintentional and unpremeditated, and came about because of his propensity for sexual violence. He is full of remorse, as well as fear, considering how he can pay for his crime (p.103); furthermore, he is an informer,

betraying his anti-Peronist companions, and he weeps on that score
(p.103). He is ashamed that no one wants him as a friend (he refuses to
go to the theatre since he will be alone in the interval (p.107)), feels guilt
because it is his fault that a homosexual colleague is sacked (p.109), and
is envious of María Esther, who claims that she never feels regrets for
her actions (p.152). Like Gladys, he is aware that he is not what he
should be. All his troubles have come about because of what Marta
Morello-Frosch has called his 'oppressive sexuality'.[21] The only period
of contentment he has ever had, in fact, was when he was convalescing
after pneumonia. The doctor prescribed complete abstinence from sex,
and 'fueron las semanas más felices de su vida' ('they were the happiest
weeks of his life') (p.109). Perhaps Gladys's well-documented passion
for cleanliness (p.234, for example) and her desire for sweet-smelling
sheets on her bed every day (p.126) represent the same kind of aversion
to what obsesses them both.

So it is that both protagonists are neurotic. Their lives are recounted
using expressions such as 'postración nerviosa' ('nervous prostration')
(p.12), 'llanto histérico' ('hysterical tears') (p.47), a 'crisis nerviosa'
('nervous crisis') (p.56), and an 'ataque de nervios' ('attack of nerves')
(p.217); and there is no shortage of references to suicide, lack of
concentration, fury, nightmares, sedatives, sleeping pills and
insomnia. In Freudian psychology, the causes of neurosis are twofold,
and both are apt where *The Buenos Aires Affair* protagonists are
concerned. The first reason for this state is largely social, and it is
particularly relevant when we consider the peculiarly Argentine
features of Puig's fiction, with its first-generation, rootless immigrants,
manipulated by foreign models. It was in 1908 that Freud observed that
patients often pointed out that all their families were neurotic because
they had wanted to become something more than their origins would
allow. And he added then that psychiatrists were familiar with the
condition in the descendants of peasant families who had gone to big
cities and achieved a notable improvement in their social level.[22]
The second, and more obvious, reason for nervous instability —
repressed sexuality — is perhaps also more acceptable.[23] There is no
doubt that Puig himself portrays this as its main cause in this novel. In
another 1908 essay, Freud emphasized the intensity of the sexual
instinct in the constitition of neurotics, but pointed out that thay were
human beings like everybody else; this seems exactly to reflect the
Argentine author's view of his characters. Freud also tells us that
impotence may well attack individuals with an intensely strong libido,

even that an incestuous inclination may be repressed in this way. Two currents in the immature child — the affective and sensual — have not fused.[24] Leo himself at one point refers to cheap 'simbología freudiana de bolsillo' ('pocket Freudian symbolism') (p. 152), but it is clear that, despite his awareness, he is a perfect example of the Freudian type in question: his precocious sexual maturity, its obtrusive nature, his early games with his sister, the fact that his innocent sexual activity as a child is strictly forbidden (as Freud says, the psychic importance of any instinct increases if its indulgence is prohibited),[25] all lead to his perverted behaviour as an adult, to his unhappiness and, indeed, to his neurosis. As one psychiatrist has put it, 'the study of sexual deviation is very largely the study of sex divorced from love',[26] and this is true of Leo. Among others, Adler has pointed out that the word 'neurosis' covers a multitude of sins. Indeed, the English translation of one of his own chapter headings is 'What Really is a Neurosis?' and in it he provides a long list of possibilities.[27] The common denominator would seem to be an inability to live with the world, often with an intense feeling of inferiority. Symptoms are chronic and extremely distressing.

The Freudian view of the outcome if the libido is suppressed includes artistic and cultural activity as well as neurosis, and this is what has happened with both Leo and Gladys — another feature that they have in common. They are both concerned with the same kind of art, even though Leo is not a practitioner. The world of sculpture has brought both of them the only success they have ever known, but there is conflict between the senses and the creative, aesthetic life. Sometimes these can go together, and all is well: the subject will be an artist, and will lead a satisfying erotic existence. Perhaps Freud overstated the case somewhat when he claimed that an abstinent artist is scarcely a possibility,[28] but in any case, in *The Buenos Aires Affair,* no such happy state has been reached. Even the satisfaction that artistic activity might provide is sullied and even cancelled out by the oppressive nature of the characters' drives and their inability to satisfy them. Neither of them has enough freedom to live a reasonable life.

Leo and Gladys not only have so much in common that they could be seen as parts of the same person, they also complement each other. To begin with, they are interlocking because they are exaggeratedly male and exaggeratedly female, two halves of a whole. The frequent references to the size of Leo's penis suggest several interpretations, one of which is the oppressive nature of all sexuality, another the heavy burden of masculinity. Leo is too much of man. For Libertella, the

novel is basically made up of 'un ojo postizo' and 'pene desmedido' ('a
false eye and a disproportionate penis'), and he goes on to say that 'la
relación entre esos dos elementos permite leer *The Buenos Aires Affair* a la
sombra de cierta sugestiva ayuda psicoanalítica' ('the relationship
between these two elements allows us to read *The Buenos Aires Affair* in
the light of certain helpful and suggestive psychoanalytic points').[29] He
is undoubtedly right, but his memory deceives him over one important
detail of the narrative: this is that after her horrendous experience,
'Gladys *rechazó la colacación de un ojo de vidrio* y el cirujano logró que el
párpado pareciera cerrado pero no hundido' (Gladys *refused to have a
glass eye fitted* and the surgeon succeeded in making the eye look closed
but not hollow') (pp. 48 – 49). What we actually have, then, is an orifice,
and this is even more suggestive: there are countless examples in art and
mythology of the eye representing, or replacing, the female sexual
organs.[30] In this case it is now non-functional. The symbolism is all too
obvious. Then, if it is true to say that Gladys and Leo are larger than
life, how much more so is the sex maniac who made her suffer. He
represents sexual lack of control and violence taken to their frightening
limit.

Complementary, too, are Leo's macho sadism and Gladys's
masochistic tendencies, which reflect the woman's role in socially-
dictated heterosexual relationships. She is a girl who has had a stupid
upbringing, Puig once said ('una muchacha que ha sido educada mal'),
and who has acquired a dubious view of the relationship between the
sexes, in which the woman will necessarily be dominated and
manipulated in some way by a superior being who holds her in his
power.[31] Even if she is not a real masochist, Gladys takes it for granted
that she will be the passive partner. Everything about her alliance with
Leo echoes the juxtaposition of positive and negative. Leo is powerful
inasmuch as his writings influence people, his choices are accepted, his
judgement respected; conversely, even in this context, Gladys is a
victim — she is the pawn of her creative urges and the extent of her
success is dictated by others. Society, yet again, creates her role for her.
Then there is strength in Leo's being a theorist, with all that that
entails. He makes use of his reason and his intellect, he draws on
erudition and knowledge, he is trained, he thinks and therefore he
knows. Gladys, on the other hand, is intuitive, ruled by her feelings, not
in control. If it was the resemblance between the two characters that
caused us to connect them in the first place, it is those areas in which
they are diametrically opposed to each other that make them fit even

more closely together. Their names reveal this opposition — Leo, with its connotations of strength and force, its alchemical connection with the sun, with masculine power in a number of other symbolic areas, with instinct and appetite when it is a sign of the zodiac, and with triumphant virility. Gladys, on the other hand, means 'lame', and suggests colourlessness and inferiority. And all that most people know about Hebe, the goddess from whom she takes her second name, is that she was cupbearer to the gods — another subservient role is suggested, while at the same time her mother's pretentiousness is demonstrated with the choice of this name. With some of Leo's and Gladys's 'sensations', in Chapter Thirteen, this Rorschach-type symmetry is underlined, and the preceding dialogue, taken from the 1931 Marlene Dietrich film *Dishonored* fuels our sense of the fatalistic nature of everything: indeed, the film's title for Argentina was *Fatalidad,* and the disasters suggested in the scene are thought to be inevitable.

There are other areas that reflect Leo's extreme masculinity too. One of his 'sensations', or mental pictures, is of the Praxiteles statue of Hermes. While it is the beauty and general proportions of the statue that would seem to make it of interest to him, he also reflects on the fact that the missing penis muct have been life-sized, unlike so many earlier representations of the male body; this is clearly important. More details about Hermes help us to understand Leo better. For example, he remembers that the god was 'primitivamente símbolo de la fecundidad' ('originally a fertility symbol') (p. 205); in fact, he was often portrayed as no more than a phallus, or as a pillar with a human head on top of it and a phallus half-way up it. In alchemy, too, he is usually seen as ithyphallic, and in his 'Dark Mercurius' identity there are hints of mother-son incest,[32] which may be echoed in Leo's relationship with María Esther (the god's partner was Ishtar, and another version of this name is Esther). His name is connected with rock or stone; sometimes he is a dangerous power that dwells in stone. Since he is a messenger, he has access to the Underworld, and is somewhat ambiguous on that score. He was precocious, according to legend, walking away from his cradle to commit mischievous acts, then claiming innocence. Lastly, he is said by Ovid to have fathered, with Aphrodite, a bisexual child, Hermaphroditos, and other genealogies attribute the paternity of Priapos to him.[33] There is no more literal connection between the narrative and the so-called sensations of the protagonists than there is between it and the film scenes, but the associations that can be made afford us extra insight. Leo himself is ithyphallic and associated with stone. The size of his genitals, frequently emphasized, causes him to see himself as superior (p. 136), his sexual urges are uncontrollable, and almost invariably insatiable, from a very early age. He is hard, therefore metaphorically like stone (it was the Marquis de Sade who advocated that those who wished to enjoy a libertine life should become insensibly hard, emulating the ancient Stoics with their erotic archetypes that included stone).[34] But real stones, too, are key elements in the story of his life, and the image also crops up in the terminology used in its telling. Most important of all, he kills his homosexual victim with a stone — or, more accurately, a brick (p. 101). Later, in an analytic session with his psychiatrist, he describes his reaction to the news that a terrible drought will leave the land stony: '. . . yo no le deseo a nadie la muerte, pero a veces sí he deseado a alguien que padezca . . .' he says '(I don't wish anyone dead, but I have wished someone to suffer'), and he goes on, 'no sé qué pasa cuando queda al descubierto la piedra . . . Quisiera llorar, toda la tarde, no moverme de aquí y llorar . . .') ('I don't know what happens when you get down to the stone . . . I feel like crying all the afternoon, just staying here and crying') (p. 139). Then, in his mind's eye, he sees underwater coral plants which are 'cartilaginosas' (gristly) and which make him want to touch them; they're like lace, he says, smooth lace borders on old-style dresses. 'Son plantas,' perhaps, but he adds, 'No, son piedras' ('They're plants; no, they're stones') (p. 141), and he goes on to refer to fossils, plants that are stone, and to recall how, lying in his bed, he stretches out his hand and touches a 'piedra filosa' (a 'sharp-edged stone') (p. 141).[35] When he imagines killing his psychoanalyst, it is with an ashtray 'de piedra coloreada, cuarzo, más liviano que un ladrillo' ('made of coloured stone, quartz, not so heavy as a brick') (p.183), clearly remembering the crime that continues to haunt him. (Freud, of course, established that shocked patients frequently relive the episode that produced their neurosis in dreams, while discarding it and forgetting it in everyday life.)[36] Strength can become weakness as easily as Leo sees stone turning into dust (p. 141). He himself is the victim of his 'strength', itself only a slightly exaggerated version of what society finds not only tolerable but admirable.

It can all go both ways, and even in Leo's name there is a suggestion of ambiguity or duality. The lion that it connotes may be an emblem of the Lord because of its magnanimity, according to St. Gregory, but it is nearer to the Devil with its ferocity. As a sign of the zodiac it suggests animality, strong desire, instinct and passion, as well as majesty.[37]

Then, as we saw, the connection with Hermes shows that though we are dealing with gods, the Underworld is not far away. Our impression of ambivalence is confirmed when, as Leo talks to his analyst, he reveals his revulsion on the subject of bats — creatures that have a horrid side to them: 'lo miramos por las alas que nos atraen, y después descubrimos que es una rata, que como todas las ratas siempre está entre la mugre y nos da rabia haber mirado a un bicho asqueroso que habría que extinguir' ('we look at them, attracted by their wings, and then we find out that they're rats, and that like all rats they live in filth, and it infuriates us to think we've been looking at a revolting creature that should be wiped out') (p.136).[38] For him, a bat is a filthy *bird* (p.136), and we connect this with the moment when, during the scene in which Leo has Gladys imprisoned in his flat, María Esther (again like a mother, and repeating his sister's games with him in childhood) takes hold of his genitals, covered only by a towel, and says, '¿Qué tenés acá? ¿un pajarito?' ('What have you got here? A little bird?') (p. 204): sexuality has its repulsive side. One or two more examples of duality before returning to the question of Leo's sadism: in the course of the catalogue of 'sensations' in Chapter Thirteen, Leo conjures up a mental picture of Michelangelo's St. Sebastian, apparently fierce and powerful in his role as captain of the Emperor Diocletian's guard and physically robust and forceful. Yet his face is sensitive and his hair long and curly, and this is an aspect of him that is out of keeping with his extra large penis, 'de volumen decididamente mayor al de las otras figuras masculinas imaginadas por Miguel Ángel' ('of much greater volume than those in other male figures imagined by Michelangelo') (p.206). He is also a victim, as everyone knows from the many representations of his martyrdom, and he has often been portrayed as homosexual. One other figure that Leo projects on his mental screen in the same scene is the Wagnerian hero, Siegfried, fearless and blameless, but cursed at birth by an 'enano malvado' ('a wicked dwarf') (p.206). It is not without interest that he never knew his parents (p.207), and there are other details that apply to both Siegfried and Leo, inviting comparison. It is, of course, tempting to see the 'enano' of the Wagner opera — which, incidentally, begins in a cavern, a standard Freudian symbol for the womb[39] — as the so-called 'phallic dwarf'. As Rupert C. Allen has pointed out, 'every man is confronted with the problem of how he is to deal with himself as phallus bearer — else the phallus bearer within will deal with him in ways ranging from the mischievous to the massively destructive'. He continues, 'The manikin is frequently symbolized by his ithyphallic *magic gifts* — daggers, swords, guns, cannons, spears and wands', and this is the case with Siegfried, for whom a magic sword is forged. Furthermore, the phallus 'consistently seems to have purposes and desires of [its] own, whether or not they are in the service of the ego', it represents 'materially creative libido', and it is 'concealed, but it confers upon the possessor a heroic power'. Allen then refers to the Trickster figure in folklore, proud at first of his enormous appendage, but 'as consciousness grows, the biological urge is recognized as a burden'.[40] There is ambivalence again in the fact that, according to H.G. Schenk, 'Siegfried's character is meant to embody the ''purely human'' element which is idealized in a manner reminiscent of Rousseau's noble savage'; Schenk sees this as somewhat incongruous.[41] Something that could be of incalculable advantage to a man may also be uncontrollable and hostile to his best interests.

Leo is both sadist and victim. What passes for love in his life causes pain and distress to others, but he too has been wounded by a kind of love arrow: we should not forget that Hermes and Cupid are often judged to be one and the same character. Michelangelo's St. Sebastian, a soldier, is characterized by the bundle of arrows that he holds in his left hand (p.206), but he himself became the victim of arrows, according to legend. Leo may be superhuman in a way, but he is reduced to a common level by his sexuality, like the gods in his 'obscene' version of Siegfried's story (pp.208 – 9).

Leo falls into the category, so often remarked upon by psychiatrists, of sexual deviants who feel inferior and unlovable because of an early failure in the relationship with their mother.[42] There is almost certainly a further explanation for his behaviour, but we shall come to that later. For the moment, let us consider his childhood. His father was never there and could not therefore act as a model for him. He did not find love later on, so that nothing replaced the auto-erotic practices that had become a habit: he turns into a sado-masochist because he is unsatisfied.[43] Although most psychologists now agree that the two conditions are almost invariably combined in the same person, it is Leo's sadism that comes to the fore, and because he is only half a human being, in a sense, it is not difficult to determine which side is operating at a given moment.[44] There are few examples of masochistic pleasure in Leo's story. One is when he is tortured by the Peronist police (p.103): he feels more and more at peace and compares himself to the Christian martyrs, including, perhaps, St. Sebastian. The only other time that he is conscious of 'una total calma de espíritu' ('complete spiritual tranquillity') is when he gives himself up to the desire to sacrifice his life in order to save that of his desperately-ill sister (pp.107–8). His motivation in both cases may well be a need for the expiation of his sins, or even altruism, but this does not preclude masochism for, as Fromm points out, masochistic phenomena are frequently considered to be expressions of love. Storr states categorically that whereas sadistic behaviour relieves a sense of inferiority, masochism assuages feelings of guilt,[45] and this is interesting, since it might make us doubt whether we can, after all, always determine which side of Leo is in action. After all, it is Leo who feels guilt, and Gladys who is obsessed by her inferiority. Nevertheless, it seems to me that it is Leo's sadistic instinct that is in evidence most of the time. The other half of this divided self is Gladys's predominant masochism.

Superficially and in the first place, Leo's sexual strength and superiority give him a sense of power, even where other men are concerned, for they are his rivals (p.136). What we soon realize is that strength and power are not the same thing. In his struggles, he manifests all the classic symptoms of sadistic perversion, which Fromm judges to be an escape mechanism, an attempt to flee from an unbearable feeling of aloneness and, indeed, powerlessness.[46] He is committed to force, and this may well result in dangerous, even criminal, behaviour.

The person who is predominantly a masochist will go in a different direction. It was Adler who claimed that while active child failures may well turn into criminals, passive child failures frequently become neurotic.[47] This applies unreservedly to Leo and Gladys, for Gladys's childhood was unsatisfactory too, with no success in her later affective life to compensate for it. Conversely, Leo is an 'active type', 'easily excited sexually', as Adler somewhat simplistically puts it. In Freud's view, sadism comes about as the result of arrested development, and Leo represents those who find it impossible to progress further than a certain stage in their psychosexual growth. Although the sadist does not necessarily have to be neurotic too, Puig tells us on many occasions that Leo is. His emotional situation is intolerable in a chronic sense, and he suppresses his urges both consciously and unconsciously. His early attempts to control his masturbation are an illustration of his conscious efforts, while his whole cultural and artistic life is the result of unconscious sublimation: some, at least, of his energy is desexualized.

But is Gladys an authentic masochist? Much depends on how we decide to classify her. First, for her to be accepted as the other half of a divided self, she must have a certain 'authenticity'. Second, if there is any social comment here, as there has been in the previous novels, that is comprehensible only if we truly understand her. The reason that the author himself denies that she is an authentic masochist is that he is using the word to denote those that actually derive pleasure, even sexual satisfaction, from suffering. But though that is the sexologists' definition, there are other ways of demonstrating masochistic tendencies, and, as Mario Mieli has said, a sadistic libertine does not choose a masochistic partner, since he would find little pleasure in hurting someone who enjoys it.[48]

It is Fromm who is most helpful on this subject, pointing out 'the ultimate futility of the means adopted to solve an untenable emotional situation' in the masochist, and adding that pain and suffering are not what he wants, but that 'pain and suffering are the price he pays for an aim which he compulsively tries to attain'. 'The price,' he says, incontrovertibly, 'is dear'. Gladys's aim is to be loved, but, as Fromm says, 'love is based on equality and freedom. If it is based on subordination and loss of integrity of one partner, it is masochistic dependence, regardless of how the relationship is rationalized'.[49]

In the light of this definition, Gladys *is* an authentic masochist, and there is a lot of evidence in her childhood that makes this outcome inevitable. She was always a typical Jungian introvert, hypersensitive and afraid of looking foolish, never likely to turn into the active partner in any relationship. Indeed, if we continue with Jungian terminology, we could see her as the anima in the divided self, producing moods, while Leo is the animus, producing opinions. In any case, what she is aiming for may well be unrealistic. Michael Wood certainly believes that she wants 'good financial prospects *and* romantic love *and* a satisfactory physical relation'.[50] Thwarted desires, as we all know, and as Freud was the first to point out, may well lead to neurosis.[51] But if she is over-ambitious, it is because she was brought up with the same values and aims as Choli, in *La traición de Rita Hayworth,* and she is just as ineluctably bound to be disappointed. Her insomnia makes it clear that she is doomed to facing up to reality, but she still half-believes in her conditioned dreams.

There are two reasons for her state, and they correspond neatly to the constitutional and accidental causes laid out by Freud. It is the subject's constitution that dictates what might be called his 'choice' of neurosis, but then there are also circumstances that affect him or her further.[52]

Presumably the constitutional cause where Gladys is concerned is the fact that she is an 'over-developed' human being, an intensified introvert. So many of her characteristics are common to everyone, but are exacerbated. Her fear of sex and her terror when she considers how weak she is in comparison with men (p.131) are exaggerated forms of normal female apprehension. Young girls see the male sex as aggressive, and any aspect of sex that they may hear about or witness is considered an attack. Among the accidental causes, but again intensified, we are told that girls often suffer from feelings of hostility towards their mothers: Gladys actually hates hers. When she is determined on suicide and cannot get through to her on the telephone for a last word, she is delighted: 'canceló la llamada con alegría', we are told, 'pues ya nunca más oiría la voz de su madre' ('she cancelled the call joyfully as she would now never again hear her mother's voice') (p.238). The feeling is very largely reciprocated. Clara Evelia clearly recognizes the threat her daughter poses as a rival,[53] and Puig himself has described how he wrote and rewrote Chapter One, so as to try to introduce the presence of evil: 'Hay un aspecto tremendo en esta madre y es que desea la muerte de la hija, no tanto por malicia sino para terminar con un problema que le parece no tiene solución' ('There's a sensationally awful side to this particular mother, and that is that she wants her daughter dead, not so much from malice as to get rid of what seems to her an insoluble problem') is how he put it. He went on to point out that Gladys's death would mean that her mother could go on writing poems and reciting. In the end he settled on the version in which Clara Evelia is desperately trying to remember a half-forgotten Bécquer poem when she discovers that her daughter is missing. Like the film dialogue that precede the chapters, this poem creates a kind of emotional climate which provides information (the poem is about a young girl's death), and in this way Puig communicates what Clara Evelia actually wants.[54]

In the 'sensations' of Chapter Thirteen, Gladys shows herself, yet again, to be the obverse side of Leo. In his case, we were presented with heroes, an indication of his sense of importance. Gladys identifies with the barren earth; then when she is filled with alarm, thinking that Leo is about to murder her, she sees herself as a victim in a film scenario, fleeing through the streets of what is probably New York, terrified of an attack which will come from someone she knows.[55] The attack, in real life, turns out to be sexual, and ultimately provokes pleasure. The humble earth opens up and promises to bear fruit. It is worth noting that the farmer who is imagined as sowing his seed has features that are at first impossible to distinguish, but that as Gladys's fear and lack of confidence recede, his face is clearly seen as being suffused with tenderness.

Gladys is conventionally and romantically ambitious where Leo is concerned. She wants to spend the rest of her life with him (p. 123), and her sublimated creative urges can then be diverted towards their true goal. She notes that he does not wear a wedding ring when they first meet (p. 125), so she is obviously determined on something more than just an affair. She is quick to attribute his nervous state to the fact that he has still to find 'la compañera ideal' ('his ideal mate') (p. 124), and she now believes in God, she says, for love makes faith possible (p. 131). As in the Dorothy Lamour song (p. 190), love destroys fear, male strength is protective rather than menacing (p. 131), and a plain woman can become beautiful.[56] The Hollywood film dialogues emphasize the exclusivity of romantic love, with references to the 'único hombre que quise. Y lo perdí' ('the only man I ever loved. And I lost him') (p. 113) for example, and Gladys believes this as much as Nené, in *Boquitas pintadas*, ever did. Art may be a substitute for love, but that is all it is (p. 117). In *Algiers* (1938), the film at the beginning of Chapter Eight, a criminal, Pepe le Moko, is actually redeemed by love, and in *And Now Tomorrow* (1944), before Chapter Nine, we find that without her dead lover, the heroine has ceased to exist: 'esa nada soy yo' ('I am that nothing'). Touchingly, Gladys is convinced that when Leo finds out that she truly loves him, his need for her will grow (p. 131). In the event, as we have already seen, he judges her love a trap (p. 160), and identifies her with both the disgusting and potentially dangerous *galgo sarnoso* (mangy greyhound) of his imagination and the oppressive and repellent bat of his nightmares (p. 143).

Therefore Gladys is a masochist: although she is not sexually excited by pain, she is pitiful enough to believe that suffering and humiliation may bring her what she really wants. And they do not. Yet she and Leo are inescapably and fatally joined together, and the only thing that can separate them is death — either hers (Leo claims that she is a suicidal type, and wishes she would kill herself, pp. 157 and 161) — or his, which in a conversation with María Esther he says he is longing for (p. 153). There is little to choose between their attitudes. Gladys feels great relief and her headache disappears when she finally decides on suicide (p. 238), and she convinces herself that she has motives for it other than her frustration (pp. 230, 237). We cannot help being reminded of Leo's assertion that *his* nervous condition is entirely due to business worries (p.140). The only way out for them both seems to be extinction, though they do not understand why this should be so. And in the end, Gladys does not actually die.

When a sadist and a masochist come together, each invests the other with a great deal of power. For the sadist, there is someone who must be dominated, and he must force his partner to accept him. It is true to say, in fact, that he even fears his partner. For the masochist, there is obvious strength and power to submit to. This combination is a metaphor, too, for the inseparability of the two sides of each person. Male and female, positive and negative, sadist and masochist, all need the other half in order to function. The whole being, Freud said, is originally bisexual. In the 'whole' made up by Gladys and Leo, we have extreme forms of masculinity and femininity, partly dictated by innate human conditions, partly by social pressures. In the case of the male, the result is Fromm's sadistic *pervert,* while in the case of the female it is a masochistic *character,* rather than a pervert. There is hope for the female but not the male half if anything resembling an ideal is to be achieved, an absolute being that has not been divided into two or corrupted once that schism has taken place. It should be clear now what the significance of the paternity of Hermaphroditos is, why it is necessary to draw the attention to the fact that masochism and sadism exist within the same person, and why Gladys and Leo are virtually interchangeable in many ways. (There are many more minor examples: for example, Leo identifies with St. Sebastian, who was murdered with a cudgel, while Gladys was mutilated with a cudgel.) The Platonic idea that everyone is seeking his lost other half, which Freud refers to approvingly in 'Beyond the Pleasure Principle', is relevant here, but the ironic twist is that Gladys and Leo gain nothing from finding each other. The lesson that can be learned from their encounter and relationship is available only to the perceptive reader of their story.

Even if Puig had never commented on his aims in this novel, it is true to say, I think, that they can be deduced. Nevertheless, it is helpful to see what he actually said:

> Está comprobado que los roles sexuales están aprendidos, que el bebé tiene un comportamiento bisexual. Por lo tanto, una aceptación más tranquila de la complejidad de la sexualidad humana daría otra flexibilidad a la conducta. Para desmachizar al hombre, para hacerle perder sus vicios de dominador, veo como una conveniencia la aceptación de su parte femenina, que el hombre aprenda a *abandonarse,* y, por otra parte, que la mujer aprenda a *actuar* . . .[57]

> It is an established fact that gender roles are learned, that babies behave bisexually. Therefore, if we accepted the complex nature of human sexuality more calmly, there would be more flexibility in our behaviour. In order to get rid of machismo in men and free them from the vice of having to be the dominating partner, I think it would be a good idea for them to face up to their feminine side; men should learn to *let go* and, conversely, women should learn to *act* . . .

This is one of the many instances when Puig reveals his interest in Freudian theory. Though it has been argued that Freud was often mistaken, even wrong-headed, this is not the present issue: what *is* important is that Manuel Puig is not among his detractors. Moreover, he evidently feels a strong desire to at least consider the theories of the post-Freudian idealist sexologists — Reich, Marcuse and Norman O. Brown — on the possibility of an unrepressed sexual condition. This is made even more obvious in his next novel, *El beso de la mujer araña,* as we shall see, but there, as here, there is a point at which this 'solution' fails.

In the first two novels, we noted how sympathetically Puig writes about women, how he feels for them and condemns their exploitation and suffering at the hands of men (a position, incidentally, not inherited from Freud). Yet we realized, too, that he is not entirely condemnatory in his view of the male sex. Now, in his third novel, we can see latent bisexual tendencies in both the protagonists, and this is especially interesting, since another major cause of neuroses according to many psychiatrists is the individual's inability to 'identify with the current role assigned by society to male or female'.[58] The ambivalence in the characters points to this, and we can add Freud's claim that neurotic women are very often repressing masculine sexuality.[59] It may even be true that this is why so many masochists are women — that they are denying their bisexuality with an effort to intensify the differences between them and their partner, and this is encouraged by social mores. Then there is an explanation for Leo's sadism which sees his pre-orgasmic violence as the result of forcing himself to be more of a man, using society's criteria of what that concept means.[60] He has been endowed with exaggerated male characteristics and he has to use them. Furthermore, his concern with the size of his genitals is not uncommon among homosexuals. Gladys's fear of men may also be based on her bisexual tendencies, and Leo's ambitious side, his desire to show himself as superior to his rivals, may stem from a need to prove his heterosexual orientation. There are further examples of sexual ambivalence. For example, though the epigraphs for each chapter are usually consistent — that is, those with a female protagonist apply to Gladys — before Chapter Six we have a scene from *Blossoms in the Dust* (1941) which, although dealing with a heroine, creates a kind of parallel to Leo's situation. Perhaps, too, an additional interpretation of the loss of Gladys's eye is worth considering: two orifices, proper to a woman, have become one, as if she were a man.[61]

Sex, then, should be innocence, society should be more comfortable and behaviour should be less inhibited by arbitrary rules that cause immeasurable suffering. There is room for improvement in the short term. In the long term, of course, death is the only outcome, and here, as in *Boquitas pintadas,* there is no way that the reader can ignore this. There is a particularly effective and chilling reminder of the fact in Chapter Fourteen, with its autopsy report on Leo, and, as if that were not enough, an added section entitled, 'Referencias omitidas en la autopsia médico legal' ('Details omitted from the autopsy report') (p.224). The (literally) clinical style of the report and its factual nature are at the same time unemotional and horrifying, even emetic. But Puig is concerned with people's lives, not with death, and forces us to consider what could be done here and now in the fields of sexuality and politics. As we have pointed out before, there are some grounds for claiming that they are interchangeable.

The relationship between the sexes could be improved by the feminization of the macho man. 'La normalidad de la sexualidad sería más fácil a partir de la bisexualidad y el abandono de los prejuicios impuestos sobre las imágenes de "macho" y "hembra"', Puig has said, 'lo que traería como consecuencia superar el peso moral de la homosexualidad' ('Normal sexuality would be much easier on a basis of bisexuality and the abandonment of the loaded nature of the "male" and "female" images; this would bring about the lifting of the moral burden of homosexuality').[62] And homosexuals themselves, we might add, would not have to imitate the defects of heterosexual women as they have done for so long.[63] Gladys's disfigurement was the result of an attempt at the sexual act, as Alicia Borinsky has noted; her mutilated face is a constant reminder of the possibility of this.[64] It also signals an extreme case of suffering because of sexual violence. If sadism is a form of immaturity, with masochism the sadistic force against the ego, then this human immaturity is totally unacceptable. Instead of regressing to the point at which our development was arrested, we should progress. Both Freud and Lacan distinguished between need and desire: need is based on purely organic energy, while instinct and desire are different

in that instinct is a constant force of a biological nature, and desire the
directing force of the psychical apparatus.[65] Ironically, therefore, the
way to progress *is* a form of regression: 'regression' from desire to
instinct to a large extent, since desire is often the result of distasteful
accidents whereas instinct has constitutional causes. Supporting this
argument is the fact that, in the end, it is Gladys who survives. She
survives in spite of herself and because of the normality of a neighbour.
Life goes on; after any melodrama, the everyday struggle continues,
helped along by the touching faith that human beings somehow find in
themselves in the face of all the odds. It seems a pathetic happy ending,
a metaphor for hope in the future residing in feminine qualities. Even
the neighbour's baby is beautiful and appealing and holds promise for
us all.

Yet Puig's lack of sentimentality is too striking in his previous novels
for us to be able to accept this straighforward solution without
reservations; there are no easy solutions. Man is given to neurosis
whatever happens, and there is no chance of total happiness even in the
most enlightened of societies. Furthermore, it is debatable whether the
so-called feminine qualities — gentleness, humility, generosity,
serenity — are the inherent property of all women. Women who act will
become individuals, and individualism can often lead to lawlessness
and anarchy. Alienation is found everywhere, and men and women will
have to find other escape mechanisms to rid them of their intolerable
sense of isolation. It is unlikely that human guilt or fear will ever be
eradicated. History — and Puig's next novel — show us that when one
form of exploitation is wiped out, it is frequently replaced by another.
The sexual instinct is never without a component of sadism, and it is
connected to the ultimate truth that affects us all: the existence of death.
The appealing baby at the end of *The Buenos Aires Affair* is an innocent
and charming contrast with the sexually-mature child who shocks his
blind mother in one of Leo's 'sensations', but he, too, is a phallus-
bearer, even a potential sadist, and sooner or later he is destined to die.
There is no religious consolation either — even Nené's faith, in *Boquitas
pintadas,* was no more than socially-conditioned conformity, and in this
third novel religion is not even mentioned. The only hope seems to be
that if the Leo-Gladys paradigm is a valid one, and the oppressor and
the oppressed are basically one and the same person, the oppressor can
be wiped out and only the oppressed element will survive. The problem
is that survival will be anything but blissful, for in order to take part in
life, both elements are necessary. That was the root of the trouble in the

first place. The image of blindness is used with a certain amount of frequency in *The Buenos Aires Affair,* and Freud, of course, equated this with the mutilation of the sexual organs.[66] But there is another lesson to be learned: if we are clear-sighted, instinct itself will not be blind, and somehow it will be possible to go on tolerably. When Gladys sees the face of the good farmer who impregnates her, there is a sense of joy. The frequently-found image of *brotes* (buds) takes on a new meaning, with hope for the future of the nation, couched in Peronist schoolbook terminology, too: personal and social matters interlock and Gladys's projected suicide jump, which represents childbirth in Freudian terms,[67] is turned into projected fruition. Gladys herself, at thirty-seven and alone, is unlikely to be a mother, but the shift of focus onto the sexually-satisfied neighbour, a form of displacement, suggests human kinship. Indeed, the pregnant young wife might well stand for the best anyone can hope for, for even her contentment is not untinged with preoccupation; it is significant that she hates being apart from her husband and that her greatest fear is of bereavement. Death is ever-present, and again, the only way to combat it is by a meaningful relationship with someone else; the death of an individual is the final castration[68] and the loss of a love object is yet another cause of neurosis.

Sexual, social and political oppression are all organized by human beings in order to prosper at the expense of others. Violence, the extreme form of sexual injustice, is highlighted in this novel. Machismo and its offshoots are the social side of the situation; this was more explicitly dealt with in *Boquitas pintadas.* The political level comes closer to the surface in *El beso de la mujer araña* and in *Pubis angelical,* as we shall see, but it is never far from our attention in *The Buenos Aires Affair.* All three levels are linked, and our understanding is not aided if we consider one without the other two. It would be equally foolish to suppose that the solution is any more obvious in the political field than it was where sexual and social behaviour is concerned. Obviously political oppression, like sexual violence, is wrong, but justice is a somewhat elusive absolute. Nevertheless, the extreme forms of political abuse are easily located. Leo — even Leo — refuses an appointment in South Africa, for example, (p.109), and though it is not explicitly stated, his objections may have been based on humanitarian considerations.

As in the previous two books, there is conflict here between unfruitful sentimentality and 'real life' — 'real life' may be manifest in philistine provincial tedium, as in *La traición de Rita Hayworth,* in the suffering of deceived women, as in *Boquitas pintadas,* or, as in all three novels, including *The Buenos Aires Affair,* in physical as opposed to asexual, romantic love. In the third novel, though, it is also the political situation, a situation that many of the characters prefer to ignore, immersing themselves in their own 'necessary dream'. Gladys's mother, for example, is uninterested in the terrorism that is part of the world she is living in (p. 17). Gladys's political ignorance is also referred to (p. 46), but at that point is more excusable on the grounds of her youth. But when we add to this the smug, conservative, conventional attitude of María Esther, typical of the middle-aged, middle-class Argentine woman,[69] we are back at Puig's wish for women to be active, rather than passive, to think as well as to feel. This is elaborated on in his fifth novel, *Pubis angelical.* The women who do express opinions on the subject are those who find themselves on the fringes of society. They are not convinced by the same manipulators as people like Gladys are, and in that setting, particularly, their views are daring and unconventional. Not for them the kind of absurd ironies that reach their peak when a desperate woman is so imbued with magazine culture that she gives herself a facial massage and puts on clean underwear before committing suicide. They are people like Gladys's friend Alicia and her lesbian lover, previously forced by convention to hide their relationship, but now happily open about it. It is they who accentuate their lack of conformity with a bohemian appearance (p. 46) and go against middle-class values and the political views of the establishment by condemning the United States blockade of Cuba. In yet another example of the affinity between sexual and political oppression, they refer to the 'strangulation' of a small, would-be independent Latin-American state by a more powerful nation. Neo-colonial aggression and patriarchal exploitation are not dissimilar, and strangulation is an image of male aggression towards women that often crops up in psychological symbology.

There is also an emotional basis for the characters' and the author's attitudes towards politics. A clear, though not over-emphasized, area of distaste for Puig in this novel is Peronism, but there is perceptiveness and sympathy in his treatment of some of its followers. His own experience of the régime was not happy even before this book came out, and it was no great surprise to him when *The Buenos Aires Affair* fell foul of the censors.[70] In it, he draws attention to the movement's populism above all things (it is the servant girl who is distraught at the fall of the government in 1955), as he had already done in *La traición de Rita*

Hayworth by highlighting Esther's dreams. The sympathetic but deceived boarding-house dwellers who gain Leo's affections are yet another example of Peronist manipulation of the poor and destitute, so that nothing is clear-cut and straighforward. Leo is careful on most occasions to cover up his anti-Peronist views because he likes his companions. He is so touched by one of them that he gives him some money, but it is perhaps significant that this backfires, his companion spending it on a prostitute with whom Leo himself has no success. Everything is so confused. Instead of being clear-sighted, he is moved by sentiment, but on this occasion it is hard to blame him. Like Puig himself in his attitude towards his own underdeveloped characters, Leo is touched by the *cabecitas negras* who have come into Buenos Aires to find work. They are ignorant and misguided but they are not unappealing. Emir Rodríguez Monegal has commented on the fact that so many of the characters in *The Buenos Aires Affair* have recourse to the same models as Evita Perón herself, and these are taken from the field of popular culture. And the *cabecitas negras* — those who flocked into the capital from the provinces, encouraged by Peronist grants — saw that her ambitions *were* realized. Even though the end was close at hand (she died young, in 1952), the dreams still go on.[71] Puig observes and describes this phenomenon, and we shall consider his attitude towards it in more detail in Chapter VII. He does not spare us the horrors of the system (Leo is tortured, for example), and it may be that Gladys's vision of the future of Argentina in her orgasmic ecstasy — '¡Oh buen hombre! labras con tu sudor el porvenir de nuestra patria . . .' 'Oh, my good man! With the sweat of your brow you are cultivating the nation's future . . .') (p.212) — is an echo of what was preached to admiring *descamisados* by Perón and Evita on many occasions. But though the régime may be repellent, those who are deceived are not. However, Peronism's promises are no more reliable than those of Hollywood.

According to Adler, 'all the questions of life can be subordinated to three major problems — the problems of communal life, of work, and of love'.[72] *The Buenos Aires Affair* reflects this dictum, and demonstrates how impossible it is to separate the three areas. The most obvious and dramatic of them, of course, is the protagonists' erotic dreams and experiences, but we have seen, too, how their creative work is dependent on these — at least according to Puig's Freudian theories — and how 'communal life', or social patterns, also largely depend on sexual attitudes. It is clear that an extension of this, the political field, is inextricably connected to them. The link is a double one. There is the fact that people's behaviour and opinions are actually affected by their sexual propensities and their relationships with others, and there is, too, a possible metaphorical interpretation.

Many critics have pointed out that the basic theme of this novel is not political reality. It is incontrovertible, though, that the social and political observations are important to the text. Puig tends to describe, not prescribe, and it would be an overstatement to suggest that there is a clear message in what he sees and delineates. Nevertheless, there is a lot more to *The Buenos Aires Affair* than at first meets the eye, and if it is one of his most misunderstood books, this is surely because it is also one of the most complex. One of its facets is the metaphorical import that could be attached to it by means of a political reading. We have already seen how María Esther Vila plays an important part on a psychological level: a substitute mother, with the hint of incest indicated by the Mercurius-Ishtar connection; a woman who poses no real sexual threat and who is preferred to one who does (Leo's mother fixation is still with him, since he never had a mother and was unable to make normal progress as a child). This means that he finds it impossible to escape from a stage in his development that belongs in the past. If this is the case, he will never establish a stable, loving relationship with a woman, and we could see his early death as the only way out. At the same time, María Esther represents conservative obscurantism. If her second name reflects the classical, incestuous mother figure, then her first name denotes the standard, Catholic establishment mother figure, which is equally engulfing. To go forward and become an independent adult, Leo has to turn his back on both these aspects of the object of his fixation. Part of Puig's liberation theory must surely involve a wish for the country to do the same thing: to turn its back on past values and out-of-date thinking and standards, especially as the alternative is a terrible one.

On a narrative level, there are many points at which the author's view that political oppression and erotic violence have much in common is evident. As María Esther is reporting her fear of Leo on the telephone, the policeman skims through the newspaper, and the articles that catch his eye create the same kind of climate for the text as do the film scenes at the beginning of each chapter. They are almost all to do with fear, conflict and oppression: fighting in Vietnam, tension in Northern Ireland, Communist infiltration in Latin America, and Russian accusations against the Chinese. The two exceptions are to do with football (conflict in a minor key) and efforts for national progress juxtaposed with news of North-American 'interest' in Latin America (p.85). The next time she telephones we have a repetition of the scene, but this time the newspaper items are reports of crimes mixed up with political news, and her discourse, too, is much more explicit and sensational (pp.169–73). When Gladys imagines that she is being interviewed by *Harper's Bazaar,* she refers to the incomprehensible pleasure men derive from violence — in the boxing-ring, for example (p.122) — and this macho bloodlust pervades everything: sport, politics and sex. The most obvious example in the text of overlapping is the discovery in 1969 of the tortured corpse of a Peronist subversive on some waste ground (p.144); twenty years earlier, another corpse had been found on waste ground, that time the victim of a violent sexual assault. This demonstrates not only that oppression is the same in every walk of life, but that each individual is both exploiter and exploited. Leo was once tortured by the Peronist police; now a worker for the Peronist cause suffers the same fate.

In the end, life goes on and art goes on. When Leo was being tortured there were cheerful songs on the radio in the background (p.103). When Gladys plans suicide, she knows that the opera performances at the·Teatro Colón will go on as if she were still alive (p.233). Society does not come to a halt just because two people die. Because when all is said and done, and in spite of Gladys's apparent survival, two people do die. Her future could never be more than a kind of death in life, and hope is transferred to Leo's well-adjusted neighbours. Gladys has to die because she has lost her other half. Like all the 'double' stories in the literature and folklore of countless countries, the whole being is doomed because one half— either a portrait or a mirror reflection or, indeed, a double — is annihilated. Her 'double' had become so extreme, so distorted, that life for him was impossible, and again she is a victim. The reasons for Leo's condition were partly constitutional but partly accidental, and something can be done at least about the accidental causes. Nevertheless, this is not politically and socially committed writing, any more than *La traición de Rita Hayworth* or *Boquitas pintadas* were. Fundamentally, it is the vision of a man who is saddened by what he sees, but never condemnatory. This reflects what was once said of Freud himself: that he looked upon human frailty all his life without revulsion and without contempt.[73]

CHAPTER V

'The Kiss of Death':
El beso de la mujer araña (1976)

> El hilo que une la araña a su tela es un lazo mortífero y vital a la
> vez . . .

> The thread that joins the spider to the web is a bond that is at the
> same time lethal and vital . . .
>> Annie Perrin and Françoise Zmantar Pez, *'La telaraña'*

El beso de la mujer araña[1] has attracted more critical attention than any
other Puig novel. Its reception has been, and continues to be, such that
1976 — the year of its publication — might well be judged the key
moment in the author's career. It was then that his place in
contemporary Latin-American literature was irrefutably established
and universally recognized. The book impressed everybody, even
those who had not been his most fervent admirers up to that date. For
those who had, it confirmed their previous judgments as a
consolidation of everything that had gone before it; not only did it make
clear where all this had been leading, but it also demonstrated what the
earlier novels had really had in common.[2] For Juan Goytisolo this is
Puig's masterpiece; indeed, for virtually all its critics, both journalists
and academics, it is the best of his work.[3] It is the only one of his novels
to have a whole book dedicated to it (albeit a short one), it has been the
subject of at least one Round Table symposium, and of the ten papers
delivered at a Colloquium on Puig and Mario Vargas Llosa in France
in 1982, as many as nine dealt with *El beso de la mujer araña*.[4]
Furthermore, the theatrical version, an adaptation made by the author

himself from the original narrative, has been well received in several
Latin-American countries as well as in Europe, and a different version
has been turned into a very successful film.[5] It is perhaps worth
mentioning at this point that this has led to a situation that may well be
unavoidable: there are not a few critics who judge everything that came
after 1976 as inferior. Juan Manuel García Ramos is a case in point.
His book on Puig's narrative goes up to and includes the fifth novel,
Pubis angelical (1979), and already, with this last book, a lessening of his
previous enthusiasm can be detected. In a later newspaper article which
deals with the subsequent work, he expresses his disappointment
explicitly.[6] This, of course, is a point we cannot avoid returning to in
later chapters.

It is not difficult to see that *El beso de la mujer araña* is part of the same
oeuvre as the other novels. It repeats a number of the author's favourite
images and ideas, and it can also be claimed with some justification that
one of the two protagonists, Luis Alberto Molina, is a version of a
previous character: he is Toto, from *La traición de Rita Hayworth*, grown
up. Both Molina and Toto find consolation and search for identity by
means of Hollywood and other films, and there is comfort for each of
them, too, in thinking about 'cosas lindas' ('beautiful things') (p.85).
They both selectively and revealingly restructure those films that they
have enjoyed, and in true Lacanian fashion they make progress in life
by means of narrative discourse, either internal or directed at an
interlocutor. Both are victims of spatial limitations, of a mother fixation
and of the imbalance caused by the absence of a father figure. Then,
although there are many points of divergence between them, we should
not forget that almost everything in Toto's childhood points towards
homosexuality in his adult life, and effeminate homosexuality at that.
As Walter González Uriarte has said, 'a su manera, Molina es un Toto
adulto, menos cultivado y de origen más humilde' ('in his own way,
Molina is a grown-up Toto, though less cultivated and from a humbler
background').[7] Like Toto he is by no means stupid, and though
uneducated and far from being an intellectual, he possesses the same
kind of talent as his young prototype for copying and re-creating, both
in his profession as a window-dresser or display artist ('vidrierista'),
and in his beguiling capacity for remembering and elaborating on
cinematic décor, atmosphere and characters in order to entertain and
seduce (in both senses of the word) his cell-mate, Valentín. Many critics
have emphasized his total lack of culture, but their views are
undoubtedly distorted by their distaste for the *kind* of culture that he is

knowledgeable about. Here, once again, we are dealing with the so-called 'géneros menores' ('minor genres') that Puig has so often defended, likening them on one occasion to women in *machista* countries: 'se goza con ellas pero ne se las respeta' ('you have fun with them but you don't respect them').[8]

Puig, like his fictional character, is deadly serious about his favourite art form — one, incidentally that is nowadays acquiring more respectability — and it seems to me that Frances Wyers is right when she says that Puig's art is not cannibalistic and ironic but integrative, and that his use of film is 'anything but tongue in cheek'. This is not to say that there is no irony in the novel, as we shall see later, but the author's use of mass media paradigms is certainly not an example of it.[9] In any case, to return to Molina, he is not actually uncultured or ignorant. His background is incontrovertibly modest — no 'apellido' ('famous surname') in his case, unlike his cell-mate (p.125) — but he has heard of Pascal (p.263), knows more about opera than Valentín does (pp.25,72) and, like Puig himself, is not unacquainted with Freudian theory (p.25).[10]

There is no way in which concrete evidence can be adduced to show just why this fourth novel is so successful. One can only say that the pace is right, even if some critics have found the footnotes that constitute eleven per cent of the text somewhat distracting; the narrative line holds the interest — indeed, is gripping; the characters, though extreme, are credible, and they actually develop and mature as the story progresses; furthermore, there is a splendid narrative surprise half-way through the book. The six recounted film plots themselves hold the reader's attention, of course, with their 'mythopoeic power which neither ineptness of language nor banality of ideas can impugn', as Leslie Fiedler once put it,[11] and there is intriguing interplay between these and the personalities and circumstances of the two protagonists. In addition to all this, there is the fascination of a voyeuristic view of the psychology and lifestyle of an effeminate homosexual, or *loca*, and there are learned footnotes on the subject of sexuality and, in particular, homosexuality.[12] Perhaps most important of all the novel's many qualities is its fundamental air of ambiguity; we should not forget that this is extremely carefully calculated, for Puig made his views very clear when it was published:

> Yo no sé cuál será su suerte [he said in an interview] pero te voy a decir una cosa disparatada y es mi creencia de que esta novela puede ser útil,

en un aspecto didáctico. Es decir, que se ventilen, que se conozcan cuestiones de las que no se tienen la suficiente información. Verdaderamente, la novela tiene una intención didáctica y no me avergüenzo de decirlo.[13]

I don't know how it will be received, but I'm going to say something crazy, and that is my feeling that this novel might be useful from a didactic point of view. What I mean is that subjects about which we haven't got enough information may be recognized and aired. Actually, there is a didactic aim behind this novel, and I'm not ashamed to say so.

In spite of this basic ambiguity, the storyline is quite simple. Molina (he is always referred to by his surname)[14] has been sentenced to eight years imprisonment for corruption of minors, and is now sharing a cell in the Villa Devoto penitentiary in Buenos Aires with a young Marxist activist, Valentín Arregui Paz. In order to while away the long hours of inactivity, the thirty-seven-year-old homosexual tells the younger man (Valentín is only twenty-six) the stories of films he has seen and enjoyed. The age gap is obviously important, and in the theatrical version Puig places even more emphasis on it by increasing Molina's age to forty-one. In this way, as Maryse Vich-Campos has noted, all the films that are referred to are not only part of a culture that would be totally alien to the upper-class intellectual Valentín, but are also from an epoch that he could not possibly remember.[15]

Once again we have a novel with sixteen chapters. This time it is divided into two parts, with the plot laid out so that in the first seven chapters, in addition to hearing — for again it is spoken language that is reproduced — Molina's version of the 1942 film *Cat People*, an invented Nazi propaganda film and his recollection of *The Enchanted Cottage* (1945), we get to know the two protagonists and witness the gradual breakdown of Valentín's reserve. From total incompatibility, symbolized in the play by an opening scene in which the two men are looking away from each other, a friendship gradually develops. Molina is kind to Valentín, panders to his narrative taste (p.118), and even cares for him physically, performing the most degrading tasks when he is suffering from food poisoning and is helpless and incontinent. He shares his provisions with him, and is patient and seemingly altruistic. Valentín becomes more human, even affectionate, as he becomes weaker, and with physical debility comes the diminution of his resolve and even of his courage. It is only when the reader, too, has been lulled into an attitude of complaisant indulgence that the bombshell is dropped. In the strategically-placed Chapter Eight, we discover that

Molina had in fact been planted in Cell 7 in the previous April (the action begins in September) to try to get information from his companion about his fellow urban terrorists. The stakes are as high as they could be: Molina is playing for his freedom and, too, his peace of mind and happiness, for if he serves out his full sentence it is almost certain that he will never again see his old and infirm mother. This revelation obliges the reader to reconsider, if not re-read, everything that has gone before it, and this has the same effect as a second reading of a mystery story, when the criminal's identity is known.

In the first seven chapters Molina has come across as a spontaneous and attractively naïve character, in strong contrast to Valentín's sceptical worldliness and demythifying cynicism. He is gentle and tolerant beside Valentín's rigid self-discipline and cold intellectualism, and flexible and receptive where Valentín is firm, dogmatic and even fanatical — however much justice and right may be on his side. There is no doubt that Valentín sees himself as superior to Molina, if only because the cause he represents, and is prepared to give his life for, is sublime. Both characters are in gaol for what is most distinctive about them, as Milagros Ezquerro has pointed out,[16] both of them are victims of some form of oppression — governmental in the case of Valentín, social and even religious where Molina is concerned — and it is perhaps surprising that it should be Molina who originally wins more sympathy from most readers. Yet he *is* appealing: he is not without a sense of humour (p.35, for example), he is unaware that he is the butt of Valentín's scornful comments (p.13), he is full of genuine remorse for the suffering he has caused his mother. Perhaps this devotion should not be judged a virtue, since his love for his mother is excessive, but he nevertheless seems to be generous and affectionate by nature. And he apparently does not deceive himself: when he speaks of his sexual orientation and his position *vis-à-vis* society, it is difficult not to feel for him. His most disarming trait is his total lack of self-righteousness, and this goes hand in hand with an unwillingness to indulge in self-pity and a capacity for self-mockery. How disconcerting, therefore, when it is disclosed that all this forms part of a calculated plan of deception.

Nevertheless, we soon have to reconsider the situation yet again, for in Part Two we find that Molina gives away nothing at all to the authorities. So it is that the text continues to hold our attention: we, too, have been trapped by a spider woman. And there are many questions left unanswered as the narrative progresses and Molina breaks down Valentín's reserve completely, seducing him physically as well as metaphorically, and at the same time playing cat and mouse with the authorities. When, ultimately, he is released and tries to make contact with Valentín's revolutionary comrades, he dies a melodramatic death at the hands of those he is ostensibly aiding. Even after the final section — Valentín's delirious stream-of-consciousness dream after being tortured — there is no way of knowing exactly what has happened or, more important, why. Some of the unresolved puzzles are relatively unimportant, some vital to the interpretation of the novel, but all of them point to the fact that Puig is asking the reader to make an effort, to contribute his own ideas towards the formulation of a question, even if, as always, there is no easy answer. In spite of all appearances, the narrator is not actually absent; as Yves Macchi has noted, here as in all Puig's novels, 'le narrateur devient le dieu caché'.[17]

To deal with the minor questions first: one that has not, as far as I know, been discussed by critics is why Molina should have indulged in 'corruption of minors' in the first place. Since he sees himself as a woman, says that he wants to be one (p. 25), and admires what he sees as feminine sensibility, it is strange that he should be attracted to a very young boy. After all, he always identifies with screen heroines, not heroes, he rushes to the defence of women's attitudes (p. 35) and he uses feminine adjectives to describe himself and his *loca* friends (pp. 68, 133, 138) — something, incidentally, that irritates Valentín (p. 65). He is really called Carmen, he says, as in Bizet's opera (p. 72), and when he is released we find that his companions use names taken from female film stars, including Manuel Puig's great favourite, Hedy Lamarr (a name the Secret Police agents, who are tailing him and bugging his telephone, fail to recognize, p. 272). Most revealing of all is the conversation between the two prisoners in which Molina explains his particular situation. He finds no comfort in his *loca* friends, he says, but longs — as they all do — for a real man. Although there are homosexuals who fall in love with each other, he admits that he does not belong to this group: 'Yo y mis amigas somos mu-jer', he says ('My friends and I are actually women'), and 'Nosotras somos mujeres normales que nos acostamos con hombres' ('We are normal women who sleep with men'). But, of course, this can never be, 'porque un hombre . . . lo que quiere es una mujer' ('because what a man wants is a woman') (p. 207). 'No me siento hombre', he had said earlier on ('I don't feel like a man') (p. 60), and half jokingly, he had admitted that men 'son unos brutos pero me gustan' ('are swines, but I love them') (p. 35). All this points to the need for a virile, domineering, macho man

— indeed, the current object of his affections, we discover, is a heterosexual waiter, an 'hombre normalísimo' ('a completely normal man')
(p.72), who is an ex-professional footballer, married, and as handsome
as a film star. The offence Molina was charged with seems much more
appropriate for the 'male' partner of a homosexual relationship; why
this seeming inconsistency? One obvious reason for Puig's inclusion of
this particular offence is its function as a narrative device: he has to find
a way of putting his homosexual protagonist behind bars *without his
moral worth being impugned, other than by his sexual orientation.* And just being
a homosexual is not a criminal offence. Then, perhaps more important,
his incarceration with Valentín, a much younger man, leads to a
variation of the corruption of minors theme. We shall return to this.

Another problem is that there is no way of knowing if Valentín dies at
the end of the novel. The play is slightly less equivocal, but even there it
is difficult to be sure. In the play, when Valentín has disclosed the
telephone number of his political contacts, Molina begins to pack his
few belongings; then, in the background, the recorded voices of both
men are heard. First, Molina asks Valentín what actually happened to
him — Molina, that is — after his release, and he is told about his own
death. Molina, in his turn, says that Valentín was horribly tortured and
that his wounds became infected. Strangely, *he* then recounts
Valentín's last dream *to Valentín himself,* and when asked what the
outcome was, his reply is somewhat ambiguous. These are the last few
lines of dialogue:

> VOZ DE VALENTÍN: ¿Y al final me salvé de la policía, o me volvieron
> a agarrar?
>
> VOZ DE MOLINA: No, al final te fuiste de la isla, contento, a seguir la
> lucha con tus compañeros, porque era un sueño corto, pero era feliz . . .
> (p140)
>
> VALENTIN'S VOICE: And in the end, did I get away from the police,
> or did they catch up with me again?
>
> MOLINA'S VOICE: No, you left the island in the end, quite happy, to
> carry on the struggle with your comrades, because it was a short dream,
> but it was sweet . . .

(Valentín had dreamt that he was on a desert island.) After these final
spoken words there is one more stage direction:

> *Se abre la puerta, Molina y Valentín se abrazan con inmensa tristeza, Molina sale, la
> puerta se cierra, cae el telón.*

The door opens, Molina and Valentín embrace with great sadness, Molina leaves, the door closes. Curtain.

This does suggest that Valentín survives. Molina, of course, dies, but the struggle against tyranny continues even if Valentín does join the thousands of *desaparecidos*. One individual is no more, but there will always be those who fight on, and the authorities do not, in this case, find out what they want to know. Furthermore, there may be a reason why Molina had to die. This is another point that we shall return to.

Perhaps the most important puzzle of all, since it leads us to the fundamental question, Molina's motivation, is to do with his agreeing to contact the revolutionary group on his release: he has, after all, frequently begged Valentín *not* to tell him anything about their mission. Does Molina know at the end of his period of imprisonment that he is almost certainly going to be killed? And if he does, why does he go on? Needless to say, critics have considered this point and come up with a variety of answers. The text, though, is not helpful. In the last chapter, Valentín dreams that the woman he loves, Marta, is inside him, and he confesses to her his feelings of guilt and his fervent wish that Molina may have died happy since he was serving the cause. Marta replies, significantly, that Molina allowed himself to be killed because this meant that he would die like a screen heroine. 'Eso lo sabrá él sólo, y hasta es posible que ni él lo sepa', replies Valentín ('Only he could know that and it's possible that not even *he* knows') (pp. 284–85). At this point, then, Puig is saying that Valentín is saying that Marta is saying that Molina died in a gratuitous melodramatic gesture; and in the play there is even more of a *mise en abyme* since it is *Molina* who tells Valentín about Marta's opinion on the motives behind his death. Gilberto Triviños, writing about Puig's first two novels, calls them 'relatos de relatos' ('stories about stories').[18] His judgment is even more apposite when it comes to *El beso de la mujer araña* and the resulting subtleties; but, as we have already observed, there is little doubt that the ambiguity is intentional. Puig refuses to judge or pronounce, or even to be explicit, and he is aided in this by stylistic complexity. It is more than ten years since he explained his position in an interview, and we have no evidence that he has changed his viewpoint; this is what he said then:

> Yo tengo mis ideas y mis convicciones pero trato de no expresarlas muy directamente sino de que los hechos que cuento las pongan de relieve.
>
> I have my own ideas and convictions, but I try not to express them outright; I prefer them to emerge from the facts that I recount.

And he added that where political matters were concerned, any explicit message would turn the work into a pamphlet, and that that would be counter-productive.[19]

Several critics have come up with the observation that, to use Gustavo Pellón's words, 'the author has refused each of them [the protagonists] the benefit of his authority; both Molina and Valentín speak for him'.[20] And although García Ramos may well be right when he claims that Molina is slightly more important than Valentín, since the author has so often written about and discussed his preoccupation with the theme of sexual exploitation, there is really no way in which either of the prisoners could be judged the hero of the novel.[21] Both of them have appealing *and* reprehensible characteristics; the problem therefore is that it is fairly easy to be selective, and make a case either for or against one of them which does not bear thorough examination. It is not difficult, for example, to list Molina's unattractive features and see him as an unsympathetic 'mujer araña', luring his prey into a position of weakness and taking advantage of this situation. One example of this viewpoint is Maurice Molho's essay. 'Tango de la madre araña' ('Tango of the Spider Mother').[22] Although he is right, in my opinion, to assume that the novel approaches activism from homosexuality, and not vice versa, he then goes on to portray Molina as calculating and single-minded in his egoistic aim of seducing Valentín. For Molho, Molina's ultimate sacrifice — he calls it a 'martirio' ('martyrdom') — is 'absurdo y a contratiempo' ('absurd and out of place'), the footnotes (which we shall come to later) seem to him to be taken from 'la biblioteca de algún homosexual inquieto de sí' ('the library of some homosexual who is unsure of himself'), and the sum total of Molina's actions, which he refers to as 'manipulaciones perversas' ('perverse manipulative acts'), is a process of *captatio benevolentiae* designed and carried out entirely for his own advantage. Molina traps Valentín by turning himself into a surrogate mother who tells him bedtime stories, cares for him when he is ill (an illness that he has deliberately connived at), and gives him good things to eat which he claims that his own mother has provided. (In fact, they are the props supplied by the authorities for the comedy that he is acting out.) The film stories, says Molho, divorce Valentín from reality, making him almost cataleptic, and in this way Molina acquires power over him, reducing him once again to helpless childhood. Very neatly, Molho draws our attention to Molina's shift from his mother fixation to *becoming* his mother when he dictates his 'shopping-list' to the prison Governor. And the items on it, he claims, are symbolic: for example, a kind of sweetmeat made from caramelized milk is judged to be 'leche materna, dulce, nutricional y placible' ('mother's milk, sweet, nutritious and delectable'),[23] and he asks for not one but two jars of it. This is seen as a parody of motherhood, and the father's role is taken by the institution, with its unassailable power; Valentín and the prison are two manifestations of virility that Molina must overcome. But in the end Molina dies, and Molho sees this as the inversion of the domination of the theme of homosexuality.

With some minor exceptions,[24] the evidence that this critic produces from the text is indisputable. The point is, though, that it does not constitute anything like the whole truth, and proof of this is that so many others have found enough evidence to support the opposite approach, convinced that Molina's appealing features outweigh his defects and that he changes as the narrative progresses. Even his treacherous pact with the authorities can be explained, if not condoned. As Claude Le Bigot has argued, when he found himself caught up in a kind of pernicious triangle, he was forced to choose between his mother and his cell-mate;[25] this may be seen as not his fault. Like the night-club singer in the (largely invented) Mexican film who is obliged to prostitute herself in order to maintain her sick lover, he had no option but to promise to betray Valentín. And then, what tips the balance very much in his favour as far as the reader is concerned is the fact that he does not actually keep his side of the bargain. Indeed, he is loath to receive any confidences (pp.135, 136, 137), and though we cannot be entirely sure whether this original refusal to become involved is a carefully worked-out, underhand feature of his strategy, his increasing affection for Valentín tends to suggest that this is not the case, and that his behaviour is based on pragmatic desperation. Indeed, it could be argued that the sincerity of his helpless romantic love for Valentín is what makes him sympathetic and affecting; after his release he makes only desultory efforts to renew his acquaintance with the waiter who was formerly the object of his affections, and he is reported by the Secret Police as spending much of his time looking towards the penitentiary where Valentín is still a prisoner.

My contention is that Molina is not a reprehensible character, only a misguided one, and in this he has much in common with several Puig characters that we have already met. Though there is certainly more to him than his sexuality,[26] this is undeniably what is most immediately distinctive about him, and at the same time, it causes him to be fatuous, pathetic and touching. In other words, he is another of Puig's *female* creations, and his approach to life is similar to that of Choli, Nené and even the young Toto.

As he tells his stories and serves the author's avowed purpose of avoiding conventional third-person narration wherever possible, he also embodies the notion of sexual exploitation. He is another ill-used woman, glad to suffer — or, at the very least, *prepared* to suffer — at the hands of a 'superior' man. Five of the six film stories that make up the book illustrate what the author himself has termed 'the various clichés of femininity',[27] and in them Molina invariably identifies with the passive, though central, character. This is very different from the orientation of the vast majority of immature male protagonists in fiction. To take just one well-known contemporary example, Holden Caulfield, J. D. Salinger's adolescent narrator in his novel, *The Catcher in the Rye,* has the somewhat bizarre ambition of becoming a 'catcher', a kind of saviour and protector, when others fall down. There is no doubt that in the same fanciful circumstances Toto would have wanted to be the one who was caught, while Molina would succour those that have been hurt, with loving gratitude his only reward. That is to say, he sees himself as cut out for a domestic, caring role, like conventionally selfless wives and mothers, or the pure and simple heroine of the radio serial *El capitán herido (The Wounded Captain),* in *Boquitas pintadas.*

The first film that he recounts to Valentín, *Cat People,* is the most important. It is the only one to survive the reduction of novel into play, and the book's very title is a slightly amended reference to a key moment in the film. Its retelling, of course, involves many changes, many of which are highly significant,[28] but whatever else is excised or distorted, the eponymous kiss remains inviolate. The kiss of the screen panther woman (in Latin America, the title of *Cat People* was *La marca de la pantera — The Mark of the Panther Woman*) is imitated much later on in the novel by the kiss of the 'spider woman': Molina.[29] There is only one kiss in the original film, even though it is a love story, and only one in Molina's re-creation of it, and in both cases it is a prelude to death. Irena, the screen heroine, falls in love and marries, but she finds it impossible to express her feelings for her husband, for sexual arousal causes her animal proclivities to come to the surface and she turns into a ferocious wild beast. Her macho analyst is the only one rash enough to kiss her, and she claws him to death. At the end of the novel, we find that Molina is happy when Valentín agrees to give him a farewell kiss, and flattered and pleased when he says, 'Vos sos la mujer araña, que atrapa a los hombres en su tela' ('You're a spider woman, catching men in her web') (p.265). But a good example of what we might term Puig's 'non-distanced irony', an element that we shall look at later, is that it is the person who desires the kiss that dies. The victim, that is to say, is the spider woman herself. It is surely important that one of the radical changes in Molina's version of the original film is found in the character and motivation of the heroine. In *Cat People*, Irena is vicious and vengeful, and Valentín is not mistaken when he sees her as a 'psicópata asesina' ('psychopathic murderess') (p.45), but Molina, identifying with her, omits any evidence that could point in that direction and portrays her as the undeserving victim of an arbitrary condition.

As Roberto Echavarren says in an admirable essay on the novel, there is another subtle reversal of accustomed roles: here it is the homosexual who indoctrinates the political activist and the active becomes passive.[30] And we might add that neither character does himself a great deal of good by means of the association between them. Like Gladys and Leo in *The Buenos Aires Affair,* they are essential for each other, but their relationship could never flourish and at least one of them is eliminated. Molina has to die. Death is inevitable, but for Molina it comes sooner than it might have done had he not become involved with Valentín. Where Valentín is concerned, even though he may not die, his immediate mission ends in failure as, presumably, Molina is killed without passing on the message he gave him. Furthermore, the modification in his outlook could mean that he will now face death with less conviction and, therefore, diminished fortitude. Weakness is appealing, but it is strength that prevails: the meek may inherit the earth, but the strong control it.

There are many parallels between Don Quixote, the idealist, and Valentín, while Molina has been seen as a latter-day Sancho Panza;[31] but the two sets of characters have a point of contact that has not, as far as I know, been elaborated on to date. This is to do with the processes of modification that Salvador de Madariaga called the 'quijotización de Sancho' ('the Quixotization of Sancho') and the 'sanchificación de don Quijote' ('the Sanchification of Don Quixote') in the Cervantes novel. Because of his master's influence, Sancho begins to see life differently; by the time Part Two is reached he is judged madder than Don Quixote himself, and his shallow simplicity has acquired subtlety and understanding; he becomes less of a servant, more of a partner, in the search for glory. But, as Madariaga has it, 'mientras el espíritu de Sancho asciende de la realidad a la ilusión, declina el de Don Quijote de la ilusión a la realidad' ('as Sancho's spirit rises from a position of clear-sightedness to dreaming, so that of Don Quixote descends from dreaming to clear-sightedness'), and his attitude as he goes forth on his adventures in the latter half of the narrative is no longer spontaneous. His approach to his activities now contains a certain element of compulsion. His later sorties are based on an unwillingness to be unfaithful to his original commitment rather than on continuing unswerving conviction. In a way, the two characters are transpositions of each other: 'parece que les forjaron a los dos en una misma turquesa' ('apparently they both come out of the same mould') says the priest in Chapter Two of Part Two of the novel, and this observation clarifies a great deal.[32] They complement each other, act on each other, learn from each other; they are, so to speak, inseparable. Sancho achieves a moving dignity with the hurtful process of *desengaño* (disillusion), and there is a final stage of *desengaño* for his master too, as his awareness of approaching death obliges him to repudiate his past fantasies. What is remarkable is that although both of them are disabused and enlightened away from different positions — fancy's excesses are tempered by the mundane in the case of Don Quixote whereas coarse materialism is sweetened by the spiritual and the philosophical where Sancho is concerned — in both cases enlightenment takes the form of an invasion by 'reality' or 'real life'; perhaps we could even call it 'truth'. Yet in the end, death is the only outcome; the two men may be inseparable, but they *are* separated, and there is infinite sadness. It is not only *El beso de la mujer araña* that suggests this comparison, but also the disabusing of Nené in *Boquitas pintadas*.

The two protagonists of *El beso de la mujer araña* have the same need for each other as the *Don Quijote* characters; even though Sancho does not make his appearance in the Cervantes novel until after the first foray is over, and the first six chapters could be thought self-contained, it is with his presence that the sense and complexity of the work begin to take shape. The same is true of *El beso*: Molina comes into Valentín's life and prison sentence (even if not into the text), fairly late in the day, since Valentín was arrested three years earlier and has still not been brought to trial. Yet it is only when the two men act as catalysts on each other for various reasons — some of them reprehensible — that the real drama begins. So it is that it would be as absurd to consider Valentín on his own as to isolate Molina. There is binarism in all Puig's writings, and this is yet another example of it. Valentín is cold and mechanical and single-minded (Molina says he has no feelings, p.110) when we first meet him, but our critical judgments should be even-handed, and we should be able to see that both he and Molina are incomplete, and that there is no real condemnation of either of them on the part of the author. Even the fact that, ironically, Valentín, whose entire life is a struggle against exploitation, immediately and unconsciously exploits his cell-mate is portrayed by Puig more in sadness than in anger. It is another example of an ironic view in which he does not distance himself.

Let us consider a few examples of irony in the novel, and we shall see that the author's involvement and identification with the situation and characters he invents are evident. Perhaps the most suitable area to begin with, since we have just mentioned it, is that of exploitation. As we said, it is the *initiator* of the eponymous, fatal kiss that dies, but not before he (originally an exploited character) has been revealed as an exploiter in his own right, maliciously seducing his victim and 'governing' the prison Governor (Chapter Eight). The perfect mother, in Molina's version of *Cat People,* is another manifestation of this kind of irony. She is a class exploiter, says Valentín, not without justification, but she in her turn is exploited by her husband. Then, we saw that a man whose life is dedicated to a fight against the humiliation of others adopts all that is blameworthy in the conventional male role in his treatment of someone weak and female: in this case, Molina. After his original superior and demanding attitude and his attempts to impose his interpretations of the film stories, which themselves constitute a kind of domination,[33] we are lulled into a false sense of security with Valentín's apparent conversion, but this security is then shaken when he *forces* Molina to promise that he will never allow himself to be exploited (p.265).

There is irony, too, in Puig's portrayal of gender and of the relationship between the sexes, even in the fact that here indoctrination comes from the homosexual. And where sexuality is concerned, we know that Molina looks like a man but, according to him, 'is' a woman, imprisoned in a *calabozo* (dungeon) (p.200). He is actually in prison for being a threat to society, but is well-behaved, pacific, conservative and domesticated, anything but a rebel — indeed, he embodies what feminists would consider all the worst elements of the female partner in a traditional bourgeois heterosexual relationship. Following from this is his unquestioning espousal of a pre-feminist viewpoint in general. No good can come of it. (In Puig's fifth novel, *Pubis angelical,* there is again the basic situation of a woman who dedicates herself, unsuccessfully of course, to the search for a superior man.) It is strange, then, that

someone who represents an oppressed minority — effeminate
homosexuals — and whose only hope of progress would appear to be an
opening up of society and a liberalization of attitudes, should be no
more and no less than another version of all the complaisant female
victims of male oppression that we have already come across. It is
Echavarren's opinion that the most striking benefit gained from the
presence of the footnotes in *El beso de la mujer araña* is the way that they
emphasize the gulf between what homosexuality might be and the
'modelo reducido' ('scaled-down model') that Molina's condition and
attitude constitute.[34] Although Valentín is undoubtedly sincere in his
belief that there, in the prison cell, 'nadie oprime a nadie' ('no one is
oppressing anyone') (p.206), he is clearly wrong; and the theories of
Michel Foucault — so hostile to the post-Freudian idealists — which see
sex as a pivot of power, are demonstrated for all to see. This is an
example of irony that is tragic indeed.[35] In the end sexuality *is* an
ineluctable pivot of power, whatever the conscious morality or
intentions of the subject may be.

It is difficult, too, to cope with the need for separation between sexual
appetite and romantic love. When we considered the apparently
insoluble problems of Gladys in the previous chapter, we saw that she
might well be judged over-ambitious in her wish to enjoy an active and
totally fulfilled sex life and (her idea of) romance. Certainly there is
something of this incompatibility in Molina. It would be difficult to
reconcile his record of sexual promiscuity with his avowed desire to
spend a lifetime of service and fidelity to one single partner. Even if the
protagonists' habits were to change dramatically with the advent of a
more liberal society, no long-term relationship is likely since, as he
himself points out (a double irony here for, ironically, he is aware of
irony), he sees himself as female and he wants a real man; yet a man's
first and *lasting* interest would be a woman, whatever the social climate.
In any case, wherever society insists on the concept of 'the couple',
exploitation is inevitable, and without this ideal there is no such thing as
romance.

The only way that Molina can even approach being loved as he wants
to be is by changing his sex. And that, in a way, is what he does. Not for
the first time in literature a homosexual relationship is facilitated by one
of the partners 'becoming', in one way or another, a woman. One
example is the 1914 *novella* by the Portuguese writer Mário de
Sá-Carneiro, *A Confissão de Lúcio* (*Lúcio's Confession*). Here, the
narrator, Lúcio, is profoundly shocked when his intimate friend

suddenly produces a wife from nowhere. The wife (who, coincidentally, is called Marta, like Valentín's lover), wastes little time in seducing Lúcio, and in spite of certain reservations on his part, the affair continues until Marta betrays him with another lover. Her husband, Ricardo, is distraught at the break-up of her relationship with Lúcio and confesses that he had fabricated Marta out of the air: she was part of him, 'sexualized'. He shoots her in hysterical despair, but when Lúcio looks down at the dead body, it is Ricardo that is lying there. This, clearly, is a fantastic story, a 'tale of mystery and imagination' or *conte fantastique,* [36] but even so, there are points of contact with *El beso de la mujer araña.* In each story we have a triangle formed by two men and a fabricated woman. In the Portuguese version Ricardo creates Marta in order to seduce Lúcio; in the Puig novel Molina creates a mother/lover (who is also Marta, for Molina and Marta are the same character in the end[37]) and he is successful in seducing Valentín. If we continue with this line of thought, we may decide that this is another reason why no good can come of the relationship. As Erich Neumann has pointed out, the anima figure, the Young Witch, is much less dangerous than the Great Mother, [38] and, of course, although Molina takes on both these forms, it is the mother figure that is predominant and more effective (Valentín, as a heterosexual, is not likely to be led astray in a definitive sense by a sexual relationship with another man). One further thought: if Molina is both mistress and mother, the physical consummation of the relationship between the two men, in many ways a liberating act, is also an act of incest. And we cannot but remember that, as we saw (n.9), Freud said that freedom and happiness in a man's erotic life can only be attained if he is able to conquer his respect for the opposite sex and his revulsion at the thought of incest with his mother. [39] It is claimed that Molina restores Valentín's faith in the maternal figure, since Valentín has been estranged from his mother for so long; if this is the case, then this compounds the basic irony. [40]

Perhaps the most fundamental irony of all is to be found in the inextricable link not only between sex and death, but also between romanticized love and death: the dream may be necessary, but it is also dangerous. The traditional sex/death connection is explicit. For example, any attempted physical contact with Irena, in *Cat People,* will prove fatal. And odder still is the fact that her name means 'peace', since, conversely, it is sex with *Valentín,* part of whose name is Paz (peace), that leads to the same outcome in the novel's main narrative ('la Ficción (1)' as Michelle Débax has designated it, calling the film

narratives 'la Ficción (2)')[41] There are countless other points at which
we are made aware of the connection, even implicitly, such as when the
drums referred to in Molina's recounting of a film about zombies on a
Caribbean island are judged both erotic and sinister (p.213). Sex may
be 'la inocencia misma' for Valentín (p.224), repeating Puig's own
words, but from the beginning the reader is aware that it is the source of
Molina's guilt, and later realizes that this constitutes the first step
towards his untimely death. According to the Hollywood ethic, love
should destroy fear. As the Dorothy Lamour song that forms the
epigraph to Chapter Two of *The Buenos Aires Affair* has it, 'En la noche de
la jungla/ me asusta la oscuridad,/ pero con tu abrazo fuerte/ mi
temblor aquietarás' ('In the jungle night/ the darkness frightens me/
but with your strong embrace/ you will calm my trembling'); and this
does happen, briefly, in the story of *Cat People* (p.20). But human love is
based on and includes sex, and only in the fantasy world of Puig's next
novel can an innocuous 'pubis angelical', a sexless genital area, exist.
The aim, presumably, of those who have been made to feel what Mario
Mieli has called 'false shame' on account of their sexuality and the
orientation of their drives,[42] is to leave these behind with a kind of
mystical journey which repudiates the senses. It is by means of
enlightened carnal activity that the problems of the flesh are forgotten.
The happiness/absence of desire equation was clear in the Leo-Gladys
combination in *The Buenos Aires Affair*. Here, after sex with Valentín,
Molina confesses that he has become someone else, 'que no es ni
hombre ni mujer, pero que se siente . . . ', and it is the heterosexual
Valentín who finishes the sentence for him: ' . . . fuera de peligro',
comprehending because he shares his feeling (someone else 'who is
neither male nor female, but who feels . . . ', '. . . out of danger')
(p.238). This desire for the *vita minima* — and this is not the first time
this is found in literature — is due to emotional exhaustion: it is too
trying to keep up a struggle against unequal odds. It could almost be
seen as a kind of suicide wish. After all, when Molina is happy, he says
that he wants to die (p.239), and this is strange since it is only when one
is happy, as he has just pointed out (p.238), that one can believe that it is
a lasting state. This kind of flying in the face of all evidence is an
example of the consoling dream that is not quite credible enough, and
Molina knows, deep down, that the only way to preserve these fleeting
moments is to stop living. In the same way that some Romantic and
Decadent writers attempted in their fiction to prolong ecstasy by
combining the moment of orgasm with the lovers' death, Molina,

somewhat less melodramatically, reveals his awareness of the ephemerality of happiness in this world.

There are far too many indications in *El beso de la mujer araña* of Puig as an ironist to consider them all. Some of them are serious indications of self-deception at a tragic level — Molina admires a self-sacrificing middle-class Marxist character in a film about Latin-American urban terrorists but accuses Valentín, a carbon copy of that character, of being without feelings, for example (p.129), while Valentín thinks that the enclosure situation of their prison cell means that he and his companion are free from external pressures. Equally important is the fact that society's view of Molina as a man means that his knowledge and experience of the feminine condition are limited to its sexual and emotional aspects: he is ignorant of the pressing socio-economic problems that are influential in women's lives. Other examples of irony are formal, to do with the framework and structure of the novel and the use of fiction within fiction, especially, of course, with reference to the world of film. For instance, there is no question about the fact that Molina is constantly aware of the artificiality of the medium, the 'trucos del cine' ('tricks of the cinema') as he calls them (p.80). As Frank McConnell has said, film is an art 'that seems at once absolutely artificial and absolutely realistic',[43] and Molina reflects this in his consciousness of how, and indeed why, he will tell a story. Molina's awareness is indubitably a reflection of Puig's awareness: Puig relates Michelle Débax's 'Ficción (1)', Molina the 'Ficción (2)'. Since this kind of writing is bound to be very consciously planned, it would be difficult for the novelist to refrain from extending patterns of reflection and self-referentiality into the text itself. The process adds a certain ludic, but not frivolous, element to the novel. It is fun for both creator and reader but it does not in any way debase the value of the serious irony nor lessen the involvement of the author. Some of the authorial game-playing has been noted by Michelle Débax, while at the same time she draws our attention to more profound connections and areas of self-reference (such as the similarity between Molina's relationship with the prison Governor and that of the heroine of the Nazi propaganda film with the French Resistance organization, the Maquis). One or two of the more light-hearted cases are that the last words before the *laguna* (gap, void) which separates the first two parts of the novel are Molina's: 'déjeme pensar un poquito, porque tengo como una laguna en la cabeza . . .' ('. . . give me a moment to think, because my mind has gone blank' — literally, 'I have a gap in my head') (p.157); then, at the beginning of Chapter Ten, almost the first words (again Molina is speaking) are that it is ten past ten. More tenuous a connection, perhaps, is that between the convention that footnotes illuminate what is above them and that, in *Cat People*, when the heroine's architect husband and his colleagues are working at night, their faces are illuminated by the light that comes through the light-table from below. The text refers to the text: 'la Ficción (1)' refers to 'la Ficción (2)'.

The irony, the observation of the gulf between what appears to be the case and what is, makes no attempt to ridicule or mock the protagonists, and there is no hint of cruelty or malice in its presentation. We are never told that Molina looks or sounds foolish, even by implication; we are never encouraged to see the stories he tells as inferior kitsch — indeed, they are presented to us at great length and, so to speak, in verbatim detail, so that we too are trapped by their spell. Though intellectually we, as readers, may side with Valentín in his original questioning of the simplistic values and events of the first story, it is not long before Molina's skill and reasonableness, sensitivity and good humour carry us along too. The unacceptability of his effeminate sexual orientation and the sexual problems of both the protagonists are at least partly based on their unthinking adherence to dubious social conventions, yet their suffering is so sympathetically described that we are never impatient with them. Perhaps the strongest indication that Puig does not distance himself is that here again there is no obvious answer to any of the problems he presents: ironic perception is usually seen as involving authorial certainty and manipulative purpose. As D.C. Muecke reminds us, irony always contains the basic concept of a purposeful deception, together with mockery, and an ironic observer will make any affecting ironic contrast painful for the actors and amusing for the reader.[44] Admittedly, Vladimir Jankélevitch claims that irony is too cruel to be really comic,[45] but that does not affect my argument, since whether or not the Molina/Valentín combination is comic is not at issue, nor is it likely to be. There is, however, an objection that could well be raised, and perhaps we should anticipate it: since this text obstinately refuses to fit into any of the apparent categories of irony, it might be claimed that is not ironic at all. Are we falling into the trap of seeing irony where it does not exist? Wayne Booth, in *A Rhetoric of Irony*, is helpful on this: he dedicates a whole chapter to the question 'Is it ironic?'[46] The chapter's first subdivision deals with 'straightforward warnings in the author's own voice', and the most immediate of these, where ' ''secret'' intentions' are often found, is a book's title. Where *Kiss of the Spider Woman* is concerned, it is at least likely to alert the reader on this score. Booth's suggested category of 'known errors proclaimed' also applies to Puig; though 'proclaimed' is clearly too strong, there can be little doubt that the author is not at one with the ignorance or — in his case — *innocence* of his characters, and he knows what he is doing in highlighting these. We could paraphrase Booth and say that Puig is communicating with us from behind his characters' backs, but we should have to add, unless I am entirely mistaken, that the omniscient state of mind that is usually attached to this activity is missing. In theatrical asides, for example, complicity with the audience and humour are achieved by means of this kind of communication, and it is invariably mocking. It is in the section of his chapter that Booth calls 'Conflicts of Facts within the Work' that we can most easily recognize *El beso de la mujer araña*, as we can see from our selection of examples, and we are made even more confident in our claim that the book is actually full of irony by reading the last subdivision of the Wayne Booth essay, 'Conflicts of Belief': he is referring here to the conflict between 'the beliefs expressed and the beliefs we hold *and suspect the author is holding*'.[47] Puig does not invent or impose irony, he recognizes it; in this sense he is not an ironist, but an aware observer who includes himself among its victims.

Although *Cat People* is incontrovertibly the key film in *El beso de la mujer araña,* the others are not without importance. The second story, *Destino (Fate),* is taken from a Nazi propaganda film which, though in fact no more than a pastiche, might well have been shown in Buenos Aires in the forties, as Molina claims. Its most striking feature is its weighting in favour of what, to us, constitutes the wrong side in the struggle. This is hardly surprising considering its context, but Puig's motives in inventing and including a story of this kind are worth thinking about, especially when we consider the amount of Nazi sympathy in Argentina during the Second World War. It deals with a beautiful Parisian night-club singer, Leni, who falls in love with a charming German officer; thus she is torn between her devotion to him and her loyalty to France. Like Molina, she belongs to two worlds: she originally comes from Alsace, so that her Christian name is German and her surname is French. The repellently cruel and exploitative nature of her own countrymen is contrasted with the irreproachable and high-minded courtesy of the German occupiers, and this intensifies her confusion even before the relationship with her lover begins.

Further complications arise when she is asked to take the place of a young Resistance worker who has been killed. This girl had found herself in the same trap as Molina does in *El beso*: her mission to discover the location of a German arsenal for the Maquis had failed because of her love for an enemy officer. It was the Maquisards themselves who had murdered her in cold blood, a deed made all the more horrifying by the fact that she was happily pregnant and felt secure in her lover's support. Leni has no option but to agree to take on the job, as a young, and totally innocent, cousin of hers is threatened with death if she refuses. Once again we have one of Le Bigot's pernicious triangles, as the heroine finds herself with two intolerable solutions. Her first step, like Molina's, is to agree to do what is asked of her: then, also like Molina, she is trapped, and furthermore an apparently unavoidable chain of death and disaster follows. The young cousin sacrifices himself in an attempt to kill the brutal maquisard blackmailer, while Leni discovers that her lover is less civilized than she had supposed. She decides to denounce him to the Resistance and is prevented from doing so only because she receives an invitation to star in a film in Berlin.

It is at this point that Valentín's distaste for the story becomes so much of an irritation to Molina that he refuses to go on. The narrative is carried on in the (invented, of course) official publicity hand-out from the Tobis, Berlin film studios, and is presented in the form of a lengthy footnote. In spite of its alleged origin, the document's tone varies little from that used in the first half of the account. The voice is clearly still that of Molina, with its plethora of descriptive detail, its excited wallowing in phrases such as 'su arrogante uniforme militar' ('his arrogant military uniform') (p.91) and its interest in the heroine's search for 'un hombre superior' ('a superior man') (p.91). The story that this note tells is of Leni's conversion to the Nazi cause, led, revealingly, by a figure referred to as the *Conductor*.[48] Werner, her lover, convinces her *by means of a film* that he was justified in ordering the death of the two Jews who have earned a reputation as the leading anti-Nazi fighters. One of these depraved master-criminals is still at large, and Leni is convinced that she has seen his face somewhere. Werner returns to Paris before her; when she joins him there, she is shocked to see how much Jewish influence there is in France, and she determines to locate the hateful anti-German terrorist. At this point we find the word 'Sigue' ('To be continued') (p.94), but in fact this story is not continued here, and the next footnote is part of the next chapter and consists of a treatise about the possibilities of a physiological basis for the homosexual condition.

There is clearly reference in the orientation of this story, as well as in its narrative style, to the necessary dream that we have considered before. Though Valentín has little time for it, Molina confesses that if he were to be offered the chance to see just one film over again, he would choose this one (p.63). For Valentín, it is an 'inmundicia nazi' ('a piece of Nazi filth') (p.63), but Molina is so deeply involved in it, so moved and thrilled by it, that his cell-mate's criticisms infuriate and offend him to the extent of making him cry. Through his tears he claims that it is a work of art. And Valentín could not possibly know anything about it since he never saw it (p.63). Molina's criterion is aesthetic while Valentín's is moral; like Leni herself, who says at first that the only thing she likes about Germany is its music (p.61), Molina is capable of suppressing his awareness of unpleasant facts and concentrating on 'cosas lindas' ('beautiful things') in order, as he puts it, not to go insane (p.85). I am in sympathy with González Uriarte when he claims that this reaction reveals 'la fascinación que siente Molina *por el aspecto externo* del nacismo. Fascinación que es compartida por todo un tipo de homosexual y por una parte de la pequeña burguesía de los países del cono sur' ('the fascination Molina feels for the trappings of Nazism: a fascination shared by one kind of homosexual and by a section of the lower middle classes in Southern Cone'),[49] if by this he is saying that there is little ideological sympathy. Leslie Fiedler, in a memorable phrase, once referred to 'the immunity of popular taste to ideology'. 'There is something profoundly disturbing,' he went on, 'about the power of vulgar works . . . to move us at a level beneath that of our conscious allegiances, religious or political'. Fiedler may well be right, in fact, when he claims that we will one day abandon, or at least 'drastically downgrade', both ethics and aesthetics in favour of what he calls 'ecstatics'. Perhaps we already have.[50] This encapsulates the most important element in Molina's point of view. The film may have been invented by Manuel Puig, but many aspects of it are based on the early, European work of the director Douglas Sirk (though not of course the Nazi viewpoint). In a perceptive appraisal of Sirk's melodramatic output, the critic David Thomson puts his finger on the reason for the appeal of these films to the Molinas of this world: what he calls their 'graphic fluency' expressed the timelessness of a genre that 'soothes away the romantic wound'. 'There are no ugly or gross shots in Sirk,' he adds, and in answer to the anticipated accusation that the material is trite, says, 'The material is style'. This could also be an answer to an accusation that the material is an indefensible 'inmundicia nazi'.[51]

In a move from footnote to the main body of the text, we find that it is Molina himself who finishes telling the story, starting from the point where he had left off, not from the last word of the footnote: 'sigue'. (In the English translation of the novel, the 'official' footnote actually runs below Molina's last recounted episode, modifying the nature of the reading experience.[52]) It all ends when a complex plan which, like Molina's own, involves seduction and apparent betrayal, backfires. Leni kills the inhuman Maquis leader and is herself shot; she dies, like Ziegfeld's wife is *La traición de Rita Hayworth*, pretending that there is nothing wrong. After her death she is honoured by a life-sized statue in the heroes' pantheon in Berlin. Luise Rainer lived on in Toto's heart; Leni lives on in Molina's; the well-intentioned, noble woman lives on in truth. The adult and the child react similarly; perhaps the only difference is that Molina is so much *more* aware of the processes involved in the creation of his response. This does not, however, invalidate it. Frank McConnell has something helpful to say on this:

> Sentimental art, the art of the romantic imagination, recognises both the necessity of recapturing the naïve perceptions of a child for the sake of a fully human, fully conscious life and the impossibility of recapturing that life without the aid of the sophistication, the intelligence, and the techniques of artifice which separate it from us so irrevocably. We are never, in other words, taken out of ourselves: we read the poem, view the film, as mature men and women; and the gift of the poem or film is not a cancellation of that maturity, but an enrichment of it.[53]

The word 'mature' begs a question, but even so Molina is undeniably older and more experienced than Toto.

The third film is one that Molina tells himself when Valentín insists on abandoning him in favour of studying. In spite of its being a fairly close rendering of the 1945 Hollywood offering, *The Enchanted Cottage*, and of an auto-reference in the narration to 'la casa del encantamiento' ('the enchanted house') (p.114), few interpreters have recognized it, and fewer still have seen it as vital to their view of the novel as a whole. Yet it seems to me revealing on several levels. First of all, we are again reminded of the Toto/Molina connection. In the same way that Toto was talking to himself when he gave his version of the Ziegfeld story, Molina here is both narrator and interlocutor. And the setting of the tale strikes a chord in our memory too — it is not all that far removed from Toto's 'cabin in the snowy forest', even if there is more evidence of authorial control ('si no hay nieve es otoño': 'if there's no snow it's autumn', p.104). Then, though less obviously than in the case of Toto's intervention in *The Great Ziegfeld*, the narrator reveals that he sees himself as one of the dramatis personae (p.106). If narrative is a sign, then it is a sign of the truth of one individual.

Here, too, we find a pervading theme in Puig: the possibility of achieving beauty with unpromising materials. In *The Buenos Aires Affair* Gladys's sculptures were fabricated from rubbish; Molina's discourse is constructed from a less than respectable genre, and from fairly lightweight examples of it at that.[54] An extension is the beauty that is found under the skin, so to speak, of the unattractive heroine of *The Enchanted Cottage* and the horribly disfigured man that she loves. One of the reasons, perhaps, that critics have paid so little attention to this film is that it does not fit in with their theories: all the films in the novel have a tragic end, claims González Uriarte, inaccurately;[55] all the female heroines are young, beautiful, dark-haired and white-skinned, says Maryse Vich-Campos, equally inaccurately, they eternally live an impossible love, are victims of uncontrollable forces and are often being blackmailed. And they die.[56] Clearly, *The Enchanted Cottage*, the story of a handsome man engaged to be married to a beautiful if unpleasant woman, who because of his own facial injuries looks beneath the surface of his 'sirvienta fea' ('plain servant') and discovers her 'fine soul' (p.111) is taking us in a different direction. By some sort of magic the couple become beautiful in each other's eyes; they marry and are blissfully happy, and we are glad to endorse the view that the oppressed and unattractive are morally superior. This is a romantic film, and that is a romantic idea.[57] All of us can identify with it since we are all insecure. Puig himself once said when a journalist from a Brazilian newspaper asked him why he had set *El beso de la mujer araña* in a sordid prison-cell, 'Porque eu procuro a beleza no feio. Porque eu sou o feio' ('Because I'm looking for beauty in ugliness. Because I am ugliness').[58] But there is more to it than that of course. We are back with the question of truly *seeing*, of distinguishing between what is and what is only superficial. The ugly, clumsy servant-girl is really beauty itself, she is loyal, self-sacrificing, even — unaccountably — cultured. The only one who recognizes this at first is the blind narrator (another *mise en abyme*: Puig narrates the tale of Molina, who narrates the tale of a blind man, who narrates the thoughts of the servant-girl, who is a reflection of the second narrator, Molina). Molina sees himself in this girl: like him, she is not what she appears to be, but the exigent gaze of the sighted is not capable of this discovery. And yet, as Echavarren has said, this is another of the metaphors that represent a 'sujeto invisible' ('invisible subject'), since the girl is actually *not* beautiful and Molina is *not* a woman.[59] This too is an aspect of the necessary dream: the individual's reliance for survival on the hope that someone, somewhere, even if it is in heaven and not on this earth, will recognize the truth of his being. For this can produce the longed-for happy ending. It will be an understanding that transcends all misconceptions and, on a deeper level, will overwhelm not only the horror and putrefaction of death but also what Puig occasionally seems to see as the horror and degradation of the flesh.

This is a moment of hope and consolation for Molina, for romantic love is liberating — not only in socio-economic terms, as it was for radical feminists, or even as far as pleasure is concerned[60] — but on a transcendental level. In the same way as Gladys, in the previous novel, was prepared to endure pain to attain what was probably an unattainable aim, Molina is capable of denying, even sacrificing, his sex life, though not his sexuality. This may be judged one of the most potent and tragic ironies of all: rejection of the flesh in a relationship that is born of the needs of the flesh, a step in the direction of the *pubis angelical* of the next novel. We remember that Molina's stated aim is to look after his lover for ever, 'day in, day out', as the hero of *La dama de las camelias* puts it in the epigraph to Chapter One of *The Buenos Aires Affair*. He frankly admires the mother in *Cat People*, at least as he imagines her, a moral person, well dressed, who has made her family happy, someone who is affectionate, fastidious, flirtatious, but almost virginal (pp. 22–23). Also, his own real-life sexual experiences have resulted in opprobrium and seem likely to result in more unhappiness, at the very least. In all the novels, the flesh is presented as repulsive, other than when coitus is accompanied by dedication and devotion. In *Boquitas pintadas* we are constantly reminded not only of death but of illness and decay: the decline of the organism. In *The Buenos Aires Affair* no attempt is made to gloss over the repellent aspects of sexual intercourse, and the autopsy report adds to the reader's revulsion, especially when we are brought to an awareness of the sterile uselessness of the protagonist's final ejaculation, post mortem (p. 226). The affective life, which for Molina, as for many women, means all there could possibly be to life, is based on sex; but sex itself is something that society condemns, by and large, and the individual may well find it reprehensible, ugly, even nauseating. Love is redemptive, sex degrading, and Molina has little option but to cloak his general masochism with the terminology of love so as to live with it. In the end, though, this too brings about death. In a way, it must be added, this is what society exacts: Molina wants what women are supposed to want, but his personal tragedy is that he is not really a woman. Feminine masochistic sacrifice is not an unknown phenomenon: this would be a very much more straightforward situation (even if it could not arise from the circumstances presented in this novel) and would lead to less thought, soul-searching and concern on the part of the reader. The answer would seem to be easier to locate: society could and should put an end to feminine abnegation by recognizing the rights and needs of women. I fear, though, that Puig himself realizes that this is only a superficial and, ultimately, unsatisfactory solution. As we have seen from *Boquitas pintadas* and *The Buenos Aires Affair*, it would be an improvement, but death must come, and the path that leads to it is not without unhappiness or frustration whatever happens. There is more genuine escapism in *The Enchanted Cottage* than in any of the other films. Their protagonists started off with something — beauty, talent, money, sex appeal, even love — and life became impossible; here the heroine starts with no obvious advantages and life rescues her.

An important feature of the last film recounted in Part One of the novel is the way it underlines Molina's orientation. As he thinks over the story he has just started telling (a complete invention of the author's, incidentally), a story that ostensibly reflects Valentín's life and position and which has a male protagonist, his mind is on the hero's sophisticated French mistress and his elegant mother. Both the woman of the world who has befriended the young radical during his period in France and his mother represent the other side of Molina's Jekyll and Hyde aspirations. Gone are the gentle, ill-used, unattractive victims of male exploitation. Here we are in the world of Choli's jewel thieves from *La traición de Rita Hayworth*: intelligent, glamorous, strong-willed and strong women. Their strength, though, is insufficient for them to avoid love and its attendant tragedies. For Molina this could be seen as the correlative of another fleeting hope — that success, glamour and elegance are possible even if the web, similar to the one that he himself is weaving, has trapped its victims. 'True love', with its concomitant devotion, exclusivity and sacrifice, does exist and should be sought at all costs, but ideally women should maintain their impassive beauty and dignity and not allow themselves to be humiliated. Like all the other comforting dreams, this one is completely impossible. As Stanley

Cavell has said, film turns our epistemological convictions inside out
because reality is known to us before the appearance of it. However,
what Molina, and those like him, desperately want to believe is that
adhesion to appearances can somehow affect, even change, that
reality.[61]

Like Valentín, the hero of this film has rich parents, but he turns
against what they represent when his social consciousness is raised by
studying politics at the Sorbonne. Nevertheless, he is unswerving in his
devotion to his mother. It is his father's capitalist views that he finds
intolerable. And he seems more concerned about his parents' divorce
and his mother's consequent loneliness than he is with the cause he
supports. He himself fits in nowhere: the people he wants to fight for
despise him because of his background of money and privilege; his
mother is about to marry again; his career as an independent racing
driver is ruined when his home-made car is sabotaged, presumably by
someone hired by one of the big names in Formula One racing. When
he has to return to South America because his father has been
kidnapped by guerillas, the usual Molina-esque complications are to be
found — with deception, when the boy convinces the revolutionaries
that he is on their side; sacrifice, when his French mistress pays a huge
ransom fee; and death, when the terrorists murder his father. There is a
police shoot-out that prefigures Molina's own death, and there is the
hero's reunion with his mother, while the French woman, whom he
really loves but who comes from another world (p.126), goes back to
Paris.

Molina elaborates on all this and parallels become even more
obvious: the hero, a boy whose wrath is aroused by social injustice,
seduces a poor girl and makes her pregnant, 'una muchacha a la que no
dan ganas de acariciarla después del orgasmo' ('a girl that you would
not want to caress after the moment of orgasm') (p.133) — at least for
Molina there is to be one post-orgasmic kiss from the man who makes
him promise not to allow himself to be exploited. Then the triangular
situation involving the young revolutionary, his mother and the
woman he loves is emphasized by the similarity in the descriptions of
the two women. The choice between them echoes all Oedipal
situations, but particularly Molina's. And we find, ultimately, that the
mother too is hiding something. She has been unfaithful to her
husband, is involved in political intrigues and was an accessory after the
fact when her husband was killed. The youth is betrayed, in other
words, as so often happens, this time not by Rita Hayworth and all she

stands for but by Neumann's 'all-powerful numinous woman' who is his mother. As we have seen before, it is not the tempting Young Witch but the deceitful Old Witch who is so dangerous.[62] Significantly, the protagonist orders his mother's execution, then dies himself. At this point we cannot help remembering the sixties view of the homosexual as revolutionary.

Indeed, this is a key moment in the novel for Molina, for it is here that, consciously or unconsciously, he prepares to discard his mother as the dominant figure in his life in favour of a lover, however unsuitable. With the waiter, Gabriel (a name reminiscent of Genet's *Notre Dame des fleurs*), he had wanted to have both, but now his mother's claims on him begin to recede into the background. Later, he is to say, 'My mother has had her life' (p.258), and this constitutes the final rejection. It is relevant that the substitute for the mother in the symbolic story should be older than the protagonist, a woman who has lived and suffered and knows the ways of the world, not altogether unlike the woman she might have replaced; for Molina, there is a related sense of having found someone who, though admittedly younger than he is, is a dominant, even a domineering character. And, for him, an 'hombre superior'.

It is at this point in the novel, too, that the controversial footnotes begin to be really obtrusive. These have been judged as carrying on 'a rather elementary symposium on homosexuality' by one critic, and as unconnected to the main text, as clarifying and explaining nothing, and as forming a separate text by another. Puig does, in fact, risk ruining his narrative with them and clearly their very length is going to constitute a practical problem for the reader since it is impossible to read two texts at once.[63] It seems to me that the explanation is a fairly simple one, but it is important because one aspect of it ultimately reveals the author's ambivalence, even pessimism. The simple answer is that Puig is prepared to take the risk of alienating his readers because if he succeeds in holding their attention, the gain will be immeasurable: he will have prepared them for what is about to happen and rendered them not only reasonably well-disposed, but sympathetic, towards what might otherwise seem a shocking scene. García Ramos is absolutely right when he claims that the author is conditioning us for the physical consummation of the love that is burgeoning in Molina's heart.[64] The reader should not ignore the footnotes, for if he does, a major key to at least some kind of understanding of the novel will have been passed over.

The more thought-provoking aspect of the relationship between the footnotes and the main body of the text demands investigation into the pattern and theme of the notes themselves. They are, with the exception of the 'factual' and intradiegetic notes to the Nazi propaganda film, a homogeneous collection, orientated towards the theories proposed by the politico-sexual liberation movements of the sixties, and at least some of the sexual idealists of that epoch. Their quasi-scientific nature gives them an impersonal, even objective air, but they are not, of course, either impersonal or objective. Like the sixties movements, they constitute an explicit plea for freedom from repression, a repression that was seen then as the pervasion of society by a ruthless masculinity.[65]

The first note of all, taken from the writings of D. J. West, is a refutation of the three possible physical causes of the homosexual condition; West supports his argument by referring to other experts. This appears fairly early in the narrative, in the middle of the Nazi propaganda film and before the note that accompanies this film. The ground is prepared. But it is almost forty pages later that the 'alternative text' is continued. This time West investigates the views of the general public as to the causes of homosexuality: could it be the result of impulses that are just wicked, corruption by other people, or enforced segregation in adolescence? All of these theories are rejected, and there are references to Freud and his views on neurosis and sexuality, on the role of society and on the family. For society, the two most inconvenient manifestations of the libido are incestuous desire and homosexuality.

Half-way through Molina's reflections on the story of the Latin-American radical and in the middle of the account of his ministrations to the sick Valentín, we find the third footnote. They are now becoming more frequent. We return to Freud and his appreciation of the need for the individual to adapt to the norms of the society in which he lives, for the couple is not everyone's ideal. There is a reference to the theory of over-repression, taken from Anna Freud, and then to the Oedipus complex and infant bisexuality. Just five pages later, the author cites Fenichel's views on the probability of a homosexual future for a child who is closer to his mother than his father, and elaborates on this with references to Freud, mother fixations, and the possibility of narcissism. With the next note we move towards the concepts of repression, domination, exploitation and female inferiority within society; the idea of sexuality as sin is mentioned, and we finally come to the point that all this has been leading to — the need for sexual liberation. We have a short summary of some of the views of Marcuse, Brown and Marcuse's disciple, Altman. Below Chapter Nine — that is, in Part Two of the novel — all this is made even clearer. Particular attention is paid to Norman O. Brown's view of the possibility of true sexuality, to Marcuse's theory of 'surplus repression' and to Kate Millett, who in *Sexual Politics* (1970), one of the handbooks of feminism, argues against the hypocritical economic exploitation of sexual alliances that makes bourgeois marriage the only possibility. The ultimate thesis is that of a certain Danish doctor, 'Anneli Taube',[66] and this encapsulates many of the theories that we have already extrapolated from the previous novels. We have worked up to this with all the other notes, even including the occasional piece of devil's advocacy, such as the anthropologist Unwin's claim that sexual liberty can be equated with social decadence, and that social vigour is born from sexual repression.

The solution, as is so often the case, is seen as a kind of happy medium, with the elimination of 'surplus repression'. And a parallel to this is the need for a role for the bisexual in society: exclusive homosexuality can itself become authoritarian, the socialist countries are notoriously hostile to it — somewhat invalidating the argument that the sexual and political revolutions must go hand in hand — and even if this could be remedied, the implication (supported by Puig himself in past interviews) is that homosexuality is as much a limitation as exclusive heterosexuality. 'Anneli Taube' claims that the male child's rejection of his natural parental model in favour of feminine characteristics — tenderness, tolerance and culture — is a deliberate, courageous act. But the model role is also submissive, and the male homosexual will learn to be submissive and accept, if not welcome, male exploitation just as his mother has done, emulating the worst characteristics of female heterosexuality. However, things are changing, we are told, especially since the sixties liberation movements, and it is becoming accepted that a strong man and weak woman no longer constitute the universal paradigm.

At the same time as the notes move towards their final argument, Valentín's reserve and hostility are being weakened. Molina starts off by telling him something about his sexual orientation; then, as Valentín shows few signs of sympathy — indeed, he is still hostile to him and insists on reading — the fact that Molina lets slip that 'his turn will come' (p.103) indicates that the next stage in the wearing-down process is to be that of physical debilitation. But in the meantime Molina tells himself the story of *The Enchanted Cottage*, the *only* film in which a misunderstood, 'misread' character finds happiness and erotic fulfilment, and before the appearance of the next footnote we are told of his interview with the Governor, in which it seems that it is *Molina's* resolve that is weakening: he is now trying to have things both ways. He is affectionate and attentive when Valentín is ill; comforts him with good things; tells him another story. But now the account is interrupted by negative mental images which force themselves into his head, suggesting his concern for the potential outcome of his actions. This violent world is one which he is beginning to be aware of through his growing love for Valentín. Valentín's vulnerability becomes clearer and clearer, and when he loses control and hurls a cake across the cell, we can see that the spider woman's web is trapping its prey just as it was intended to. Not without reason has Molina referred in passing to Sparafucile, the professional assassin in *Rigoletto* (p.25). In Act II of the opera, the jester, Rigoletto, reflects that he and the man of violence have much in common: 'Pari siamo!' ('We are two of a kind!') he sings, for whereas Sparafucile kills with the sword, he kills with words.

But will Molina actually use his power over Valentín? His vacillation is increasingly obvious. In a second interview with the Governor, he manages to postpone his deadline and he gives nothing away. Valentín is now a contrite, affectionate and grateful friend who begs Molina's pardon for his bad behaviour over and over again. When Molina tells him that his appeal is going well and that he is to be moved out of that cell, that is the end. Valentín is not only confused and shaken, but almost distraught: this is a culminating point in the 'first fiction', for Valentín is incontrovertibly trapped. But as the footnote makes clear, Molina's adhesion to feminine social models has trapped the effeminate homosexual too. In the sixth note, we find Roszak's apt claim that liberation is most needed for the image of woman that men keep in their minds, and which so many real women try to live up to. Molina is one of these 'real women'.

My contention is that although it would be only too easy to see all this as an unequivocal cry in support of the utopianism of the sixties, it would be a mistake to do so. Everything we have read so far suggests that Puig does not see the possibility of social paradise based on sexual liberation, even if there is room for much improvement. The experts that he refers to in the notes do not necessarily support the position he is portraying, and he is quite aware of this. After all, he refers to Wilhelm Reich, for example, whose 'total orgasm' theory ignored friendships between people of the same sex, the possibility of romantic love and, of course, homosexuality. Since the sixties, with the new permissiveness and the new selfishness, we now have what Charles Rycroft has designated 'neuroses of confusion'; and Rycroft adds that 'the sexual revolution has so far at least proved to be largely an upper middle-class phenomenon having little if anything to do with the class war'.[67] In Puig's writings there is not only ambivalence but also pessimism. So many people — psychologists, theologians, even poets — have seen the aim of ridding man of his neuroses as illusory, and I am sure that he shares this view. He once, in fact, commented that with the elimination of the strong man/weak woman paradigm in the United States little had been gained. Now, he said, there were 'dificultades en restablecer un entendimiento' ('difficulties in re-establishing some kind of understanding').[68] As Cavell has said of film, sometimes the narrative mode is not 'Once upon a time . . .' but 'what if one day . . .'[69] but a great deal of what Puig ostensibly hopes for and his novels plead for is as much part of the world of fantasy as are the relationships and events of the Hollywood films that inspire Molina. Like these, though, it is a dream that is necessary, and the struggle must go on.

   There are just two films left before Molina's fatal sortie into the world. The first is a very free adaptation of a 1943 horror story, *I Walked with a Zombie,* which itself was a modern Caribbean version of *Jane Eyre.* (Incidentally, it was directed by Jacques Tourneur, who was also responsible for *Cat People.*) It is interesting that in the 'first fiction' Molina no longer has to adopt the role of supplicant. At this point, Valentín not only suggests that he tell him the story of a film, but to all intents and purposes begs him to do so. He has eaten well, feels better, and says that this would be the finishing touch to the evening.

   The story is of a girl who travels from New York by ship to join her fiancé on a sinister Caribbean island. Our fears regarding the likelihood of a happy outcome are built up by the equivocal reaction of the ship's captain when she tells him her story, and are compounded by our discovery of the fact that her future bridegroom is a widower whose acquaintance she had made only a couple of days before agreeing to marry him. Furthermore, she is greeted on her arrival at the island by a less than ideal situation: her fiancé is a weak character, there is a repellent, all-powerful butler — similar to the housekeeper in *Rebecca* — and an unpleasant scene when a cask of rum, brought as a wedding present by the natives, is rejected. Things are obviously not going to go well.

   Unlike the situation in *Jane Eyre,* the male protagonist's first wife is not still alive. But neither is she dead. She has been turned into that most horrifying and significant of creatures, a zombie: a living corpse. She is, furthermore, by no means the only one of these on the island, though she is the only *woman* in this unhappy position (female weakness means that there is little to be gained in reducing women to a state of impotent servitude). The zombie workforce obeys and labours through each night, but in the moonlight their tears are visible, and it is clear that they are suffering. Indeed, there is little happiness to be found anywhere. The bridegroom is irresolute and afraid and ends each night in a drunken stupor. The heroine is worried and nervous, with at best curiosity about her predecessor, and at worst, consuming suspicions and fears which lead her into danger. And all the time we are conscious of a sinister presence that is manipulating events and circumstances, and we hear about a voodoo priest. When one day the heroine goes alone to a beautiful mansion that had caught her eye on a tour of the island, but which she had been warned against visiting, she finds that it is the female zombie's prison house and that her black housekeeper, the one sympathetic person she has met since her arrival, is this woman's nurse and gaoler. From her she learns about her husband's ambivalence and cowardice, of how he had witnessed the inhuman repression of the plantation-workers' rebellion, years earlier, by the brutal landowner who was his father. And of how that repression had taken the form of converting them all into creatures without will-power or, indeed, any power at all.

After his father's death — and there is mention of an ambush, again prefiguring Molina's later circumstances — the son tries to remedy the situation but achieves nothing. Yet another standard Molina feature now emerges; the wicked voodoo priest had blackmailed the young man's first wife threatening to kill her husband if she did not yield to him. Her husband was mistakenly convinced that she had betrayed him, so he killed her, and was then blackmailed in his turn. So we have another deceived character who is trapped by circumstances beyond his control. Now, more than ever before, Molina seems to be identifying with the male protagonist, even though it has to be added that this is in addition to his involvement with the plight and personality of the heroine and the indisputable connection between women and zombies. We are not limited to, or even greatly aware of, male/female exploitation in this film though, but rather of two innocent victims whose problems have both constitutional and accidental sources. The latter, as always, are susceptible to modification, but in none of the previous stories nor, ultimately, in the 'first fiction' of the novel, does any advantage seem to be gained by the attempt to change them. If we consider the prison/body/native country images, present throughout the book, it will help us to see this more clearly. (We remember that in the explanation of Valentín's terrorist code, it is explicitly stated that 'house' means 'native country', p.140.)

All of these images are, in a way, interchangeable, since even if they represent something accidental rather than constitutional, there is little possibility of radical and permanent change. All improvement in Puig is a question of degree; many problems are insoluble anyway. The idea of the body as a prison is by no means new, but for a woman trapped in a man's body the connection takes on a new force. It occurs to us that both the body and prisons constitute no more than temporary homes, but the price paid for freedom from the body is death, and in this story that is also the cost of freedom from the characters' 'accidental' incarceration in the Villa Devoto penitentiary: Molina moves heaven and earth to achieve release from his bonds, but has to promise to betray another human being for this purpose, and dies himself before he can enjoy his liberated state. Divided loyalties are a commonplace. Could Molina's final gesture be interpreted as an attempt to escape from the prison of exclusive feminine orientation? Is his act of courage a manifestation of his male side? Not all masculine traits are reprehensible, and it is bisexuality, not homosexuality, that both the footnotes and the author defend. That his final action is not only unsuccessful but also misunderstood again reveals the authorial pessimism that I have already referred to.

There is the same degree of failure when the young protagonist of the Caribbean film sets fire to the zombies' huts so as to liberate them. In fact, they survive, if this can be called survival. They go on half living, and suffering, and there is no liberation. In the previous story the Latin-American terrorist set fire to his own house, in the same way as political rebels apparently try to destroy their country; for them, the accepted model is actually unacceptable, heritage and the social environment are repellent, the house, the home, are incompatible with freedom. None of it is tolerable, but the liberating aim is, at least in part, unrealizable. To use Fromm's terms, 'static adaptation' — the acquisition of new habits — is all we can hope for; 'dynamic adaptation' — fundamental change — is really impossible.[70] As Stanley Cavell once said, in Hollywood films, when the hero goes home, his life is over. Home is not heaven, but a prison, and when you escape there is nowhere to go.[71]

In spite of the horror and danger and the loss of the man she (presumably) loves, the heroine of the zombie film does achieve some kind of happy ending. It is by no means a straight run, as it was in *The Enchanted Cottage,* where no one suffered (the hero's original fiancée, who soon disappears from the story, was insensitive and unpleasant, and therefore does not count). Nevertheless, in spite of a hair's-breadth escape from the clutches of the butler, who turns out to be the villainous voodoo priest and who embodies all that the insistent drums have suggested about sex, danger and the occult; in spite of violence and rejection from her drunken husband and his death at the hands of his poor, suggestible first wife, who still loves him; in spite of all this, she *does* escape, the voodoo priest is struck by lightning, the zombies' huts and the first wife's house are burned down, they at last escape into death, and the handsome captain is waiting to take the heroine away on his ship. Love will conquer all, and the future promises happiness.

There *is* now a degree of optimism in Molina, then, even if he realizes that there is a price to pay and someone will suffer if he finds fulfilment. The island — the prison, the body, the house — can be left behind. The escape by sea is an escape to happiness; the sailing-away image has frequently been used to represent this, and as well as its connotations of a new start, it often has erotic overtones. Above all it is consolatory, for in leaving behind the horrors of the island and going into exile one leaves behind one's own involvement and guilt, and an authority figure will be there to protect and guard the victim against future misery.

Yet despite the ending, this film is less than comforting, not only because death and suffering form an integral part of it, or because images of the living dead, among others, are only too distressingly relevant to both prisoners, but also because, intercalated in the tale in italics, is the series of mental pictures I have already mentioned, pictures that are not dissimilar to the 'sensations' of Gladys and Leo in *The Buenos Aires Affair.* And these undermine optimism as they illuminate the narrator's confusion and indecision: like the footnotes, these images are strategically placed in their fifty-three pages of text. A nice irony is that it is *after* the impression has been given that Molina has made up his mind to sacrifice himself for Valentín, an impression gained from the cumulative effect of these odd images as well as by one particular statement, that Valentín's strength and reserve are shown as totally broken and Molina has him in the palm of his hand (pp. 193 and 198 respectively).

It is all mixed up and surrealistic: here are the zombie film, a police ambush and a sinister, dream-like hospital — another enclosure and impotence situation. On this level, the filmic sea voyage is an escape to death: an injured heart drowns in black sea-water, the roughly-painted ship's figurehead (reminiscent of an unsuitably made-up face) is of glass, and is shattered by a male fist; at first the fist is said to be undamaged, but later this is amended. And the image of glass persists — a glass brain is hurled against a filthy wall and it is pointed out that a glass doll (like the voodoo dolls with stakes through their hearts in the zombie film) is all too easy to break. The vulnerability of the weak and fragile and the presence of death are the keys, and these are evident, too, in the hospital scenario. Someone who is very ill and weak is left alone with an infectious male patient; an inexperienced young nurse is on night duty with him — who can she turn to for help? She is a victim; she has to do something so that he does not either die or assault her. The night is long and cold: if he attacks her during the night, there is no escape. The night nurse, like the female zombie, is a sleep-walker; the patient is revolted by her. She talks in her sleep and betrays everything. There is great danger of infection and the patient is getting worse. She trembles when he looks at her. Ultimately, the gravely ill patient is reported as being out of danger.

However, this stage is not reached without a nightmare of indecision. In the poor glass brain there are picture-cards of saints and whores — they belonged to the past and are rotting and yellowing, harmful to the survival of the organism. When the brain is shattered, they fall on the floor, automatically discarded with the destruction of their container. Mixed up with all this is a young suburban girl, who is then referred to as a suburban homosexual, not actually a girl. She used to go to the cinema to avoid church-going, we learn. There is a cultured man too, but he is an executioner, and he obeys orders without knowing their source. The poor homosexual's head rolls, but — and this is the point at which it seems to me that the (literally) fatal decision has been made — when he is dead his forehead can be stroked, even kissed, after his eyes have been closed. For he will have died with his eyes open.

In a kind of coda, there is a rich man who begs a poor man for alms, only to mock his benefactor because he has often offered a counterfeit coin. So the hospital patient gets better; the rich man sleeps soundly if he gives his gold to the poor as Valentín charitably gives his love to Molina; but the homosexual's body is irretrievably broken. Little critical attention has been paid to this stream-of-consciousness section, and impressionistic interpretations of the outcome of the 'first fiction' of the novel have frequently been offered without any reference to it. To me, it seems an essential compendium of the evidence for Molina's actions, for it reveals his determination not to carry out his original plan and the reason for his lack of commitment to it.

The last *recounted* film (for Molina's death is also, in a way, a film story) is yet another in the series of elaborations on divided loyalties, apparent betrayal and the far-from-smooth path of true love; at the same time, it invites both the reader and Valentín to reflect on the subject of power, while underlining what we have always known — that for some, at least, the dream that is essential is one of exclusive devotion unaffected by death.

Though an invention, the story takes place in familiar territory, for the film is a pastiche of many that were extremely popular in the Mexican cinema of the forties and is concerned with a character who has been a stand-by in works of art in many countries and all epochs: the woman of unimpeachable morality — and great beauty, usually — who is forced into prostitution by circumstances, and then misjudged and abandoned by the man she loves. The blackmailed first wife in the zombie film is the most recent example of this situation for us, of course, but countless other cinematic and literary melodramas have been constructed around it. This version is an accurate objective correlative for Molina's present situation: by this time, Valentín has become so considerate, pliable, even submissive, that he is happy to go along with Molina's choice of film. No longer is there any rhetoric behind the story-telling. It is now no more nor less than a self-portrait of the narrator.

The lovers in his story first meet at a masked ball, for it is carnival time. As the night is ending, he asks her to remove her mask, but she refuses: they will never meet again, she says, and tomorrow is Ash Wednesday. Their encounter has been a blissfully happy dream, but it is soon to end (and in the shadow of death, furthermore). But the hero, who is a journalist, realizes that he has been waiting for her all his life, and he has no intention of losing her now. When the action moves from the lush, tropical splendour of Vera Cruz to Mexico City and he returns to work, he finds her again. She is the subject of a sensational revelatory article to be published in his newspaper, and she is newsworthy because she is a famous ex-actress and night-club singer, now the kept woman of a Mafia tycoon. He calls on her to say that he will see that the article is suppressed and she reveals how her simple faith in the seemingly good man who is her protector has been betrayed, telling of his abnormal jealousy. She is, like so many other people in *El beso de la mujer araña* and elsewhere in Puig, kept a prisoner. After a series of misunderstandings during which, among other things, the hero pens (and sings) the lyrics of appropriate sentimental songs, drowns his sorrows in ever more frequent bouts of drunkenness, and destroys the valuable presses on which the notorious article is being printed (thus ensuring that he will never work again), he goes back to Vera Cruz. The night-club singer manages to escape from the clutches of the tycoon and prepares to start up her career again, but at the last minute her jealous — and rich — lover buys the club which was to employ her, and all is lost. The hero works briefly as a labourer, but his health soon fails, and it is from a hospital bed that he calls for her; when she is found, she has to prostitute herself to pay the fare to Vera Cruz. They go and live together in a picturesque little house, and there he convalesces, supported by her immoral earnings. When he discovers that she is not a singer but a dockland whore, he leaves her. She knows that he knows the truth.

It is at this point that there is an interruption of the story-telling that is especially important. This time it is Valentín that is fascinated by it all, but Molina refuses to go on because it depresses him. Ironically, Valentín encourages him, tells him he need not feel that he is inferior and that he certainly does not have to be a martyr (p.247). To the reader, it is all too clear how closely Molina is identifying with the film situation. There is no alternative for him, but there is no hope either. He is now totally committed in his love for Valentín — 'Estás en mí . . . estoy en ti . . .' ('You are inside me . . . I am inside you . . .') says the film song (p.243), and this reflects Molina's fusion with the man he now sees as his husband (p.246).

When the heroine of the 'second fiction' locates her lover for the second time, he is desperately ill, and though he talks of their future together, she knows that the end is near. He tries to sing his latest song to her, and in his delirium fantasizes about their leaving together by sea, as in the zombie film. But he dies, and, *like a sleepwalker,* she goes back to the home they briefly shared. When one of the local fishermen asks after her lover, she replies that he has gone away, but that it is not important for he will always be with them, if only in the memory of his songs. The final close-up, Molina tells us, is of her face: she is smiling, but her eyes are full of tears. Valentín is very taken with the conclusion: it is better to have loved and lost, he says; but for Molina, it is a 'final enigmático' ('an enigmatic ending') (p.263).

The central figure in *El beso de la mujer araña* — for Molina *is* more important than Valentín — is in prison on a charge of corruption of minors. Yet it is abundantly clear that he is more of a victim of life than one of its agents. And as we listen to his discourse, it becomes more and more obvious that there are other victims too, even if they are not all in his peculiar situation; one of them is Valentín. The real 'corrupted minors' are human beings themselves, for their constitutional characteristics predispose them to imposed suffering, and this is invariably exacerbated by accidental factors. It was, perhaps, Freud who really opened our eyes to the difficulty of accepting the concept of the basic goodness of man and, indeed, to the total impossibility of perfecting his being or even his circumstances. For life itself is a kind of prison sentence. Fromm summed this up when he said that 'the child has a mother who by her love wards off all dangers,' adding, 'The adult has — nobody'.[72] The problem is that danger persists, even increases, when so-called maturity is reached, and political and socio-economic factors cannot be ignored: the avoidance of any consideration of such factors has often been judged one of the failures of psychoanalysis, and Puig, in this novel, combines the constitutional and the accidental, revealing that he is as aware as anyone of this weakness.

Constitutionally speaking, people never really achieve maturity, for all human beings are incomplete. Any solution is no more than a pipe dream. Freud once said that 'access to the halfway region of phantasy is permitted by the universal assent of mankind, and everyone suffering from privation expects to derive alleviation and consolation from it'.[73] The one consolation is that sometimes, for some people, some aspects of some dreams do come true. What Puig never lets us forget is that even if they do, death is never far away: Thanatos is always struggling with Eros for dominance in our lives.[74]

If the erotic bond is so frequently pernicious, especially for those who have been condemned to a marginal existence from infancy, if not from birth, is there any hope of happiness? The answer is that there is, but that it will either be very short-term and with a false foundation, or slightly longer-term and based on fusion: fusion of male and female (in the same body), of head and heart and of force and submissiveness. There is no escape, really, in escapism based on a sexual relationship; as we have said before, sexuality is a pivot of power, and the exercise of power is an irresistible temptation for all human beings; furthermore there is no avoidance of related constitutional conditions, such as neurosis, or of arbitrary and accidental circumstances and events, such as totalitarianism in society or wars. There are two types of power: that of some unknown force, which may be called fate, or destiny, perhaps even God, and against this there is no appeal; the other is that exploitative force used by one man against another, and something has to be attempted in order to change that. Ultimately, though, there are so many constitutional elements in the situation that little will be achieved.

It is all a question of faith in something in the face of the odds, faith in 'cosas lindas' when the world is so obviously made up of lies, betrayal, disappointment, apathy, irresponsibility, malice, egoism and cruelty. The terrible thing is that these manifestations of what is ugly and wicked may exist in the very same people who are searching for something beautiful. Man has to know himself or, at least, to know himself better in order to avoid *unnecessary* suffering, for there is no way of avoiding suffering completely. One of the reasons for the disapproval that Freudian theory has provoked over the years is the simplistic view of some of Freud's followers that, as Bettelheim puts it, 'the negative aspects of a man's behaviour are merely the consequence of his living in a bad society'.[75] Conversely, some improvement must be possible. In Antoine Vergote's words, 'what power could be assigned to the cure if analytic theory condemned man to be irremediably captive to his illusions?'[76]

CHAPTER VI

'Only Make-Believe':
Pubis angelical (1979)

> . . . el mundo real es siempre imperfecto . . . los sueños
> platónicos que los niños (y los grandes) gustan soñar, en que hay
> Héroes y Malvados, Justicia e Injusticia, Verdad y Mentira, son
> al fin nada más que sueños y . . . la áspera realidad está hecha de
> una mezcla triste e inexorable.
>
> . . . the real world is always imperfect, . . . the platonic dreams
> that children and grown-ups like to dream, in which there are
> Heroes and Villains, Justice and Injustice, Truth and Falsehood,
> are in the end only dreams, and . . . harsh reality is an unhappy,
> inexorable mixture.
>
> Ernesto Sábato, *El otro rostro del peronismo*

WITH Puig's fifth book, *Pubis angelical* (1979), a certain sourness began
to be noticeable in the reaction of at least some of his critics. To be frank,
said one, it was disappointment: even with a good theme and a good
protagonist, it turned out to be a sort of plea for something
incomprehensible, and it added nothing to the author's previous work.[1]
And (as we have already noted) even García Ramos, though in fact
rather good on this novel, is beginning to sound less enthusiastic than he
had before. Does this, then, mark the onset of a decline in quality?
Certainly *Pubis angelical* excited less interest than its predecessors.

Any assessment of quality is, of course, bound to be subjective. My
own view is that this is actually one of Puig's best books and if there is a
falling off, it has not yet started. *Pubis angelical* is a dense, cleverly-
organized piece of fiction, and though it contains themes and

preoccupations in common with its predecessors, there is also something very new. The problems are similar, but the path ultimately chosen by the protagonist is one that goes in a surprising new direction. It should be added, perhaps, that as well as the occasional expression of disappointment in what has been written about it, there is also some excellent critical writing from those who have been impressed by the issues raised and fascinated by the techniques the author employs to bring them to the printed page.[2] It may be that public and critical dissatisfaction invariably follows when a book has had the success of *El beso de la mujer araña*. Or it may be that the author is beginning to demand more of his readers and that some of them either cannot or will not make the necessary effort. In the past, after all, it was easier, and Puig's public had never been accustomed to the obscurities of, say, a Sarduy, the difficult fragmentation of some of the Vargas Llosa novels or the peculiar layout of a *Rayuela*. In spite of signs to the contrary, though, the formats that in earlier novels appeared to be there to avoid any strain on the part of the reader actually housed intricate, subtle and consciously-worked complexity. Nothing in Puig has ever been gratuitous; references are never casual or arbitrary. In this particular novel there is a web of symbols which can add immeasurably to our understanding of it, and it is worth making the effort to see where they lead.

The most obvious variation in this book is that here we are presented with a new kind of layout. Again the author is going in for formal experimentation, as he explained in an interview just before its publication. It is, he said then, a question of 'un experimento nuevo . . . tres partes separadas pero al mismo tiempo interdependientes; ninguna funciona por sí sola y, si se elimina una de ellas, las restantes se empobrecen totalmente' ('experimenting with something new . . . with three separate sections which are at the same time interdependent; none of them works on its own and if you take one away, the other two will be totally impoverished').[3]

The principal story, the one that could be said to represent 'reality', runs from the first to the last of the usual sixteen chapters. As a counterpoint, we have the other two which cover Chapters 1 to 7 and Chapters 8 to 16 respectively. The main thread is about Ana, an exiled Argentine woman who, shortly before her thirtieth birthday, spends a period in a Mexico City hospital suffering from cancer, and who very nearly dies. The second tale — with which the book actually begins — is that of a beautiful European actress, known first as the *Ama* (mistress of the house) and then as the *Actriz* (Actress). The third and last is a science fiction piece, in which the female protagonist, a descendant (it seems) of the Actress, is known as W218. The stories, therefore, are set out like this:

Ch. 1--------------*AMA*--------------Ch. 7
Ch. 1-----------------*---------------------ANA--------------------------------------Ch. 16
                                        Ch 8------------W218------------Ch. 16

The other two woman are, needless to say, projections of Ana, with the boundaries of time blurred, for the first story takes place in the thirties and early forties, while the last is set around the year 2000. And, as several critics have pointed out, it is not only impossible but actually quite unnecessary to know just how these other selves are created — whether Ana is dreaming, delirious, or just fantasizing, the result is the same.[4] What is important is to take all three stories together. Even though there is one that could be seen as 'real' while the other two are 'dreams', this time the dreams do not constitute therapeutic escapism. They are necessary, certainly, but their purpose is not self-deception: it is, rather, self-knowledge. It will be a struggle to achieve this, for it is difficult for people to shake off conditioned identities and values. We have only to recall Gladys, in *The Buenos Aires Affair,* and her attitudes towards life and love, to realize that this is a recurring theme in Puig. What he has said on the subject in interviews confirms this. In 1981 he explained his views to two French journalists: 'Il semble que malheureusement, dans la sexualité, il y ait un âge où tout se cristallise, l'érotisme en particulier. Il est par la suite très difficile d'oublier certains rôles pour en adopter de nouveaux. C'est le sujet de *Pubis angelical'* ('It appears that unfortunately, where sexuality is concerned, there is a moment in time when everything becomes fixed, particularly the erotic. It is therefore extremely difficult to forget certain roles and adopt new ones. That is what *Pubis angelical* is all about').[5] There is, of course, little doubt that for Puig's characters 'roles' are established almost entirely on the basis of sexuality, and this is a subject we shall return to.

    In the end, our knowledge of Ana will come about as the result of what links these three stories, what in a Lacanian sense is realized by discourse. If she is identifiable, it will be because a kind of 'earlier sketch which has been covered over before the canvas is used for another picture', to use Leclaire's words, has come to life and we have seen it. In other words, we shall have been granted a glimpse of her unconscious. In the same text, Leclaire went on to invalidate, somewhat, my use of the word 'counterpoint' for those other two discourses, and what he says is worth considering:

> If we use a comparison of a musical order, the unconscious is not the counterpoint of a fugue or the harmonics of a melodic line: it is the jazz one hears despite oneself behind the Haydn quartet when the radio is badly tuned or not sufficiently selective. The unconscious is not the message, not even the strange or coded message one strives to read on an old parchment: *it is another text written underneath and which must be read by illuminating it from behind or with the help of the developer.* [6]

It is this 'other text' that the reader is presented with here, and it is the insight that it affords that makes all the difference.

Ana, like so many of her predecessors in the novels of Puig, is a social outcast (in a manner of speaking) and is in prison (also in a manner of speaking). She is a marginal figure because she is ill. (It is scarcely necessary to underline the alienating effect of physical incapacity: it is a subject that has been frequently discussed in recent years. [7]) And she is a prisoner who can no more escape than could Molina or Valentín in *El beso de la mujer araña;* indeed, she is a successor to the *loca* of the previous novel. When we first meet her it is October 1975, and she has now spent five weeks in her hospital bed after an operation for the removal of a tumour. She is an artistic, somewhat frivolous woman, divorced from her husband, Fito, and to all intents and purposes alienated from her only daughter, Clarita, who remained with her father after the divorce. In spite of the critical situation in Argentina and the fact that her exile was at least to a certain extent brought about by political pressures, Ana sees herself as totally apolitical and she is far more concerned with the fundamental search of her life: for a 'superior man' (p.190), a 'worthwhile man' (pp.21, 94), 'a real man' (p.29). And it should not prove too difficult for her to attract men, even if ultimately they do turn out to be disappointing, since she bears a striking resemblance to the film star Hedy Lamarr (p.33), and was considered to be the prettiest girl in her class at school. (p.74).

Her only two visitors are a Mexican friend, Beatriz, who is a feminist, and who therefore has ideas that are entirely foreign to Ana, and Juan José Pozzi, her ex-lover, who has been forced to escape from Buenos Aires. He too is on a different wavelength, since he is an ardent left-wing Peronist (a position Ana neither understands nor sympathizes with) and an idealist (as a lawyer, he has defended political prisoners without taking any fee). Both of these characters are impatient with Ana's immaturity, and in various ways they both contribute to her development and her final moment of hope for self-recognition and knowledge, a moment of beauty since, as Ana says, it is beautiful to feel the desire for knowledge (p.90).

Like Pozzi (he is always referred to by his surname), Beatriz is concerned with justice. We are told that she is currently involved in the defence of a servant-girl who has been raped (p.21), so that she too is a fighter against the exploitation of the weak. She would seem to be an ideal model for Ana, who has thoughts of 'liberation' and was disillusioned by her role as wife and mother, being treated as no more than hostess and a mistress — a housekeeper (*Ama*?) by day, a prostitute (W218?) by night, (pp.85–86). But there are objections to emulating Beatriz: Ana is confused with regard to her own views, her social position and even her feelings towards the Mexican woman. The political side of things is difficult enough to understand. Is Beatriz right to despise and hate everything that Pozzi stands for (she has not actually met him, but Ana has told her about him)? For Beatriz, all Peronists are fascists (p.59) and she is incapable of understanding the concept of left-wing Peronism (pp.51–52). Perhaps even more important is Ana's conditioned, if not inherent, conviction that in any case politics are far removed from what should constitute a woman's world. Women, she has been brought up to think, are exclusively creatures of emotion, are aesthetically sensitive and, needless to say, lack intellectual powers. 'I'm no intellectual, no luminary', she claims (p.173), and we would do well to remember that the phrase does not represent that misleading modesty that is so common among the British: 'intellectual', for Ana, is not a dirty word. To her mind, women have their heads full of 'dresses and curtains and tablecloths, Dior boots and Gucci handbags, Hermès scarves, Cartier watches and Vuitton luggage, leopard, ocelot, ponyskin, mink, chinchilla and sable coats, platinum bracelets and emerald necklaces, extremely expensive earrings and French perfume. And Persian carpets and Chinese vases and Chinese lacquer screens and colonial furniture in your country house'. 'What else have we women got in our heads?' she pauses to ask herself (p.231). And the answer is: love, poetry, tender Rachmaninov concertos, paintings by Delacroix, the bossa nova and the 'hustle'. When she wonders how the world would be if it were run by women, she concludes that it would be as graceful and light and harmonious as a duet between Fiordiligi and Dorabella in *Così fan tutte* (p.231). This last thought is revealing, like so many of the operatic references in Puig. Ana's lack of knowledge and understanding extends to the world of opera, even though she once worked in the world-famous Teatro Colón in Buenos Aires, for in *Così fan tutte* Fiordiligi and Dorabella are far from the constant and dedicated lovers that they should be, and happiness in the end is achieved only when everyone accepts the fact that romantic illusion is worthless and that things are as they are. (It is interesting that Ana's views should represent such an extreme position: it was George Yudice who originally made the point I have already alluded to that they are not so much those of a woman, however conventionally brought up, but of a *loca*. Ana is a reincarnation of Molina and, like him, her judgments are primarily aesthetic.[8]) Perhaps, too, the fact that Beatriz appears to have made such a success of her life will make her example less attractive to Ana. She is an independent woman with up-to-date ideas, but at the same time she is happily married and has lovely children (p.21), so that Ana is jealous of her and sees her as patronizing or, more accurately, maternal in her attitude towards her. Furthermore, she is reluctant to discard the good features of her chosen way of life and afraid to leave the safe surroundings of her expectations. It seems unlikely that, when it comes to a conflict between heart and head, the voice of reason will prevail for any female character in Puig. Yet in this case we wonder: Beatriz is what Ana could, and perhaps *should* be, but there is no 'right answer' and, as everyone knows, and as was memorably demonstrated in the 1979 Pastor Vega film *Retrato de Teresa (Portrait of Teresa),* the life of a 'liberated' woman is not without its drawbacks. In the film the principal problem was male resentment and hostility; in the Puig novel there are hints at too much work in Beatriz's life and little time for anything else. Traditionally, sex objects at least have some leisure.

Pozzi is the nearest thing to a 'superior man' that Ana has ever met. He is incontrovertibly less than ideal in many ways, especially as he is married and has children and because, like Valentín in *El beso de la mujer araña,* his attitude towards those who love him is exploitative and aggressive. Yet he is educated and clever, conscientious and socially aware, devoted to the cause he believes in, physically attractive, patriotic and serious. Furthermore, he is the only man Ana has ever slept with, apart from her husband, and this is likely to make him special in her eyes. A woman's devotion to her first and continuing lover, recognized by Krafft-Ebing as a kind of sexual servitude, will be only slightly watered down in this case.[9] (The other man in Ana's life was one Alejandro, a right-wing Peronist, a narrow-minded Catholic with a mother fixation, and a ruthless oppressor; and apart from hating and fearing him, it has to be pointed out that she never became his mistress.)

Ana and Pozzi first met when, after her divorce in 1969, she went to live alone in a Buenos Aires apartment bought for her by her mother, and started work in the Teatro Colón. Although I do not want to go into links between the three stories at this point, it is difficult to resist the temptation of pointing out one very obvious one that gives us a clear picture of Ana's feelings about her life in the early seventies. In the third story, W218 looks back to what she sees as her best period: 'when I had a job, and was waiting for my ideal man to turn up' (p. 255). For Ana, he did, and it was Pozzi. Though it was she who made the running (p. 88), he soon fell in love with her and, had it not been for misunderstandings that are now referred to and clarified, they might have made a new life together. (An aspect of Pozzi's egocentric and exploitative nature is revealed at the same time as the confusions in their early relationship are sorted out: unknown to Ana, his wife had been aware of their weekly meetings even as they were going on. And she had known because he had been cruel enough to tell her, (p. 174).) In any case, they soon stopped seeing each other because of the pressure of his work (p. 55). Now he visits Ana with a purpose. Although he says he loves her (p. 39), and actually makes love to her in her hospital bed later on (p. 178), she discovers that his mission is to persuade her to entice Alejandro to Mexico, where he will be kidnapped and held hostage. Ana is not prepared to do this. First of all, she does not support left-wing Peronism. Secondly, it occurs to her (even if not immediately) that the lives of her mother and daughter would then be at risk since they are still in Buenos Aires. Thirdly, she is suspicious of Pozzi's promise that Alejandro will come to no harm, and she is, or wants to be, a generous person.[10] Probably, though, her fourth reason is the most powerful: she judges Pozzi's attempted manipulation of her as a form of treachery. Jorge Rodríguez Padrón echoes what Puig himself said on the subject when he stated that the theme of all the books is the protagonists' basic isolation when the illusions that are the product of their particular upbringing are shattered.[11] This is what happens here: it is a question, of course, of sexual exploitation. 'The theme of the perversion of erotic feelings for political aims . . . achieves the proportion of an obsession in *Pubis angelical*', another critic, Gustavo Pellón, has claimed with justification.[12] Love is betrayed, in other words.

As the story of Ana progresses, there are more and more indications that she is going to die. There seems to be no improvement in her condition, she is not receiving the usual post-operative therapy and her sense of perspective is increasingly dependent on her sense of an ending. Not for the first time in Puig, death is a constant presence in the world of the characters. Her worst fears are confirmed when Pozzi, converting his plea for her help into moral blackmail, reveals that there is, indeed, very little hope for her survival. Her operation had shown that nothing could be done for her. Identity for Ana is now linked with value to society: you think that if I help you, she says bitterly to Pozzi, my death will have some meaning (p. 222). Although he demurs, this is precisely what he does think, and to him, a man whose single-mindedness cannot be affected by personal relationships, Ana is just a frivolous, useless creature. 'You were my little luxury, Anita', he says (p. 222). It is not surprising that for Ana his revelations about the gravity of her condition constitute an act of conscious brutality. When he goes on saying hurtful things — that she despises other women, including her own mother and daughter — she rejects him definitively. *She* will not indulge in sexual exploitation and she never wants to see him again (p. 224).

But in the event Ana does not die, and Pozzi does. He returns by a secret route to Buenos Aires and is killed in the statutory shoot-out. And no one will ever know — or, more accurately, Ana will never know, and that is what concerns us as readers — what the circumstances and his motives actually were. 'Qué final más enigmático ¿verdad?' ('What an enigmatic ending, isn't it?') says Molina in *El beso de la mujer araña* (p. 263) when he finishes telling the story of the Mexican film, and the death of Pozzi is surrounded by the same kind of mystery. It constitutes a sort of blank page, and the survivor can write whatever she likes on it, remember whatever she wants to. This is an interpretative choice Puig's characters frequently have to make. In Molina's Mexican film the heroine has loved and lost, and Valentín comments that 'although she is left with nothing, she is happy because she has experienced one meaningful relationship in her life, even if it's now over' (p. 263). This is a point in the novel at which Valentín has achieved some kind of balance between his previous excessively clinical approach and Molina's fatuous emotionalism and it seems like a 'correct answer'. He goes on: 'One ought to be able to accept things as they come and be grateful for anything good that happens, even if it is short-lived. Because nothing lasts for ever' (p. 263). Molina is quick to point out that this is not really a satisfactory solution, since the emotions are rarely, if ever, so easily controlled. The heart has its reasons, he says, quoting

Pascal, and given the process of what we have previously called 'Quixotization' that he has undergone, this is now not just fatuous emotionalism.

The point, though, is that some kind of choice has to be made, and Ana elects to face up to what to her has never been reality, and to become reconciled with her mother and her daughter. The element of mystery in other people's motivation is brought home to us by means of another of the author's operatic references. When Pozzi comes to see Ana for the last time before returning to Argentina, he tells her that his undercover name is to be Ramírez. Just like the bandit in *La Fanciulla del West*, comments Ana. She tells him that though a bandit he is also the hero, and that when he is about to be hanged, the heroine rescues him. In fact, the character in the Puccini opera is called Ramerrez, but that is neither here nor there. What is relevant is that just before he is to die, Ramerrez denies the murders he has been accused of, admitting only to the robberies. And he asks that the woman who loves him be kept in ignorance as to the manner of his death. Let us compare this with Pozzi. Before he leaves, he assures Ana that he will never become involved in terrorism, only in his usual work, the defence of unjustly-arrested political prisoners (p. 216); Ana accuses him of role-playing, and enjoying the role of martyr (p. 219); when he is killed, she discovers that he did not enter Argentina by the route he had told her about (p. 242); she is unable to answer Beatriz who asks if he was a terrorist or not; it was said that he had been armed in the final shoot-out with the police (p. 243). I shall never be certain about what happened, she says, and she cannot bear to think that he died just because he was a decent person who did altruistic things. However, she wants to think that he was not a terrorist, but a martyr for the cause (p. 244). She is irremediably sad because of what has happened to her native country and, for the first time, conscious of her uselessness there in exile. This is the good that has come of an ill wind, for her first reaction to the news of Pozzi's death had been one of satisfaction: her initial *Schadenfreude* had been partly the result of a feeling of vengeance, as he had hurt her so much; then she gloated over the fact that he, who was so clever, had proved to be not so clever after all, and she was delighted that someone whose health and strength she so envied should die first. She is later horrified by these reactions, and this marks an important stage in her journey towards the beginning of self-knowledge.

In the other novels, escapism was necessary for the mental and emotional well-being of the characters. Here, the scenarios in Ana's unconscious are also therapeutic, but they do not lead to false well-being. For the first time the development of the character tends towards the apprehension of the truth — or as close a vision of it as human beings are ever granted — however painful the process may be and however lacking in comfort and consolation the various parallels are. This escapism frees the subject from self-deception, but may deliver her into a state of awareness where sadness and suffering are inevitable. The head-in-the-sand attitude that we have met before has a lot to be said for it. Ana's flashback story, which runs from Chapter One to Chapter Seven, provides no facile answers, and is distinguished by, among other things, the fact that for the very first time we are presented with the ugly side of the soothing mass media, in this case the cinema. (This echoes Puig's own disillusionment when he worked in the film industry in Italy.) In the previous novel, we noted that Molina, one of its most ardent fans, was perfectly well aware of the artifice of it all but chose to ignore it. The new, *Pubis angelical*, point of view is illustrated in the story of the *Ama*/Actress: the glamour and even the pleasure are at best ephemeral and superficial, at worst totally fraudulent.

The most obvious link between Ana and this novelettish story is found in her likeness to Hedy Lamarr, the Austrian actress, which is mentioned explicitly and alluded to indirectly; for although novelettish, this is, by and large, that actress's real-life story, as revealed in her (ghosted) autobiography *Ecstasy and Me. My Life as a Woman.* It was as early as 1931 that she achieved notoriety, appearing naked in a Czech film, *Extase,* directed by Gustav Machaty. She then married one of the world's richest men, Fritz Mandl, who to all intents and purposes kept her a prisoner. 'I had anything I wanted', she recalls, 'clothes, jewellery, seven cars. Every luxury except freedom. For Mandl actually held me a prisoner!' And she goes on: 'He had not married me, he had *collected* me, exactly like a business prize'.[13] Furthermore, it is well known that he was so obsessively jealous of her that he bought up every print of her films so that others could not see and enjoy her, and this is referred to in *Pubis angelical.* Finally, by means of a ruse that involved the drugging of a maid who closely resembled her, she made a dramatic escape to Paris, then went to London and the United States. Her American début was in *Algiers* (1938); interestingly, this film about a gangster who lives in the Algerian casbah where the police are not able to get at him, but who falls in love, leaves his safe surroundings and is shot, is referred to in *Boquitas pintadas, The Buenos Aires Affair* and in Puig's sixth novel, *Maldición eterna a quien lea estas páginas.*

In Ana's dream story, the metaphors, as it were, materialize. The beautiful heroine, the *Ama* — whose name is not given but whose designation is not all that far removed from either 'Ana' or 'Lamarr' — is literally held prisoner by her rich husband. Her father, a Viennese professor (Freud?) who had discovered the secret of reading people's minds, had died just before the Great War; her real mother had been the woman she had supposed was her wet-nurse. This poor woman, who only once found sexual favour with the Professor (who had a mother fixation) tried to murder the child. She was afraid that when, at the age of thirty, she inherited the ability to read minds, this would be used for evil purposes. In her own suicide note she says that she would rather see her daughter dead than the servant of any man (p.48).

When 'the most beautiful woman in the world', as she is often called, does make her escape from the island prison in the Danube, we come to another important and typical feature of this story: espionage. The *Ama*'s servant, Thea, turns out to be a man in disguise — Theo — and it is he who organizes their flight after they have confessed their love for each other. But all is not well: they do get away, certainly, and we hear no more of the oppressive husband, but Theo, a sinister character, had previously told his employer that the *Ama* was a German spy. He murders her double, and the *Ama* herself is obliged to kill the captain of the launch that takes them to the mainland. When they finally find themselves on board a transatlantic liner on the way to the New World and a new life, she discovers, sleepwalking, that Theo is going to kill her. Love has again been betrayed. With rough justice, since her husband had drugged her in order to have sexual relations with her on their wedding night, she now drugs Theo. And she reads his diary, in which he admits that although he does love her, he is a Russian agent first and foremost: this is where his loyalty lies. He is dreadfully afraid that at the age of thirty she will discover that all men . . . But at this moment of imminent knowledge, the wind carries off the pages of the diary, and yet again we have a situation where a character, like a non-omniscient author, will never know the truth. There is no option for her but to kill him.

Her second period of liberation is short-lived, for she is then blackmailed into becoming the virtual prisoner of a famous Hollywood producer and the Hollywood star system; a daughter is born and she is obliged to have her adopted. From now on she is referred to as the Actress. When she goes to Mexico from Hollywood, a week away from her thirtieth birthday, she meets a young man who reminds her of the most important person from her past, the 'más amado y más traidor' ('the most deeply loved and the most treacherous') (p.132). She falls profoundly in love with him, but is suspicious of his motives, especially when he insists that he wants her to have no secrets from him and to undergo analysis. In her headlong escape from him she is killed by a jealous (and ugly) rival. In fact, we discover that her lover had not betrayed her.

The most striking feature in this story is its symbolism: there is a series of images which are repeated with significant frequency. The first is the angel. As we shall see, the *pubis angelical* of the novel's title (the sexless genital area) is presented in the third story as a possible solution to the world's evils. Where there is no power, there is no exploitation and, here, as for Molina, lies (theoretically) a way in which sexual attraction, the pivot of power, can be resisted. The spirituality of angelic symbolism is ever clear, but so is the element of hidden betrayal and sinister mystery. The *Ama*'s bedhead, for example, a piece of flamboyant luxury, is made up of multicoloured clouds and floating angels, but one of these, with strange fishlike eyes, seems to be watching her. When she looks back at it, she is sure that it blinks (p.10). Conversely, the clouds and angels of white stucco — not highly-coloured this time — that decorate the doorway to a summer-house are totally pure. They are shown as worshipping and protecting a *santa* (a female saint, perhaps even a virgin), and not one of them has fishlike eyes or looks at the *Ama* or at the passing clouds. They look at each other (p.12). This leads her to think about the possibility of there being good *and* bad angels (the hateful Alejandro in the first story is almost always referred to by Pozzi as Beelzebub, and Beelzebub, of course, was a fallen angel who became, in Milton's words, 'Satan's nearest mate').[14] There is always danger: angels are beautiful, as she is, but beauty brings about vulnerability, true motives are never discernible and, worst of all, love itself is a trap. Even angels may represent maleficent forces, and the *Ama* is actually afraid (p.15). St. Augustine once said that the word 'angel' is equally applicable to good and bad spirits, and the book of Genesis tells us that some angels were expelled from paradise for lusting after earthly women; this is the reason for her fear. Like Herminia, in *La traición de Rita Hayworth*, the *Ama* considers the fate of dead virgins, for Theo has told her that angels are the souls of children who have died before losing their innocence, sacrificed by clairvoyants who could forecast future horrors for them (p.44). Since 'innocence' is almost invariably taken to be sexual, the source of their

future unhappiness is abundantly clear. Theo, incidentally, wears a
lapel badge in the form of a golden child-angel. Angels do not merely
bring peace on earth, and the Actress realizes this when she goes to Los
Angeles, the City of the Angels; she is conscious of 'esos mismos ángeles
que siempre le habían perseguido, insidiado, espiado, traicionado'
('those same angels that had always persecuted her, plotted against her,
spied on her, betrayed her') (p. 113). Here, perhaps, they also represent
the oppressive nature of the perfect beauty she has to keep up. The aim
of finding true love is one that cannot exist outside the world of
sexuality. But there is no alternative other than death. The *Ama*'s
mother preferred her to die than be sexually enslaved; the Actress
unwittingly chooses death because she does not trust love. There is no
real moral here though: Puig is not highlighting the foolishness of the
Actress's suspicions, even if they are unfounded in this instance. On the
contrary, he is showing us, through Ana's imagination, that both
alternatives open to her are heart-breaking and that everything
revolves around power. The Actress's rival, hideous and pock-marked,
is jealous of her beauty and success and, therefore, of her power. For
Ana, lying in the sanatorium, the two imagined stories constitute a
rehearsal of what she thinks she knows about life. And of course, this is
dependent on two conflicting factors: her own experience of the world
and the *Weltanschauung* of others who did not share her kind of
upbringing and conditioning processes, but who influence her. She
does not know what the answer is for her: she is not — as Choli was, in
La traición de Rita Hayworth — entirely committed to her brand of
escapism. Indeed, she secretly suspects that there might well be
something in what Beatriz says and stands for and what Pozzi believes
in. Her flight from Argentina represented the culmination of a process
of independence-seeking. She is now no longer trammelled by her
husband, her daughter, her mother, her domestic duties, her sexual
appetite, the political situation or an oppressive pursuer. On the other
hand, she is not happy. When she is the *Ama*/Actress, she is seeing her
own dilemma metaphorically, as if it were a film; and the ending of this
particular film is one in which death is the alternative to blind trust. But
no one is trustworthy: everything has an ugly side and may even be
intrinsically evil. There are even angels it would be as well to avoid.

   There are also many images of imprisonment, though at the same
time we cannot avoid references to the fact that if something is
contained, it is at least given some kind of shape.[15] Ana is preoccupied
by the formless and aimless nature of her own 'liberation'. At one

point, after combing her hair into the well-known film star's style, with a centre parting (p.109), she begins to meditate on the subject of Hedy Lamarr's real-life imprisonment by her wealthy husband, and her escaping in order to take up her career again (pp.33–34). After that, the Actress story is all about incarceration. Links are obvious: even the elaborate Venetian windows in her splendid mansion have an iron framework that imprisons them (p.10); her island house has an electrified iron railing which separates her from the surrounding water. Even more significant is the design of this railing, which is fashioned in the form of titanic arms and serpents. The description is worth quoting in full:

> Los hierros verticales figuraban serpientes paralelas, una con la cabeza hacia arriba, la siguiente hacia abajo, todas con la boca furiosamente abierta y la lengüeta rígida; las líneas horizontales eran en cambio una cadena de nudosos brazos que se iban tomando el uno del otro, describiendo un esfuerzo crispado y aparentemente sin esperanzas: en ellos se clavaban las serpientes. (pp.12–13).

> The upright pieces of iron were in the form of parallel serpents, one with its head up, the next one with it hanging down, all with their mouths open in fury and their tongues rigid; the horizontal lines, on the other hand, were a chain of sinewy arms which took hold of each other in a convulsive effort which was apparently without hope; the serpents were nailing them down.

The various connotations of the serpent are well-known: man's animal desires, the genius of evil, temptation, the seduction of (titanic) strength by the flesh, even Satan himself. And they are all relevant here as, indeed, is the often-forgotten ambivalence that the symbol possesses, for it can have positive values.[16] Even being nailed down and helpless may have certain advantages.

The references to imprisonment are too numerous to list: they range from a description of jewels that are 'imprisoned' in their setting (p.14) to the *Ama*'s husband's vengeful plan to incarcerate her, together with her jewels, in a strong-box of some rigid transparent material where she would slowly asphyxiate and he could watch (p.62). It is all even more explicit when the *Ama* meditates on the Winter Garden in the grounds of her house: 'armazón de hierro, fuerza de macho. Cobertura de cristal ¿sometimiento de hembra?' ('iron framework, male strength. Glass covering, female submission?') (p.64). And again the commonplace flesh/prison equation, hinted at in *El beso de la mujer araña*, is also mentioned (p.65). However, as we saw, if the flesh does constitute a prison, to escape is the equivalent of self-destruction. There is an indication of this in the history of the *Ama*'s mother, whose only means of egress from the asylum was to commit suicide (p.47). Ana's unconscious, illuminated by the imagery, has rejected the possibility of salvation via the flesh. Sex bars the way to freedom, like the Titan guards of the *Ama*'s Viennese house, the elaborate wrought-iron railing on the island and the heavy handle of the French window in her bedroom: she is shaken when she notices the form of this, 'cylindrical and covered in veins' (p.10).

Many images of restraint are rectangular. The glass that contains the drink that the *Ama* finds irrestistible, and which is the only thing that quenches her continuous thirst, is square. There is a wide rectangle formed by the lake in the grounds of the island house. When she is ill, she is confined to bed. Later, as the Actress, she looks back on a career in which she has always been put in luxurious showcases (p.112), and we find that she has always had a horror of rectangles, parallel lines and cages (p.12), so typical of Viennese *fin de siècle* design.[17] It cannot fail to occur to us that in addition to their similarity to cages, rectangles represent all that is static, firm, definite, rational and secure. The opposite, in fact, of romantic impetuosity and spontaneity. They are also connected with the even numbers which allow the superstitious Ana to feel safe (p.23). A woman, surely, needs some kind of shape to her life. Could it not be dangerous, even pointless, to be free? Perhaps this applies to everyone, not just women, for in a way Pozzi himself is imprisoned in his ideology: he is, so to speak, a *preso político* (political prisoner), and it is this that gives his life purpose.

There are many more significant images in this section of the novel (an emphasis on the sinister left hand, for example, later to reappear in the science fiction story, pp.10, 189), and they all point in the direction of man's duality and the ambiguity and untrustworthiness of everything, of the choices that have to be made and of the likelihood that the alternatives in any dilemma will be equally harmful, of the unavoidable realization that other people invariably hold us in their power. And the romantic desire to escape, which García Ramos has seen as involving 'el inconsciente, el sonambulismo y el ensueño' ('the subconscious, sleepwalking and dreams'),[18] leads to death and disillusion: when the metaphor materializes and the *Ama* sleepwalks, she achieves knowledge but she also discovers the hideous truth.

Ana's other Other, as it were, W218, is the heroine of a story very loosely based on the 1970 George Lucas film *THX 1138*. In the film, set in a society where emotion is forbidden and so is sex, the hero, THX 1138, tries to go against the rules of the tyrannical computer and indulge his love for a woman, LUH 3417. In *Pubis angelical,* we meet W218 after the Actress's story is over. She has been eliminated, and Ana has admitted that she no longer has any illusions. 'Es una cosa muy triste,' she has said, 'Si ya uno no se puede imaginar algo lindo ¿qué le queda? Si en este mundo no te imaginás las cosas lindas estás perdido, porque no existen' ('It's so sad . . . If you can't make up something beautiful any longer, what are you to do? If you don't make up beautiful things in this world, there's no hope for you, because they don't actually exist') (p.150). Everything has let her down, she is feeling ill and depressed, and her romantic ideals have not been replaced by other objectives. She looks back on her remaining a virgin until her marriage with something approaching shame; she feels no desire to see her mother or her daughter; she is sure that the 'superior' Pozzi has deceived himself on the subject of Peronism as much as she once did on the subject of men and marriage; she is aware that he thinks her a fool, and she knows that he is now going to renew his efforts to persuade her to trap Alejandro. Worst of all, she is convinced that she has no future and that even if she did, it would be joyless.

So it is that the society in which the third story is set is one in which male domination of women not only still exists, but has been institutionalized. There is no hope for the future here either, only a picture of what Bart L. Lewis has called 'regimented eroticism'.[19] The beautiful young heroine (this time the imminent birthday is her twenty-first), who of course closely resembles Hedy Lamarr (p.210), is a kind of sexual social worker in the colourless state that survived the cataclysm which destroyed earlier civilizations. This is now the Polar Era, after the 'Gran Vuelta de Página' ('Great Turning of the Page') (p.151), but W218 was born just before this, and feels subconscious stirrings based on the values of a previous world. There is also a certain unpredictability in her which, presumably, would not be present in her colleagues; these variations from the norm are intensified by the fact that she was born abroad, not in this town 'in the bottom of the lidless box, the Urbis valley' (p.185) where the sunset is invisible, and which is so obviously Mexico City. Finally, but unsurprisingly, she is very different because, secretly, she can already read other people's minds and because she longs for a superior man, even as she goes about her five-day-a-week sexual therapy job. Once the two-year conscription period is over, she will be allowed to involve herself in personal relationships, and her previous caring profession will give her much prestige among members of the opposite sex. On the other hand, as she often reminds herself, her looks would ensure that anyway (pp.157–58).

For the moment, though, her timetable is fixed, her duties clearly defined and she is controlled by (indeed, a prisoner of) the state, in particular because of the computer that she constantly carries with her and which can theoretically answer all her questions. The stage that she has almost completed consists of providing sex for old men, and has few compensations other than the knowledge that some of them, at least, are grateful. Soon she will go on to the crippled and deformed. This may be better, but she takes leave to doubt whether there will be any improvement based on generation: if the old peasant was brutal, as he was, there is nothing to suggest that his son will be any less so (p.158). In other words, no progress will have been made. One should be grateful to the state, but there is still no happiness or justice. Consciousness of the past is aroused when W218 sees on her 'teletotal' set in her clinical, modern apartment, a documentary on the submerged city of New York, with a poster of the face of a famous actress of the epoch, which she seems to recognize. Few powers of deduction are needed to work out that the face is that of Hedy Lamarr; the poster is for *Algiers,* though the film itself would be unknown to W218 since 'pre-polar' films are banned because of their antisocial elements. There are no romantic illusions any more.

W218's life changes when she meets someone who is indubitably her ideal man, even to the extent of having the two characteristics she sees as beautiful: green eyes and a pointed beard (pp.180, 181). This is LKJS, an emissary from her home country, and his accent makes her remember the bad things that have happened, just like Ana with Pozzi (p.166). They go out together in a style reminiscent of the ideal romantic settings of thirties and forties Hollywood films, and in tempting contrast to the lack of colour and luxury in her everyday life, he provides her with exquisite clothes, jewels and furs, and a bottle of costly perfume like the one that Ana asks Beatriz to buy for her in the main story (p.177). She is able to tear her gaze away from this wonderful man just long enough to be disillusioned by the knowledge that the night club, with its decadent décor and music and forbidden food and drink, is frequented by members of the government (p.188). But it is all very romantic, and she and LKJS fall madly in love. She is, of course, deceived: he is a married man with children, on a mission to find out all about her potential mind-reading capacity (he does not know that it is already functioning), and his brief is to visit her, so as to control her, every year until she reaches her fateful thirtieth birthday (p.238). When he returns to his country, she obtains permission to visit him, and it is there that she discovers the truth.

Like the Actress, to whom she is undoubtedly related, the only outcome of all this is death. She attempts to murder LKJS, and elects to be sentenced to a region called 'Hielos Eternos' ('Eternal Ice'); there she will give sexual solace to hopeless, contagious patients in an underground isolation hospital, and there she will inevitably contract some horrendous disease and die. But among the political prisoners who are also being despatched to this Siberian region she sees LKJS; he weeps at her suffering, calms the lust of the others, is full of remorse, and is distraught at the thought of the pernicious triangle he had found himself in, with a choice between his family and country and W218. And he feels pity for W218, even though his first loyalties lie elsewhere; far from being a 'superior man', he regrets his previous exploitative role and says, 'no quiero estar por encima de nadie' ('I don't want to be above anyone') (p.254). [20] It is she, a poor, generous victim of fate, that has made him realize this.

When, eventually, W218 falls fatally ill, she meets a dying but rebellious patient who tells her that someone did once escape from this area, so desperate was she to be reunited with her daughter and to return to her homeland, which was in the middle of a civil war. As the other patient tells the story, the not entirely unknown Puig phenomenon of a change from the third to the first person occurs in her narration. It was actually she, it seems, who went home by means of some kind of magic, and with her angelic body, her *pubis angelical,* brought peace: as she materialized next to a pyramid — usually seen as symbolic of the maternal aspect of the earth[21] — in the middle of the main square of the city, the sight of her sexless genital area caused the combatants to lay down their arms. She met up with a man whom she had long thought dead, and he begged her to forgive him for once having judged her frivolous, as Pozzi judged Ana (and, indeed, as Valentín once judged Molina). Now he thanked her from the bottom of his heart for the miracle she had wrought (p.266). And, to her utter joy, she also found her daughter, another pure, sexless angel, with no 'punto flaco . . . en medio de las piernas' ('vulnerable point between her legs') (p.162), so that she could never be enslaved by a man. Her contentment was such that she came back by magic to the hospital; and she warns W218 not to believe the staff if they claim that her daughter is actually dead and that her grief has made her insane.

As García Ramos has so rightly pointed out, the science fiction story highlights Ana'a three major obsessions: the condition of Argentina; the possibility of being reunited with her daughter; and being liberated from her attractiveness to men and, therefore, from being exploited by them.[22] All of these are evident in the other two stories too, and furthermore, it is hard to avoid the conclusion that at least the first and the last are major themes in the other novels. Even the question of the relationship of Ana/the *Ama*/W218's hospital companion and their respective daughters, echoes preoccupations mentioned briefly, if not elaborated on, in the author's previous writings. And in each area, there is the need for choice, and there is deceit and self-deception. Ana claims that women are always obliged to choose between two evils (p.194); my contention — and it seems to me obvious that Puig has been concerned with this in the novels we have already considered — is that *everyone* has to make difficult choices, even if conditions for women are usually worse.

It is, I think, somewhat surprising that so few critics have noted the extent of the interdependence of the three stories, some of them even going as far as to claim that there are no explicit links between them and that the effect of their juxtaposition will be exclusively based on the reader's impressionistic reaction. In fact, there are countless repetitions and much overlapping, and it is this that will influence the way in which any reader reacts.

The basic link is that between the three women: all of them are used by men — the *Ama* is idolized, but used just the same, and her 'liberation' is nothing of the kind — and all of them find the strength to carry on by imagining that they will some day find a superior man. This is their 'necessary dream'. They are all imprisoned in various ways, all worried about reaching the age of thirty, and two of them are subconsciously, if not always consciously, haunted by the fact that they have allowed themselves to be deprived of their daughters. Even in the case of W218 the same story is told, and perhaps she could be said to have 'become' the woman to whom this tragedy has happened.[23] All three women are in Mexico, all three are living in the shadow of death. And of course, there is the element of espionage, which represents deception and the terrible problems of, on the one hand, the victim's misplaced trust and, on the other, the agent's divided loyalties. It could even be seen as misleading to talk about three heroines. The men, too, are obviously interchangeable. Pozzi is the *Ama*'s Theo and W218's LKJS, and none of them is what he appears to be. They may seem superior, but all are traitors to those who love and trust them and who have created a false image of them.

That the women are all one is underlined over and over again. 'The most beautiful woman in the world' wakes after her wedding night having dreamt that she has undergone an operation: Ana, of course, really has been operated on. The *Ama* is sure that instead of a heart, she has some kind of clockwork mechnism, Pozzi calls Ana a machine (p.91), and one of the questions that W218, much later on, asks her all-knowing computer is cancelled because she refuses to reveal to it that she suspects this of herself (p.179). All of them suffer from nightmares, particularly on the subject of unprotected women. All of them have been forced to kill the man they love: the *Ama* murders Theo, W218 stabs LKJS (and although he survives, he has no future in the barren regions of Eternal Ice), and Ana is partly responsible for Pozzi's death (he blackmails her by stating that if she will help him catch Alejandro he will stay in Mexico City, (p.219)). Then — and this is one of the points that superficially but strikingly links them all with Molina — they are incapable of resisting beautiful luxury goods. We have already seen the list of elegant items that, according to Ana, fill the heads of all women, and as she looks back on her relationship with Alejandro, we discover that his minimal charm was decisively enhanced by the fact that he showered her with presents of clothes: when parcels began to arrive from Yves Saint Laurent she was incapable of refusing them. The Hedy Lamarr version of Ana is invariably surrounded by beautiful things (this was why she married her husband), and in the grey, cold city of the future where W218 lives and works, a sure way of attracting and seducing her is to present her with a lilac-coloured pleated chiffon evening dress à la Fortuny, transparent sandals with high heels, a full-length chinchilla coat, an evening bag made from tiny purple tube-like beads and a bottle of the world's most expensive perfume, just for one outing. It makes her think insubordinate thoughts (p.184) and turns her into a 'frivolous female' (p.185). In all three cases, too, there is the need for a man who will provide a sense of direction, who knows all the answers, who will make vital decisions unhesitatingly. Even in her fantasies Ana claims she could not be attracted to someone who could not find his way along an unknown road (p.87), she deeply regrets the early death of her father, who might well have helped her in her approach to life and men,[24] she admires Pozzi's grasp of Lacanian psychoanalysis, is impressed by his sense of justice and generosity (p.29), has been known to reproduce his opinions (p.54), and is ultimately convinced by him that she is incapable of thinking seriously about anything (p.245). In her diary, she directs all her questions to her dead father; but of course, there is no answer from him. It may be that in the end, like so many others, her best advice will come from her mother, but we shall return to that point later. Ana wants, among other things, protection, but there is too great a price to pay for it: after all, prison guards are protective. Ana's husband certainly did not fail her in this, and the *Ama*'s warders protect her only too well. When she finds happiness with Theo, it is short-lived, and he makes it plain that he must be the master. Finally, her romance with the young man she meets in Mexico is equally fated, since he wants nothing less than total possession of her in return for his love. As for W218, her computer provides the knowledge that she needs, but that is dangerous since she makes herself constantly vulnerable, and she realizes that if only her knight in shining armour would appear, she could consult him instead (p.158). In fact, she actually drops her computer when she first is attracted to LKJS (p.180), but it is all an impasse, for the 'superior man', in the sense that Ana uses the expression (and she is is so incapable of thinking really clearly that she cannot define what she actually wants when Beatriz asks her to, nor can she counter Beatriz's objections to the concept, (pp.19–20)), will always exact a terrible payment.

   There are so many reflections of each of the three stories in one, or both, of the others that the novel is like a carefully laid-out gallery of mirrors, with the reader seeing himself accurately, or even inaccurately, represented and reproduced, ultimately acquiring a certain amount of uncomfortable knowledge and awareness. Some more repeated elements are worth looking at. One is the desire on the part of the women to avoid sex altogether, thus releasing themselves from its painful consequences. The *Ama* does her best not to look at the concupiscent angel on her bedhead (p.15), but looks to the 'good' angels instead for compassion and protection (p.14). She (literally) felt nothing during her first sexual experience with her husband since she was drugged by him and unconscious, and this illustrated the fact that Ana felt nothing for Fito after a while, and nothing *at all* when Pozzi made love to her in hospital (p.190). This is taken to its logical conclusion in the fable of the *pubis angelical,* and it repeats Molina's hoped-for love without sex in *El beso de la mujer araña.* We have already pointed out the obvious objection to that solution. Here, too, as Gustavo Pellón observes, 'the fable itself contains the seeds of its own failure, since the best it can offer us is an end to exploitation when the object of exploitation itself ceases to exist'.[25] An absurd solution, indeed, and yet one that those concerned with the problems of sexuality in the modern world will understand, even sympathize with. For as Jeffrey Weeks points out in his thought-provoking book *Sexuality and its Discontents,*

> Sexual behaviour would transparently not be possible without physiological sources, but physiology does not supply motives, passion, object choice or identity. These come from 'somewhere else', the domains of social relations and psychic conflict. If this is correct the body can no longer be seen as a biological given which emits its own meaning. It must be understood instead as an ensemble of potentialities which are given meaning only in society.[26]

There is always an element of blackmail: between Pozzi and Ana, of course, but the same sort of situation arose with Alejandro (p.105) and even, to a lesser extent, with Fito. As for the *Ama*/Actress, she is blackmailed both by her husband and by the famous film producer. A sure sign that Puig sees no easy way out of all this is his indication that the 'escape' from the servitude and impotence of marriage is a mirage. There is no such thing as liberation.

This knowledge does not take away the desire for freedom *and* happiness, unfortunately, or indeed the need for sexual fulfilment, often seen in the image of thirst (though in the main story this is also an aspect of the post-operative condition of the patient). References to Ana's thirst and her sedation are echoed in the mention of the *Ama*'s wonderful tranquillizing liquid. The fact that these interrelated references are not, so to speak, chronological (the *Ama*'s thirst comes long before Ana's and that of W218) underlines the pointlessness of trying to clarify the three stories in a conventional way. Their juxtaposition is a literary technique based on psychoanalytic foundations.

Colour is another important element, with the most obvious contrast that between the subtropical lushness of the story of the Actress and the cold grey, brown and black of the Polar Era of W218's adventures; colour disappeared at the time of the polar inundation, we are told (p.159) and, with two exceptions, the whole of her environment represents the sterility of her existence. The exceptions are the lovely clothes LKJS presents her with and his irresistible green eyes, a colour referred to again later in the perennially green oak tree that he says he can see from his home in the Avenue of the Aurora Borealis in Aquarius City (pp.27, 205). But all vital colour is at least partly fraudulent, and — like the angels — connotes hidden deception and danger. In Mexico, the glorious plumage of the peacocks constitutes 'el hastío' ('tedium') according to the sentimental song that is quoted (pp.128, 133), and even the tropical palm-groves are bad omens (p.136). We find this image repeated in the night-club that LKJS takes W218 to, and the visit is a prelude to disaster. Indeed, the old cliché holds: one has to take the rough with the smooth, and the rough is often intolerable even if it has to be tolerated. The fraudulent nature of everything is constantly illustrated: the green of LKJS's eyes brings death, not life, and when he removes his contact lenses his eyes are seen to be black or, later, the colour of 'barren earth' (pp.209, 252). At that point, W218 no longer finds him so irresistible, As for the green oak tree, we find that though it does exist (there is always a positive side), it is no more than a painted street sign (p.207). One more example: when W218 and the political prisoners are condemned (and the constant use of the word *condenado* for 'prisoner' is not without significance) to a sojourn in the region of Eternal Ice, they are given spectacles to protect them against the glare, and these make everything look blue, the colour of passivity and debilitation and sacrifice in an area where life — water — is petrified and its life-giving potential denied.[27] But here, as in *The Buenos Aires Affair,* the positive side is represented by the continuation of life, and Ana, through W218, does not think about dead blue flesh but about young children with blue eyes (p.256)[28] Then, LKJS's home city is knowingly named (Aquarius, with his two amphoras, represents the active and the passive, and although related to the Flood — and ending — he also contains the promise of a new beginning[29]). Even the name of the street in which he claimed to live — Aurora Borealis — represents something which seems like a beautiful new dawn, but which misleads not only the human eye but the compass needle. It turns out that he does not live there anyway: a double deception. And the imagery of the shepherd and lamb, which LKJS sees in his mind's eye when he and W218 are making love, suggests protection *and* sacrifice, not only to the reader but to LKJS himself, when he admits that later he will use her skin to protect himself (p.240). Everything has its harmful side. The tragedy is twofold: it is not the intellect but the emotions that come into play when human beings make definitive choices, and what seems like the 'right' choice may bring suffering in its wake.

Much of this repeats not only the basic preoccupations but also the actual imagery of the previous novels. The sleepwalker reminds us of the nurse in *El beso de la mujer araña,* for example, as well as of the zombie woman in the same book. The doll is found there too, in what I have called Molina's 'sensations' (the string of images in italics) as well as in the zombie story. Here, the *Ama* is 'a broken mechanical doll' (p.9) and W218 a rag doll thrown to the floor (p.239);[30] a woman, it is claimed, is no more than a sentimental doll anyway (p.24). Happiness that stems from sexual pleasure is short-lived: in *El beso de la mujer araña,* the metaphor is of a short but happy dream; in *Pubis angelical,* the *Ama* thinks it was all literally a dream when she wakes up on the transatlantic liner after spending a night of love with Theo (p.77). Then, also in *El beso de la mujer araña,* an absurd hope is implied that Valentín might renounce the violence and fanaticism of his brand of politics for the sake of 'feminine' values, introduced to him by Molina. The same, perhaps, applies here to Theo. In the previous novel it was love that involved Molina in politics. (As Alicia Borinsky has wisely pointed out, for his sacrifice to be genuinely 'feminine', it has to take place without his really believing in the cause.[31]) Ana's relationship with Pozzi is a parallel (whether she likes it or not, and before her conscience is moved by how little she can do for her country there in Mexico, Pozzi implicates her by hiding out in the Buenos Aires apartment that had been their love-nest). She is like Molina, too, in that she is forced to consider the possibility of a worthwhile, meaningful death (p.222), and even — on a more frivolous level — because she thinks that the love of opera is a sign of culture. Pozzi is unconvinced (p.168), again illustrating the incompatibility between aesthetics and ethics which we first noted in the previous novel. Another example of this is found in *Pubis angelical.* In spite of his fascist leanings and cold ruthlessness, Alejandro is the possessor of a 'feminine' sensibility, and he is very artistic. Then the power of men as shown in the initiation scene that LKJS imagines ('Males of the world, unite!' (p.239)) is not all that far removed from Leo's exaggerated and brutal masculinity in *The Buenos Aires Affair.* And echoing the realization of the deceptive quality of both people and things, we find that W218 is kind to a disfigured patient, like the hero of *The Enchanted Cottage* in *El beso de la mujer araña,* and like the *Ama,* who embraces a man who is dressed as a servant girl (p.71), and Valentín, who makes love to a man who is — to his own satisfaction anyway — a woman.[32] All are blackmailed, in pernicious triangles. Toto, Herminia, even Berto, (in *La traición de Rita Hayworth*), Nené,

Celina (in *Boquitas pintadas*), Molina (in *El beso de la mujer araña*) and now Ana and Theo (with their secret diaries) go in for discursive cures. There are song lyrics to substantiate love scenes in several of the books, and there is always, of course, the question of utopian ideals, be they obvious and 'feminine' or more subtle and political. Perhaps the second category is even more pernicious and deceptive than the first.

So we come to the first of Ana's major obsessions, as pin-pointed by García Ramos: conditions in Argentina and the possibility of its pacification. It may be reasonable to claim that *Pubis angelical* is not only a political novel, but also a historical novel. For Juan Goytisolo, it is certainly the first and, if I am not mistaken, he at least would also judge it to be the second. Puig, he says, has given back:

> su rázon de ser y dignidad a la tan justamente desacreditada novela política. *El beso de la mujer araña* y *Pubis angelical* son en efecto dos testimonios demoledores, implacables del mal que corroe no sólo a Argentina, sino a la totalidad de Latinoamérica: la monstruosa pirámide de opresión política, social y moral que aplasta a los hombres y mujeres del continente en nombre de unos valores cuya inanidad y mentira resultan cada día más flagrantes.[33]

> a *raison d'être* and dignity to the justifiably discredited political novel. *El beso de la mujer araña* and *Pubis angelical* are indeed two pieces of ruthless, demolishing evidence against the evil that is not only eating away at Argentina, but also at the whole of Latin America: the monstrous pyramid of political, social and moral oppression that is crushing the men and women of that continent in the name of values, the inanity and falseness of which become more and more striking every day.

He goes on to observe that, generally speaking, Puig's characters are not in possession of a raised political consciousness (even if we do meet two militant revolutionaries in Valentín and Pozzi), but are people who represent the daily drama of life in Argentina under, say, Onganía or Videla better than the writings of any explicitly committed author could. The important feature of this is that because of what Goytisolo calls the books' 'apoliticism' any genuine coming-to-awareness takes place in the reader, not in the characters. This is a feature that we have already noted where other serious issues are concerned, and it is García Ramos who underlines this authorial delicacy when he claims that though, as Puig himself has said, the political panorama of Ana's life is a vital element in *Pubis angelical,* and though too Peronism constitutes the political framework of all Puig's work, the author carefully avoids Manicheism.[34] He is only too aware of the contradictions of Peronism, and his characters are either unconvinced or are 'retratos desmitificadores' ('demythifying portraits'), to use Goytisolo's words.[35] The present and the future of Argentina are major preoccupations of the exiled Puig as they are of his exiled character Ana, and we have already noted, in Chapter Four, that Peronism interests him deeply. It has been present in all the novels so far, but it is only with *El beso de la mujer araña* and *Pubis angelical* that it becomes so vital an element that the whole construct would collapse without it. In the earlier novels, with one exception, the characters see themselves as apart from popular demagogy and they have no real interest in Peronism or in what it might come to mean to them. In the later two, they are either in it up to the hilt (Valentín, Pozzi, Alejandro) or implicated in it by others (Molina, Ana, and even Beatriz). But both groups of people are equally important as the author reveals their priorities. We discover how it feels to live in a given place at a given time. Whether people were right or wrong in their attitudes towards what was being offered to their country is neither here nor there for the purpose of this argument. What is important is that our understanding of what it was like at the time makes these historical novels: apathy, unrewarded faith, misguided fanaticism, even a misunderstanding of the situation, are all part of history.

In *La traición de Rita Hayworth,* there are only two references to the first wave of Peronism, but they are both revealing. The first, as we have seen, is the 1947 diary of Esther, whose education is being paid for by a Peronist grant. The other constitutes a clear indication of the social class to which Peronists were invariably thought to belong. In the foul-mouthed sexual fantasies of Cobito Umansky, Toto's great enemy, he makes passing use of the word 'peronista', and it is obviously not meant to be complimentary. The subject is a voluptuous, large-breasted washerwoman who excites him. She is a 'gorda peronista del carajo' ('fat fucking Peronist'), he says, the lowest of the low (p.200). The chapter dates from the first few months of 1946 and, of course, the first Peronist administration had been elected in the February of that same year. From his position as a kind of Minister of Labour in the previous régime, led at first by Ramírez (the name, incidentally, that Pozzi was to assume when he returned from his Mexican exile) and then by Fárrell, Perón had kept a canny eye on the poor and underprivileged classes. They would constitute a guaranteed constituency for him should he achieve power. In the meantime he issued decrees favouring the workers and promising them what would nowadays be designated civil rights, he created new trade unions and then purged these, together with those already in existence, of dissidents. The oppressed had faith in him, and the *Confederación General del Trabajo,* the biggest representative body of the working man, actually held the country to ransom when they demanded his release from prison just before the 1946 elections which changed the face of Argentina. The fact that it was the military and the Supreme Court, both of which were seen as ultra-conservative, who were against Perón, worked in his favour. He was the defender of the workers and, to add to his acceptability, he was endorsed by the Church. (During the second administration the Church was among his bitterest enemies, but those days were still to come.) The opposition, as Ernesto Sábato has pointed out, dangerously misjudged the strength of his support; those who, like him, issued warnings about what was happening, or likely to happen, were said to be callow inexperienced youths, and perhaps the most mistaken view of all was that real, responsible workers would never support Perón and that he could never win an election.[36] In the event Perón won fifty-five per cent of the popular vote, became one of the most consummate populist (with all this word's pejorative connotations) leaders, exploited class warfare and made economic and social justice his warcry. The two faces of Peronism echo the duality of so many other issues in Puig's world. On the one hand, the new 1949 constitution marked a move towards a more democratic election process; on the other, the executive's power was increased over that of the legislature and the courts, and this was a sinister move. Then dissidents were removed, the unions neutered, student organizations repressed and people began to lose their jobs; furthermore, two top newspapers, *La Prensa* and *La Nación,* were silenced. But, on the credit side, there were efforts to make Argentina economically independent and to help the working class. Although for various reasons, some beyond Perón's control, some based on his misjudgement of international affairs, his economic ambitions remained unrealized,[37] the negative aspects of Perón's character and policies did not matter to the people: they were fully behind him, and they adored Evita. As I have already pointed out, with her humble origins and dubious past, her success demonstrated irrefutably that their wildest dreams *could* come true. What did they know or care about Perón's Nazi sympathies during the war, or what Sábato calls his total lack of scruples?[38] The year 1951 saw him re-elected with an even greater majority than he had received in 1946.

One of the phenomena of the first Perón régime was the influx of poor people from the neglected provinces into Buenos Aires, the so-called *cabecitas negras* (literally: 'little black heads'). We met some of these simple and (according to Leo) misguided souls in their state-aided boarding-house in *The Buenos Aires Affair,* but migration to the capital is already evident in earlier novels, and is a manifestation of the wish to go up in the world. In *Boquitas pintadas,* Nené is one of the many hopefuls arriving in the big city. For her it is a new life in more ways than one: marriage and fulfilment awaited her. Needless to say, her optimism, like that of the Peronists who saw Buenos Aires as the new Jerusalem, was ill-founded.

In *The Buenos Aires Affair,* we have the first hint of the real complexity of the subject, of the fact that everything cannot be seen in terms of black and white, rich and poor. For the first time we have references to terrorism; the political situation has changed, and we realize that it is no longer a question of a clear-cut class struggle being carried on by the workers, but of the active participation of young intellectuals who came to the fore in the crisis years following Perón's downfall in 1955. His decline had come about as so many of the groups that had hitherto unquestioningly supported him became disillusioned. Even the workers lost some of their enthusiasm for him as his disastrous economic policies made holes in their meagre incomes. Peronist violence, the movement's worsening relations with the Church, the alienation of the powerful nationalists, the absence of the charismatic Evita, all contributed to the formation of militarily-based conspiracies. The second military uprising, which began on 16 September 1955, was the one that was successful, and the General agreed to abdicate. Under President Aramburu, the Peronist party was abolished. The problem then was that economic conditions did not actually improve with the departure of Perón; indeed, they got worse, and the workers were even more hostile and bitter than they had been when he was in power. As one president succeeded another, there was an atmosphere of discontent, and at each election the blank voting papers of the Peronists were greater in number than those of any of the other parties. The common thread, as elections and *coups d'état* changed the faces of those in the *Casa Rosada,* was the clandestine power of the Peronists, in overall majority and constantly alive. Many historians of the epoch feel that Perón's final return to power was the culmination of a chain of events that started in May 1969 with the terrible violence that accompanied the so-called *Cordobazo,* a strike launched by the unions in Córdoba, Rosario and elsewhere, that escalated into a small revolution which

Onganía's forces put down only with difficulty.[39] It was this, they claim, that made the military realize that it would have to allow an *elected* president to take over the reins, even if this should turn out to be Perón. And, of course, ultimately it was.[40] A direct result of the *Cordobazo* was the launching of the ERP, a paramilitary offshoot of the Trotskyite PRT.[41] (We remember that Pozzi, in *Pubis angelical,* actually started his political career a a Trotskyite (p.51), and that later he admits that his hatred of Trotskyite extremism was one of the reasons for his joining the Peronists (p.119). He disapproves of the ERP, but in spite of his aversion to them, based on their lack of nationalistic fervour and their desire to turn Argentina into another Vietnam (p.123), he and his companions are happy to adopt one of their most notorious practices when they decide to attempt to kidnap Ana's admirer, Alejandro.) The other guerilla group to come into being after the *Cordobazo* was the one with which Pozzi is dealing (p.122), the *Montoneros.* Indeed, by the time of the action of *Pubis angelical,* the *Montoneros* had absorbed more or less all the other Peronist terrorist groups.

This, then, is the background period to the 1973 novel, *The Buenos Aires Affair,* with the use of armed force a deliberate and calculated stratagem of *civilian* groups, and Perón managing to ride two horses simultaneously. While never publicly dissociating himself from his more violent supporters, such as the *Montoneros,* he maintained a kind of working relationship with many who were strongly against all their activities. Urban guerillas were now very much part of the scene, and though many people were prepared to help them, even if only as passive supporters, many others were very worried by the way things were going. There was a feeling of polarization, and Leo is just one of those whose sympathies do not lie with the Peronist cause. This situation is indicative of Puig's wish to avoid the obvious; though no supporter of the *Conductor* or his methods, he refuses to draw simplistic conclusions and presents us with a frankly unappealing man who, nonetheless, may hold reasonable political views.

It is with *El beso de la mujer araña* that the political activist and theorist comes into his own, again illustrating the impossibility of understanding, to say nothing of being sure about, anything. The class element is no longer in evidence: Molina, though of far humbler origin than Valentín, feels unsympathetic towards the movement; Valentín, a professional man with promise for a brilliant future, sacrifice everything for what he judges a sacred mission[42] (he is charged with being involved in workers' demonstrations, so has abandoned his class in favour of his ideology). This, we recall, is 1975: Pozzi, from *Pubis angelical,* and Valentín are fictionally coetaneous, living through the disastrous epoch that followed Perón's death, with its renewed political violence and the *Montoneros* accusing the new president, Isabel, of betraying the revolution while issuing death threats to officials of her government. Perón's *Justicialismo* now belonged to the past. It was in March 1976 that the military coup that meant the end of official Peronist power took place; then the new junta launched into the ruthless eradication of all guerillas and the left wing in general, and a great many others became its hapless victims. But in 1975 this has still to take place, and the setting of both the fourth and fifth Puig novels is the interregnum, as it were. Isabel is on the throne, the government is at best inept, at worst corrupt, the country's economy is on the rocks, inflation is soaring, the unions are demanding higher wages, harvests are bad, beef production is in decline, and civil revolution and urban violence make up the order of the day.

Like Peronism, and like everything else in the novelistic world of Manuel Puig, Valentín has two sides to him. He is both good and bad, high-minded and misguided, selfless and narcissistic. A 'demythifying portrait' indeed. And though it is Molina who could most obviously be accused of running away from reality, Valentín is also doing so, in a way. Valentín avoids the destructive isolation that his alienation from his family, and particularly his mother, would otherwise have caused by establishing a sense of oneness with others of the same persuasion; he refers to this explicitly. He thinks that political consciousness and action are the best method of combating alienation; Molina thinks the answer is affective contact (p. 24). In fact, they have more in common than they think, and they certainly complement each other. (Later, in *Pubis angelical,* a decisive factor in Pozzi's conversion to Peronism is his realization that with so many anti-Peronists he feels that he is in bad company, (p. 115).)

The situation in Argentina was a factor in the first three books, a kind of vague framework that gradually became more and more visible. In the fourth novel it became an important element, but where the fifth is concerned it could, and I think should, be said that it is vital: it constitutes Pozzi's *raison d'être* and Ana is created by it. Ultimately even Ana renounces the position that had previously been so much a part of her. She too wonders what she can do for her country and for other people. Like Molina, her motives may be mixed; her new awareness may be less a question of having been intellectually persuaded than of emotional solidarity with someone she has loved and cannot have. (In the W218 story, she reads in her lover's mind that although he feels great tenderness and compassion for her, his greatest love has always been for his wife and family, and for his country, (p.254).) The only thing Ana simply cannot tolerate is treachery, so she will refuse to believe badly of Pozzi, and will open her mind to what he stood for, following the dictates of her heart.

He had tried to explain his position to her, and — in all fairness — she tried to understand. But it was difficult, especially as he classified her as a pre-feminist political ignoramus in the first place (p.38), and criticized her for having turned her back on Argentina in the second (p.39). Even if he had treated her as an intellectual equal, Peronism would be difficult for her to understand, and her good will was not increased by Beatriz's hostility to it, or by what she herself had suffered at the hands of its right wing, as represented by Alejandro, in a position of authority in the new Perón and Isabelita government. Nevertheless there *was* good will on her part, and she is not blindly and unreasonably hostile to the movement. (In the same way, Puig has shown his own flexibility on the subject in previous novels — in his case, perhaps, loving the sinner while hating the sin.) Ana remonstrates with Beatriz when she queries Pozzi's selfless goodness: 'an enormous number of good people became Peronists', she says (p.57). She repeats Pozzi's affirmation that Perón had been the first leader to produce a national, or nationalist, policy that was worthy of respect (p. 58) and points out that he rightly judged the labour movement important (p.58). Indeed, we might add that Perón expressed a concern for the lower classes that had not been heard in Argentina since the epoch of Rosas.[43]

When Pozzi explains his views as best he can, his utopian idealism becomes clear. He sees Peronism as a struggle for justice; when he says, 'Yo me metí en el peronismo, pero fue después que me hice peronista' ('I got involved in Peronism, yes, but it was afterwards that I became a Peronist') (p.114), he is implying, surely, that its formal, organized aspects were no more than a kind of superstructure, and that all the time that he had been flirting with other parties he was a Peronist at heart. It is the nearest thing to what he truly believes in in this imperfect world, a stage in the progress of socialism that was historically necessary in the Argentine (p.59) and, in spite of its faults and confusions, infinitely preferable to the *Partido Socialista* (Socialist Party), with its exclusively middle-class orientation and its lack of unity and continuity (p.117), and the Communists, who supported Stalinism and the invasion of

Hungary and condemned Fidel Castro and the Cuban Revolution in 1959. For him, Peronism is greater than any political party (p.121) and he realizes that the real thing will not exist in the future: all there will be is the name (p.122). Fundamental to his beliefs is the attitude he brings to bear on the subject of exile. He is desperate to return to Buenos Aires (p.147), but it is not just because of homesickness and a sense of rootlessness, something that the Mexican novelist Carlos Fuentes once summed up in a memorable aphorism: 'El exilio es un homenaje maravilloso a nuestros orígenes' ('Exile is a wonderful homage to one's origins').[44] It is, rather, the realization that changes have to be effected from inside the country. And it is the same where the Peronist party is concerned. 'Dentro del peronismo hay gente de lo peor,' he admits, 'pero si te da asco pertenecer al mismo movimiento les dejás el campo libre' ('In Peronism there are the worst kind of people, but if you are revolted by the thought of belonging to the same movement as they do, you will leave the field clear for them') (p.124). And when Ana says that the present government is genuinely Peronist, as far as she can see, in other words a gang of thugs and Nazis — this is 1975, of course, and Perón is dead — he admits that this is *not* the Peronism that he had worked for (p.148).

Once again all the reader can do is to try to formulate a question. And there is no more chance of a clear-cut and obvious answer this time than there ever was. The question, really, is formulated for us by Ana's view of Pozzi's political stance, and, ultimately, boils down to how different his attitudes are from hers. This is what she says:

> — Pozzi, vos te imaginaste el peronismo a tu antojo, y te casaste sin conocerlo . . .

> — Lo que sos es . . . un inocentón, un iluso, que te metiste en todo este lío por qué sé yo . . . por romántico. Igual que yo me metí en el lío de casarme con un hombre que no sabía quien era. Y sos también un irresponsable, porque colaborás con gente que toma las armas sin saber lo que hacen. Tan irresponsable como yo, que traje al mundo a mi hija porque sí nomás. Así que somos los dos iguales, unos ilusos y unos irresponsables.

> 'Pozzi, you made Peronism what you wanted it to be, and you got married to it without knowing what it was like . . .

> 'You're hopelessly . . . naïve, deluded, and you got into this mess because you're . . . oh, I don't know, a romantic. It's the same as my getting into a mess marrying a man I didn't know. And you're irresponsible too, because you collaborate with people who use force without knowng what they're doing. As irresponsible as I was, bringing

my daughter into the world just because. So we're the same, you and I, deluded and irresponsible.'

And she accuses him of actually enjoying the role he has chosen for himself in life: he finds pleasure, she says, in martyrdom (p. 219).

Like Leo in *The Buenos Aires Affair* and Molina in *El beso de la mujer araña*, Ana is a character who is misguided on many points, unhappy in many ways, insecure, muddle-headed and lonely, but who may be less short-sighted than she seems. The author had the help of a militant left-wing Peronist in the preparation of this book, and transferred verbatim the answers to his questions onto the printed page; he changed, he has said, his questions only slightly, just so that they might be more appropriate for a heroine like Ana,[45] and we can detect his own puzzled reaction in hers. Well-intentioned, altruistic people were misled by the movement as they are by so many areas of faith and belief in life. And this is the cause of sadness and sympathy, a sympathy which may well be Manuel Puig's most striking characteristic. When writing about Esther, the young Peronist in *La traición de Rita Hayworth,* Jorge Panesi signals the presence of parody in this section, but goes on to point out that it is not Peronism itself that is being parodied, but that populist sublimation in it, which spiritualizes the notion of 'the people', granting them a soul, a heart and breath. In Panesi's opinion, this is a sentimental, paternalistic and, in the end, reactionary ideology.[46] He is almost certainly right. And the middle classes unwisely and unjustifiably excluded from his policies by Perón, as Sábato has noted,[47] could react in one of two ways — either falling into what was, after all, the trap of defending and sacrificing themselves for 'the people', as Pozzi did, or ignoring genuine social problems, like Ana, wrapped up in her own world and dreams of her own destiny. But even the most unaware among us have to live in the world with other people and may be drawn into the struggle; we may start as spectators, but we may have to become active participants in it. Conscience demands a point of view. However, each of us is just as likely to be wrong as right, even when guided by high principles. We are all wrong *and* right: countries, movements and individuals.[48]

The second of Ana's preoccupations can actually be bracketed together with the third, since both her concern for her relationship with her daughter and that for her own female condition are based on how women judge their role in life and how they are treated by men in a particular society. Indeed, all three obsessions are inseparable in the sense that they are all to do with identity. Can anyone know who they are without asking someone else to tell them their name?

Ana's daughter, Clarita, although not an active member of the dramatis personae of the novel is, nonetheless, a key character. It is important that Ana's only child is a girl, for there is more to this than a highlighting of the unavoidable feminine condition of motherhood, something that no amount of pleading for the acceptance of bisexuality can avoid.[49] The fact is that Ana has abandoned her daughter in her pursuit of liberation, and this preoccupies her terribly, however much she justifies her actions by saying that Clarita does not love her (p.34), that in any case her ex-husband adores the child (p.27), and by referring back to occasions when her best efforts went unappreciated — the visit to Alejandro's *estancia* which bored Clarita to death (p.96) for example, or the trips to the Teatro Colón which were not much better received (p.92). We trace the obsessive concern on the subject of what she has done via her uneasy unconscious (and it has to be remembered that Clarita was left with her father immediately after the divorce, it was not that Ana was forced to leave her when she fled the country). In the story of the *Ama*/Actress, the conditions of the choice are made explicit: freedom in a new country, with an exciting career and the accompanying glamour and riches, or the burden of a child to bring up without the support of its father. (In another of the numerous *mises en abyme* of the text, the Actress herself has to play the part of a woman who has left her husband and in so doing lost her daughter, (p.109).) For the Actress the real-life 'consolation' consists of clandestine, impersonal sex with the chauffeur and the fleeting sense of power she experiences when she succeeds in exciting her unbearable co-star during a love scene. This is such small comfort that she loses her control and expresses her grief in public (p.111). And connected with all this is the extreme version of this situation: her own mother had actually attempted to kill her, though apparently for her own good. Her motive provides another very small crumb of comfort for the Actress, and she thinks about other stupid actresses who have only their careers. She is haunted by what she has done, so much so that after a night plagued with bad dreams she is wakened by what seems to be the crying of a little girl (p.127), and when she meets the man she falls in love with in Mexico, she confesses her shame to him. She finds out that he, too, is the father of a daughter, but in contrast to her situation it is not his fault that he can see the child only infrequently: he adores her, but she is with his ex-wife (p.135). The comparison is echoed in the continuation, so to speak, of this story, with the thoughts and worries of W218. When she is mortally ill in her hospital-prison, the fellow patient who recounts her fantastic journey back to her home country, and who 'is' W218, emphasizes the desperate need she feels to see her daughter, comparing her isolated situation with that of another patient whose daughter loves her and can go on living in her place (p.262). Shortly afterwards (p.263) it is made clear that a gradual perception of the claim to immortality that motherhood gives is dawning on Ana: the body dies but the soul goes on living.[50] The realization that descendants may represent survival echoes Nené's wish in *Boquitas pintadas* to have keepsakes from her children buried with her rather than the old love letters written to her by her *príncipe azul*, (Prince Charming), Juan Carlos. And the underground location of W218's hospital may also bring to mind the maternal body. The mother (W218? Ana?) refuses to admit that her daughter could be dead; this would be enough to cause her to lose her mind.

These feelings and thoughts have been further fired by Pozzi's forcing Ana to consider her relationship with members of her own sex, and with Clarita and her mother in particular. (We have already mentioned that one of the reasons that she feels hostile towards Beatriz at times is that she treats her in a way she judges 'maternal' (p.75).) We discover that far from being indifferent to her child, Ana was so intensely worried about her well-being as a baby that she almost made herself ill, and had to employ a nanny (p.91); that she feared for the safety of both her daughter and her mother if she became involved in the plot to kidnap Alejandro (p.191); that her mother has been generous to her and desperately concerned about her, refusing to rent out the flat she bought for her in the hope that she would come home; that perhaps there is something in female solidarity. Ana's final choice is one which reveals some hope of a relationship with the women in her life, as well as (and this for the first time) concern for her mother's distress on the subject of her illness. Perhaps, like the Actress, there was a woman's voice — a mother's voice — giving her advice all the time, and perhaps it would be as well to listen.

This is not to say that she has found the answer. Her mother's voice is not that of divine knowledge, and comes from someone who is misguided, empty, perhaps just wrong. But that is all there is, and it need not be a question of going to extremes, rejecting a whole known world for the sake of an unknown and uncertain substitute, for the one does not automatically exclude the other. Ana wants to understand and be understood, and to understand one has to look with the look of love.

Knowledge and love do not have to be incompatible. But there is no guarantee that any of this will happen; life is a risk, and where there is risk there is failure. If one chooses knowledge, not pleasure, one may achieve neither. Perhaps, ultimately, what has to be changed in us all is the level and direction of our expectations. Even to seek out a 'true identity' may be an error, as Jeffrey Weeks points out: it can be 'a threat and a challenge, because it is the negation of choice. It claims to be finding out what we really *are,* or should be. Its reality is of restriction and force'.[51] Ana is doing precisely this: she wonders if 'in this world each of us is a blank, and we have to choose some role that we fancy. To entertain ourselves, pass the time, or fill that empty space inside us — I don't know' (p.195). And she is sure that everyone she knows is only too happy with their chosen role: Pozzi the left-wing martyr; Beatriz the feminist; her mother a lady living for her friends (pp.195–96). She is sure, as she was in her self-projection as the Actress, that everyone in the world is happy except for her (p.114) and she does not know which path to choose; her record thus far has not been very good, and several illusions have been shattered. Pozzi seemed to be the incarnation of common sense when he said to her that 'en política como en la vida no se viva de utopías sino de realidades' ('in politics as in life, you don't live on utopias but on realities') (p.118), reminding us of Valentín in *El beso de la mujer araña.* But it is not true, of course, and we have already considered the utopianism of Pozzi's own view of the future of society. Again, it is Jeffrey Weeks who has something vital to say on the subject, advocating 'a vision of an alternative society in which exploitation and oppression can be tamed, in which a real equality and genuine self-determination for all can be achieved', and emphasizing the need for hope.[52] According to Raymond Williams, there are two relevant imaginative utopias left: first, a 'systematic utopia', which suggests that human beings can live in radically different ways, and which Puig seems to think is unlikely to be achieved; but there is also the 'heuristic utopia', and this is as near as we can get to a focus for hope. Weeks paraphrases this as the 'education of "desire" in its widest sense, an imaginative encouragement to feel and relate differently in a better future'.[53] This is what Ana chooses; but it is a path full of pitfalls.

The nature of these pitfalls is only too obvious. How can she conquer the hostility she has felt towards her mother for so many years? And the resentment towards a child who appears to be indifferent to her? How can she rethink her relationships with other women, when for as long as she can remember she has found them tiresome? 'I'm not interested in talking to women', she once confessed (p.94). How will she join in any movement of female solidarity if she has always seen feminists as *marimachos* (viragos, p.86)? Or believe that men can be changed? How can she stop wanting what she has always wanted: beautiful things and a superior man?

But perhaps the most important impediment is going to be that, whatever the new theorists may say, and however justified their views may be, it will be virtually impossible for her to stop looking for an identity, a part to play in life. Her constant self-analysis when confined to her hospital bed underlines this; indeed, it may well be a universal need. Her interest in Lacanian psychoanalysis is another indicator of her desire for self-identification, and this key element in the novel represents a focus of interest in Buenos Aires intellectual circles in the epoch (Pozzi recalls that when Lacan was still little known in France he was appreciated in Argentina, p.167), and one that, as we have seen, in real life aroused sympathy in Manuel Puig. The wish to achieve selfhood is also reflected in her passion for analyzing Argentina, and comparing it with other countries — she claims that the Argentines want to be distinguished, for example, accepting Beatriz's view that the Mexicans aim to be rich and Pozzi's that the Spanish value courage and generosity most (p.54). The categorization habit is one that will be very difficult to break, especially as there seems to be no harm in it: on the contrary, one may well ask how improvements can possibly be made unless the nature of the problems is understood.

García Ramos claims that Pozzi's Lacanian exposition contains the key to the unravelling of *Pubis angelical*.[54] Even if this were not so, it would at least serve to underline two features of the novel that we have already noted, Pozzi's superiority to Ana in her eyes, and the problem of identity. It was when Ana went back to studying after her divorce from Fito that she met Pozzi, and we discover that their first outing together was to his weekly seminar on Lacan. He refused to miss it, but Ana understood nothing, and wept with shame (p.89). When he explained it all later, though, she understood perfectly, and they played games applying Lacanian theory to people they knew to prove this. The stereotyped stupid woman is a role Ana has hitherto been content to play. In hospital, she asks Pozzi to explain the theories to her over again and he does so, from his elevated intellectual position, finally giving up in exasperation because, he says, she converts Lacan into something banal, and it is impossible to hold a serious conversation with her (p.172). Her image of herself, therefore, is partly created by him.

This is the aspect of Lacanian theory she is clearly interested in, and Puig's own interest is the source of hers: the whole novel is permeated with it, as we shall see. In the scene where Pozzi rehearses what is for Ana an area of previous study, he reminds her of the well-known mirror stage in a baby's development, the mythical moment when it identifies with its reflection. According to Lacan, this stage represents 'an ideal unity, a salutary *imago*',[55] and the image is localized, for the first time, in time and space. Previously there had been a sense of fragmentation, with the consequent fear that part of the body may be lost. Pozzi refers to the possibility of this fear cropping up in adult life as a form of *Angst*. This happens when someone loses control over something, or someone, they considered to be part of them. And it is vital, as far as *Pubis angelical* is concerned, for us to bear in mind that for Lacan the mirror image constituted a 'homologue for the mother-child symbolic relation'.[56]

Then Pozzi goes on to say that in fact 'lo que te devuelve tu propia imagen es la mirada de los demás' ('what actually reflects your image is the gaze of other people') (p.170).[57] Their subjective view turns you into what suits them. And the subject is actually grateful, just like Lacan's small child, for whom it is necessary to recognize in another child someone who is able to recognize him. This is the world of the Lacanian *regard*, and it haunts Ana's unconscious in a most revealing way.

There is duality in all looking, Lacan tells us. Desire is present in everything that is seen (though this involves error, *méconnaissance*), but there is also the so-called 'scopic drive', when desire is present in the act of looking. As Elizabeth Wright puts it, 'the eyes, as one of the modes of access for libido to explore the world, become the instruments of this drive'. And when the infant's sexual drive is deflected from its primal object, the mother, it searches for an object 'always out of reach, to be found only by discovering its trace as an absence in every signifier. This signifying process comes to affect all looking, every recognition at once a finding and a failure to find'. Fantasy is always missing from what is actually seen, therefore; 'its absence looks through its wished-for presence'.[58] Ana finds, to paraphrase Lacan, that what she looks at is never what she wants to see. Her ideal is not hidden, but absent. But one area in which the self can see the image of itself that it wants to see is the cinema, as Christian Metz's theories proclaim,[59] and Ana identifies with screen images.

The ideas of Lacan are notoriously subtle and elusive, but in *Pubis angelical* they are used as a basis for two simple points: that the subject is created by the eye of the beholder, and that the subject's own gaze is an instrument of (doomed) desire. In the first case, the question of sexuality and identity are involved, and this leads us to Ana's third major obsessive preoccupation, the avoidance of exploitation because of her condition as a woman. (All this can also be seen to link up with the socio-political aspects of the novel, since women's problems are not to be divorced from general political problems.)

It is in Ana's *Ama*/Actress projection that there are the most references to the gaze of others, and this is frightening. To see is to know, even to possess and, later, W218 is actually able to read people's minds when she looks into their eyes. But the Actress is not yet at that stage, and she is ever conscious of hostile looks: the unattractive bad angel, for example, or the handsome dancing partner who unswervingly stares at her (p.44). She is beautiful and desirable, and the gaze of others not only reveals this to her, *but makes it so.* The outcome is that the subject's centre of gravity is dictated by this alien creative power, and it makes for the acquisition of some sort of identity. It may even lead to delusions, and a false sense of security caused by *méconnaissance*: the Actress is so often referred to as 'divine' that she begins to believe that she is; in the science fiction story, the old librarian recalls that Hedy Lamarr had a face so beautiful that it did not seem to be human (p.211), and W218 herself glimpses something superhuman in her own lovely face when she looks in the mirror (p.185). As for false security, ecstatic, adulatory glances make the *Ama* feel protected (p.44); like Ana, she tries to separate desire and love, and does not at first realize that the admiring look is a preliminary stage in the process of possession.

The process works both ways, and in practice the subject's gaze can be defensive. The *Ama*'s husband thinks it necessary to drug her before they first make love, for example, as he could not have done what he did if she had been looking at him (p.11); then, she can stop her servant looking at her by staring at her (or, in fact, him, since it is Theo, disguised as a woman) (p.13). The statues of smiling women look only at each other: they are apparently knowledgeable and safe in their unity (p.45). And of course, constant reassurance of the identity that has been imposed by others is gained by looking in mirrors. These defence measures always fail, though, and all there is left is the hope for escape — either in an acceptance of new attitudes and relationships, the desire of the mother, which is what Ana chooses (and we remember that the double genitive means that the phrase works, and moves, in both directions), or in the denial of sexuality itself, which is postulated at the end of the W218 story. Ana actually becomes the Other of Lacanian theory several times. She even writes her diary in the first-person plural.

The trouble is, of course, that there is a vast difference between female liberation and sexual liberation. Much contemporary thinking claims that sexual and sexological traditions have ascribed an inflated importance to sexuality, and the sixties sexual liberation movements brought little more than disillusion, 'a god that failed', in Weeks's phrase.[60] And, as Michel Foucault has observed, this is hardly surprising: 'si la répression a bien été, depuis l'âge classique, le mode fondamental de liaison entre pouvoir, savoir et sexualité, on ne peut s'en affranchir qu'à un prix considérable . . .' ('if repression has been the means of linking power, knowledge and sexuality since the Classical period, the cost of any emancipation will be considerable'). It is so alien to us, he goes on, to talk frankly about sex and to see it in an enlightened way, so opposed to intrinsic power mechanisms to do so, that it cannot fail to be an extremely slow process. And 'le pouvoir s'exerce à partir de points innombrables, et dans le jeu de relations inégalitaires et mobiles . . .' ('power is exercised from countless points of origin and with non-egalitarian and shifting relationships in play').[61] We have constantly affirmed that there are no easy answers; one reason for my claim that *Pubis angelical* marks a heightening of quality rather than a decline in Puig's work is that we now discover that there are no easy questions either. Weeks agrees with Foucault's rejection of the simplistic binary opposition between dominant and dominated based on sexuality. This is what he says:

> The erotic acts as a crossover point for a number of tensions whose origins are elsewhere: of class, gender, and radical location, of intergenerational conflict, moral acceptability and medical definition.[62]

There is not much of a happy ending for Ana, then. The solution of the renunciation of a sexual identity, the *pubis angelical,* would be inefficacious even if it were feasible. And, furthermore, though it may be perverse on our part to remember this, all Ana's past happiness has come from make-believe, anticipation and, with her early sexual experience with Fito, the short but happy dream of temporary and partial fulfilment of desire. It is hard to forget, too, when thinking about this woman who has lost all desire (p.56) and who feels nothing (pp.75, 87), that fantasizing had once been a solution to this problem (p.53).

Now, she says, she has no more imagination (p. 31).[63] We are consoled, if consoled we are, by one consideration: this is *not* an ending, but a beginning. We would be foolish to be optimistic, but the struggle has to go on. The *pubis angelical,* after all, would be the equivalent of death.

As in *El beso de la mujer araña,* Puig here enjoys himself from time to time by playing with language. There are puns, sly references to external, often extra-literary elements, and clever internal patterns, in addition to the symbolism, some of which we have already considered. And as in the previous novel, this does not reveal an uncaring, frivolous attitude on the part of the author. It is important, for more than one reason, to be aware of these linguistic games. First, they serve to underline and confirm the conscious artistry of Puig's composition. In achieving a huge popular audience for his books, often — in the first place — because of the misleadingly conventional framework (the detective story, for example), he has been unfortunate enough to attract a number of critics who have failed to appreciate their complexities. The word-play is amusing for the reader who becomes aware of it; it may well have provided enjoyment for the author; but it is also a sign of craftsmanship in the writing. Then, too, it is important because, like the symbols, and like symbolism in general, especially in poetry, it can make allusions that are not limited by explicitness, it can help to create atmosphere. It also makes all kinds of connections accessible, not least of which, in *Pubis angelical,* are those between the three stories.

One source of allusion is the names of the characters: Ana, connected with the mother of the Virgin; her daughter, Clara, bringing to mind St. Clare who refused marriage and gave up the world (taking her widowed mother, incidentally, into her order). Then there is Pozzi, whose name means 'wells', which in Christian symbolism represents salvation, especially in their function as restorative bathing-places for the sick. Has Pozzi helped to 'save' the sick Ana? He certainly provokes her into thoughts of a new life, patriotism, and a realization of the unacceptibility of her relationship with her mother and daughter. In spite of Ana's — and Pozzi's — refusal to see Alejandro's name as appropriate, we might remember that Alexander the Great often conquered by means of generosity. It is interesting, too, that according to Evita, Perón admired Alexander the Great. And Beatriz, of course, means blessed, fortunate and happy. The *pubis angelical* fable is clarified and, indeed, destroyed, by several points at which the angels, and everything angelic, are alluded to in their connection with death. Angels, we saw, are dead innocent children; a pact has been made with the dead — with the angels, in fact — to relieve human suffering, and this, significantly enough, concerns clairvoyants. And Clarita, like Herminia in *La traición de Rita Hayworth,* adored *Giselle,* with its dead virgins. These connections leap out from so many of the pages, and there are plenty of others. Pozzi judges Mexico to be a dream, and in the same breath says he is now interested in women again (p. 169). Ana's Buenos Aires apartment is bugged, like W218's computer. Blindness is ever present too. With the power gone, the blind person becomes defenceless and no longer exigent. He or she may actually understand and love more. One of Puig's many puns is that W218 and LKJS go out on a blind date (a 'cita a ciegas') (p. 152).

Other puns both create atmosphere and link stories. As we saw, the blind date takes the potential lovers to a glamorous night-club, with 'un palmar de cocoteros' as part of the décor, reminding us of the world-famous Coconut Grove in Hollywood. When the desperately ill and unhappy Ana complains about the Mexico City rainy season dragging on ('Qué larga . . . la estación de lluvia . . .') (p. 247), the words themselves survive the scene. Five pages later, when W218 has just been condemned to what is undeniably certain death, she leaves by train, and we find, 'La estación de trenes se veía severamente patrullada, lluvia torrencial caía . . .' ('The railway station was heavily guarded, torrential rain was falling . . .') (p. 252), the pun, of course, depending on the two meanings of the word *estación.* Then, because of the blue-tinted spectacles that have been distributed to everyone, it is a 'tren azul' ('blue train') that takes W218 away from LKJS (p. 256). The connotations of any hope of pleasure and colour in life are removed with the departure of the glamorous-sounding train. And when W218 arrives at her destination, she finds that it is underground, and it is impossible to ignore the connections between this and Pozzi's underground activities: in the hospital, as in these, there are false dawns (p. 263).

There are so many examples that could be given, but perhaps just one more would be enlightening. It is an instance of how an abstract concept materializes from one story to another, making for a pattern. In their talks about Lacan, Pozzi has told Ana of the theory that the unconscious is structured like a language. Ana glosses this in an uncomprehending way, much to Pozzi's irritation, by talking about everything being classified and filed, as in a computer: 'todos tenemos la maquinita de calcular adentro', she says ('we all have a calculator inside us') (p. 171). When we pass into the area outside Ana's immediate conscious control, we find two manifestations of her attempt to understand this principle: first, W218's 'víscera electrónica' ('electronic viscera') (p.161), which echoes the *Ama*'s dream that an operation has revealed a clockwork mechanism in her rather than a heart (p.9); then there is the library image, where information is sought, where meetings take place, and where — theoretically — everything can be explained by consulting the hitherto-concealed records.

Perhaps in the end nothing can be explained. But Ana is going to try, for surprisingly, she is going to live after all: what was eating away at her has gone. Beatriz, at least, thinks that 'a veces las cosas salen bien, aunque cuesta creerlo' ('sometimes things do turn out well, even if it's difficult to credit it') (p.269).

CHAPTER VII

'Les Liaisons dangereuses':
Maldición eterna a quien lea estas páginas (1980)

> No se debe contar jamás todo lo que se sabe porque se pierde poder
> One must never tell all one knows or power will be lost
> *Apud* Rosa Montero, *La función delta*

THE strength or otherwise of all Puig's books will depend to a large extent, it seems to me, on whether their innovatory features are merely formal or whether there is something new and provocative in the fields of theme, character and ideology as well. The interest of *Pubis angelical,* for instance, is very largely — though not entirely — centred on the last-minute change of viewpoint on the part of the principal character: its layout is by no means everything. *Maldición eterna a quien lea estas páginas,* the author's sixth novel,[1] is certainly totally different as far as its construction is concerned, but it also contains notable variations from the previous works, and that bodes well. This is not to say that old preoccupations are not rehearsed here, but one change that is immediately striking is that the two protagonists are men and that neither of them could be judged a female character 'in disguise'. The old preoccupations rise to the surface by means of what these two characters say and, perhaps more important, in what they choose to leave unsaid. Other vital variations are found in their attitudes towards themselves, each other, and life in general.

Puig's confessed interest in formal variety constitutes an area of risk as far as critical reception is concerned. If the results are seen as successful by his readers, all is well: *Boquitas pintadas,* with its indebtedness to the *folletín,* is a case in point. New formats are by definition original, and may well turn out to be seminal. Sometimes, though, they can produce confusion, even hostility and incomprehension, and as we have seen in the previous chapter the three interdependent stories of *Pubis angelical* had this effect on some people, with certain critics dismissing it out of hand. Differences of opinion are almost entirely based in varying reactions to *form,* and are concerned with the elusive element sometimes referred to as pace. When this is imperfectly achieved the reader may lose interest and find it difficult to keep his attention on the text. It is particularly ironic if this happens in the case of Manuel Puig since he has always striven for what he calls 'accessibility' in his writings, and judges boredom the only really illegitimate factor in art.[2] Obviously, then, he is on the horns of a dilemma: he can stick to a tested formula, which will undoubtedly meet with a certain amount of critical fatigue and which will not satisfy him, or he can try something else. The problem is that his innovations may alienate his audience: it is almost certainly true to say that he has by now left his mass audience behind anyway. As he matures and becomes increasingly conscious of the actual process of novel writing, the question of his relationship with the reader assumes more and more importance: he demands maturity as well as offering it. He is not unaware of this. 'Suelo escamotear partes de mis relatos', he has said, 'Es una forma de . . . no subestimar la inteligencia del lector. Es una forma de buscar la participación más profunda del lector' ('There are always gaps in my stories. In that way I avoid underestimating the reader's intelligence. It's a way of demanding greater participation on the part of the reader').[3] He has always done this, but it is now increasingly evident and it makes him more vulnerable: there are fewer concessions made to the reader in the later works.

The danger is that readers may not want to, or indeed be able to, participate in the creation of an integral work of art to the extent that the author would like and, 'serious' critics or not, they will then justify their reaction by laying the blame on the text. *Maldición eterna a quien lea estas páginas* is an example of this. It takes an enormous risk because of its form, and has therefore provoked even more unfavourable comment than its immediate predecessor. Its layout — a dialogue between the two male characters with no relief at all until the very end, when seven more or less explanatory letters are reproduced — and its consequent lack of pace have proved too taxing for many of its critics, and they have found little else to compensate for this in other features of the novel.

This is hardly surprising, perhaps, since several old concerns are re-examined here. What is surprising, as Nora Catelli has noted, is the virulence of some of the later Puig criticism. As she points out, this seems to be based on personal animosity rather than on a desire to illuminate or add something to our reading of the works.[4] Could this indeed be the case? Is there always, as we suggested in a previous chapter, an unfriendly backlash in the face of success? If this is so, then of course it is an intolerable as well as a disagreeable situation, and one which devalues the art of criticism. On the other hand, it has to be admitted that some people have felt, apparently in all sincerity, that *Maldición eterna a quien lea estas páginas* is far from being the best of the author's creations, and it would be as absurd to explain away their aversion in terms of laziness or the inability to contribute enough to the receptive experience as it so obviously is to attack a work of art on personal grounds. Taste is subjective. There is, after all, no denying the lack of humour in this book or the denial of comfort and consolation; the absence of any sure footing in this bitter encounter between two alienated and, in a way, exiled men, when added to the monotony of the form, does little to encourage the reader. In previous Puig novels we have been aware of the therapeutic effect of facile optimism and various kinds of escapism where at least some of the characters were concerned, and we have attributed the values of 'subliterature' to them, even if not to their creator. We have, perhaps, vicariously enjoyed these values, as I suggested in Chapter I, while at the same time reserving for ourselves a position of clear-sightedness. In Puig's sixth novel though, the characters overtly reflect what I have always seen as the author's basic pessimism, and their escape routes are always blocked, never providing even temporary respite from unhappiness. Not only is there no facile solution to life's problems, but the characters themselves are aware of this. They have both 'lost' their past and, like mentally-disturbed children, have no hope for the future (at least for most of the duration of the text). Furthermore, as always, they are ever conscious of the existence of death.

So it is that the book's innovatory characteristics have found little favour in some quarters. The dialogue form has been judged 'played-out' and 'hackneyed' as far as Puig is concerned. And in the same review he is dismissed as a *guionista* (scriptwriter).[5] García Ramos claims that in the last two novels (he is referring to *Pubis angelical* and *Maldición eterna a quien lea estas páginas*) there is a lack of verbal craftsmanship,[6] and Eduardo Mejía says, with some justification, that at times it is difficult to know which of the two men is speaking.[7] The fact that there *are* only two characters has been seen as limiting, and the unrelieved gloom of their environment and their world-view, their pessimism and their isolation, has been branded unoriginal as well as unattractive.[8] 'Las casi trescientas páginas desorientan, fatigan, angustian, golpean como un sordo taladro en un mismo lugar, son una cruel búsqueda en el túnel oscuro sin salida' ('For almost three hundred pages we are disorientated, wearied, distressed and hammered as if by a noiseless drill on the same spot; the pages constitute a cruel search in a dark, interminable tunnel'), says another critic,[9] and the prospective reader might be forgiven for giving up there and then. Yet this last judgment is actually part of a favourable account of the novel. In other words, while the effectiveness of the form is something that can only be judged subjectively and one reader's opinion is as valuable as the next, the atmosphere and subject matter of a work have absolutely nothing to do with its quality. We *are* hammered and distressed by *Maldición eterna a quien lea estas páginas,* but this does not make it a bad novel.

Indeed, to redress the balance it must be pointed out that it has also received much praise. It has been described as 'fascinating', 'masterful', and as the crowning work in a series that places Puig in the front line of modern Latin-American novelists.[10] It is also worth repeating that many of the hostile accusations and assessments are not really defensible. Just one example: the label 'badly-written', which some have attached to the novel, and criticisms of the actual Spanish (especially the anglicized syntax), have little value with regard to literary quality. The dialogue formula, reproducing what people actually say, renders the first accusation meaningless, and the fact the the conversations must have been in English makes the second irrelevant.[11] It would surely be more acceptable to acknowledge subjectivity in critical judgments than to justify a negative reaction by referring to, for example, incorrectly conjugated verbs.[12]

The novel's protagonists are Juan José Ramírez, a name that cannot fail to remind us of Pozzi in *Pubis angelical,* and Lawrence John (Larry), whose Italian grandfather's name had originally been Giovanangelo: he had been obliged to change it by 'the authorities' (p.31). Ramírez is seventy-four years of age and he is in exile in New York City; he is very ill, and is being supported in an old people's home by the American Human Rights Reception Committee, which also funded his journey from Buenos Aires after his release from gaol there. He was once, it seems, an important left-wing activist in his native country: like Pozzi, he was a lawyer; like Valentín in *El beso de la mujer araña,* he organized syndicalist rebellion and was imprisoned and tortured because of these activities. The phrase 'it seems' is not an idle one, at least at the beginning of the novel, for this is only what we suppose to have been the case. Ramírez himself flatly denies this version of his past and claims that he was imprisoned on a false conviction for larceny and that his brother is paying for his convalescence in the United States. There is no firm ground in this text, and this is the first example of this. The characters contradict themselves and each other all the time, playing a cat and mouse game. They conceal as much as they reveal. Furthermore, we discover that Ramírez has, or claims to have, lost his memory, and at times he appears to be delirious.

The action — if we may use that word — of the novel takes place in the winter of 1978 – 79. We meet Ramírez when he has been in New York City for just a week; this is the moment of his first encounter with Larry, who is an out-of-work history teacher, thirty-six years of age, divorced, and eking out an existence with odd jobs. This one involves taking the old man out for walks in his wheelchair. From their very first exchange we are aware of the distance, the apparently unavoidable lack of communication, between them, a certain reciprocal hostility and impatience and, above all, the generation gap. They indulge in verbal struggles over a period of weeks, with a final skirmish that results in a definitive break. From the letters at the end of the book we discover that Ramírez was then moved to the better climate of California for the sake of his health, but that he was immediately transferred to a psychiatric hospital where he died. As is so often the case in Puig novels, the text ends with a note that may (or may not) be thought hopeful: Larry is preparing to begin again, to restart his professional life, and he writes to an employment agency as the first step towards working in a university again. This time, though, he wants to be a researcher, not a teacher. Earlier he had said that he was not interested in resuming his career. 'No me siento en condiciones' ('I don't feel I'm in a position to') had been his explanation (p.66). We shall return to this point.

The fact that the two men are of different nationalities is not without importance in the interpretation of their relationship. It represents mutual incomprehension, intensifies their need for information, and constitutes a plausible motive for self-exploration and analysis. There is undoubtedly a meeting of 'culturas inconciliáveis' ('irreconcilable cultures'), as they have been called, here,[13] and the continuing dialogue would be far less acceptable if the two characters shared the same geographical and social background. The real-life model for Larry was in fact a young man that the author met in New York during his second period of exile there, beginning in 1976. Like Larry, the prototype was a Marxist; like Larry, he was troubled, insecure, even — says Puig — a potential suicide.[14] In spite of their long conversations, no real friendship ever developed between the author and his New York acquaintance, and Puig has said that the original ending intended for the novel was one that was unrelievedly sad, 'um final preto, sem saída nenhuma' ('a black outcome, with no hope whatsoever'). When the model for Larry later telephoned and told him that he was going to rejoin society, to re-enter his profession, the last two pages were added. But how much real optimism there is in this looking towards the future, how much the tone of the book is modified by these last pages, is another matter. And, as Puig says, even the phone call did not bring about any feelings of friendship in either of them: it was too late and they were totally incompatible.[15]

Ironically, though, in the fictional version the men are indispensable to each other for a short time. There is no love lost between them but each is necessary, it seems, for any hope of fulfilment in his interlocutor. Not for nothing did Ángel Rama call his perceptive analysis of the novel 'El diálogo imposible' ('The impossible dialogue'), and not without justification does he sum up the relationship as *vampirización* (vampirization): 'el diálogo es imposible', he admits, 'y simultáneamente ineludible' ('dialogue is impossible but at the same time unavoidable').[16] The most convincing reason for this paradox is that the two are acting out a power struggle, not between a North American and a Latin American (although the history and culture of the two regions are so different, this is something of a red herring), but between a father and son. Like Gladys and Leo in *The Buenos Aires Affair,* like Molina and Valentín in *El beso de la mujer araña,* even — to a certain extent — like Ana and Pozzi in *Pubis angelical,* there is a bond between two people which does not actually work in practice, but which is apparently essential to the continuation of life.[17] As Larry comments acidly at one point, 'seguiremos viviendo, sin necesidad de ser felices' ('we'll survive without having to be happy') (p. 154), and there is more in that statement than meets the eye. It is obvious enough that happiness is a rare commodity, but 'seguiremos viviendo' is true only if the plural form of the verb is emphasized. The father-son relationship is frequently one of struggle and pain, though, with the father torn between affection and apprehension, and the son, though admiring the father, the prey of jealousy, resentment and fear. It was ever thus, psychologists tell us.

Ramírez is a father-figure, but he is also an author, a priest and a god, a fount of knowledge, and we remember that Ana, in *Pubis angelical,* was always seeking the incarnation of omniscience (or a substitute machine or institution) too. Larry found this in Marxism at one point in his life but, as we shall see, that no longer seems to be the whole answer. Rightly or wrongly, Larry judges Ramírez 'una persona superior' ('a superior person') (p. 26) at the beginning, and is conscious of his past sacrifices and selfless suffering. He even weeps when Ramírez promises to keep some food for him (p. 26). He asks for the older man's help and, more important, enlightenment (p. 26), for 'los padres saben las respuestas' ('fathers know all the answers') (p. 40), and he has not been in touch with his own father for five years. Even as a child he had seen little of him (p. 41). At first he sees himself as ideologically in tune with Ramírez and he suggests that they look at books on Marxism together (p. 48); his favourite reading is Marx and Lenin (p. 49) and, like the older man, he has been a political activist in his time, advising union members and leading strikes (p. 200). Later we discover that he also identifies with Ramírez' neglect of his wife and son in favour of the cause he supported (p. 258) since his own marriage foundered for this reason, among others (p. 241). In theory the relationship between them looks promising.

But there is a barrier. The very first page of the novel is made up of two people talking at cross purposes, and their lack of affinity is summed up when Larry, already impatient, comments that not everyone judges the same things important. When Ramírez refuses to drop the subject of what is or is not important, Larry points out that he is paid to push his invalid chair, not to expound on philosophy (p. 9). There is an edginess, a sense of mutual distrust, and the generation gap is always in evidence. Ramírez suffers from periodic bouts of pain, something that he claims (implausibly) Larry is too young to know about (p. 33); Larry is concerned about losing his hair and his good looks, and the older man presumably will find it hard to sympathize with this (p. 34); Ramírez is totally immobile while Larry is an active, athletic character, happy to spend all day running if he could (p. 36); Ramírez wants a *vita minima* (p. 192) while Larry is rebellious and breaks rules on principle (p. 55). There are very many moments when our attention is drawn to the difference in their ages, either implicitly or explicitly, as when Ramírez points out that he is twice Larry's age. 'Así que fácilmente podría ser mi hijo', he adds ('So you could easily be my son') (p.40). We would do well to see this statement in conjunction with something that Larry says a good deal later on: 'En una familia nadie está satisfecho con nadie' ('In families no one is ever satisfied with anyone else') (p.123).

We have therefore two cultures and two different generations, and my contention is that the first symbolizes the second: the two men do not speak the same language and their lives have been formed by experiences, values and social mores that are foreign to each other. Even words like 'Marxism', which ought to be directly translatable, produce very different reactions. This reflects the basic incompatibility of the relationship, and their warfare is full of stratagems. First we have Ramírez' amnesia, real or feigned; and second, and certainly connected with this, we have the almost intuitive way in which both of them cover up facts and attitudes, even going as far as actually lying. These skirmishes may form part of all interpersonal relationships to a certain extent, but they are particularly common where fathers and sons are concerned. Each of the protagonists needs something that only the other man can provide (in Ramírez' case, he wants to regain the ability to feel, to be alive), but each is thwarted by the resistance he is faced with. Larry admires the older man's record, but Ramírez either denies that he is the man Larry thinks he is or claims to have forgotten his past. Larry wants answers, but Ramírez is reduced to reading the encyclopedia in order to find out the simplest things; he has taken notes, we learn, all his life, but now he has lost them and he knows nothing without them (p.19). Larry is a political animal, but Ramírez says that he never had anything to do with politics, a field he despises (p.56). He cannot even remember if he ever had a family (p.40). He refuses to talk about Marxism (p.224). Though he speaks English, French, Italian and Spanish (p.10), he is constantly asking what words actually mean, indeed, he asks many more questions than he answers. He is, in short, an enigma, and an unapproachable enigma at that. Though he seeks illumination (he often starts his sentences with 'I need to know . . .') he is ever fearful of treachery. He is watchful and secretive and unfathomable. But then, so is Larry. There is little to choose between Ramírez' saying he has a secret (p.33) and then denying this (p.35) and Larry's talking about his adventures as a marine in the Vietnam War in one breath (p.71) and claiming he was a conscientious objector in the next: 'Nunca salí del país' ('I've never been out of the country'), he now says (p.73). He is even evasive on the subject of whether he has a pet cat or not, and although he seeks information, he resents Ramírez' questioning him in his turn. Each is aware that the other is hiding a great deal and each suspects that this hidden something is important. But there is no common ground, and for each of them the only means of escape from the other's power seems to be to locate its source.[18] There is no hope of fusion, nor even of any rapport. It is a war to the death and, unsurprisingly, it leads to the old man's death, for as Bruno Bettelheim points out, the child always wins in the long run.[19]

Ángel Rama has linked this novel to a letter that Kafka once wrote to his father, but which was actually received and read by his mother. He points out that when she kept it in her possession this was no more than just, since *she* was really the person for whom it was intended. When Kafka refers to the omnipresence of his father in his life, his fear of him, and the fact that they had always been at odds, this constitutes a father-son dialogue via the mother. *Maldición eterna a quien lea estas páginas* is the desire for, rather than the experience of, this dialogue.[20] While in no way dissenting from this interpretation, I would add that in this novel something *is* achieved, and furthermore it is achieved by both characters. This may sound like a contradiction of my previous assertion that there is no hope for the future and that the novel is pessimistic, but this is not actually so. The words 'future' and 'hope' in that statement connote *personal* success and happiness, but what is achieved, I suggest, is the continuation of the life cycle. In a kind of ritual progress the individual forms part of cosmic continuity, but there is no happy ending. This is the significance of Larry's planning to start all over again at the end. It would be naïve to find this reassuring.[21]

I have used the word 'ritual' deliberately, for the protracted conversation could be seen as a kind of initiation rite. What both men gain by means of it is the possibility of survival that maturity brings. Let us consider each of them in turn. It would be as well to begin with Ramírez since the idea of initiation may seem inappropriate for him, given his age, the state of his health and, indeed, the fact that he dies soon after his rupture with Larry.

He is a man whose existence has reached a point of inertia. His past no longer exists and he has to learn vital functions all over again if he is to rejoin life. His condition could be compared to the pre-initiation catatonia of fairy-tale characters such as the Sleeping Beauty and Snow White, and he shares with these a (false) state of innocence. The impression of temporary death is underlined when we learn that he was born under Capricorn, an earth sign; he is physical and receptive

therefore, but associated with the winter solstice when there are as yet
no signs of the possibility of renewal. He has died, like pubertal children
in tribal initiation ceremonies, and he must be rescued if he is to go on.
As Vladimir Propp reminds us in his well-known writings on folk-tales
and fairy stories, in these there is invariably a disaster, the hero is forced
to leave home and he goes into a kind of exile. He is then magically
aided by someone or something so that he can escape from the
Kingdom of the Dead. One cannot, says Propp, exclude the subject of
death from consideration of these *rites de passage*. When the initiation
period is over, the dead person is resurrected, but only after suffering all
kinds of physical pain, even torture, and not before essential secrets
have been imparted to him. Then he has no option but to go forward,
for the abyss now separates him from his paternal home.[22]

The 'magic helper' for Ramírez is Larry, and the first thing that the
young man does is to restore mobility to him. This is limited, and does
not bring him independence; nevertheless it stands for progress, since
movement and death are incompatible. Something or somebody
outside himself wants him to live and instigates a process of
revitalization; in the rituals practised in primitive societies it is the tribe
or clan that is responsible for the protection and education of the
initiate, but in the old man's case it is the Committee for Human Rights
which pays for him to try, at least, to rejoin society. Larry's company is
another vital aid: without him he would be in complete isolation, for his
companions in the home are so stupid and ill-informed as to be beneath
his contempt (p.61).

That they *know* nothing makes them useless from a therapeutic point
of view, and his only other contact is a young nurse. Although she is
kind to him and her part in the story is ultimately important, like that of
all the nurses in Puig novels, for the moment she is not in a position to
supply what Ramírez needs. She is too busy to spend much time talking
to him for one thing, but also it is essential that the therapist be a young,
or at least a younger, man. The two protagonists are therefore thrown
together in the first place for practical reasons, convenient for them
both,[23] but it is psychological factors that keep them together. Rama
sees Ramírez' position as one in which the 'father', weak and
diminished, 'occupies the son's lap'.[24] Discourse is the only thing that
can help him, and the conversations of the two men resemble
psychoanalytic sessions not only in their content but also in the
circumstance that at first the 'analyst' is behind the motionless 'patient'
as he pushes his chair through the streets of New York. This reminds us

that Erich Fromm, when discussing psychoanalytic techniques, once pointed out that the analyst's position, sitting behind the analysand, 'actually results . . . in the analysand's feeling like a little child'. The difference, of course, is that usually in psychoanalytic sessions the analyst does not speak, so that the patient is not conscious of conflict. As Fromm says in his condemnation of this, it is this very conflict that would be conducive to improvement or change.[25] Where Larry and Ramírez are concerned there is plenty of conflict and, therefore, some hope of advancement.

Like all little children, Ramírez asks what seem to be silly questions, and the parallel maintains its validity when we realize that these often reflect areas of great profundity. One area of fundamental ignorance, based on Ramírez' amnesia (and partly explicable on a narrative level by his having to speak in a foreign tongue) is the meaning of words. By means of discourse both characters are trying to re-create themselves, and words are the key to understanding — of the world and of themselves. This is particularly true where Ramírez is concerned, since an (apparently absurd) aid has been lost: his notes. 'No sé nada,' he says, 'Todo lo que tengo . . . es una esperanza mínima, de encontrar mis anotaciones' ('I don't know anything. All I have is . . . the very slight hope of finding my notes') (p.94). And the codified signifier points to an elusive signified: emotion.[26] This is what he is trying to rediscover. The further and most terrible difficulty is that emotion itself is but a signifier, for behind it, somewhere, lies the most elusive concept of all — the truth. There is a whole world of potential treachery between the two extremes. This can be something as simple as the gulf between a *politesse,* such as an apology (when Larry says he is sorry if he is pushing the wheelchair too fast, for example, (p. 12)) and what lies behind it, or as complex as the distance between non-formulaic discourse and what really lies behind that. Overt contradictions of what has previously been claimed to be factual, such as Larry's ambivalence over his Vietnam experiences, are clearcut examples. But there is so much more: the question is one of great subtlety.

One important aspect of all this is that for Ramírez the written word has little value without a voice and a face, and this confirms our view of the vital nature of his search. Fresh air is better for his health than books are, he says (p.39), and in his circumstances going out into the fresh air is the equivalent of being with another human being. He realizes that there is a choice, of sorts. When he is particularly irritated by Larry's guarded, perhaps mendacious, answers, he points out that he could learn everything that Larry tells him from an encyclopedia (p.55). Truth and facts are not the same thing though, and he has to carry on with the dialogue. For the time being he has faith in the power of words to restore the memory of what is essential to his fallow mind: he wants to hear about sex, not see it on the screen in a pornographic cinema (p.74); he is interested in the 'voice' of the narrative of a novel (p.49), something that presumably will humanize it; when he talks to Larry about his conversations with his father, he wants to hear the actual words (p.42); and much later on, he admits that he understands more if the speaker is looking at him (p.213) and this is clearly a principle that he has tried to transfer to written texts in the past. As his relationship with Larry continues — one could hardly say 'progresses' — he becomes disillusioned with the ability of words to reveal the knowledge that he is seeking. Yet what is the alternative? Silence, he says, makes him ill (p.80) and action is impossible. Like life itself, words are deficient, and when a voice *is* distinguishable its effect is unknowable and its motives untrustworthy. As Larry says, one hears two voices in one's head, and one of them (like the Actress's angels in *Pubis angelical*) is often malign (p.50); this holds for external voices too. Nevertheless, in a novel entirely made up of spoken dialogue, representing a period in two lives that is almost entirely made up of dialogue, words are all there is.

In the end words betray Ramírez. He does discover what he wanted to and he does learn to feel again, but with the irony often found in life and not infrequently in the writings of Manuel Puig, what he discovers are unbearable facts from his past (that his wife, son, and daughter-in-law were all murdered because of their connection with him, (p.259)), and what he feels is vengeance, resentment and hatred, together with a touch of *Schadenfreude* — spiteful satisfaction in the face of Larry's misfortunes. Emotion, James Hillman tells us, after sifting through the writings of countless psychologists, psychiatrists and philosophers, is 'a way of perceiving, a way of knowing, a way of adapting and a way of being in the world. It intends a specific object, goal, or end result. In short, there is reason in emotion'.[27] What Ramírez had forgotten was the capacity to perceive, the ability to know, and he seeks a means of entering the world again. But the emotions he relearns can only provoke despair. Then death is inevitable. As in Gestalt psychology, the incomplete searches for completion, but here 'completion' is intolerable, and total alienation is the last stage.

This does not invalidate my contention that Ramírez achieves something, or that the process by which he does so can be compared to a process of initiation. He is exiled and independent (for the first time); he is in the hands of others and he has a 'helper'. He suffers physically, he has a kind of vital secret imparted to him and, very briefly, he comes out on the other side. But because of the number of years he had spent on this earth before the enactment of this rite and because the knowledge he acquires is totally destructive, any new life is impossible. Furthermore, and I shall return to this point, he has fulfilled his function. He turns his back on life as an individual. It is he who loses his head — in insanity — as the primordial son fears *he* must do at the hands of his father.

Larry represents the young initiate, although — as he is at pains to point out — he is not all that young, at thirty-six, and is preoccupied with evidence of ageing, combating this by means of physical activity and a healthy diet. His sense of imminent old age is increased by the fact that he too has arrived at what is (paradoxically, considering his athleticism) a moment of inertia. He is away from his family and alienated from his original social background, living in a district of New York largely populated by people on their own: Greenwich Village. He has turned his back on his profession. He is divorced, he is unemployed and he is aimless. In this state of idleness, every little task is too much trouble (p.36). He cannot go on like this. He, too, has to acquire the right sort of knowledge in order to break out of his 'exile', but it is a special kind of knowledge that he needs. At first glance, there would seem to be little that he does not already know. *He* has not forgotten his past: in fact, he remembers everything. At least, this is what Ramírez claims (p.53), and later Larry does admit that he has an excellent memory (p.221). He is well educated and widely read. A historian, trained at New York University, where he was judged an excellent student (pp.15, 221), he has studied St. Augustine and other theologians (p.144), he has read philosophy, including the existentialists (he mentions Sartre (p.145)), and he is knowledgeable on the subject of psychoanalysis (p.54) as well as Marxism, on which he used to lecture, dealing too with Hegel and the German idealists (p.238). Then, on a social and human level, he is also experienced. His work with trade unions has provided him with insights into the class struggle in a practical way, and he has been married to a woman he loved. Yet he is now alone and at a standstill and can progress only if he is able to appropriate the secret of continuity. This he must glean from somebody else.

This other person must be his father, though not his real father, for the moment when that might have been possible is long past, but a surrogate: Ramírez. Needless to say, Ramírez, like all fathers, is going to safeguard his position, his dominant role, by jealously protecting his secret. It is a rehearsal of the primordial clash which signifies a son's attempt at creating an independent identity by sucking the blood of his father, emasculating him, too, in true classical fashion.[28] This makes for an equivocal situation. The son actually wants to be free of the father, but at the same time he subconsciously fears retaliation. According to Bettelheim, this fear is manifest in all those fairy tales in which a pubertal child is evicted from home because he has posed a threat to the father's power or even to his self-respect.[29] We remember that there is some talk, at least, of Larry's actually having been thrown out by his parents (p.99). That Larry fears and mistrusts the father-figure is incontrovertible. When pressed, he recalls that his real father was often irritable, even violent (p.43), and he apparently transfers his implied fear to the paternal image in general. When he had felt hatred for his father, he had wanted to destroy him (p.44), and his attitude to Ramírez often reflects this. Even in a contrapuntal story of how he rescues a strange woman, the villain who is threatening her is described as a *viejo* (old man, p.110). In a transposition of the time scale, for the real-life situation occurred many years earlier, Larry asks Ramírez' advice about how he should conduct himself with his family, and Ramírez tells him to trust his father, to confide in him. But if he does, Larry objects, his father could annihilate him and tear off his limbs (pp.206–08). Larry feels that Ramírez is the possessor of 'the secret' (p.18), and admits that what he hates most in his life is betrayal (p.245). He thinks again about being mutilated, about having his head pulled off (a standard torture in magic initiation rites) (p.267), and it all starts to make sense. Fear, suspicion and a sense of rivalry go hand in hand with admiration; a wish for independence, individuality and freedom combine to suggest that this is a classic filial situation. Freud considered this in *Totem and Taboo* (1913): the primitive, violent and jealous father keeps all the females for himself, driving out the sons as they grow up. They retaliate by killing and devouring this man that they both fear and envy, so that each of them achieves identification with him and acquires a portion of his strength. This is seen as a parallel to the contradictory feelings and ambivalent father-complex of all children. Freud adds — and this is a point we shall return to — that the root of every religion is based on longing for the father.

However, although it is beginning to make sense, it is not all that straightforward. Much of what Larry says fits in with Freudian theory, but close scrutiny of the text reveals that just as the two protagonists fence with each other, covering up, inventing, refusing to clarify anything, so Puig teases his readers. For at least some of the time we can be reasonably sure that the reported conversations actually did take place. The problem arises when we bear in mind that Ramírez is both psychologically and physically ill. Some of the dialogue may belong to his delirious wanderings. There are several hints that this is indeed the case, such as when we are told that Larry appears at dead of night, having come through the window: he comes, what is more, through *closed* windows and doors, says the older man (p.105). On another occasion, Ramírez cannot tell whether Larry is there or not (p.67), and then there is a night when Larry is found sleeping on the sickroom carpet on the fifteenth floor of a hospital which forbids night entry. When Ramírez asks how he got in, he answers simply, 'No sé' ('I don't know') (p.165). How significant for Ramírez the conversations between the two of them are is indicated by the fact that whenever the reader has any doubts about whether Larry is physically present, it is the younger man that takes the initiative, claiming that it is he who needs to talk. In other words, it is not unlikely that several of the scenes are no more than part of Ramírez' delirium in extreme weakness, and in these he assigns to Larry what he thinks he ought to want, feel and think.

The reader, therefore, cannot be expected to distinguish between what Larry says and what Ramírez has him say in his imaginary scenarios. The father appears to know, perhaps does know, more about the son than the son himself does. It has often been observed by psychologists that parents know everything about their offspring apart from what these are ultimately capable of, and this is applicable here, even if Larry is not actually Ramírez' child. It is the older man, for example, who elaborates on Larry's (possibly invented) adventures in Vietnam, insinuating that he had been disillusioned and shocked by the existence of sexual desire in a previously admired, middle-aged superior officer, that he had seen him as a rival in a Saigon brothel, and that he had actually recognized the officer, so to speak, as his father. This man saved his life, and Larry may have killed him. This reciprocity where the two men's experiences are concerned is a phenomenon that we have come across in Puig on more than one occasion — for example, when Valentín and Molina recount each other's stories in *El beso de la mujer araña*. Here Larry asks, '¿Me balearon o no?' ('Did they shoot me or not?') after the recounting of the Saigon incident (p.83).[30] Conversely, the older man wants the younger to tell him his own life story, for he cannot get better unless someone reveals what happened to him in Argentina (p.86), and the authorities refuse to do so (p.70). It takes two people to establish one identity, and when these two people are father and son, it is inevitable that the identity that is forged will be that of the son. The father not only can, but must, now withdraw from the scene, and since what Ramírez has created is a source of bitter disappointment and disillusion to him, he descends into insanity before he does so. Larry only just manages to come out on the other side; there is no triumph for him, and he does not share the consolatory escape routes of other Puig characters. Certainly he entertains ambitions now, but they are moderate and realistic. The aim is survival in the world, and the poignancy of the last pages of the book lies in the reader's reservations as to whether even this is feasible. During the painful initiation process, our belief in the Lacanian principle that discourse makes the whole man has often faltered. The frequent contradictions arose because as the person the words were creating gradually emerged, the characters had to reject what they were discovering about themselves and start again. Ultimately Ramírez has to concede.

What I have called Puig's old preoccupations are the question of identity, human relationships, the parent-child situation, frustration and unhappiness and, when all is said and done, fear: the continuous threat of the void, into which each individual has to step. Although all of these have appeared in various forms in the previous novels, some of them are approached differently in *Maldición eterna a quien lea estas páginas,* and certain aspects of them are aired for the first time. One of these is fatalism with regard to the question of personality and, indeed, identity. This is manifested in references to astrology, which appear explicitly in the first part of the novel and implicitly as it progresses. It is, of course, a singularly apt area of study in connection with the present work since, as Richard Cavendish observes, it is 'concerned with the future, but its predictions are always based on analysis of the past'.[31] This is complicated in one sense by the fact that to all intents and purposes one of the principal characters is devoid of a personal, experienced, remembered past; actually, though, this makes the astrological details more interesting, and decidedly more significant, for the absence of verifiable facts leaves the field clearer. Birth signs and their resulting influence are seen against an almost blank backcloth.

We have already noted that Ramírez' amnesia does not extend to his forgetting that his zodiac sign is Capricorn. The nurse who is kind to him is Virgo, we are told, and Larry was born on 27 February (p.276), which makes him a Pisces subject. One other important date is that of Ramírez' death: 2 February. Before looking at these in more detail it is, perhaps, necessary to anticipate possible accusations of making capricious connections. Any defence will, and must, be based on the author's intentions. First of all we have established in other chapters that Puig is a very knowing writer and that his references and allusions — to books, operas, films, etc. — are never arbitrary or gratuitous. This leads us to suppose that we are not, in fact, seeing imaginary pointers. Then there are enough explicit mentions of astrology to suggest that it would be worth our while to follow them up. Once this has been done, we find that several surprising, even bizarre, images take on meaning and some puzzling pieces of apparently arbitrary information slot into place.

Very early on we are told that people who try to explain life by means of horoscopes get on Larry's nerves (p.16). In spite of this, Ramírez tells him about his connection with the Virgo nurse: they were both born under earth signs (pp.16–17). Larry thinks that those who have faith in astrology are ignorant and, more often than not, he claims, they are women: it is just a question of chance what happens to you and how you are, as far as he is concerned (p.17). That might have been the end of it, but Larry brings up the topic of conversation again on more than one occasion, claiming that Ramírez understands horoscopes, for example (p.50), and suggesting that they look at books on the subject in the public library (p.47). The older man assumes that Larry's insistence on what, after all, was just a casual remark reveals a desire to see him as ignorant, and to feel intellectually superior to him (p.51). Now this may be true, but at the same time it does mean that the subject has been introduced, it is in the reader's mind, and this acts as a basis for what follows.

The fatalism connected with man's astrological orientation should not be over-emphasized. Astrologers see their interpretations as an aid to self-knowledge, to be used for the good of the individual. On the other hand, there is a parallel between this kind of determinism and Freud's references to constitutional as well as accidental factors in human beings. Aspects of the future may be avoidable, but the constitutional make-up that points in one direction or another is based on the past, and is not.

Ramírez has gone north, although he cannot stand the cold, he says (p.250). For a Capricornian this is a journey towards essence, and since Capricorn, which represents winter, is a so-called 'cardinal' sign, the subject is travelling towards the polar star. In a story of danger and flight set in pre-Revolutionary Russia which probably forms part of Ramírez' delirium (and which we shall return to), this is made explicit. As the old man rescues the young, sacrificing himself by pulling the sleigh in which two people are travelling single-handed (the faithful, protective, parental dogs have been killed), they go ever northward and the star is ahead of them (pp.232–33). The journey, for Ramírez, is towards death, and a last-ditch attempt to provide him with the warmth of life by taking him to Palm Springs fails. The choice of this particular resort is not fortuitous, given its name. Capricorn is a constellation in the form of a goat, and it is said to have fed a god;[32] in this sense it is a creator, almost a progenitor, and the god — which in the myth was Jupiter — is a kind of *regius filius*. In this second myth, as Jung explains, the son is 'a rejuvenated form of the Father-king', and in some of its versions he is eaten by the father.[33] Ramírez attributes this fear to Larry in one of the imagined dialogues (pp.267–68). But he saves him because, in a way, he has no option: Larry is part of him. Capricorn is a goat with a fish tail, and Larry's sign is Pisces. The son survives and the father dies — on 2 February, traditionally the date on which Jesus became independent of his earthly parents by being presented at the Temple. It is a moment of renewal, for the zodiacal year is about to begin. The Capricornian's dual tendencies, towards the abyss and the mountains, have resolved themselves, and Ramírez goes to the abyss, to the Kingdom of the Dead. His emergence from this had been short-lived.

Larry fits in with the usual view of a Pisces subject: changeable, dependent on others, nervous (he admits to 'terrible tension' and his hands are constantly shaking (p.35)), and incapable of making decisions. At the same time he is evasive, as Pisceans are said to be.[34] In his case, his birth sign makes one feature of his revelations to the older man comprehensible: when talking about his dreams, he says that he has had many in which fish play an important role. There are two in particular, one about an 'atún jorobado' (a hump-backed tuna fish) (p.59) and one which featured a Nova Scotia mackerel (p.60). He is undoubtedly teasing Ramírez when he refers to these ludicrous images, but the very fact that he chooses to recall or invent them is not fortuitous. The Pisces character also tends towards spirituality, and while this in itself may not seem relevant, it could be judged appropriate if we return to the myth of the *regius filius*. The father in this represents the body, the son the spirit. Ramírez' death may bring with it a hint of progress since the descent of spirit into matter, the devouring of the son by the father, does *not* take place. The spirit survives and there is some promise of life: in the astrological Great Year, the Piscean Age, which began with the birth of Christ, signifies the triumph of the spirit; in Christianity, the fish is the symbol of spiritual redemption. It is important that the narrative indication of this in the novel, Larry's application for a post as a researcher, makes it clear that he is no longer interested in teaching. His transformation means that he is now knowledgeable enough to reject the assumption that he is knowledgeable. He is humble, and feeling, enough to see what he calls a 'responsible' job (p.277) as one which will be a quest, so as to avoid the mistakes of the past (pp.277–78). Something has been gained.

The role of the nurse has psychological implications, but for the moment we shall confine ourselves to the fact that it fits in with the astrological aspect of the book. She too is typical: Virgo subjects are generally involved in service to others, we are told, and they are dependable and reliable and practical. Furthermore, those born under this sign and Pisceans are said to be mutually attractive, and Ramírez has the idea that Larry and the nurse have felt this. The connection with the psychological aspect, needless to say, is that she is a mother-figure. This is underlined when we remember that Virgo is often equated with Isis, who is the Divine Mother as well as the goddess of medicine.

These features of the foundation of personality and identity are not universally applicable: they serve to prepare the ground for particular existences and particular circumstances. While every human being is part of a family, has to adopt his innate tendencies to the society he lives in and, ultimately, has to face death, not everyone starts with the same qualities or has to cope with the same circumstances. Before coming to those elements in the novel that could be judged universal, there is one other personal point that can be made and which may add to our understanding. That is that the father-figure's role as author is unusually emphasized. In a way he creates the character of the surrogate son by means of words and, through them, aims at the son's integrity as well as his own. We have already noted that Ramírez is intent on finding out about life by means of what people say. He does not confine this to Larry, but is also interested in his doctors' use of language (p.10), and dialogues between people he has never met. For example, he asks Larry what the favourite topics of conversation had been for him and his ex-wife (pp.182–83). He attempts to live other people's lives in order to understand himself, and he does this to such an extent that Larry calls him a voyeur (pp.89, 176), an appropriate insult since many of the older man's questions are on the subject of sex and, more important, because what he ultimately wants is to *see*. But time is passing and he is losing his sight (p.137): this is tragic, since seeing means understanding (p.138). The nearest approach that can be made to this now is in his mind's eye, aided by traditional literary devices (metaphors and objective correlatives). It has to be admitted that Larry does do his best to help at one point, translating the emotions and sensations of sexual experience into 'lomas, lomas suaves, verdor y lagos' ('slopes, smooth slopes, greenery and lakes') (p.76), but most of the time he resists his companion's prying. He will not ask him in to his apartment, which would have provided a kind of setting for Ramírez' mental scenarios (p.20), refuses to tell his tale until Ramírez does so (p.26), is reluctant to talk about his ex-wife (pp.62,179), and is determined not to join in the silly game in which the roles are reversed and Larry has to speak the father's lines (pp.42,45). Ramírez' circumstances are also significant. Some of them are based on his condition as an invalid and ex-prisoner, of course, but they are equally applicable to authors. In fact, some make real sense only when considered in this context. An example of the former is that he is 'imprisoned', alone: 'paso muchas horas, todo el día casi, en este cuarto diminuto' ('I spend hours and hours, practically all day, in this tiny room'), he complains (p.57), as so many writers have done before and since. Even more telling is his admission that he never appears in his own dreams (p.58). He is an observer and an interpreter and a seeker, not a principal. His preoccupation with his notes is now explicable too, and so is the fact that when he hides his meagre collection of books (which contain these) from Larry, the younger man accuses him of being a *maquinador* (schemer) (p.140). Even in his extreme weakness, the parts of these texts that he has chosen to formulate as a coded message give him power. They represent his 'secret'. All of us possess mystery for other people, and this may cause apprehension, if not fear. It was Mircea Eliade who once talked of the importance of discovering the origins and history of a thing in order to be able to dominate it,[35] and this is true of people too. In this novel it is constantly in evidence.

Interchangeability of verbal subjects is something else that suggests the author-figure, and so is the way that the two characters recount some anecdotes together, if only in Ramírez' imagination. They even use each other's vocabulary (p.231, for example). Perhaps it is not going too far to suggest that some of Ramírez' reactions to unpleasant revelations — as when he feels unwell immediately after Larry tells him about loveless, aggressive sex, (p.244) — are those of a writer in the face of life's distressing aspects. Puig has actually said that Ramírez is a transposition of himself.[36] He and his fictional character were both exiled and ill, desperately trying to comprehend the alien situation that they were observing. On a more general level, all authors seek even more that that: they are looking for their own identity.

It does no harm to repeat that for Puig satisfactory relationships with other people are not only a means to this end, but are essential in themselves for the achievement of happiness. This is another of his standard themes, his old preoccupations, and it is often illustrated by the conflict between social and political duty and individual preferences, affections and ties. In *El beso de la mujer araña*, Valentín admits that in spite of his principles the girl he really loves and wants belongs to the bourgeoisie, a class he despises. Pozzi, in *Pubis angelical*, is also prey to divided loyalties. Here, both protagonists have faced the same problem, and it seems to be insoluble.

Ramírez' amnesia may be seen as partly due to his feelings of guilt at having neglected his family in order to dedicate himself to the cause of social justice. This is compounded by the fact that they were ultimately murdered (p.87). The only way for him to survive has been for him to wipe this memory from his consciousness and his conscience, and this he has done. It will not go away, however: certain things upset him, such as when he admits that Larry reminds him of someone he has forgotten (p.52). He may have forgotten how to feel, but there is underlying remorse. He maintains that he is not inoffensive, for example (p.55), and when Larry accuses him of having a persecution complex he promptly feels ill (p.70). Even his oft-expressed concern about betrayal can be seen as referring back to his own past and is evidence of his sublimated guilt feelings. 'Usted se desentendió de su esposa e hijos,' Larry says to him 'y de las carencias diarias de ellos, de los reclamos de ellos. Y eso ahora no lo deja vivir en paz' ('You washed your hands of your wife and family, of their daily needs and their claims on you. And now you can't rest') (p.156), Earlier, Larry surmised that Ramírez was afraid he had hurt someone very badly, but could not remember who (p.70). In his dream of escaping from Moscow Ramírez' guilt complex is made explicit. He imagines, in a moment of wishful thinking, that the young man at last recognizes the truth, as he sees it, behind the appearances. Weeping with gratitude, the surrogate son admits that the older man has saved his life by risking his own, that he has worked hard in his profession and that, instead of falling into the trap of being entirely wrapped up in his duty, with a 'tarea socialmente válida' ('a socially-useful job'), seeking glory and sacrificing his loved ones, he actually did the opposite. He thanks him from the bottom of his heart (pp.230–31).

History repeats itself, and we are told that Larry has also neglected his family for the sake of work and the cause. In his case too it was his wife who suffered (p.241) and once, in fact, towards the end of their marriage, when she interrupted his work, he actually struck her (p.246). Long before this he had been faced with the choice between betraying some union members who were about to strike and who needed his counsel, and his parents and fiancée (pp.201–2). The irony of this is indicated when he realizes that the last person on earth to be interested in his struggle for the rights of the working class was his own working-class father: although exploited and frustrated, he felt no sense of solidarity with his fellow-workers, and merely wanted to rise above the level of his origins. The problem may be insoluble, as I have suggested, but if there is any hope of alleviating the suffering caused, this could lie in some kind of compromise, one which would be similar to the fusion of opposites or the blurring of boundaries and limits that we have seen in the other novels. This time the conflict is not between the sexes, as in *The Buenos Aires Affair,* nor between socially-dictated gender roles and natural inclinations, as in *El beso dela mujer araña,* but it is not all that different either: the individual cannot serve two mutually-exclusive and time- and emotion-consuming causes at the same time. Larry's final reluctance to teach (if by that we mean to pontificate) signifies a weakening in the strength of his Marxist convictions, even if he still yearns for social justice. His doubts have grown over the years. At first he had been overwhelmed by the doctrine of Marx, falling under its spell at the end of his undergraduate career and judging it the answer to everything (p.221), convinced that it was a language in which one could express oneself. Now he is disillusioned by the behaviour of North-American Marxists who, he says, are always squabbling among themselves (p.223), and by the low level of political consciousness and the social apathy of those for whom he was fighting, and sacrificing himself. Perhaps most important of all, he now sees that blind faith in Marxism removes the need for self-examination; it is aggressive in theory but passive in practice (p.224).

He has been strongly influenced by three apparently incompatible sets of beliefs. First of all there was the Catholicism in which he was brought up and which as a young boy he found inspiring and comforting. He soon found, though, that for him there was something missing in religious faith. Then came his conversion to Marxism, but his personality problems were not alleviated, and it goes without saying that he was not popular in the Catholic University (p.240). Finally, he turned to psychoanalysis, which he now thinks is a somewhat inconvenient bedfellow for Marxism, and while not completely unhelpful, that was not the complete answer either. Since he underwent analysis there has been no striking improvement in his ability to live with himself, or any relief from nervous tension. There must be another avenue to explore, and there is: finding oneself by means of the Other. This forms part of psychoanalytic practice and theory, so he is not actually leaving them behind, and according to certain psychologists it is not incompatible with aspects of Marxist ideology.

Perhaps the most helpful of these is Henri Wallon, who was influenced by Marx and who propounded original theories on the connections between psychology and dialectical materialism.[37] In two seminal articles, dating from 1946 and 1956,[38] he gives his own, very personal view of the role of the Other in the human psyche, based on the social nature of the personality. For him it is not a question of biologism, as Freud largely maintained, or of sociologism, as in the theories of Durkheim. He refuses to accept the opposition between the two positions, and sees each human being as the repository of both biological and social impulses. This is what he says on the subject:

> Je n'ai jamais pu dissocier le biologique et le social, non que je les croie réductibles l'un à l'autre, mais parce qu'ils me semblent chez l'homme, si étroitement complémentaires dès la naissance, qu'il est impossible d'envisager la vie psychique autrement que sous la forme le leurs relations réciproques.[39]

> I have never been able to dissociate the biological from the social, not because I think that they are mutually reducible, but because in man they seem to me to be so closely complementary from the moment of birth that it is impossible to consider the life of the psyche other than by means of their reciprocal relationship.

This avoids the narcissism traditionally associated with self-examination, which usually separates the individual from others and increases his sense of isolation. For Wallon, understanding between the individual and other people in general is established by means of the Other that each one of us carries within us. He calls it the *alter,* and he was first attracted to this idea in his studies of mentally disturbed patients who suffered from a condition that has been called 'mental automatism'. This is relevant as far as the present novel is concerned in spite of its abnormality, for Ramírez descends into total alienation just before his death. Even earlier, the symptoms are discernible from time to time:

> Le malade s'entend interpeller, insulter, on lui vole ses pensées les plus intimes, on lui en impose d'étrangères, on lui dicte ses actes: il est persécuté et possédé par un être à la fois intime et étranger.[40]

> The patient thinks he is being challenged and insulted, someone is stealing his most intimate thoughts from him, and imposing their own, someone is telling hin what to do; he is persecuted and possessed by a being who is at one and the same time an intimate and a stranger.

This is neither uncommon nor abnormal when not taken to extremes. Talking to oneself, or to the Other in oneself, is not necessarily the sign of a pathological condition. For Wallon, man is genetically and essentially a social creature. As a baby and throughout childhood his existence depends on other people. He is incomplete: 'L'infirmité biologique du nouveau-né suppose une société, un milieu, un autre être qui veille sur lui et qui le complète' ('The biclogical weakness of a new-born baby presupposes the existence of a society, an environment, another being who will watch over him and make him complete').[41] As time passes, a situation of affective symbiosis arises within the growing child. With the development of the Other he experiences a sense of duality *vis-à-vis* his surroundings which is based on his emotions. As he becomes an individual with a particular identity, the Other becomes objectivized in the people who cross his path. Communication and communion with other people is thus guaranteed. The principle is summed up in this way: 'Toi et moi nous ne sommes pas des êtres séparés, des consciences closes' ('You and I are not separate beings, with a closed-off consciousness'), and that is consoling. However, there can be a schism between the *toi* and the *moi,* either 'd'un instant' ('for a moment') or, as in the relationship between Ramírez and Larry, it can be an 'éloignement irrémédiable' ('irremediable rupture').[42] Even so, the experiment had to be attempted, and for one of the participants some good comes of it.

The initiation rite involves tremendous risks and profound suffering for Larry. Understanding does not come easily and may not even be the final answer even if it is acquired. His development has been painful for everyone, but this was unavoidable: his parents, his wife and, of course, Ramírez have played their thankless part in it. It is a question of *liaisons dangereuses,* and it is not irrelevant that this is the title of one of the four books that contain Ramírez' famous secret. On a narrative level, the first step towards his, and Larry's, enlightenment is when a parcel containing some French books arrives for him. Three of these are identified. They are *Les Liaisons dangereuses* by Pierre Choderlos de Laclos (1741 – 1803), *Adolphe* by Benjamin Constant (1767 – 1830), and *La Princesse de Clèves* by Mme. de La Fayette (1634 – 93). At first he denies that they are intended for him and claims that some mistake must have been made. Then he appears to be less convinced that this is so and allows Larry free access to them, whereupon the younger man immediately discovers a coded message. It is to do with politics, and concerns the organization of illegal strikes; it begins with the words 'maldición eterna a quien lea estas páginas' ('an eternal curse on the reader of these pages'), though this is, of course, written in French. When asked if this curse is aimed at the Argentine police, Ramírez refuses to answer. Indeed, his first reaction is to deny the existence of the message, and he claims that some child must have written on the books. As the text progresses these gain importance: Larry's interest in politics revives, and he contacts the Universities of Columbia and Montreal with a view to undertaking research based on what they contain and reflect. Ramírez reluctantly begins to show an interest too, and there seems to be some hope of a future for him. It is a chance for them to work together, for if his health improves he can accompany Larry to Montreal. But their relationship is so unstable and the latent hostility between them so great that the books are converted into a tangible source of power, and Ramírez hides them away. The projected trip to Canada begins to loom large in the game they are playing with each other: first Ramírez wants to go (p. 224), then he is not able to (p. 235); he is definitely going, then he is not (pp. 249 – 50). And ultimately there is no question of it. On his death Larry is to inherit the four annotated volumes (p. 271), but Ramírez repents of this promise when overcome by the fury and disappointment that result from his final encounter with his companion. He leaves them to the hospital library (p.272); he has taken the most intimate part of his secret to the grave. Larry 'wins' because it is he who survives, but Ramírez has withheld at least some of what the younger man needed to know.

Why *Les Liaisons dangereuses, Adolphe* and *La Princesse de Clèves?* What was the fourth book? What is the meaning of the epigraph 'maldición eterna a quien lea estas páginas'? Why does Puig highlight this by using it as the title of the novel itself? The answer to the first question is, perhaps, the easiest one to guess. All three books are strikingly relevant as they are the forerunners of the modern psychological novel and they therefore prefigure the investigations into the inner man that exercise Puig. Furthermore, they contain elements that are by no means unfamiliar to his readers. There is treachery, overwhelming emotion and the manipulation of those who feel this. In *Les Liaisons dangereuses,* for example, the exploitation of those who are blinded by their feelings and are unable to detect and recognize the unscrupulous motives of their deceivers, ends in death for one woman and in the living death of incarceration in a convent for the other. Their attempts at self-knowledge and the understanding of others are doomed to failure because of an internal enemy. They betray themselves, when all is said and done. The book's relevance is underlined by its being put at the top of the list although it is not the first of the three books chronologically; its *liaisons* are as pernicious as those in *Maldición eterna a quien lea estas páginas.*

Adolphe is no less relevant. Its theme is the divided self and, as one critic has put it, it portrays a character who, in a bid for freedom, 'breaks an innocent heart to death'. He adds that 'the conclusion is pessimistic',[43] and the same might be said of the end of the Puig novel. *Adolphe* has also been described as the 'analyse [d'un] esclavage par un homme qui a la vocation de la liberté' ('analysis of an enslavement perpetrated by a man whose vocation is freedom'), and that is not an unfamiliar situation in Puig novels either.[44] The conflict is between emotion and judgment and Adolphe is another character who is involved in politics.

La Princesse de Clèves, the earliest of the three books, treats of the complexities of human motives and emotions too. Thematically, all three novels are reflected in the present work. Even stylistically there is a connection between what is probably the most significant of them, *Les Liaisons dangereuses,* and *Maldición eterna a quien lea estas páginas.* This is found in the formal limitations that each of the authors has chosen to observe: the French novel is entirely epistolary. There may be something to be learned from the dates of the French books: the *Liaisons dangereuses* and the *Princesse de Clèves* are pre-Revolutionary and describe a society that, we now know, was soon to disappear. *Adolphe,* on the other hand, dates from 1815, and is therefore set in the post-Revolutionary period, but political and social reform have done little to improve the individual human situation or to increase man's knowledge or control of his inner self.

We are not told what the fourth novel was, and it may seem otiose to ask why this is so. Nevertheless, given Puig's thoroughness, we may be forgiven for assuming that there is a reason for this omission. Could it be a kind of game on his part to withhold secret information in his turn? Ramírez' role as author is, after all, manifest in the fact that *his* secret is codified in his books, and it is not accessible without his aid. The title of the fourth text is withheld from us, and this leaves the real author in control of the amount we are able to decode and decipher.

The opening curse in the coded message is intended for snooping eyes: there is little doubt that Larry is right and that, superficially, it refers to the Argentine authorities. Spying and deception are obsessive themes in Puig though, not just narrative features, and there is more to the curse than that. We have only to recall how many times betrayal is mentioned in this particular novel to realize this. Even the amiable nurse has two sides to her, and is accused at one point of being a thief and of reading other people's private papers (p.69). It is intolerable to Ramírez that other people are in a position to know one's secrets, steal one's thoughts, infiltrate the fortress of one's being; we are back with the concept of 'vampirization', with the life-blood at risk. In the final dispute between the two men, Larry reveals that he has read and understood many more personal extracts from the coded text in the French books: Ramírez' attitude towards him is entirely based on the old man's concealed past. Ramírez has wiped the floor with him, accusing him of being ungrateful, selfish and mercenary because he intends to go to Montreal alone, and Larry is stung into spelling out what he has discovered, that history is repeating itself in Ramírez' treatment of him. He had failed to establish a satisfactory bond with his own son, who had hated him because of his cruelty to his mother and because of his fearful rages, and now he is trying to make amends. He knows that Ramírez found it impossible to love his son (p.257), but that when he was in prison, his son had admitted that he had misjudged his father, and had felt guilty at the thought of his imminent execution. Larry says categorically that he is *not* Ramírez' son, even if he treats him as if he were, and adds that the old man is clearly going insane (p. 259). He is unbearable, he says. This is the point at which Ramírez gives up, once and for all; Larry was never his friend, he claims, and though he always gave him what little he had, Larry never gave anything at all. He goes to his grave hating the young man who has read pages he should not have read and who is therefore cursed. But he is cursed because that is the fate of each new generation as it penetrates the armour of the previous one. Life goes on as our knowledge and power are wrested from us by our children in their turn. This means they have won, and we shall be destroyed.

Now all this is a harshly pessimistic view. Even the word 'curse' smacks of bloody mythological stories and the Old, rather than the New Testament. The most striking omission from all this is love. Christ's forgiving grace is not a satisfying concept for Larry, and Ramírez ignores it all together. And human love, whether between a man and a woman or within family life, is tainted with self-interest and jealousy in at least one of the partners. The answer may be that this extreme image of the primitive struggle between the sexes and between rival generations is an intensification, even an exaggeration. In some relationships there may indeed be love, but Puig does not write about these.

It is probably true to say that our first reaction to this novel will be amusement at the apparently jocular nature of the title and consciousness that the author-as-father also has his secrets. Perhaps we will be aware of the prying, bloodsucking role that we take on once we start to read. Perhaps we will feel that if we understand our authors too well we too will be cursed: we could be accused of cannibalistic interference as we feed on other people's knowledge and experience. We may even destroy them. R.D. Laing has said:

> They are playing a game. They are playing at not playing a game. If I show them I see they are, I shall break the rules and they will punish me. I must play their game, of not seeing that I see the game.[45]

But there is little danger, in fact, of the reader being cursed because of his acquisition of the author's power in this case: there are too many secrets, and the text is too dense for us thoroughly to understand the 'game'.

Human relationships depend very largely on sex and sexuality, and again in this novel this is an area fraught with problems and dangers. It is hard to avoid the conclusion that life without sexual desire and the difficulties that arise because of sexuality would be preferable for the characters. We are back with the concept of the *pubis angelical* of the previous book. Ramírez has no memory of sex (p.73), and although his desire to live again means being rejuvenated (he hears a young voice in his internal dialogues, he says, (p.50)), this does not alter the fact that he can no longer understand why sex is so important (p.77). He knows about it, but he does not know it. But, as we have already been told, what is important for one person is not important for another, and there is no doubt that Larry is not devoid of sexual feelings or sexually-orientated memories. Also, given his knowledge of psychoanalysis — even if it is 'psicoanálisis sintético' ('synthetic psychoanalysis'), as Ramírez sceptically comments — he is bound to be greatly involved with theory as well as practice.

In the course of one conversation he admits that he feels nervous and inferior when he meets a woman who attracts him (p.53), and this is echoed in what is, probably, Ramírez' invented story of Larry's impotence when a strange young woman faints in the street (p.106). '¿Qué debí hacer entonces, señor Ramırez?' ('What should I have done then?') Larry is made to ask (p.106). We discover that all he had to do was to reach out and embrace her; she would then reveal his identity to him, for she knows who he is, and for that reason she loves him (pp.108–12). This is the way that Ramírez construes the situation, since Larry himself has confessed that for him the idea that someone else can make one complete is no more than an illusion (p.78). He undoubtedly has grounds for his cynicism and disenchantment. As a child he had felt ashamed of his penis, and he was mortified if his mother made him wear a little pointed cap on his head, which made him feel he was exposing it in public (p.127). Even at that tender age conflict was already in evidence, since the Phrygian cap traditionally symbolizes both the phallus and liberty.[46] As time passed, his sense of guilt increased with social and family pressures. His mother threw his copy of Sartre's *L'Être et le néant* away because it contains a chapter called 'Le corps' and she thought it was pornographic (p.145), and later he feels 'muerto de vergüenza' ('desperately ashamed') when he is sexually excited in the company of an attractive young girl. The results, in adult life, were and are distressing. He is now revolted by the smell of female flesh after sex (p.82); his sexual performance with his wife was far from satisfactory (p.219); he constantly used to feel inferior to some invented rival, who would be a superman, and would please his wife in a way he could not (p.219). He became madly jealous (p.217), and after a while their sex life was as mechanical as their marriage was boring (p.239). He was attracted to a neighbour, and his wife started to have affairs with other men (pp.239 – 40). Ultimately, before their definitive separation and divorce, when he felt that he could not admit that he was incomplete without her (p.96), he had listened in the next room while she had sexual intercourse with someone else. This had excited him more that it ever had when he had been making love to her (p.247).

With his experience of psychoanalysis, he now believes that he understands the reason for his attitudes, and he projects these back into his childhood. He is conscious of his Oedipal relationship with his mother and he feels guilty at the thought of his lack of affection for his father (p.157). The juxtaposition of the image of landscape beauty and sexual intercourse that we have already referred to takes on new significance when he observes that the attractions of the beauty of nature are a substitute for something else (p.79), and his arousal when listening to his wife and her lover suggest a voyeuristic child witnessing his parents' love-making. Freud maintained that in normal development the child eventually substitutes a member of the opposite sex of his own generation for the desired mother, but we cannot help recalling that he also claimed that there is no hope of an ideal relationship with substitutes. He was actually referring to cultural substitutes as outlets for the libido on that occasion,[47] but Larry may well feel that the result will be the same where a real person is concerned. He sees the arguments he used to have with his wife and those he had with his mother as strikingly similar (p.101), and he has no difficulty in explaining his present fear of women. He how rejects the idea that another person can make him whole, and attributes all his problems to his early desire for his mother who, he is sure, also desired him (p.128). He has already said that mothers will always have sexual feelings towards their sons (p.99), and it follows that the father will be a usurper who has to be eliminated (p.100). He remembers that he was blissfully happy one day when he went out alone with his mother and she confided in him, talking to him as if he were an adult (p.160), and the obvious interpretation of this is that on that occasion he saw himself in the role of the father. He is only too aware now of the part parents play in the formation of a child's personal identity, and how this develops so that individuality will be achieved when other people recognize this: even as a teacher he had depended on the admiration of students and colleagues in order to be sure of who he was (p.238). Oedipal desire and adult desire are closely connected, and he rejects the banal (but comforting) concept of the ideal mother (p.98), knows what effect his father's absence has had on his life (p.41) and refers to his, perhaps excessive, devotion to his mother (p.43). He now knows why he is as he is, and in articulating all this to the older man he is making progress, for verbal expression of his knowledge of himself is the opposite of repression.

But *Maldición eterna a quien lea estas páginas* is not just the story of Larry. Ramírez has an important role to play too, and the two men complement each other. In the face of Larry's self-examination he is sceptical; he accuses Larry of repeating prefabricated ideas almost unthinkingly, and pours scorn on his explanations. At the very end, just before he announces that he wants no more to do with him and to have no more influence over him, he comes out with what he judges to be the truth. Larry's mother-complex, he says, is something he admits to, even proclaims, in order to cover up something far worse. In fact, he adds, it would be better to feel shame, and personal guilt, and all the other emotions that Larry now eschews than to be as he is: incapable of feeling anything at all (p.248).

This, then, is something else that the two men have in common: Ramírez has, perhaps unconsciously, suppressed the ability to feel, while Larry has done so deliberately. This is another way in which this novel varies from its predecessors, neither man having any hope at all of affective bond with another human being. Those critics who have objected to there being too much theorizing analysis in the book,[48] justifying this opinion with phrases such as 'la novela se convierte en mero panfleto' ('the novel just turns into a pamphlet'),[49] demonstrate that they have not read it with sufficient care. What they do not appear to have noticed is that *none of the analysis serves any purpose as far as the well-being of these characters is concerned*. The 'theorizing' does not actually work. The author's attitude here is not just ambivalent (as I suggested it was in the footnotes to *El beso de la mujer araña*) but pessimistic and disillusioned. Lucidity does not bring happiness, even if it is authentic. Indeed, as the comparative contentment of some of the characters in earlier novels shows, it is not just a question of necessary dreams, however short, but also of having some faith in these, even if it is clearly misplaced.

As the title of the book suggests, human beings cannot afford to think, to understand, to know too much. However unsuccessful family life or sexual relationships are, however many risks have to be taken, life has to go on. No one (other than a total amnesiac) can live in perfect ignorance of the fact that as T.S. Eliot said in *Murder in the Cathedral:*

> We do not know very much of the future
> Except that from generation to generation
> The same things happen again and again . . .

Yet there is no real option but to persevere. As we saw when discussing socio-political conditions in previous chapters, this is not to say that no improvements can be made, but man will always be incomplete, and the various solutions to his problems are at best only partial and at worst, mere palliatives. Certainly knowledge without love will fail. The obvious objection to this is that love, too, fails, especially in the novelistic world of Manuel Puig. It is exploited and betrayed, it is often an actual impediment to happiness, it is restricted and dictated by constitutional eccentricity, it is oppressed by society, it conflicts with duty. Furthermore, it is an emotion that seemingly cannot exist in isolation from other destructive, pernicious emotions, such as anger, jealousy and fear. In spite of all this, man cannot live without feelings, even negative feelings. And emotions themselves have a cognitive function, according to many theorists. To repeat Hillman's words, this is 'not mere perception, but a tendency to achieve something'. They constitute,

> a way of perceiving, a way of knowing, a way of adapting and a way of being in the world . . . There is reason in emotion. "Le coeur a ses raisons que la raison ne connaît pas".[50] The relation of emotion and reason is an ancient problem solved usually by splitting them asunder. The meaning of this breach in our civilization is a subject for itself, but its tragic effects are everywhere present in the violence of emotion unmitigated by reason and *the sterility of intellect uninformed by emotion.*[51]

Since Larry has not rejected the value of psychoanalytic insight, it is safe to assume that he still accepts the Freudian view that emotion is connected with instinct, or 'drives' (*Triebe*), and that love and aggression are 'an affect charge of the libido'.[52] Nothing could be more basic, and he will have to feel again, as well as realize the source of his feelings, if there is to be any hope for him at the end of the novel. He — and we — must bear in mind that, as Bettelheim tells us in his *Freud and Man's Soul,* psychoanalysis is a 'demanding and potentially dangerous voyage of discovery', and while the consequences of acting without knowing what one is doing can be utterly destructive, Freud himself was never really enthusiastic about psychoanalysis as therapy. All it claims to do is to free us from *unnecessary* repressions and *unrealistic* anxieties. Bettelheim maintains that Freud did not want it to become the exclusive domain of doctors, but rather that he wished for 'a profession that doesn't yet exist' to entrust it to.[53] Perhaps poets, novelists and philosophers could be seen as paving the way for this non-existent profession. Even if, as T.S. Eliot says, 'human kind / Cannot bear very much reality', William Carlos Williams's lines:

> It is difficult
> to get news from poems,
>   yet men die miserably every day
>   for lack
> of what is found there

may be judged even more apt in this context, especially if the connotations of the word 'news' include rational understanding, and 'poems' are defined as the linguistic manifestations of vital truths.

A major lack, therefore, in the lives of both the protagonists is the sort of love that ought to exist between members of a family. Larry's attitude towards his parents is now clinical and resentful. The surrogate mother is the Virgo nurse, and there is rivalry between her and the young man for Ramírez' time, attention and money (p.63). Ramírez' attitude towards her is also one that fits with this theory. He sees her as caring and sacrificial, and he illustrates this in a dream about Edith Cavell, who will not abandon the wounded (that is, him), and is shot because she refuses to have sex with a German officer (p.59).[54] She is faithful and she is doomed; he cannot save her as she cannot hear him. He calls the nurse an angel, but we already know that angels are not necessarily benign, and there is a moment when he thinks she has betrayed him. She is an ambiguous figure for Larry, too, and there is a link between him and two older, ugly nurses who are interested in him: there is duality inherent in the mother-figure. The young nurse certainly betrays Larry in the end, if only unwittingly, as it is she who repeats Ramírez' complaints about him to the authorities, thus ensuring that he will not inherit the all-important books. The surrogate parents are united against the child, and this is seen by Larry as the generation battle: 'Tal vez toda la gente mayor decepcione a los más jóvenes' ('Perhaps old people always let young people down') he comments (p.261). Though parents care for their children like the sparrows that Ramírez reads about in the encyclopedia, they too fail to recognize them once they grow up (pp.115, 117). The reaction of the offspring is equally provocative and hurtful. Larry has already mentioned the anti-authority behaviour of young people (p.178), talked of his unwillingness to emulate his parents (p.215) and has opted for freedom from any bond with them. There is a parallel in Ramírez' past. When his son returned from abroad because his mother was alone, he found that she was still loyal to her husband. He could not replace his father in her affections.

The love of God is also missing from the protagonists' lives. At first glance, religion does not seem to play a large part in Puig's novels. Only one of his characters, Teté in *La traición de Rita Hayworth,* has any strong religious faith, and that is more of a preoccupation than a comfort. Nevertheless, I would go as far as to claim that religion is a major theme, with the emphasis on the Old Testament God as a jealous and chastising father, not averse to acts of arbitrary cruelty. Toto, in Puig's first novel, articulates the suppressed anger felt by puzzled and deceived mankind in typically adolescent fashion. He is simplistic and brutal, seeing things in black and white, but it is my contention that his basic philosophy lies behind all the novels. He is talking to his piano teacher, Herminia, and during the conversation he points out the absurdity of life — a profound enough observation for a boy in his very early teens, though not perhaps all that surprising when we recall his sense of alienation from his immediate environment. He condemns the pointless cycle of working in order to eat and eating in order to work (p.282), and then shocks Herminia by questioning her faith, claiming that she believes only so as to stop herself from committing suicide. Like his fictional heir Molina, in *El beso de la mujer araña*, he recounts the story of an unnamed film, and this reflects his feelings and ideas on the subject. In it, a feudal lord who has two sides to his nature, is benevolent towards the children in his territory by day, educates them and trains them for warfare. But at night he injures them and harms them, debilitating them in every possible way. Among these children is his own son. When the appropriate moment arrives, he puts them to the test by hiring a band of evil mercenaries, and the battle that ensues, like all initiation rites, takes place in a thick forest. The forces of darkness are victorious against their deliberately weakened opponents, and those that do return to the feudal seat are reviled for having fallen into all the traps that the world has set for them. They are punished according to their particular sin, and the patriarch abandons them and turns his attention to the new generation, still asleep in another part of the castle (pp.282 – 85).

As Ángel Rama has pointed out, in *Maldición eterna a quien lea estas páginas,* the reader is aware of a tendency towards allegory, but this, he says, is combated by the author's perspicacity and vitality and by the text's ambiguity.[55] The latter factor seems to me to be the more telling and defensible. Clearly, Puig is tempted by allegory in this novel, but this is not by any means fully developed. The father-son relationship has always been used to reflect that between God and man, and the two situations invite comparison. Ramírez *is* a God-figure, in a position of power. He dreams of a tree with only one branch bearing fruit (p.11), and while this represents his family circumstances on a narrative level,[56] it could also work allegorically, with the tree signifying the cross. The dream at the end of the novel, which is brought about, at least in part, by the fact that Ramírez has just been talking about Marxism with Larry, is one in which he rescues a young man and a girl from the Tsar's henchmen in Russia, although at first it looks as if he is betrayed by them (p.229). He advises Larry to trust his father at another point (p.208), and talks about paternal tolerance (p.267). But at the very end, when he asks Larry to postpone his trip to Montreal, the young man replies: 'Usted no me puede pedir ese sacrificio' ('You can't ask that sacrifice of me') (p.251), and there is no more to be said. He abandons him.

Larry is a son of God, and his grandfather's name, Giovanangelo, links him with the angels as well as with the various biblical characters who bear the name of John.[57] But there are also times when he could be seen as Christ. His father (who is largely ignored, like Joseph) was a carpenter, according to Ramírez (p.254). He insists on bowing his head in the old man's presence and cannot look him in the eyes, and deep down he knows that there is a strong chance that he is going to be destroyed and that his flesh will be eaten. But the God of this quasi-allegory is incomprehensible, and the ways in which he moves are impenetrably mysterious. He does not want to be worshipped (p.64), seems to offer no love and is unforgiving: Ramírez is wild with fury if people get away with things (p.70). The outcome of the story is very different, too, for the son refuses to die.

The allegorical nature of the relationship between the two men is underlined when they translate their earthly father-and-son game into a religious context. Since their comprehension, imagination and, as a consequence, the language they have at their disposal cannot cope with the eternal mystery, all they can do is attempt a journalistic 'day in the life of God', and its tone is both preposterous and pathetic. On a general level, it illustrates the impossibility of human understanding of the

nature of God; in this particular case, it reveals their impatience with
the concept of a benevolent Father. Larry judges his earlier religious
faith an aspect of the repression that he used to be subject to, and he
claims that worshipping God involves the suppression of all
individuality (p.148). One of the things he had admired in his father
had been his indifference to religion: for him it had nothing to do with
reality (p.142). He now rationalizes his adolescent fervour, seeing it as
a phase that was replaced by sexual energy (p.148) and the
manifestation of an egocentric wish for attention. He is surely aware of
the Freudian view that religion is born of the longing for the attention of
a lost father. This is what Larry actually says when Ramírez asks him if
he had ever imagined himself as the crucified Christ:

> Al principio tan sólo [quería ser] uno de los ángeles. Después alguien en
> especial, señalado por Cristo, por su bondad, que más tarde suplanta a
> Cristo o se vuelve Cristo mismo . . . en virtud de su generosidad y
> sufrimiento. Pero así me convertía nada menos que en el hijo de Dios, y
> Dios y todo el mundo me miraban favorablemente. La aspiración
> religiosa responde a la psicología del sufrimiento. Sufriendo tan bien, tan
> pacientemente, tan desinteresadamente se alcanzaría la protección y la
> admiración de Dios. (p.149)

> At first I only wanted to be an angel. Then someone special that Jesus
> singled out for his goodness. Then I wanted to take Jesus' place, become
> Jesus himself . . . through selflessness and suffering. But in that way I
> would actually be the Son of God, and God and everyone else would look
> on me with approval. Religious aspirations go hand in hand with the
> psychology of suffering.[58] If I suffered properly, patiently,
> disinterestedly, I would attain the protection and the admiration of God.

There follow all kinds of bizarre projections of God and his son, of their
getting up early, drinking coffee, getting dressed and going out to work,
and some important pointers emerge: that Larry has never before seen
himself in the role of the Father, that religion is seen as an obsession
with power, and that the Father is asking too much of his son in sending
him down into a world that he himself describes as a *cloaca* (cesspool)
(p.152). God is authoritarian but, in his own way, he too is trapped and
frustrated (p.152). Like Ramírez he is unpredictable, and the only way
to keep out of trouble is to refrain from causing him problems (p.154).

Religion is therefore like sex as far as this novel is concerned: we have
a man who may once have felt its call but has now forgotten the
experience and the emotion behind this, and one who was once
comforted by religious faith, but who now knows better. Larry's
disappointment with sex has removed one chance of human love in his

life, and his rationalization of religious feeling has destroyed any consolation in divine love. It is another unsatisfactory solution.

It is like Toto's film story. God creates, tempts, debilitates, tests and abandons his creatures, and if the love of the Father is anything like parental love, then it is so beset with pain and disappointment that it is no foundation for happiness. As Larry says, happiness is in short supply (p.153). Yet how can we disregard imponderables such as love and death, or ignore thoughts on God and the beyond? The consciousness of life's great mysteries is frequently represented in Puig as being aware of the void, and we are all cursed from birth by the eventual necessity of facing up to this. There are many examples of the use of the term. For example, in *El beso de la mujer araña,* when Molina talks about the heroine singing in the Nazi propaganda film, he adds: 'a mí me da miedo cada vez que me acuerdo de esa pieza que canta, porque cuando la canta está como mirando fijo en el vacío' ('it terrifies me every time I think of that song that she sings, because when she is singing it it is as if she were staring into the void') (p.58). Here, there is explicit reference to its presence in a delirious dream that Ramírez has towards the end of his life. In it, there are two old dogs, male and female, who demand his affection, protect him and Larry from three murderous thugs who come into his hospital room and, before he can risk his own life to save them, hurl themselves from a top-floor window: 'un salto al vacío' ('a leap into the void') (p.171). That this is a descent into death is made even more explicit when Ramírez sums up what they have done by saying that they sacrificed themselves that he might live. 'Esos pobres animales sabían cuidar a su cría' ('Those poor animals knew how to look after their young') is Larry's supposed comment (p.171).

This is by no means the first time that Puig's characters have been aware of the presence of death, and a passing reference to Sartre's *L'Être et le néant,* when Larry was talking about what he read as an adolescent, points us in the direction of a possible interpretation of the author's viewpoint. Puig seems to have some sympathy for Heidegger's way of avoiding the apparent absurdity of an existential understanding of death by seeing it, as John McQuarrie says, not as 'the once-for-all observable fact at the end of life', but as an awareness throughout life that one's being is 'a being-towards-death'. This is not to say that life should consist of morbid brooding, but there is 'an *anticipation* of death, a realistic inclusion of the death-factor among our projects and the way we evaluate them'. And of course, 'there is a great difference in existential attitude between the man who lives in the face of an end and the man who systematically excludes the thought of death', like some of Puig's less mature characters. For Sartre, death constituted the ultimate absurdity, 'neither more nor less absurd than life itself', and he said that during his lifetime man is — like Larry — prey to the desire actually to be God. For this reason 'interpersonal bodily relations are inherently self-frustrating'. Sartre sees the inefficacy of interpersonal and sexually-based relations in the same way as Puig appears to do in the present novel. In McQuarrie's words:

> It is in exploring these relations that Sartre brings out what he supposes to be the inescapably contradictory and frustrating character of the interpersonal and sexual relation. I try to escape being object to the other through love. In this context love is understood as possessive love. It is the desire to assimilate the other to myself. But in order that this may happen, the other has to love me; and to make the other love me, I have to become an object to excite love. So the relationship becomes endlessly ambiguous and frustrating, oscillating between love and hate, the desire to possess and to be possessed . . .[59]

Nevertheless Puig has some reservations. There is, I think, a hope that love need not be possessive, that the attitude to the other may not be based on self-seeking, exploitative motives. There may be justification in seeing death as nothingness, but if there is to be any happiness at all in this world, we have to live as if this were not so. Perhaps he shares Unamuno's view that if that is indeed what awaits us, then the least we can do is to act in such a way that this will be an unjust fate.[60]

It is not much, though, and it takes little knowledge of the world to realize that there is plenty of injustice in it; Puig sees this only too clearly. His maturity is manifest in this sixth novel, and it is quite wrong to assume, as some have, that he is now distancing himself from his characters.[61] I would go as far as to say that he is more involved with Ramírez and Larry than he has been with any of his previous creations. *Maldición eterna a quien lea estas páginas* is the most sombre of his works because we cannot allow ourselves to be soothed any more. The characters have lost their capacity for dissociation, and so have we.[62] We cannot avoid seeing and talking about the abyss, however much we would like to, and the formula behind the book is no longer the fairy tale, where peril is successfully overcome, even if only in dreams, but myth, where there is only 'insurmountable difficulty and defeat'.[63] Mythology, according to Joseph Campbell, is 'psychology misread as biography, history, and cosmology',[64] but within its framework the hero regenerates society. This is not very comforting on a personal

level, but this, together with the desire for love in a world that
continually shows us how love can fail, is how life is. The author,
previously sympathetic and touched by the plight of his pitiful fellow
men, has changed his standpoint: now he is sympathetic and angry.
Life betrays us all, but unlike Larry, who claimed that when his wife
deceived him he felt anger so profound that words could not express it
(p.245), Puig communicates his emotion by means of appropriate and
— because there is only dialogue in this book — real language.

CHAPTER VIII

'Life's a Dream':
Sangre de amor correspondido (1982)

> Nur der Irrtum ist das Leben,
> Und das Wissen ist der Tod.
>
> Only in error is there life,
> And knowledge is death.
>
> Schiller

MANY of the characters and situations in Puig novels are elaborations on people and circumstances from the author's own life: Toto, in *La traición de Rita Hayworth,* is based on his childhood self, as we have already seen; the chorus at the beginning of the same book is the result of his attempt to reproduce the voice of an aunt;[1] real people were used, to a greater or lesser degree, as models for *Boquitas pintadas, The Buenos Aires Affair, El beso de la mujer araña* and *Pubis angelical;* and the character of Larry, in *Maldición eterna a quien lea estas páginas,* was born from a New York City acquaintance. But it is probably *Sangre de amor correspondido,* the seventh book,[2] which most closely reproduces and reflects a real person. The hero, Josemar, is a portrait of a Brazilian stonemason who enlivened the period of time that he spent working in the author's Rio de Janeiro apartment by recounting his life story, ultimately putting the varying (and, indeed, self-contradictory) versions of it on tape for him. Puig has told of this encounter and his reactions to it in more than one interview, and before becoming acquainted with the text, the reader might be forgiven for assuming that the resulting novel will be little more than a verbatim account of the Brazilian workman's confessions and personal fantasies. In fact, this is by no means the case. There is obviously no slavish dependence on the source material, for the homogeneous nature of the novels is not affected, and Puig's own world-view is still very much in evidence.

Once again, though, there is plenty of novelty in the text. Indeed, its originality is so striking that critical reception, as much based on the reviewers' incapacity or unwillingness to cope with stylistic experimentation in this case as it has been in the past, was largely uncomprehending and hostile. That it is form, and not content, that provokes adverse comment is clear from even a cursory glance at the reasons given by those who condemned the book: parts of it are 'unintelligible', claims one;[3] there is 'leaden monotony', says another.[4] In the end, it is worth repeating the obvious: that each reader has to come to his own conclusions where value judgements are concerned. Furthermore, *Sangre de amor correspondido,* like its predecessors, has been seen by many as both impressive and complex.[5]

This is the only Puig novel to be set exclusively in a non-Spanish-speaking country, and the source tape-recordings were in Portuguese. The Brazilian version, needless to say, is more faithful to the colloquial language used by the original narrator, and the author has talked about his problems in translating this into a language which would not limit it to a particular Spanish-American setting.[6] Critical opinion is divided on this too: is the setting vital to the integrity of the novel or is it not? Brazilian reviewers have judged it all-important, one going as far as to say that it is the most typically *carioca* piece of writing that he has read for a long time.[7] Others, mindful of the fact that to classify it in this way might suggest that it could be seen as regionalist literature, and therefore inferior, have claimed universality for it, and think that the Brazilian background is irrelevant. In fact, although there is incontrovertibly less of a gulf between *Sangre de amor correspondido* and the other six novels than might at first appear to be the case, there is one very important element of Brazilian society that constitutes an innovatory feature as far as Puig novels are concerned, and that — as Jorge Rodríguez Padrón was the first to note[8] — is poverty. It is true that the story could equally well be set somewhere other than Brazil, but only in a country where a significant section of society lives in conditions approaching destitution and, even more important, only where these conditions are accompanied by a rigid and oppressive social code.

The novel takes the form of a monologue in which the hero, prompted by a series of brief questions and comments from various characters from the dramatis personae of his life, attempts to explain and come to terms with his current situation and, in so doing, with himself. It is relatively short, and it would not be impossible to read it in one sitting, as one critic has said,[9] but its complexity is such that little would be gained by such an exercise. There is no doubt that all Puig's books yield their more intimate secrets and transcendental themes only after several readings, and that the immediate surface appeal of the earlier novels has proved counter-productive where reaction to the later ones is concerned. What can be read quickly and with unconsidered enjoyment carries a built-in handicap: it is so easy to think that its entertainment value is its only virtue, and in Puig's case this error may well be compounded by so many somewhat misleading references to mass culture — misleading in the sense that the values of the characters may be automatically attributed to the author. If subsequent novels make increasing demands on the reader and there is less immediate appeal, this may result in disappointment or, at worst, resentment and even condemnation. *Sangre de amor correspondido* makes unprecedented demands; it is not an easy text to come to grips with straight away. First of all, it is different from most novels, as well as from the others in Puig's output, in that there is really only one voice from beginning to end (hence the accusation of monotony). In spite of the fairly numerous queries and objections that punctuate the narrative, when all is said and done Josemar is talking to himself. What is worse, the story that he tells is both confused and confusing, and it is difficult to reduce the text to a set of clear-cut, unassailable facts. Still on a stylistic level, the linguistic inelegance and repetitive verbal tics of the narrator (many of which are more typical of Portuguese than of Spanish)[10] can prove taxing. And ultimately, as always, the theme provides little consolation, even if Josemar's capacity for cheerfulness and his skill in creating a tolerable fantasy-reality for himself out of intolerable facts could be judged almost moving in the way that it reflects human adaptability and powers of survival.

It is not immediately apparent that Josemar's tale is almost irreducible to a simple linear narrative, even though there is a challenging note in the voice of his first interlocutor, who is Maria da Gloria, the young girl he pursued and, he says, seduced some years earlier in his home town of Cocotá, in the State of Rio de Janeiro. There seems little reason to doubt the veracity of what he is saying, that in spite of her protestations of love for him and the fact that, once deflowered, she was his slave for life, he abandoned her in order to make his way in the world. We can also accept that when he left, she went out of her mind with grief. It is not long, however, before we realize that much of what is being narrated does not ring true, and some of it is subsequently contradicted by the speaker himself. For example, it is surprising that someone so meticulously concerned with the time of day at which past events took place, as well as their exact duration, should be so vague on the subject of when he last saw the girl who is now so important in his life. Perhaps it was ten years ago, perhaps eight (p.9). (Later in the novel we are given information that reveals that it must have been thirteen years since the couple last met.) Then details of the story of their sexual encounter are suspect, to say the least, and the conscience-like voice of the girl points out their implausibility. According to Josemar, they spent a night together in a hotel after attending a dance at the Municipal Club. When his mental reproduction of Maria da Gloria's voice says how unlikely it is that a girl of fifteen, as she then was, would be admitted to a local hotel in his company, he hastily amends his account, saying that actually they went to another town. Her implicit and explicit denials of almost everything that he claims once happened are less acceptable than his version of events because of the strangeness of her asking him what she herself once did, and what they did together:[11] this strangeness is confirmed when we learn of her mental illness. If she has had a breakdown, we assume, then any incompatability between what Josemar claims and what Maria da Gloria says must be based on her alienation. The confident tones of the hero (it is impossible not to think of this as an aural text) lull our suspicions for a little while longer, and the girl's comments appear to be those of a typical amnesiac. But at the same time it becomes increasingly difficult for the reader to avoid a feeling of disbelief as the text progresses, for progress it does, in spite of its somewhat repetitive nature. And this unease proves to be justified. For example, at first Josemar says that on the fatal night they went to the hotel in his car. He even remembers the make: a Maverick (p.9). Later, he says he had a Gordini (p.41). Later still, as he looks back on his life and thinks about the plans he made at that time, he recalls that one of them had been to own 'su automóvil, *que nunca tuvo*' ('his own car, *which he never did*') (p.201, my italics). Then, apart from his sexual prowess, his greatest talent used to be for football, and we discover that he was the star of the Cocotá Sporting Club, adored by the fans and even admired by the manager, Maria da Gloria's father, in whose eyes he could do no wrong. Yet, disconcertingly, the voice in his ear denies this. 'Esto no es

cierto', it maintains, 'En el equipo del pueblo no dejaban entrar a los de
las chacras' ('That's not true. The town team didn't admit poor farm-
labourers') (p.50). Maria da Gloria contradicts so much of what he
says. According to Josemar, he had once gone on a memorable
excursion to the country with all her family. But her memory of the
event is that although he had wanted to go with them, they had refused
to let him (p.53). And his account of a celebratory party that he had
attended in her house is demolished by her assertion that he would
never have been allowed to enter it (p.19). There are so many cases of
ambivalence and the blurring of detail, to say nothing of complete
invention, that it would be tedious to list them all. Nevertheless, it is
hard to resist mentioning a few more. First of all, did Josemar treat
Maria da Gloria violently? She says that he never did, but he angrily
contradicts her (p.54). And when he refused to be seen with her in the
street on one occasion, was it — as he claims — because he did not want
all the women he was sleeping with at the time to see them together, or
was it due to some kind of fear on his part (p.104)? Is he just teasing her
when he tells her that he has two children by another woman
(pp.105–6)? This is what he says at first, but it appears that there is
more to it than that, for we find that this is true, and that he has never
lived with, or properly supported, any of them;[12] he cannot give the
children anything because he is too poor, and as for their mother,
'cuando él se asquea de algo es para siempre' ('when something starts to
disgust him, that's an end to it') (p.153). At first, Josemar tells Maria
da Gloria that the two children were born of two different mothers, but
this is not confirmed by later revelations. Even less convincing is his
description of them as being well-behaved, educated and affectionate
(p.107), especially since he then admits that he has been told that they
are constantly fighting, break things, throw everything on the floor and
make a terrible mess in their mother's house (p.152). And what are we
to believe about Josemar's temperament? Is he never (unlike his father,
(p.122)) *nervioso* (agitated, upset, nervy), as he claims (p.139)? Is he
never afraid ('El es hombre y no tiene miedo a nada': 'He is a man and
never feels fear' (p.118))? He certainly weeps at one point (p.157), and
on more than one occasion his hands shake — during his last meeting
with Maria da Gloria, for example (p.189), and when he went back to
Cocotá (p.166). But did he ever go back to Cocotá? And, most
important of all, why did he ever leave there, and what happened
between him and Maria da Gloria?

On close inspection, we discover that the text contains several vital

pieces of apparently incontrovertible information that serve towards
the elimination of fantasized episodes and invented 'facts', helping us
to piece together some kind of reliable story. There are two of these that
are essential to any interpretation of the novel, and it is unfortunate that
they should have been missed by so many of its critics. The first, and
more important of the two, is that Josemar never actually had sexual
relations with Maria da Gloria. The second, that he is the natural son of
the local landowner. Let us consider the evidence for these two
assertions.

First of all, as we have noted, the memories of the two protagonists do
not coincide on the subject of the seduction of Maria da Gloria. Even
more significant, what Josemar himself later admits to and what he
originally asserts are quite different. This is less surprising if we see the
interlocutory voices as *created* by the narrator to act as self-imposed
checks on his wilder imaginative exercises. The story of the night of love
in a hotel is repeated in the Epilogue to the novel, which is Chapter One
all over again, with a few minor omissions and changes, but even so
(and we shall discuss the reason for this repetition later), by the time the
Epilogue has been reached, that version has been superseded by what
really happened when Josemar, after at least three years of chaste
courtship, decided to force the issue. By means of promises of marriage
(p.111), he persuaded Maria da Gloria to agree to what he wanted. In a
large shed behind his house he prepared the scene, making up a bed
with a mattress that his mother had discarded (which is particularly
interesting, given Puig's interest in Freudian theory). Then, after
boasting to his brothers about what was going to happen, he brought the
girl there and, in this version, there she lost her virginity, shouting and
crying with pain, joy and love (p.113). Nevertheless, when he
summons up her voice in his head, her reaction is that she cannot
remember the pain of that first sexual encounter at all. His self-
consoling answer to this unpalatable challenge is that the voice belongs
to someone who has lost her mind. This being so, how could she
remember?

Throughout most of the novel, Josemar's devotion to his mother
seems to be almost unnaturally strong, yet towards the end he turns
violently against her. It is at this point that what has previously been
claimed by another interlocutory voice (this time that of his black foster-
brother) is articulated by Josemar himself. What his foster-brother had
said was that his mother had managed to achieve what she wanted,
'separarlos' ('to separate you'). 'Te jodió bien, esa vieja puta,' he had

added ('She screwed things up for you well and truly, the old whore')
(p.125). Now, with bitterness welling up in him, Josemar blames his
mother for all that has gone wrong in his life. He insults her roundly,
and admits what actually happened in the shed:

> . . . ella estaba entrando al galpón. ella me quería, ella estaba decidida
> esa noche, y yo la iba a preñar i bien preñada! i ése era mi plan! ya después
> los padres no iban a poder decir nada. Pero ese día la asustaste, se
> arrepintió ¿no te das cuenta de eso? y la hiciste sentir como una puta, ese
> día que por fin me iba a dar lo que tenía, guardado para mí, *y después ya
> nunca más la pude convencer* . . .(pp.196 – 97, my italics).

> . . . she was going into the shed, she loved me, she was ready that night,
> and I was going to make her pregnant, well and truly pregnant! That was
> what I was going to do! Then after that her parents wouldn't have been
> able to say a word. But you frightened her off that day and she changed
> her mind. Do you realize that? And you made her feel like a whore, that
> day when at long last she was going to give me what she had been keeping
> for me, *and afterwards I was never able to persuade her again* . . .

A little later Maria de Gloria told him that her mother had forbidden
her to see him again. His mother admits that she interfered (p.181), and
he now wishes that she would die (p.198).

If this is indeed the truth, then several otherwise inexplicable
elements slot into place. For instance, if Josemar really had been the
uninvolved Don Juan that he claims, it would be difficult to reconcile
this with his romantic, even sentimental, vision of how marriage would
be, with the fact that he once told Maria da Gloria that they would sleep
apart at first, so that she would come in search of him, desperate with
longing (p.168), and that he would bring home little presents for her
and their baby (p.169). Josemar's macho boastfulness is part of what
Elías Miguel Muñoz has referred to as 'el discurso del poder masculino'
('the discourse of masculine power').[13] But it may not represent the
situation as it really was. We also learn that now, after this long period
of deranged dedication to Josemar's memory, Maria da Gloria has
turned down the offer of a teaching job and is going to be married
(p.185). It is unlikely that this could happen, bearing in mind the
rigidly conventional views of her family, if she really had been
dishonoured by a *chacarero* all those years earlier. Everybody knows that
women's lives are doomed when they commit the sin of indulging in
pre-marital sex (p.191); Josemar's mother says this in the course of
talking about Olga, a middle-class girl who is now grateful that she
failed to seduce Josemar when they were young, because she was able to

go on to make a good marriage. It is as much a question of social honour, the famous ¿qué dirán?, as of finding oneself abandoned and destitute with illegitimate children to bring up, which is the situation of so many poor girls. Would Matías, Maria da Gloria's future husband, have asked for her hand, as the text puts it, if she was no longer a virgin? There was no *sangre* at the time of Maria da Gloria's deflowering by Josemar because it never actually took place. What he now sees as his love for her was certainly requited (*amor correspondido*), but any bleeding was — and still is, in the case of Josemar — metaphorical.

Blood has another vital connotation, that of caste, and this is the area that must be investigated in order to clarify the picture. Officially, Josemar is the third son of a poor *chacarero*, Astolfo,[14] for whom he feels absolutely no affection, a fact underlined by Maria da Gloria's voice: 'El que es incapaz de querer al padre es incapaz de querer a nadie' ('Anyone incapable of feeling love for his father is incapable of loving anybody') (p.32). There was always unremitting conflict between father and son, so much so that the reader soon begins to harbour suspicions on the subject of Josemar's true paternity. Although the father-son relationship is never without difficulties and ambiguity in Puig novels, here more evidence is soon presented that reveals the motive for the excessive hostility between Josemar and Astolfo.

When Josemar slaughters a cow belonging to his father, 'el padre empezó a mirarlo peor que antes todavía, de sólo ver al hijo ya se enervaba todo. La vida pasó a ser una guerra continua entre ellos dos' ('his father started to look on him with even more aversion than he had before; he had only to see his son to become completely overwrought. Life began to be a continuous battle between the two of them') (p.33). He suggests that since Josemar is now old enough to look after himself, he leave home, but the boy refers the question to his mother. Her reply reveals everything: 'Nadie se va de acá,' she says, '*mi hijo es tan hijo mío como de él,* y se va a quedar acá como los demás hijos' ('Nobody is going from here, *he's as much my son as his,* and he's going to stay here like the others') (p.33, my italics). Later, Josemar himself reveals that there are those who have doubts as to the identity of his true father: 'porque él es más blanco dicen que no es hijo del padre verdadero' ('since he is whiter, they say that isn't really his father's son') (p.52). We learn, too, that Astolfo always slept well, 'aunque pensaba que le tercer hijo no era hijo de él' ('although he thought the third son was not his'), always treating him as if he were adopted (p.73). Astolfo never came out with accusations, but he did make the odd joke on the subject, and the boy's

paternal grandmother once said categorically that he was really the son
of Astolfo's employer (p.74). At the time that these revelations are
made, Josemar's adulation of his mother is still so intense that he flatly
refuses to believe anything against her: 'su madre era una persona muy
honesta, correctísima' ('his mother was a very respectable person,
always impeccably behaved') (p.74). In any case, he adds, he is not
actually all that different from the rest of the family, even if his hair is
light brown and wavy and his skin fair. If he is right, and there is less of a
contrast between them than the neighbours claim, this may well be
because his maternal great-grandmother was an Indian (p.75): there is
no doubt that he is his mother's child, at least. If Josemar is not Astolfo's
son, then the occasion on which Astolfo tries to kill his wife, Carminha,
simply because she has taken her son's part against him, is less difficult
to understand. Otherwise, as Maria da Gloria implies, it seems
incredible: just because she defended you? she asks, just for that (p.36)?
It is easier, too, to realize why, when Josemar and his parents moved
away from the countryside, his father soon abandoned them and went
back again (p.97): he was never at ease alone with them. And Josemar's
view that fathers who abandon their sons cannot really call themselves
fathers (p.161) now makes sense on several levels. Not only does it
reveal pangs of conscience because he himself has never done anything
for his own children, and resentment because Astolfo left him and his
mother, but there is also an underlying bitterness because his true
father, whom he closely resembles, has never recognized him. After all,
fathers and sons should live as friends (p.170), and all fathers should
leave the book of life open for their sons (p.171). 'Un hijo siempre
quiere al padre,' his mother says, 'es la ley de la sangre' ('A son always
loves his father; blood will out') (p.176). But which father is he
supposed to love? The one whose blood runs in his veins but who has
ignored his existence since the *habladurías* (gossip, pp.24, 190) of so
many years earlier, or the man who has brought him up? If all these
hints are not enough to convince us, we can turn to the author himself.
In an interview with Milagros Sánchez Arnosi, he states that Josemar's
real father 'es un terrateniente' ('is a landowner').[15] Maria da Gloria
seems to know all about this (though we must always remember that he
himself creates the script of the dialogue). Your father (that is, Astolfo),
didn't love you, she says, because you were different from the others.
'And I know why you were different' (pp.30–31). But every time the
subject crops up, Josemar makes an effort to avoid it. When Maria da
Gloria begins a sentence with 'Pero decían que . . .' ('But people used

to say that . . .') (p.35), or something of the sort, he switches off, and
concentrates on the present: should he go out and buy a packet of
cigarettes? Has he enough to last him the evening? The dialogue is full
of evasive *non sequiturs;* if there were continuity, unacceptable facts
would immediately come to light instead of lying repressed at the back
of Josemar's mind.

One of the most interesting features of *Sangre de amor correspondido* is
also the one that has attracted the most criticism. This is the often
incorrect colloquial speech of the narrator, which Puig's 'técnica
transcriptora' ('transcribing technique'), to use Luis Suñén's phrase,[16]
reproduces. It is a mixture of popular language and what has been
picked up from rhetorical school textbooks. (This, incidentally, is not
the first time that this excessive, purple style is used by a Puig
protagonist. We remember that Gladys, in *The Buenos Aires Affair,* is
prey to it when her subconscious comes to the surface under the
influence of drugs.) There is a parellel between critical objections to the
style of this novel and the reactions of some 'serious' readers to the mass
media elements utilized in its predecessors. It is all a question of
hierarchy, and linguistic inelegance is judged reprehensible and to be
avoided at all costs, as are the superficial values, sentimentality and
stereotypes of popular fiction. The author, of course, is aware of this
problem and has commented on it: 'este tipo de lenguaje,' he has said,
'[es] un código de signos como cualquier otro', and he then added that
'lo que gusta de una prosa culta no es el hecho de que sea
gramaticalmente correcta, sino que tenga valores musicales y
expresividad de todo tipo' ('this kind of language is as much a sign
system as any other. What is attractive in cultured prose is not the fact
that it is grammatically correct, but that it contains all-round musicality
and expressivity').[17] However, not only does he reject the idea that
popular speech is unacceptable, but he sees its use as a positive factor.
'Inspirei-me em sua linguagem' ('I was inspired by his way of
speaking'), he said, referring to the stonemason whose story he is
repeating,[18] and indeed, the work has been called an 'exaltación del
lenguaje' ('a celebration of language').[19] It is not the reproduction of
vulgarity that Puig is seeking here, as Joaquín Marco would have it,[20]
but of reality and truth.

Reality — a difficult enough term to define — is subjective, and in
this novel it is ultimately a tolerable amalgam of what was and what
ought to have been. In other words, the narrator creates a version of it
for himself, his only means of survival, from everyday circumstances

and conditions that he has lived through, together with events that he would like to have lived through. These contribute to what he now is. One aspect of his past is the language that he now uses, and it would be absurd were he to express himself in locutions foreign to his background. So it is that he is clumsy, repetitive, coarse, and at the same time sentimental and vulgar (after all, he adores the *samboleros* of the Brazilian singer, Roberto Carlos, pp.9, 100) in everything he says. This may be tedious for some, but it is undeniably realistic. And the sentimentality, like the values of the novelette that so greatly influenced the characters in Puig's second novel, *Boquitas pintadas,* does not permeate the story itself. At the end, we are left with a sense of bitter frustration towards life, and our only slight comfort lies in the misguided perseverance and ill-founded optimism displayed by the narrator.

Popular language is, of course, always ungrammatical, repetitive, incoherent, and plagued by linguistic tics. What is important for the novel in question is what constitutes these characteristics, what makes up the 'sign system'. Grammatical mistakes may seem to be unworthy of comment: Josemar is an uneducated *chacarero* (even if he has been to school), and is unlikely to speak well. It is also worth bearing in mind that spoken language is always, and for obvious reasons, very different from written language, full of *lapsi linguae* in even the most cultured speaker. Yet his mistakes and his inability to express himself take on extra significance if we consider that they serve to emphasize the social gulf between the hero and Maria da Gloria. She is a girl who has never known hunger (p.67), and she lives in one of the prettiest houses in Cocotá (p.93). Conversely, he has often been hungry, went barefoot until the age of twelve (p.161), and has Indian blood: Maria da Gloria does not hesitate to point out that he is a descendant of savages who use bows and arrows (p.75). His background is impossible to live down: *chacareros* are the laughing-stock of the townspeople (p.85), they are afraid when they go into town (p.86), and they are easily recognizable as their hair is always full of dust (p.86). Josemar does try to cover up his poor origins, even to himself, when he denies that his mother ever went out to work. (Later he admits that she took in washing and became a servant, 'y a mucha honra' ('to her great credit') (p.67). She, however, knows her place and declines an invitation to visit Maria da Gloria after Josemar has left (p.180).) Furthermore, while the courtship is going on, he always washes his hair before going into Cocotá so that no one will suspect that he comes from the *chacras* (p.164). It is all to no avail, though, since apart from any other consideration, poor farm-labourers speak badly, as he himself says:

> Los del campo hablan diferente, hablan mal, cuando tienen a una persona delante no le dicen las palabras que deben . . . (p.85)

> Country people speak different, they speak badly, when they are with somebody they don't use the right words . . .

Since to a large extent this is what Jorge Campos has called a 'novela de la pobreza' ('novel of poverty'), then it is impossible to disregard Puig's own statement, quoted by Campos, that the protagonist 'no tiene otro medio de expresión que su propio decir' ('has no means of expressing himself other than through what he says').[21] And the way that he says it is bound to be clumsy and ungrammatical.

The repetitive nature of Josemar's discourse also takes a significant form. There are two aspects of it: one is that he uses the same phrases over and over again; the other, that he tells the same story more than once. The constant use of the same locutions, many of which could be described as verbal tics, is not only based on the paucity of his vocabulary and his incapacity to verbalize his memories fluently, but is also the result of his underlying motivation for verbalizing everything in the first place. The same motivation lies behind the limited nature of the content of the text, the rehearsal of the same 'facts'. If the narrator is employing words as a means of survival, then, given the lack of success in his life, he has to rewrite — or, more accurately, recreate — history. His cheerfulness is the result of invention, rather than of the recollection of what is objectively true. Thus many of the interpolated phrases are to do with truth and (though the word is not ideal) lies. Of course, expressions such as '¿no es verdad?' ('isn't that so?') come naturally and frequently to every speaker and are employed unthinkingly in all languages. It is their excessive use that is both taxing and revealing. Josemar's interlocutors, the voices he creates, whether they be his foster-brother, Lourdes ('the mother of his children') or Maria da Gloria, challenge him and have to be persuaded. He needs their approval in order to believe what he is saying. So it is that the word 'verdad' is used *ad nauseam* against the counterpoint provided by these voices, and at the same time the confident narrative is punctuated by expressions such as '¿está claro?' ('you see?'). The interlocutors vary in their willingness to be convinced. He sees Maria da Gloria as enough of a submissive woman to go on 'listening', even if she is unconvinced where anecdotal detail is concerned and keeps asking him to tell the truth: 'Te pido que jures decirme la verdad,' she says ('I beg you to swear to tell me the truth') (p.117). Josemar's black foster-brother is another whose position (in this case his social inferiority) is such that his version of events can be largely disregarded by the narrator. The real challenge comes from Lourdes, who has washed her hands of Josemar many years earlier. A woman of character and independence, she has no reason for ingratiating herself with him, and in an ironic phrase, accuses him of not being a man of his word. She goes on to say what might well be taken as the key to this novel: 'que él nunca le había hecho frente a la verdad de las cosas de la vida', adding, '¿qué clase de hombre le tiene miedo a la verdad?' ('that he had never faced up to the true nature of life. What sort of man would be afraid of the truth?') (p.117). This accusation worries him, especially as it impugns his manhood, his macho image, but he has to ignore it, together with all the other accusations of mendacity. Later, when he is about to recount an implausible story to his foster-brother, he displays a characteristic approach: 'si no lo cree', he says, 'que se vaya a la mierda' ('if he doesn't believe it, he can go to hell') (p.143).

There are many swear words and obscenities in Josemar's discourse, and again their frequency has a profounder cause than his linguistic conditioning. The image he is creating for himself reflects his need for a sense of self-respect that it has been impossible to achieve in any other way. The illusion of power is created by words that signify aggression (especially sexual aggression, since virtually all the swear words are sexually based) and strength. He uses signifiers for violence and independence even more than one would expect from a man of his background precisely because he is actually neither violent nor independent. Furthermore, it is possible to see his inability to name things directly when he is boasting about his sexual conquests as a reflection of those social taboos that he claims to scorn and which reveal fear of sin and its consequent punishment.[22] There is internal conflict in Josemar, deriving from what Otto Rank has seen as 'the duality of actor and self-observer' in man,[23] and this is manifest in the incompatibility between his inner reality and that of his milieu. He obviously belongs to the second of Rank's three categories: the first is made up of those that accept reality, are dependent on it, and are 'duty-conscious'; then there are those who, like Josemar, defend themselves against the compulsion of reality, the 'guilt-conscious'; the third category is made up of those who accept themselves, creating for themselves against the compulsion 'a reality of [their] own which makes [them] independent, but at the same time enables [them] to live in reality without feeling in conflict with it'. These are 'self-conscious', or 'creative', individuals. The second group, according to Rank, are neurotic, and for them therapy must consist of obliging them to affirm, rather than deny, their will. This is not the first time that there are elements in Puig's novels that make us suspect that the will psychology of Otto Rank is an appropriate framework for understanding the characters, in spite of the many explicit and implicit references to Freud. Rank's theories suggest that the individual's reaction to outer reality is creation, not adaptation (as Freud maintained), since his emotional life is uncontrollable and insatiable. 'To be able to live one needs illusions', says Rank, 'the necessary dream' of all Puig's protagonists. People strive for personal enrichment not only biologically, at the cost of the species, but — more relevantly — 'ethically at the expense of the fellow man', and in spite of the importance of explicit allusions to the role of parents by Puig, we can perhaps accept that 'ethical judgements are something more than introjected parental authority'. Josemar, like everyone else, wants what he cannot have; in this case, the reasons for his failure include one very obvious social factor — his poverty. Nevertheless, he does win through, in a way: surviving, though totally alone. If the content of willing arises primarily from rejection, then this is a clearcut case of its being exercized by a rejected individual. He creates a new reality, finds a partial cure for his neurosis through discourse, and combines what was with what ought to have been by means of his will. This is not to say that he is no longer neurotic at the end, especially if we accept the Freudian judgement that the separation of sensuality and tenderness is a characteristic of neurosis. In spite of all the facts that have come to light, the Epilogue is just his original version of his seduction of Maria da Gloria. He has managed to pass, though, from Rank's second category to his third: he is now a creative type who 'affirms [his fantasies] for himself and reveals them to the world'; 'He creates a whole world in his own image, and then needs the whole world to say "yes" to his creation'. The problem throughout the novel has been that 'the whole world', in the form of the interrogative voices, has refused to approve it and has denied its truth, but the Epilogue proves the power of the narrator's will against theirs. The striking irony in this particular case is derived from the paradox that in winning through, what Josemar achieves is the ability to believe that he belongs to the *first* category. 'Will', says Rank, 'as the constant driving force strives . . . to prolong its pleasurably perceived affirmation through consciousness, to make the feeling of happiness lasting, that is redeeming'. It is all subjective, as we have pointed out before: 'exactly what we pretend consciously to be the truth, that it actually is psychically'.[24] So Josemar swears in order to boast and lie, and he survives.

The incoherence of the text is also explicable on this level. Whenever the invented 'truth' looks as if it is going to be undermined, even denied, by the unpalatable facts of outer reality, a simple solution is to go off at a tangent and concentrate on something else. As one psychologist has put it, with totally unrealistic fantasies the individual feels 'chronically frustrated and chronically invisible' — a point we shall return to — 'in human relationships, because the feedback he receives is not compatible with his pretensions'.[25] This is what Josemar has to fight against. He cannot avoid disturbing information being imparted to him if he does not change the subject. If we bear this in mind, we are less surprised that someone who is so obviously obsessed by the memory of one particular woman, who wants her to love him still, should refuse to talk about her, returning to the eternal subject of the whereabouts of his cigarettes whenever her name crops up. The normal incoherence of spoken dialogue, especially that of popular speech, is exacerbated by the hero's need to go on creating.

One other aspect of the language that cannot fail to attract the reader's attention, and which could prove a negative distraction for some, is that Josemar always refers to himself in the third person. Muñoz points out, incontrovertibly, that this means that the discourse achieves a certain objectivity.[26] We are back with Rank's idea of the actor and the self-observer, of human duality; furthermore, this objectivity is essential in the creative process that the hero is putting into function. But there is another aspect of this device that may well aid our understanding, and that is that it is typical of small children. The fictional individuation process is a reduced, temporally speaking, version of the maturation of the human being. That its results are far from ideal is neither here nor there. As is always true of Puig characters, the individual achieves what he or she can with the available materials. Life is a dream because other people are in control of it, and it has to be turned into another kind of dream to be lived. Josemar, though reprehensible in so very many ways, is not judged too harshly by his creator. Calderón's lines in *La vida es sueño (Life's a Dream)* apply to him as much as to life's more obvious victims: 'pues el delito mayor / del hombre es haber nacido' ('man's greatest crime is being born').

However charitably Puig, and his readers, may view Josemar, it has to be admitted that his behaviour has never been exemplary, and it has always been based on his acceptance of the macho values imposed by the society he grew up in. Machismo is common currency in all the Puig novels, but here it is inextricably linked to the hero's social position. He compensates for his inferiority with the illusion of power that brute force and what he sees as manliness provide, even if at times he is fundamentally aware that there is more to an *hombre derecho* (an upright man, a real man) than that. The aim of those who feel that they are despised by others is invariably to have someone below them in the hierarchy. Josemar is, in a way, lucky: he can judge himself superior to black people, to Indians, and to real *chacareros* (since his true father has money and a certain breeding) and, like everyone else in his position, he can use and exploit women. He is aware, for example, that Astolfo has mistresses (p.34), and although it is he who causes trouble between his parents by telling Carminha about these clandestine affairs (p.35), he does this in order to spite Astolfo and make an ally of his mother. He certainly does not disapprove of this kind of behaviour; married men always have several women, he says (p.80), and he himself emulates the models that he sees around him. Needless to say, he does not see himself as married, since he has not committed himself legally. But he has committed himself physically to one woman, by fathering two children, and verbally to several, swearing that he loves them ('él era hombre y tenía que seguir contándole mentiras a la Azucena, diciéndole que la quería': 'he was a man and had to go on telling lies to Azucena, saying that he loved her' (p.93)). Maria de Gloria is the special woman who stands out from all the rest in that he did actually seduce them. If he does have any pangs of conscience on the subject of his promiscuity, he consoles himself by deciding to believe that women do not object and that they are all friends together (pp.104, 107). As far as he is concerned, women are grateful for what they can get, and the mother of his children still lives in hope that he will return to her (p.106). It may even be true that he *is* married: his mother tells Maria da Gloria that he is, but that he is separated (p.179). In any case, responsibility plays no part in his attitude towards the opposite sex.

The famous double standard is always in evidence, and it is accepted by the women too. They know that they should be chaste — 'una mujer no debe andar . . . regalándose' ('a woman should not go around giving herself to everyone'), says Josemar's mother (p.177). It is probably true to say that this willingness to accept an inferior, submissive and unjust position *vis-à-vis* men is based on women's age-old guilt feelings inculcated by patriarchal societies and, according to many feminists, legitimated by the institution of the family.[27] Elías Miguel Muñoz[28] sees this novel as a denunciation of the Jewish-Christian socio-religious principles that have perpetuated this situation in the western world. Woman is treacherous and, rightly, full of shame, and Muñoz refers to Kate Millett's analysis of female guilt based on the loss of Eden,[29] going on to provide incontrovertible evidence of Biblical and religious references that the author indulges in. (Even the illustration on the cover of the book is a reproduction of a painting of Adam and Eve by Tamara de Lempicka.) The story itself is clearly one of paradise lost; each of the two parts of the novel is made up of six chapters, or days of creation, and there is an epilogue that corresponds to the seventh day, when God rested. Then there are countless Biblical images: the serpent, the tree, water, etc., and even the place names seem to be consciously chosen: Josemar now lives in Santísimo, for example. For Muñoz, 'el texto [recrea] los mitos bíblicos para mostrar sus mecanismos y técnicas represivas' ('the text recreates Biblical myths in order to highlight their mechanisms and their repressive techniques'), and it not only exposes the injustices of the social system but also denounces the concept of an ideal, benevolent father-figure. We might add that this is another example of the homogeneous nature of the whole *œuvre* of Manuel Puig. We have only to look back to *La traición de Rita Hayworth* and *Maldición eterna a quien lea estas páginas* to find explicit examples of uncomprehending criticism of the divine Father, while all the other novels query the function of earthly fathers and point a finger at their manifest and far-reaching defects. That so many of the books are based on the absence of the father reflects back to the theme of the demiurge who abandons his creation and his creatures. And the creator is, of course, always seen as male (as indeed are the Devil, and Christ the bridegroom).[30] Woman must therefore work and accept and in order to be redeemed, bear children: St. Paul, in I Timothy 2, xiv – xv, says this only too clearly: 'the woman being deceived was in the transgression. Notwithstanding she will be saved in childbearing'. And since Catholic belief has it that the Virgin never knew sexual relations,[31] she cannot hope to approach this image of an ideal woman if she expresses and uses her sexuality for its own sake and for pleasure.

Josemar's problem is that he finds himself between two stools. Of course he accepts the macho principles of his society: this is only too evident in the fact that the ultimate version of his past life is the one in which he embodies them completely. But he does not really fit in, and he is another Puig character who demonstrates that where machismo reigns, men are not happy either. He wants to see himself as powerful and he is not. While in no way dissenting from Muñoz's interpretation of the novel — indeed, many of the religious allusions are very knowingly elaborated[32] — it seems to me that Josemar's duality is the sign of a condition even more universal than Muñoz claims. If we judge it in the way that I suggest we should, we will also find that there is even more connection between *Sangre de amor correspondido* and its predecessors than has so far seemed to be the case. Let us first consider the nature of the hero's internal conflict in more detail.

There is little need to draw attention to all the macho vocabulary related to his sexual prowess: it stands to reason that he will talk of lovemaking as 'hacer sus cosas' (like the current English expression 'to do your own thing', this euphemism has narcissistic connotations, implying inborn individual rights). It is no surprise either that the sex act is referred to in terms of aggression, even using military metaphors, that he calls the phallus a *garrote* (club, cudgel) or a *sable* (sabre), or that he talks on more than one occasion of the physical pain he has caused and the blood that has been shed as he deflowers his victims. (Even when it is not a question of a young virgin, he is so violent that he is accused of venting his anger in the sex act (p.92)).[33] It is not only the way that he treats his partners that is emphasized, but also his exceptional virility. He is highly-sexed, needs frequent relief, was sexually active at a very early age, is a man of few words on these occasions, and never flags: even when he is weak with hunger, he claims, it makes no difference to his performance (p.136). He has even had sex with a cow, not because he was uncontrollably aroused, but — significantly — in order to hurt and punish the animal (p.34); in fact, this is the cow that he later kills (p.33) and which is clearly associated with the mother-figure.

His masculinity is not in doubt in other areas either, it seems. He says little because ('as is well known') women talk more than men (p.21). He sees himself as courageous (p.44), fights with Astolfo to protect his mother (p.37), threatens to beat up Maria da Gloria's father (p.52), and defies the father and another lover of one of his mistresses, Azucena, during a bullfight, causing such an uproar that the event has to be cancelled (p.84). Like all ideal men he is an excellent athlete (p.50) and, since this is Brazil, his sport is football: boys ought to be footballers, he maintains, and they should never marry (pp.106, 108).

Needless to say, he himself is not just any footballer, but so much of a star that when he made his début with a new team in Baurú, his reputation had preceded him. People flocked to see him at the training sessions, and for the first match the makeshift stand was so crowded with his fans — more than 10,000 of them — all shouting his name, that it collapsed and many were injured (p.130). This marked the beginning of a new life for him: 'tres años de triunfo' ('three triumphant years') in Baurú (p.131).[34] Another characteristic of a 'real man', according to the rules of society, is that he should be hardworking, and Josemar cannot be faulted on this count: he has always been industrious (p.192). And neither can his attitude towards his parents, his children and his friends be judged anything other than that of an 'hombre fuera de serie' ('an exceptional man') as he often calls himself (e.g., p.142). His hatred of Astolfo is justified, he thinks, and he has spent all his money on medical treatment for Carminha (p.149). As for his friends, he enjoys the typical camaraderie and male pair-bonding that is traditionally acceptable: one of his later regrets is that (contradicting what he had said about Baurú) when he left Cocotá he was never again part of a team (p.17). Finally, there is the question of masculine independence and freedom. When he was young he asserted his individuality with trendy clothes and long hair (p.41), and the one item of clothing that he draws our attention to is his 'camisa Vuelta al Mundo' ('Round-the-World T-shirt') (p.12), which indicates his refusal to stay in one place. And this, of course, is what marriage would force him to do. To take Maria da Gloria's virginity would tie him down, he says (p.13), he does not need her (this is repeated, e.g. p.80), and he had to escape, since in Cocotá, 'le querían . . . echar el lazo al cuello' ('they wanted to tether him by the throat') (p.65).

There is no need to read between the lines to discover that this is largely fantasy. The text itself contradicts almost everything as it progresses. His callousness at the thought of shedding virgin blood is more than suspect when we find out that he is in fact almost unnaturally squeamish at the sight of blood. He hates it, he admits, it drives him mad and makes him feel sick. He cannot bring himself to eat rare meat; even talking about it upsets him (pp.62–63). As for his strong, silent image, his verbosity, especially compared with other people's contributions, belies this, as does his certainty that Maria da Gloria cannot have forgotten him because she hears his *words* in her head (p.24). That he is courageous is not always evident either: he has never really stood up to anybody, least of all to his mother. And his glorious

years in Baurú are pure invention. When the facts impinge on the
narrative, we discover that he lost his menial job there with the
electricity company, that the *pensión* where he was living was closed
down without warning, and that he then had so little money that he
could not even pay the bus fare to another town (p. 155). Little wonder
that in spite of his apparent capacity for total recall he cannot now
remember how many goals he scored during his phenomenally
successful début with the football team. It is equally hard to believe that
he has always worked hard; indeed, the real reason for the fact that
Maria da Gloria's family disapproved of him was not that he was poor,
but that he was idle, and never helped his father. All he did was show off
about his footballing talents and indulge in profligate behaviour
(p. 197). Later on, when his mother is ill in hospital, the house is left
dirty and untidy: clearly, as a macho Brazilian, it would be
inappropriate for him to do anything about this. Even if he has very
little free time, as he claims, we cannot help remarking that he does go
out in the evenings, and he spends all his money on beer (p. 199). When
he comes to terms with life towards the end of the narrative, one
consolation for him is his 'knowledge' that his mother now realizes that
he is *not* a *sinvergüenza* and an *aprovechador* (a good-for-nothing and a
parasite, (p. 199)). Clearly, he did not invent these derogatory terms.
His father, he feels, also knows now that he is 'un hombre trabajador y
honesto' ('a respectable, hardworking man') (p. 174), which seems to
be something new. His devotion to his mother could hardly be judged
manly either, for he is worried that she will go away and leave him alone
(p. 150). Not for nothing does her voice enjoin him to free himself from
her, after he has imagined that she has failed to recognize him: '¡Basta!
ia levantarse y trabajar!' it says, '¡que tanto mamá y mamá! ni que
fueras un niño recién nacido' ('That's enough! Get up and go to work!
All this mother this and mother that! Anyone would think you were a
newborn baby') (p. 42), Friends and companions are now non-existent,
and perhaps they always were. He cannot remember a boyhood friend
who died (p. 19), and it is years since he saw another *amigazo* (great pal)
who, in any case, was actually a friend of his parents (p. 27). He got on
well with his black foster-brother, admittedly, but only because he
could protect and patronize him, as their later encounter proves. Now
he has nobody: one of his clients treats him as if he is destitute (p. 79),
and he does not belong to a union so has no one to share and help with
his practical difficulties; he could not, he says, talk freely with his
assistant (pp. 132–33). He no longer plays football, justifying this by

pointing out that injury on the field would jeopardize his capacity to work (p.200). His independence and freedom, inextricably linked to his machismo, are also mythical. He wanted to be an electrician, but he is a builder (pp.13, 38). He left Cocotá because he had no decent clothes (p.124); now he admits that he has never been well-dressed (p.201), and his foster-brother fails to recognize him (or his true worth) because he is unshaven and dirty (p.134). He has never really travelled, as he had hoped to, and his thoughts are all based on the past, in Cocotá. His sexual triumphs were not what he pretends either. He *does* need Maria da Gloria, of course, or at least his memory of her, and he cannot forget that she once wound her long hair around his throat (pp.150, 172). Even his bombastic claims of untiring and indiscriminate sexual activity are diluted when his mother reveals that when Olga made sexual advances towards him, all those years ago, he rejected her (pp.189–90). The piece of information that causes the most suspicion on the part of the reader is that in Santísimo he has no sex life at all. He accounts for this by observing that he works too hard, and that his mother is ill (p.101). Josemar is not Don Juan who, as has so often been pointed out, was the man of the eternal present.[35]

We should also consider the symbolism and the images used by the author. The hero's name has significance other than that suggested by its religious origins, for Josemar is a combination of Joseph and Mary, male and female. The provides an important clue. It is not the first time that Puig has written about bisexuality, a subject on which he has also expressed himself in interviews. He is convinced that 'exclusive homosexuality and exclusive heterosexuality [are] cultural results, not . . . a natural outcome',[36] and it seems that in *Sangre de amor correspondido,* he is describing the results of basic bisexuality being in conflict with exclusive heterosexuality and the artificially-created norms of society. This is not to say that Josemar is homosexual, even if his foster-brother does cheerfully address him as *maricón* (queer, (p.133)). What Puig does highlight is the presence of feminine characteristics in the hero, and these are at odds with the way in which he feels he has to behave. The challenging voices shake his confidence in this image for a while, but he clings to it at the end. Maria da Gloria (Mary of Glory) is the virgin that he might have possessed (Lourdes is the virgin made flesh, and this was disastrous). Since she eluded him, he can console himself with the idea that he rejected paradise, not that it excluded him. Furthermore, he 'knows', in spite of all the evidence to the contrary, that it is still there, waiting for him. It is the spirit of the

Alfredo Le Pera tango that colours his attitude:

> Sentir . . .
> que veinte años no es nada,
> que febril la mirada
> errante en la sombra
> te busca y te nombra

> Feeling . . .
> that twenty years are nothing,
> and my feverish gaze
> roaming in the shadows
> searches for you and calls your name

and this is a repetition of Nené's situation in *Boquitas pintadas*. To have won Maria de Gloria he would have had to betray his virility. We know better: her parents spoke ill of him precisely because of his view of what constituted manliness, and his inability to challenge his mother's power is also an indication of his feminine (in the conventional sense that society brings to this word) weakness and dependence.

The point about the imagery used by the author is not just that much of it coincides with that found in the Bible, but that it is all natural, and indicates the concept of primitive, essential man. The tree and water of life were indeed lost in Eden, but so was the primordial symbiosis between humanity and nature. What followed was not just a socio-religious code, but alienating civilization. Cocotá, with its symbolic name, was full of trees (p.14); when he is in Santísimo, Josemar is aware that the trees there are quite different (p.147), and we cannot help recalling, too, that the *santísimo* is also the sacrament given to those who are dying. He looks back on the big tree outside Maria da Gloria's house, where they used to meet and from which he gained sexual potency (pp.26–27), with aversion: he cannot bear to think of that now (p.195). Before reaching this stage he remembers the tree that had meant most to him. It was strong and sweet-smelling and produced water from its roots (pp.36–37). But his mother told him that it might conceal cobras and that it was dangerous to embrace it (p.37). Water is constantly linked to lovemaking, and its masculine qualities are underlined when Josemar sees his departure from Cocotá as similar to the effect of fire on water (p.102). He was torn between two dangers: his essential nature and society. Both of these are unsatisfactory in themselves.

Nature has its own pitfalls. There are animals that sting and bite and kill. The beasts may have been friendly towards man in the prelapsarian world, but their treacherous hostility is not in any doubt since his fall from grace. There is no option but to exploit them or destroy them in order to defend oneself and to survive.[37] The most dangerous are the cobra and, because they have two sides to them based on their maternal instinct, cows: woman as a sexual partner and woman as mother, in other words. The cobra is the greater enemy of the two here. Sometimes it can be heard (p.64), but it cannot be seen (p.77). A cobra may be trapped by mistake (p.65), and once caught, it has no choice but to sting (p.64). It is possible to defend oneself against it (p.77), but it is eternal: one of Josemar's friends buried one, and when he uncovered it much later, it stung him to death (p.99). It is green in colour, as green as the leaves of a tree (p.77), and as green as the dress Maria da Gloria wears on the night that Josemar claims to have seduced her (p.12). (When he first saw her he was misled, as she was wearing an innocent combination of pink and white, (p.44).)

Clearly, then, the cobra represents the death-dealing power of female sexuality, the eternal serpent. When Josemar and his mother run away from Astolfo's violence, they sleep together under a mandarin tree, totally safe as cobras refuse to go near it (p.36). He is secure with his mother but, as the name of the tree suggests (mandarin is originally *mandarim* in Portuguese: one who gives orders), he is avoiding one form of submission by accepting another.

What is interesting and surprising is that the symbolism is not consistent, and many of the cobra's characteristics apply as much to the male as to the female. This is true in various forms of iconography too: for instance, in Kundalini Yoga, the tree of life is envisaged with an erect serpent climbing through its branches, and the connotations are not female.[38] Woman may be the indestructible serpent, but in this novel we are given details of its activities and qualities that correspond to the hero as well as to the female characters. Maria da Gloria is terrified, for example, when Josemar throws (harmless) snakes at her (p.21). Astolfo's setting fire to a cobra (p.66) can also be seen as much as a manifestation of his hostility to Josemar as of his disapproval and fear of women; this seems all the more likely if we bear in mind the fact that it is an action that parallels Josemar's setting fire to one of his father's agricultural machines. That the cobra's biological make-up is applicable to both sexes is not in doubt, and when Josemar points out that it stings with its tail and bites, this may well indicate masculinity (p.77): he himself talks about biting as a form of aggression on one occasion (p.80). Maria da Gloria is certainly a cobra: he 'hunts' her, he says (p.45), and the traps he prepares for snakes are not all that far removed from the trap he hoped she would fall into when he lured her into the shed.[39] Also, if a cobra cannot sting, it is obliged to consume its own venom, and this is what has happened to the girl, who has been poisoned by her own aroused but unfulfilled sexuality into a state of alienation from life. In fact, though, this is what has happened to *him,* and alienation is a major theme in the novel.

Puig's contention, it seems to me, is that Josemar's femininity and masculinity are at odds because of the distance civilization has put between modern man and his essential nature. This is represented by Edenic and post-lapsarian imagery, and the incompatibility of his two sides is exacerbated by his particular social circumstances. In Cocotá, natural functions were limited by the claustrophobic strength of a moral code, handed down via the family unit; but in addition to this there was also the dangerous, limiting nature of the maternal bond. Josemar remembers that the thing he hated most about his house was the *tranquera* (enclosing fence), while its plants constituted its most agreeable feature (p.201). He had to escape, but everywhere he goes he is haunted by failure and poverty. Society does not provide freedom, and a change of location makes no difference; it does not provide happiness either. If this is to be achieved, it will have to be in the exercise of the will, and Josemar goes back to the beginning in a process of self-preservation, choosing the lesser of two evils as a framework for his personality. The book, in fact, is a circular journey.

In the course of this, many explicit references to the hero's feminine characteristics come to light. Maria da Gloria is not the only one who loves flowers, for example (p.61), and Josemar claims that his erstwhile girl-friends used to bring him roses. One of them was Maria da Gloria, and he makes a point of remembering that she always chose pink for him, not red, the colour of blood (p.63). His garden, he used to say, needed flowers (p.165), and the image of the garden always represents femininity in symbology, suggesting as it does the fertility of nature. The image works both ways, as he makes Maria da Gloria imagine that he is going to bring her flowers (p.118). Then there is Josemar's passion for looking at the heavens: he uses the sky at night as a substitute for the beauties of vegetation and he teaches Maria da Gloria to enjoy this activity too (pp.60, 112). Like his zodiacal sign, Leo, he has two sides to him. He knows that lions are the most fearful animals in existence, but he also knows that they can be tamed; indeed, they are easier to tame than man, even if they are still treacherous. He himself, he says, is a 'león calmo' ('tranquil lion') (p.161). This does not coincide with his self-image at the beginning and the end of the book; like primitive man, he is part of nature and often at odds with it, but he is also part of civilization and at odds with that.

One fairly obvious objection can be anticipated here, and that is that all men are in more or less the same position, but that by no means all of them suffer in this way. The answer is one that can be formulated only if the true paternity of the hero is taken into consideration. The point is that Josemar has great expectations. His real father's social class gives him an inborn right to move up in society. And his continuing bachelorhood and freedom from responsibility towards the child he has fathered make his son realize that this happy state is a possibility. The author himself has said that the reason why Josemar picks on Maria da Gloria as the object of his affections in the first place is because she is the symbol of the class he is attracted to,[40] and there is no escaping his concern for status. The heaven/earth connection is also present in his wish for advancement, personal benefit and the rights of inheritance, and echoes what Puig has said in other novels. On a religious level, the heavenly 'real' Father is absent; on a day-to-day level, the natural father is also absent from his son's life. Like Larry, in *Maldición eterna a quien lea estas páginas,* who indulged in fantasies about replacing Christ, Josemar is thwarted of his inheritance and, also like Larry, his heart is dried up (p.35). In this case there is a further link which could be seen as almost allegorical, and that is that Josemar's official father, Astolfo, finds himself in the same circumstances as Joseph. The connection is not all that tenuous, for we recall that the Book of James, or *Protoevangelium,* an apocryphal work widely enough known to have been commented on by Origen, claims that Joseph had children by a previous marriage.[41] Astolfo is only too human, as his name suggests, with its connotations of a great horn. Although Josemar points out that he is not God (p.59), he may well see himself as the child of God, and the combined nature of his name supports this argument.

As with all his other failures in life, his social inferiority has to be denied and forgotten, and the only way to do this is to compensate with positive signs of superiority, even in the worst moments. Thus Josemar pretends, from time to time, that he has once been well off; his machismo is part of this process, and when even this appears to be inefficacious, he has recourse to the vaguest of self-consolatory thoughts that cannot be proved or disproved. The rich boys in Cocotá used to envy him, he says (p.101), and if that seems implausible, he hears his mother's voice telling him that he has qualities that make up for his not having money: 'es como si fuera rico', ('it's as if he were rich') (p.203).

All this is based on his need to be somebody, but it has to be pointed out that it is a question of basic identity, not just of social standing. This too has been a frequent theme in the other novels, and the acquisition of identity is invariably the result of seeing, and recognizing oneself, by means of other people or, more often than not, one other person. When he was young, people recognized Josemar, even if their recognition took the form of disapproval: that Azucena's father hated him (p.81) at least confirmed his existence. Now, in spite of his trying to convince himself that he is still alive because everyone remembers — and therefore sees — him (p.100), he is beginning to lose his sense of selfhood, and his theory that people forget what they have not seen clearly (p.53) points not only to the awareness that he has been misjudged because his true worth was never recognized, but also to the desolate suspicion that he has been forgotten, and is therefore invisible. Even his mother, he thinks, does not know who he is (pp.39, 42) and this, exacerbated by her actually abandoning him, lies behind his discourse. After all, as Maria da Gloria asks, why does he suddenly start thinking about her again, after so many years during which he hardly gave her a thought (p.28)? He has to find a substitute object for his Oedipal fixation, and he can do this only by resuscitating memories of the past, coloured by his life-saving macho image of himself, which includes the belief that Maria da Gloria remembers him and 'sees' him at all times. This is essential if he cannot now see himself. The text is punctuated by references to mirrors and by his realization that he does not know what he looks like. Sometimes these references are apparently entirely practical, as when he wonders if he needs to shave (p.126), but at other times he admits that he cannot recall his own features (pp.121, 204). When he was young he had had no need of a mirror as he had been able to see himself in Maria da Gloria's shining hair (p.172).

There are, in fact, clear signs of alienation in the state that Josemar finds himself in before he makes the unconscious decision to begin again what Muñoz designates 'the invention syndrome';[42] in other words, the Epilogue of the book. The depersonalization indicated by his inability to see himself as an individual is one of them. But there are others, and it is not unreasonable to conclude that it is Josemar whose mind has been affected by past events, not Maria da Gloria,[43] and this has come about because there is ultimately no other single person that reflects and complements him. She, after all, is now better and has someone who loves her. One of his symptoms is the inconsistency of his memory. It is he, not Maria da Gloria, who has no clear idea of what actually happened between them, and his fantasizing is, as we have seen, therapeutic. He claims, in keeping with the ideology of *machista* societies, that once a woman's sexuality is aroused, she is lost for ever and becomes obsessed by her first lover (p.54), but Maria da Gloria is still a virgin, and it is he who is now obsessive, though he cannot remember her features (p.66) or something vitally important that he once said to her (p.170). It is the *idea* of her memory that haunts him. Then there is the fact that he hears voices in his head. This may not seem all that significant at first, since it is clearly a technical device on the part of the author. But why should the author pick on this particular device? It is invariably associated with mental abnormality, and the phenomenon of talking to oneself is often linked with insanity. In any case, the word 'madness' is used on many occasions — too many, one might think, if it were not meant to be noticed. Josemar suspects his alienated state himself, and justifies it by saying that people can go insane from lack of money (p.193).

If we ask ourselves who is to blame for this unhappy situation, we are obliged to come to the conclusion that there is no easy answer, and we remember that this was our reaction to the previous novels too. Let us consider the basic story (for in spite of everything, the text *is* ultimately reducible to a linear narrative). We are presented with a small-town womanizer (in the tradition of Héctor, from *La traición de Rita Hayworth,* and Juan Carlos, from *Boquitas pintadas*) who suffers from a mother-fixation, failing to make the transition from his Oedipal condition to a permanent affective relationship with the girl he has chosen because of the active intervention of his mother, whose power he is unable to defy. Put like that, there is little to distinguish this narrative, but we must remember that the proposed relationship was one based on a sense of social rank which was unjustified in practice because of a lack of responsibility on the part of the true father, and which was bound to lead to disaster. When the narrator eventually becomes aware, as he must do, of the inefficacy of his relationship with his mother, he discovers that he is without identity and he can survive only by dreaming that the girl he once knew, but never seduced, still remembers him, recognizes him and loves him. Like Nené, in *Boquitas pintadas,* he dedicates himself to thoughts of a past that never existed, precisely because in that epoch there was still hope for future fulfilment.

What is the alternative? Like Nené, he can give up and die, with the knowledge of what reality consists of. Like Astolfo, he can sink into despair: he has already had moments of hopelessness, just gazing at the wall (p. 182). Or he can be 'wrong', as the Schiller epigraph puts it, and go on living. This is what, subconsciously, he chooses to do. Muñoz sees this as giving up, in fact: Josemar is not a fighter, like Valentín, in *El beso de la mujer araña* or Ana, in *Pubis angelical,* he maintains. They are able to change their approach to life and, in particular, their sexual orientation.[44] This is undeniably true. Josemar merely goes back to the beginning. But I would claim that 'the necessary dream' *is* a form of fighting back for those who, either temperamentally or because of their social impotence, are unable to contribute towards changes in society. For them, like the female characters in Puig's first two novels, this is all they have and life would be intolerable without it. As the author himself has said when talking about the seductive charm of the cinema, 'el despertar no era placentero; el sueño sí, el despertar no' ('waking up was not pleasant; the dream was, but waking up was not').[45] Like Josemar, we are back where we started in Puig's novelistic trajectory, and the question of blame is still one that cannot be answered. As before, what the author hopes to do here is oblige us to ask the right questions. If a clear-cut answer is provided by any author, then the possibility of understanding and advancement is removed.

Notes

Notes to Chapter I

[1] *La traición de Rita Hayworth* (Buenos Aires, Jorge Álvarez, 1968). The 'complete' edition is: Barcelona, Seix Barral, 1976. All quotations will be taken from the 1981 edition.

[2] *Boquitas pintadas* (Buenos Aires, Editorial Sudamericana, 1969). *The Buenos Aires Affair* (Mexico City, Joaquín Mortiz, 1973). *El beso de la mujer araña* (Barcelona, Seix Barral, 1976). *Pubis angelical* (Barcelona, Seix Barral, 1979). *Maldición eterna a quien lea estas páginas* (Barcelona, Seix Barral, 1980). 'No soy un *best seller* impresionante en ninguna parte' ('I'm not much of a best seller anywhere'), says Puig himself, especially as the profitable Argentine market was closed to him for a long time, but the facts speak for themselves. See Jorgelina Corbatta, 'Encuentros con Manuel Puig', *Revista Iberoamericana*, 123 – 24 (April – September 1983), 591 – 621.

[3] The author also considered *Una noche de amor correspondido (One Night of Requited Love)* for the title. The 'original' is the Portuguese version, which was the result of the transcription and adaptation of tapes made by the novel's real-life protagonist. *Sangue de Amor Correspondido* (Rio de Janeiro, Editora Nova Fronteira, 1982); *Sangre de amor correspondido* (Barcelona, Seix Barral, 1982).

[4] To date the novels have been translated into about thirty languages, including Japanese and Hebrew.

[5] Between July 1980 and January 1981, more than 25,000 copies of *O Beijo da Mulher Aranha* were sold in Brazil (where Puig now lives) according to *IstoÉ* ('O Novo Romance do Carioca Manuel Puig', January 1981).

[6] For a recent account of Camp, see Mark Booth, *Camp* (London, Quartet Books, 1983). Also very relevant is the classic piece by Susan Sontag, 'Notes on "Camp"' in 'Against Interpretation' (1964), reprinted in *A Susan Sontag Reader* (Harmondsworth, Penguin Books Ltd., 1983), pp.105 – 19.

[7] Severo Sarduy, 'Notas a las notas a las notas . . . a propósito de Manuel

Puig', *Revista Iberoamericana,* 37 (July–December 1971), 555–67. In fact, Sarduy's claim is a debatable one, as we shall see later.

Notes to Chapter II

[1] Carlos Alberto Cornejo, 'Sin límites fuera de Chile', *Ercilla* (31 May 1967), p.62.

[2] *Panorama* (30 July 1968).

[3] Alfred J. MacAdam, 'Manuel Puig's Chronicles of Provincial Life', *Revista Hispánica Moderna,* XXXVI (1970–71) 50–65, p.61.

[4] Alfred J. MacAdam, *Modern Latin American Narratives. The Dreams of Reason* (The University of Chicago Press, 1977). The chapter dedicated to Puig is aptly entitled: 'Things as They Are'.

[5] Saúl Sosnowski, 'Manuel Puig. Entrevista', *Hispamérica* (May 1973), 69–80, p.69.

[6] In conversation with the author, July 1981.

[7] Teresa Cristina Rodríguez, 'Manuel Puig — O Rio é o verdadeiro paraíso terrestre, sonho de beleza e humanismo', *O Globo* (30 August 1981), p.8. My italics.

[8] Jean-Michel Fossey, *Galaxia latinoamericana* (Las Palmas de Gran Canaria, Inventarios Provisionales, 1973). The interview with Puig, part of which was originally published in the Uruguayan weekly *Marcha* (14 July 1972), is pp.137–52.

[9] *La traición de Rita Hayworth,* 1981 edition.

[10] *Modern Latin American Narratives,* p.93.

[11] Ricardo Piglia, 'Clase media: cuerpo y destino', in *Nueva Novela Latinoamericana,* II, compiled by Jorge Lafforgue (Buenos Aires, Paidós, 1972), pp.350–62. The quotations are found on pp.362 and 351.

[12] Fossey, *Galaxia,* p.143.

[13] *Modern Latin American Narratives,* p.92.

[14] Nevertheless, some critics have judged the position of Berto's letter as vital, seeing in this manifestation of the hitherto absent father an indication of Toto's first understanding of him.

[15] Emir Rodríguez Monegal, '*La traición de Rita Hayworth.* Una tarea de desmitificación', in *Narradores de esta América* II (Buenos Aires, Alfa Argentina, 1974), pp.365–80. This particular article is dated 1968. The quotation is found on p.379.

[16] Michael Wood, *America in the Movies* (London, Secker & Warburg), 1975.

[17] *America in the Movies,* pp.8, 9, 11 and 19.

[18] For example, Rodríguez Monegal, in 'Los sueños de Evita: a propósito de la última novela de Manuel Puig', in *Narradores de esta América,* II, pp.381–93, says: 'aunque Toto es el centro de la novela, no es el protagonista' ('although Toto is the centre of the novel, he is not the protagonist') (p.384). This article is dated 1973. Donald L. Shaw, in his *Nueva Narrativa Hispanoamericana* (Madrid, Cátedra, 1981), says something similar. According to him, the position of Toto in the centre of the group of characters 'da una vaga unidad a la novela' ('gives a vague unity to the novel') (p.198), and the implication is that this is all. But D.P. Gallagher, in a brief but perspicacious reference to

Puig in his *Modern Latin American Literature* (Oxford University Press, 1973), refers to 'Toto, the young hero of *La traición de Rita Hayworth*' (p.188).

[19] In *O Globo* (16 May 1982), p.3.

[20] Ricardo Piglia, 'Clase media', claims that 'si el tema de esa carta (escrita y destruida por Berto en 1933, que reaparece en 1948) es el destino pensado para Toto por su padre, el "tema" de la novela es la traición de ese proyecto' ('if the theme of that letter (the one that was written and destroyed by Berto in 1933, and which turns up again in 1948) is Toto's intended future as his father sees it, then the "theme" of the novel is the betrayal of these plans') (p.356). Piglia also refers to Mita as a 'traidora' (traitress) in her double-dealing between Toto's world and that of the adults. For Evelyne Minard, in '*La traición de Rita Hayworth:* Violence et mort dans l'Argentine de Manuel Puig', *Caravelle,* 39, pp.75–80, the betrayal of the hero in the film *Blood and Sand* symbolizes Toto's betrayed hope of ever becoming a man like his father. At what she designates a key point in the novel, after the only excursion Toto and Berto ever make together to the cinema (see n.24 below), their incompatability highlights the child's nascent homosexuality (p.78).

[21] Bruno Bettelheim, *The Uses of Enchantment. The Meaning and Importance of Fairy Tales* (London, Thames & Hudson, 1976).

[22] Sigmund Freud, *Zur Einführung des Narzissmus* (1914). Quoted by J. Laplanche and J.B. Pontalis, *Diccionario de Psicoanálisis* (Barcelona, Labor, 1971).

[23] See 'Ideal y yo', in Laplanche and Pontalis, *Diccionario,* pp.186–89.

[24] *Blood and Sand* certainly was to his liking, of course: 'ahora voy a venir siempre con ustedes al cine', he says to Mita and Toto ('from now on I'm going to go to the cinema with you always') (p.87). Toto is pleased because Berto had lost himself in the film. This is, perhaps, the only moment when Toto is not disillusioned with regard to his father. It is worth noting that the macho Héctor is also very much more blasé about the cinema than Toto and the female characters.

[25] *Enchantment,* p.151.

[26] Freud first used the term in an article that formed part of Otto Rank's *Der Mythus von der Geburt des Helden* (1909). In English: 'The Family Romance of the Neurotic', *The Standard Edition of the Complete Psychological Works* (London, The Hogarth Press, 1953), Vol. X. All references to Freud will be taken from this edition.

[27] 'Novela familiar' in *Diccionario,* p.269.

[28] *Enchantment,* p.69. It is interesting to recall that Puig has said that 'la clave de la novela está en la ausencia del padre' ('the key to this novel lies in the father's absence') (Saúl Sosnowski, 'Entrevista', p.72).

[29] This is a particularly significant example since Toto's jealousy is probably not without foundation, so to speak; as Rodríguez Monegal has pointed out, it is likely that 'en sus rituales siestas con Mita [Berto cumpla] sus funciones conyugales con toda propiedad' ('in his ritual siestas with Mita [Berto fulfils] his marital duties as he should') (*Narradores,* p.375). It is worth noting, too, that as far as one can tell, Berto is not among those who are saved in Toto's apocalyptic vision of the end of the world (pp.101–3).

[30] *Enchantment,* p.133.

[31] *America,* p.23.

[32]See Erich Neumann, *The Great Mother,* translated into English by Ralph Manheim, 2nd edition (Princeton University Press, 1963), p.41.

[33]Jorgelina Corbatta, 'Encuentros con Manuel Puig', p.608. My italics.

[34]Oxford University Press, 1960.

[35]Quoted in Frank McConnell, *The Spoken Seen. Film and the Romantic Imagination* (Baltimore, The Johns Hopkins University Press, 1975), p.15. My italics.

[36]There was never a film with this title, but Puig has said (in a letter to the author dated 25 July 1982) that when he invented it he did think of *Desiderio* (1943), directed by Roberto Rossellini and Marcello Pagliero.

[37]Emir Rodríguez Monegal, 'El folletín rescatado', *Revista de la Universidad de México,* XXVII, no.2 (October 1972), p.27.

[38]Rodríguez Monegal, 'El folletín rescatado', p.31.

[39]A desire for elegance and finery is typically Argentine, according to Puig. See Fossey (*Galaxia,* p.148).

[40]Jorgelina Corbatta, 'Encuentros con Manuel Puig', p.600.

[41]Juan Goytisolo, 'Manuel Puig: una novela política', *El Viejo Topo* (Barcelona, December 1979), 63 – 64.

[42]*Enchantment,* p.10.

[43]*America,* p.16.

[44]Joseph Campbell, *The Hero with a Thousand Faces* (Princeton University Press, Bollingen Series XVII, 1973), p.26. First edition: 1949.

[45]*The Hero,* p.28.

Sharon Magnarelli has published an interpretation of *La traición de Rita Hayworth* in her book *The Lost Rib. Female Characters in the Spanish-American Novel* (London and Toronto, Associated University Presses, December 1985) called 'Betrayed by the Cross-Stitch', pp.117 – 46, in which she ingeniously connects the novel's opening conversation about embroidery, defined as decorating or embellishing rhetorically, especially with fictitious additions, with the whole of the text. Unfortunately the book came out too late for me to incorporate any comments on it here.

Notes to Chapter III

[1]*Boquitas pintadas* was finished six years before its publication date, which was delayed as the result of censorship problems.

[2]See my article: 'The First Four Novels of Manuel Puig: Parts of a Whole? *Ibero-Amerikanisches Archiv,* IV, 4 (November 1978), 253 – 63.

[3]Rodríguez Monegal, 'El folletín rescatado', pp.25, 27 and 28.

[4]M. Osorio, 'Entrevista con Manuel Puig', *Cuadernos para el diálogo* 231 (1 October 1977), 51 – 53. Quotation: p.52.

[5]Bella Josef, 'Manuel Puig: reflexión al nivel de la enunciación', *Nueva Narrativa Hispanoamericana,* IV (1974), 111 – 15. Quotation: p.115.

[6]Marta Morello-Frosch, 'La sexualidad opresiva en las obras de Manuel Puig', *Nueva Narrativa Hispanoamericana,* V (1975), 151 – 57. Quotation: p.152.

[7]'El folletín rescatado', p.32.

[8]Saúl Sosnowski, 'Entrevista', p.74.

[9]Margery A. Safir, 'Mitología: otro nivel de metalenguaje en *Boquitas*

pintadas', *Revista Iberoamericana,* 90 (1975), 47 – 58.

[10]Juan Manuel García Ramos, *La narrativa de Manuel Puig. (Por una crítica en libertad),* (University of La Laguna, 1982), p.197.

[11]Alicia Borinsky, 'Castración y lujos: la escritura de Manuel Puig', *Revista Iberoamericana,* 90 (1975), 29 – 45. Quotation: p.39.

[12]In the English translation of the novel, *Heartbreak Tango* (New York, Dutton, 1974), the epigraphs are taken from Homero Manzi, not Alfredo Le Pera. Puig has explained that the Le Pera lyrics turned out to be virtually untranslatable since their charm lay in their musicality rather than in their imagery. See Sosnowski, 'Entrevista', p.79.

[13]*La narrativa,* p.197.

[14]Ernesto Sábato, *Tango. Discusión y clave* (Buenos Aires, Losada, 1963), p.11. He claims, too, that the sadness of the tango is often accompanied by desperation, rancour, threats and sarcasm (p.15).

[15]Quoted by Sábato, ibid., p.11.

[16]Ibid., pp.18 and 14.

[17]*Trago amargo,* lyrics by Julio Navarrine, music by Rafael Iriarte. See Noemí Ulla, *Tango, rebelión y nostalgia* (Buenos Aires, Editorial Jorge Álvarez, 1967), pp.67 – 68.

[18]*Volver,* lyrics by Alfredo Le Pera, music by Carlos Gardel. Other well-known tangos have titles such as *Amores viejos (Old Loves), La he visto con otro (I've Seen Her with Another), Qué lindo es estar metido (How Wonderful to be in Love), Derrotado (Defeated), La carta que me dejaste (The Letter You Left Me), Lloró como una mujer (He Cried like a Woman), Nunca es tarde (It's Never Too Late), En mi pasado (In My Past), Fiel (Faithful), La novia ausente (The Absent Love), Olvidado (Forgotten);* the list is endless, but the themes limited and consistent.

[19]Alfred J. MacAdam, 'Manuel Puig's Chronicles of Provincial Life'.

[20]Iris Josefina Ludmer, '*Boquitas pintadas:* siete recorridos', *Actual* (January – December, 1971), 3 – 21. Juan Manuel García Ramos, *La narrativa,* pp.198 – 209.

[21]David Thomson, *A Biographical Dictionary of the Cinema,* (London, Secker & Warburg, 1975), p.563.

[22]See M. Osorio, 'Entrevista', p.51.

[23]V.S. Naipaul, *The Return of Eva Perón* (Harmondsworth, Penguin Books Ltd., 1981), p.150. The articles that constitute this chronicle were written between 1972 and 1975.

[24]Ibid., pp.148 – 49, my italics.

[25]Marjorie Rosen, 'Popcorn Venus or How the Movies Made Women Smaller than Life', in *Sexual Stratagems,* ed. Patricia Erens (New York, Horizon Press, 1979), pp.19 – 30.

[26]Marco Denevi, *Rosaura a las diez,* in *Obras completas,* I (Buenos Aires, Corregidor, 1980), pp.197 – 98. Ironically, this judgement of the character turns out to be totally erroneous in the Denevi novel.

[27]*La narrativa,* pp.195 – 96.

[28]See M. Osorio, 'Entrevista', p.52.

[29]Rosa María Pereda, 'Exilio solo y fané. Manuel Puig no es profeta en su Buenos Aires querido', *Cambio 16,* 633 (16 – 23 January 1984), 84 – 85.

[30]Pauline Kael, 'The Current Cinema: Dreamers', *The New Yorker* (21

December 1981), 122–33. Quotations: pp.123 and 122.

[31] Andrés Amorós, *Subliteraturas* (Barcelona. Ariel 1974), pp.142, 14 and 15. See too Noël Arnaud, Francis Lacassin and Jean Portel, *Entretiens sur la Paralittérature* (Paris, Plon, 1970), Segundo Serrano Poncela, *Literatura y subliteratura* (Caracas, Universidad Central de Venezuela, Colección Temas, 1966), Francisco Ynduráin, *Galdós entre la novela y el folletín* (Madrid, Taurus, 1970) and Amorós's own *Sociología de una novela rosa* (Madrid, Taurus, 1968); the title alone of the earlier Amorós work (on the writings of Corín Tellado) reveals the sociological orientation of most criticism of 'subliterature'. Needless to say, my interest in it is as a *psychological* indicator.

[32] *Boquitas pintadas*, pp.43–48. All quotations are taken from the Barcelona, Seix Barral (1982) edition.

[33] Emir Rodríguez Monegal, 'El folletín rescatado', p.27, and Sosnowski, 'Entrevista', p.73.

[34] Mikhail Bakhtin, *Rabelais and His World*, trans. Helen Iswolsky (Cambridge, Mass., The MIT Press), 1968.

[35] Mikhail Bakhtin, *Problems of Dostoevsky's Poetics*, translated and edited by Caryl Emerson (Manchester University Press, 1984), p.124 *et seq.*

[36] *Rabelais*, p.11.

[37] Emir Rodríguez Monegal, 'El folletín rescatado', pp.29 and 30.

[38] Sosnowski, 'Entrevista', p.73.

[39] Ibid., p.77.

[40] Richard Collins, 'The Film', in *Discrimination and Popular Culture'*, ed. Denys Thompson, 2nd edition (Harmondsworth, Penguin Books Ltd., 1973), pp.211–12.

[41] Luis Rafael Sánchez, 'Apuntación mínima de lo soez', in *Literature and Popular Culture in the Hispanic World*, ed. Rose S. Minc (Gaithersburg, Hispamérica, 1981), pp.9–14.

[42] Emir Rodríguez Monegal, 'El folletín rescatado', pp.32–33.

[43] Susan Sontag, 'Notes on "Camp"', pp.105–19.

[44] Ibid., pp.110–112.

[45] *Camp*, p.17.

[46] Ibid., pp.181, 164, 179, 70 and 57.

[47] 'Notes on "Camp"', p.115.

[48] Bryan Appleyard, 'A risky stand against the ironic mode', *The Times* (14 February 1984), p.17.

[49] 'Notes on "Camp"', p.119.

Notes to Chapter IV

[1] Michael Wood, 'The Claims of Mischief', *The New York Review of Books* (24 January 1980), p.43.

[2] 'The Film', in *Discrimination and Popular Culture*, p.211.

[3] Emir Rodríguez Monegal, 'Los sueños de Evita', *Narradores*, II, pp.391 and 392. Even the exoticism of a title in English is less a hint of cultural colonization than an example of the use of one of the components of the detective story genre: the English language.

[4] *La narrativa*, p.301. García Ramos draws on Alberto del Monte, *Breve historia de*

la novela policíaca (Madrid, Taurus, 1962).

[5] 'El folletín'. p.35.

[6] 'Los sueños', p.392.

[7] *La narrativa*, p.276. The original Spanish is 'detonante'.

[8] *The Times Literary Supplement* (31 August 1973).

[9] M. Osorio, 'Entrevista', p.52.

[10] I am thinking of the faultless logic behind the false theories in stories such as 'Emma Zunz' and 'La muerte y la brújula'.

[11] *La narrativa*, p.331.

[12] *Rabelais*, pp. 90 and 83.

[13] One interesting and amusing aspect of Puig's use of language here is the frequency with which he gives us negative information: 'there is no sign of violence' (p.22), 'the knife blade cannot reflect and refract the rays of light because it is hidden by the coverlet . . .' (p.23), 'it is impossible to hear what he whispers in her ear' (p.60), 'turning her back, it is impossible to see what he is doing' (p.65), etc.

[14] Included in this group are authors such as the Cubans, Severo Sarduy and Guillermo Cabrera Infante. See Héctor Libertella, *Nueva escritura en Latinoamérica* (Caracas, Monte Ávila, 1977), p.49. The term *novela del lenguaje* was not, of course, invented by Libertella but by Rodríguez Monegal.

[15] *La narrativa*, p.261.

[16] 'Los sueños'. Rodríguez Monegal points out, for example, how the epigraph to Chapter One gives a third level to the emotional atmosphere of the scene. Clara Evelia's discovery of Gladys's disappearance is a fact, her preoccupation with the Bécquer poem on the death of a young girl adds to our understanding of this fact, and the identification of Gladys with Marguérite Gautier adds a further dimension (p.387). Among other revealing observations, Roberto Echavarren, in 'La superficie de lectura de *The Buenos Aires Affair*', *Espiral/Revista*, III (1977), 147–74, points out the connection between a film scene and the pivotal chapter thirteen that it heads. The scene involves a traitor and a spy, and Echavarren judges these terms as suitable descriptions of Leo and Gladys respectively. He has betrayed a homosexual partner, as well as his political friends; she is a spy in the house of love (p.148).

[17] All references and quotations are taken from the 1973 edition (Mexico City, Joaquín Mortiz).

[18] M. Osorio, 'Entrevista', p.52.

[19] At one point we are told that with one of her lovers 'su organismo se había habituado at ataque de un cuerpo masculino' ('her system had become accustomed to being assaulted by a male body') (p.50).

[20] We never discover if his victim actually dies, though it seems that he did: 'a la mañana siguiente entre las noticias policiales del diario figuraba el caso de un amoral encontrado en fin de vida en un baldío, por aparentes motivos de hurto' ('the following day among the police reports in the paper there was the case of a person of easy virtue found dying on some waste ground, the motive apparently robbery') (p.102).

[21] Marta Morello-Frosch, 'La sexualidad opresiva en las obras de Manuel Puig'.

[22] Sigmund Freud, '"Civilized" Sexual Morality and Modern Nervous Illness'

(1908), *The Standard Edition,* Vol. IX.

[23] Erich Fromm, for example, in *The Fear of Freedom* (1942), claims that 'most of Freud's applications of psychology to social problems were misleading constructions': p.6 in the 1961 edition (London, Routledge & Kegan Paul).

[24] Sigmund Freud, 'On the Sexual Theories of Children' (1908), Vol. IX, and 'Contributions to the Psychology of Love' (1910–12), Vol. XI.

[25] 'Contributions'.

[26] Anthony Storr, *Sexual Deviation,* p.35.

[27] Alfred Adler, *Social Interest: A Challenge to Mankind,* translated by John Linton and Richard Vaughan (London, Faber & Faber, 1938).

[28] '"Civilized" Sexual Morality'.

[29] *Nueva escritura,* p.86.

[30] It would be tedious to list very many of these, but they range from the violent pornography found in Georges Bataille's *L'Histoire de l'oeil* (Paris, Fernand Lefèvre, 1928) and the clearly symbolic substitution of an eye for the female vulva in Ernesto Sábato's *Abaddón el exterminador* (Buenos Aires, Editorial Sudamericana, 1974) to the Victor Brauner drawings where the same substitution is made, and the many mythological versions of this interchangeability in the iconography of exotic religions, where the genital area is often referred to as 'the other face'.

[31] M. Osorio, 'Entrevista', p.52.

[32] C.G. Jung, *Alchemical Studies,* translated by R.F.C. Hull, Vol. XIII (London, Routledge & Kegan Paul, 1967), p.232.

[33] H.J. Rose, *A Handbook of Greek Mythology* (London, Methuen, 1928).

[34] Quoted by Octavio Paz, *Conjunciones y disyunciones* (Mexico City, Joaquín Mortiz, 1969), p.15. Stone as an indication of power is found in the Tibetan version of the Buddha's title, the translation of which is 'Lord of the Stones' (ibid., p.16).

[35] This is not the first time that Puig has made the connection between submarine and sexual images. See *La traición de Rita Hayworth,* p.41, etc.

[36] Sigmund Freud, 'Beyond the Pleasure Principle' (1920), Vol. XVIII.

[37] See G.A. Gaskell, *Dictionary of All Scriptures and Myths* (New York, The Julian Press Inc., 1960), pp.454 and 449. Conversely, it has been thought that Gladys means 'brilliant' and 'splendid'. See Helena Swan, *Girls' Christian Names* (Rutland, Vermont, Charles E. Tuttle, 1973).

[38] It will be remembered that in alchemy the bat is a creature of duality.

[39] Sigmund Freud, 'Introductory Lectures on Psychoanalysis' (1916–17), Vol. XVI.

[40] Rupert C. Allen, *Psyche and Symbol in the Theater of Federico García Lorca* (Austin, University of Texas Press, 1974), pp.9, 10, 11, 12 and 14, the latter reference quoted from Paul Radin, *The Trickster: A Study in American Indian Mythology* (New York, Philosophical Library, 1956). Allen points out, too, that in at least one fairy tale *the malevolent dwarf is released from under a stone.* The reference is to Joseph Jacobs (ed.), *More English Fairy Tales* (New York, Schocken Books, 1968). Then his investigations into the phallic significance of birds, and particularly the sunbird, are relevant here: we have already briefly mentioned bird symbolism. Leo, of course, can be seen as a sunbird since the zodiac sign from which he takes his name represents solar power, and in its alchemical

connection, the sun denotes male strength. Yet another connection with the story of Siegfried is that suggested by the death of the dragon. According to Jung (in *Psychology of the Unconscious. A Study of the Transformation and Symbolisms of the Libido*, 1917) (London, Routledge & Kegan Paul, 1951), the fear of incest is transformed into a fear of being devoured by the mother, who is often shown as a dragon.

[41] H.G. Schenk, *The Mind of the European Romantics* (Oxford University Press, 1979), p.227. Like the other figures that Leo considers, Siegfried is a man with a 'vigorosa, pujante, extrema masculinidad' ('vigorous, powerful, extreme masculinity') which should be hidden from view (p.208).

[42] See Anthony Storr, *Sexual Deviation*, p.29.

[43] *Sexual Deviation*, pp.33, 34, 35 and 39.

[44] *The Fear of Freedom*, p.136.

[45] *The Fear of Freedom*, p.138; *Sexual Deviation*, p.46.

[46] *The Fear of Freedom*, pp.127 and 130.

[47] *Social Interest*, p.129.

[48] Mario Mieli, *Elementos de crítica homosexual* trans. Joaquín Jordá (Barcelona, Anagrama, 1979), p.178. (Originally: *Elementi di critica omosessuale,* Turin, Giulo Einaudi Editore, 1977.) The same logic forms the basis of the joke about the masochist who refrained from self-flagellation because he enjoyed it. That Freud and his successors use the term differently from the sexologists is pointed out by Laplanche and Pontalis in their *Diccionario de Psicoanálisis.*

[49] *The Fear of Freedom*, p.132, 133 and 138.

[50] 'The Claims of Mischief', p.43.

[51] Sigmund Freud, 'Types of Onset of Neurosis' (1912), Vol. XII.

[52] Sigmund Freud, 'The Disposition of Obsessional Neurosis' (1913), Vol. XII.

[53] See Freud's 'Group Psychology and the Analysis of the Ego' (1921), Vol. XIII.

[54] 'Entrevista a Manuel Puig', *Zona de carga y descarga*, 7 (September 1974), p.10.

[55] This prefigures a scene from the film *Cat People* (1942), which Molina, one of the two protagonists of the novel, recounts to the other — his cell-mate — in Puig's fourth book, *El beso de la mujer araña*. In this, too, there is a sense of menace as a young woman tries to reach home across New York, knowing that she is in mortal danger.

[56] This looks forward to another film recounted in *El beso de la mujer araña, The Enchanted Cottage* (1945), in which a plain woman and a disfigured man are literally transformed by love. In Latin America the title was *Su milagro de amor (Their Miracle of Love).*

[57] M. Osorio, 'Entrevista', p.53.

[58] See Storr, *Sexual Deviation*, p.29.

[59] Sigmund Freud, 'The Disposition of Obsessional Neurosis'.

[60] In *El beso de la mujer araña*, the homosexual and the heterosexual protagonists discuss the question of what constitutes a man. It is interesting that in this novel, too, the characters become fused.

[61] A kind of sexual ambivalence (in the sense that she does not fit in with standard gender patterns) may even be indicated by Gladys's lifelong assumption that she will have to buy her own house (p.47). Of course, there is no reason why she should not do so in an ideal society, but her upbringing has

not been in an ideal society and her outlook can be judged accordingly.
[62]M. Osorio, 'Entrevista', p.53.
[63]Michael Wood, in 'The Claims of Mischief', is convinced that this is Puig's opinion, and that *El beso de la mujer araña* confirms this.
[64]'Castración y lujos', p.43.
[65]See Anika Lemaire, *Jacques Lacan,* translated by David Macey (London, Routledge & Kegan Paul, 1977), p.61.
[66]See Freud's essay on E.T.A. Hoffman's story 'The Sandman': 'The Uncanny' (1919), Vol. XVII.
[67]Sigmund Freud, 'The Psychogenesis of a Case of Homosexuality in a Woman' (1920), Vol. XVIII.
[68]Freud's interpretation of 'The Sandman' is referred to by Elizabeth Wright in a section of her *Psychoanalytic Criticism. Theory in Practice* (London, Methuen, 1984) that includes this phrase (p.149).
[69]We discover that María Esther disapproves of abortion and divorce and that she rejects the role of the unconscious in creative work.
[70]In Spain, too, it was banned until after Franco's death.
[71]'Los sueños de Evita'.
[72]*Social Interest,* p.42.
[73]David Stafford-Clark, *What Freud Really Said* (Harmondsworth, Penguin Books Ltd., 1965), p.201.

Notes to Chapter V

[1]*El beso de la mujer araña* (Barcelona, Seix Barral, 1976). All page references are to this edition.
[2]See my 'The First Four Novels of Manuel Puig: Parts of a Whole?'
[3]Juan Goytisolo, 'Manuel Puig: una novela política'. For an example of one of the many favourable comments from influential journalists, see Valerie Brooks, 'Movie Dreams in Argentina', *Newsweek* (7 May 1979). Her review begins: 'Superb novelists are alive, very well indeed, and thriving away from their native continent — Latin America'. (Puig was living in New York City at the time).
[4]Milagros Ezquerro, *Que raconter c'est apprendre à mourir* (Toulouse, University of Toulouse-Le-Mirail, 1981). This was originally a chapter in a doctoral dissertation for the University of Paris IV-Sorbonne that was presented in January 1981. Although perceptive and illuminating, no real attempt has been made to turn it into a self-contained book and it remains very much part of a thesis. See, too, *Organizaciones textuales,* and the *Actes du Colloque sur l'œuvre de Puig et Vargas Llosa* (Fontenay-aux-Roses, Les Cahiers de Fontenay, 1982).
[5]Puig's own adaptation of *El beso de la mujer araña* for the theatre was first performed in Valencia on 8 April 1981. It starred Pepe Martín as Molina and Juan Diego as Valentín. The director was José Luis García Sánchez. It has been published in the same volume as Puig's only other published play to date: *Bajo un manto de estrellas* (Barcelona, Seix Barral, 1983). The film was directed by Héctor Babenco and starred William Hurt and Raul Julia. That, too, was well received, and in 1986, William Hurt won a Hollywood Oscar for his portrayal of Molina.

[6]Juan Manuel García Ramos, 'Manuel Puig, final de itinerario', *El País*, (8 August 1982).

[7]Walter González Uriarte, *El beso de la mujer araña* y el cine', *Actes du Colloque*, pp.101–05. Quotation: p.104. See, too, García Ramos, *La narrativa*, pp.334–35: 'su antecedente más obvio es el Toto de *La traición de Rita Hayworth*'('his most obvious precursor is Toto in *La traición de Rita Hayworth*').

[8]M. Osorio, 'Entrevista', p.52. It is disturbing to note that Freud saw this situation as irremediable. He claimed that there is total incompatibility between sexual pleasure and a man's respect for his wife. See Sigmund Freud, 'Contributions to the Psychology of Love'. On the subject of popular culture, it is clear that nowadays many critics are in agreement with Puig that there is no real hierarchy of values. For example, Richard Collins ('The Film') points out that 'the source of the confusing distinctions between "culture" and "popular culture" may lie in attitudes formed when "culture" was distinguished by ownership and "popular culture" was unequivocally of the folk' (p.212). See, too, Leslie A. Fiedler, *What Was Literature? Class Culture and Mass Society* (New York, Simon & Schuster, 1984). Fiedler sees the 'separation of song and story into High Literature and low, or as some prefer to say, into literature proper and sub- or para-literature' as 'an unfortunate distinction' (p.13). Later he says, 'In terms of the "standards" of the critics, all song (especially if it appears in print), like all story, is still classified as "junk" or "mere entertainment" if it opts for sentimentality instead of irony, the literal rather than the symbolic, the commonplace rather than the recherché' (p.95).

[9]Frances Wyers (Weber), 'Manuel Puig at the Movies' *Hispanic Review*, 49 (1981) 163–81. Quotation: p.173. See, too, Gustavo Pellón, 'Manuel Puig's Contradictory Strategy: Kitsch Paradigm *versus* Paradigmatic Structure in *El beso de la mujer araña* and *Pubis angelical*', *Symposium*, XXXVII (1983), 183–201.

[10]García Ramos, in hs article in *El País*, is censorious on the subject of Puig's erstwhile connections with what he calls the Freudian school of Buenos Aires and its most enthusiastic members, among whom were two of the editorial board of the journal *Litoral*, which was dedicated to the propagation of the Lacanian version of Freud's theories. It is worth repeating, perhaps, that what is important as far as Puig's novels are concerned is not the validity of the Freudian viewpoint but the fact that it often forms the basis of the author's fictional *Weltanschauung*; it would be perverse to ignore this.

[11]*What Was Literature?* p.231.

[12]*Loca* (madwoman) is the Spanish equivalent of the French *folle*, as in the well-known play and film *La Cage aux folles*.

[13]Luys A. Díez, '*El beso de la mujer araña:* parábola de la represión sexual', *Camp de l'Arpa*, 40 (January 1977), 23–26. Quotation: p.26.

[14]Milagros Ezquerro, in *Que raconter . . .*, explains this by pointing out that whereas a Christian name indicates an individual (as in the case of Valentín), a surname represents what has been inherited. Molina is thus distinguished by his 'attachement filial' (p.39). Ironically, though, it is Valentín that has suppressed his individuality.

[15]Maryse Vich-Campos, 'L'Invention de Molina (à propos du film *Cat People* dans *El beso de la mujer araña*, de Manuel Puig)', in *Actes du Colloque*,

pp.107–13. The action of the novel begins on 7 September 1975, so that Valentín must have been born in 1949. All but one of the recounted films are set in the forties, the exception being the invented story of a young Latin-American urban guerilla.

[16]Milagros Ezquerro, *Que raconter . . .*, p.22.

[17]Yves Macchi, 'Fonction Narrative des notes infrapaginales dans *El beso de la mujer araña* de Manuel Puig', *Les Langues Néo-Latines*, 76 (1982), 67–81. Quotation: p.78. See, too, Jean Alsina's article on the structure of the novel, '*El beso de la mujer araña* de Manuel Puig como relato. Algunas sugerencias', *Organizaciones textuales*, pp.279–85.

[18]Gilberto Triviños, 'La destrucción del verosímil folletinesco en *Boquitas pintadas*', *Texto Crítico*, IX (1976), 117–30. Quotation: p.122.

[19]Saúl Sosnowski, 'Entrevista', p.78.

[20]Gustavo Pellón, 'Manuel Puig's Contradictory Strategy', p.187. See, too, my 'The First Four Novels', p.258.

[21]Juan Manuel García Ramos, *La narrativa*, p.382. Puig has commented on sexual oppression as a theme on many occasions. One instance is found in Luys A. Díez, '*El beso . . .*'. See, too, Anne-Marie Vanderlynden, 'Hacia una semiología de los discursos referidos en *El beso de la mujer araña*', *Organizaciones textuales*, who bases her judgement that the essential message of the novel is to do with homosexuality, not revolution, on the fact that the footnotes refer only to Molina's problem and not to what Valentín stands for (p.275).

[22]Maurice Molho, 'Tango de la madre araña', *Actes du Colloque*, pp.161–68.

[23]Ibid., p.165.

[24]For example, Molho considers the allusive value of the *pollos* (chickens) that Molina orders, reminding us that the word is used jocularly to mean luscious young men. This is not entirely convincing: the critic has forgotten that although Molina does indeed order two roast chickens, *both are for Valentín* (p.161). His theory that the mole on Valentín's face symbolizes the penis is also difficult to accept. Immediately after the two men make love, Molina is under the impression that it is now on *his* face, and this transference suggests fusion. As in *The Buenos Aires Affair,* the two characters can be taken as reflecting opposing aspects of the make-up of the individual human being.

[25]Claude Le Bigot, 'Fantasme, Mythe et parole dans *El beso de la mujer araña* de Manuel Puig', *Les Langues Néo-Latines*, 75, no. 3 (1981), 25–26.

[26]This point is made by Yves Macchi, 'Fonction Narrative'.

[27]See Eduardo Chamorro, 'Manuel Puig secuestrado', *Cambio 16*, no. 289 (20–26 June 1977), p.83.

[28]'En réalité, Molina ne raconte pas *Cat People*', says Maryse Vich-Campos. 'Le film n'est qu'un point de départ . . .' Then: 'Le recit de Molina fait naître un nouveau film, que l'on pourrait intituler *La mujer-pantera*'. 'L'Invention', p.112.

[29]Though as the narrative covers only twenty-two days of the protagonists' imprisonment, Molina's physical reproduction, so to speak, of the screen kiss follows fairly soon after his verbal reproduction of it.

[30]Roberto Echavarren, '*El beso de la mujer araña* y las metáforas del sujeto', *Revista Iberoamericana*, 102–3 (1978), 65–75.

[31]See, for example, Valerie Brooks, 'Movie Dreams': 'They are a modern day

Don Quixote and Sancho Panza riding across the Technicolor pampas, whose hope lies only in their shared humanity'. García Ramos (*La narrativa*) finds the parallel between Cervantes' treatment of the truth/illusion dichotomy and that of the Argentine author a fruitful topic; he also points out the relevance of Leo Spitzer's well-known references to the effectiveness of intercalated narratives in the Golden Age novel (pp.343 – 46).

[32] Salvador de Madariaga, *Guía del lector del 'Quijote'* (Mexico City, Editorial Hermés, 1953). Quotation: p.135. Another similarity is that Don Quixote unwisely sends Sancho with a message to Dulcinea, despite the fact that his faith has by this point been somewhat shaken. In *El beso de la mujer araña*, Valentín entrusts a message to Molina, and there is equally little likelihood that any good will come of this. Then there is the parallel between the Cave of Montesinos episode in *Don Quijote*, which Madariaga sees as a case of *creating* a dream, rather than defending a 'quimera ya creada' ('a chimera already in existence') (pp.149 – 50), and the final, romantic adventure story of *El beso:* instead of recounting someone else's love, sacrifice and death, Molina acts out the story of his own, and there is no sympathetic, identifying narrator any more. Now the cold, clinical and uncomprehending agents of the repressive authorities constitute 'the narrative voice', and the story it tells is, in a way, the seventh 'film' in the novel.

[33] Annie Perrin and Françoise Zmantar Pez ('La telaraña') also make this point (p.265).

[34] 'Metáforas', p.75.

[35] Michel Foucault, *La Volonté de savoir* (Paris, Gallimard, 1976).

[36] See my *A Alma Amortalhada. Mário de Sá-Carneiro's Use of Metaphor and Image* (London, Tamesis, 1984), especially pp.149 – 50. Sá-Carneiro also wrote a short story called 'Ressurreição' ('Resurrection'), in which a dead girl is, so to speak, 'resurrected' by means of an act of homosexual intercourse between the two men who had been her lovers (*Céu em Fogo*, Lisbon, s.d.).

[37] Milagros Ezquerro (*Que raconter . . .*, p.66) agrees that in the end 'Marta et Molina ne forment plus qu'un seul personnage'.

[38] *The Great Mother*, p.35. Later, Neumann refers to Jung's observation that 'the perilous way' is often represented by a net, with a spider at its centre.

[39] 'Contributions to the Psychology of Love'.

[40] See Michèle Ramond, 'La Femme ombilicale. Quelques réflexions sur la Femme araignée à partir de l'image de couverture', *Actes du Colloque*, pp.155 – 59. As she says, 'Molina réhabilite aux yeux de son compagnon l'image maternelle', and 'Le retour manqué de Valentin à la mère, par l'entremise de Marta, se répare en prison à travers sa nostalgie de Marta . . .' (p.157).

[41] Michelle Débax, 'Autorepresentación y autoferencialidad en un texto narrativo. *El beso de la mujer araña* de Manuel Puig', *Organizaciones textuales*, pp.287 – 94.

[42] *Elementos de crítica homosexual*, p.9. In the second film recounted by Molina, it is love of one's country — another 'safe' form of love — that may make a person fearless (p.62).

[43] *The Spoken Seen*, p.15.

[44] D.C. Muecke, *Irony* (London, Methuen, 1970). Muecke takes the phrase 'a

purposeful deception' from Eleanor Hutchens, *Irony in 'Tom Jones'* (Alabama, 1965), p.20, and refers to A.R. Thompson, *The Dry Mock, A Study of Irony in Drama* (Berkeley, 1948) when discussing the painful and comic nature of an ironic contrast.

⁴⁵Vladimir Jankélevitch, *L'Ironie* (Paris, Flammarion, 1964), p.9. He also claims that irony 'est bien trop morale pour être vraiment artiste' (p.9) and this statement, too, is inappropriate in any discussion of Puig's novels.

⁴⁶Wayne C. Booth, *A Rhetoric of Irony* (The University of Chicago Press, 1974). Chapter Three, 'Is it ironic?', pp.47 – 86.

⁴⁷Ibid., p.73, author's italics.

⁴⁸Perón was usually referred to in this way in Argentina.

⁴⁹'*El beso de la mujer araña* y el cine', p.102, my italics. See, too, Duarte Mimoso-Ruiz, 'Aspects des ''média'' dans *El beso de la mujer araña* de Manuel Puig (1976) et *La tía Julia y el escribidor* de Mario Vargas Llosa (1977)', *Les Langues Néo-Latines*, 76, no.1 (1982), 29 – 47, who refers to Latin-American 'colonisation spirituelle' and the 'fascination dangereuse éprouvée pour les fascismes et les dictatures militaires' (43 – 44).

⁵⁰*What was Literature?* pp.197, 195 and 139. Hermann Broch, in *Poesía e investigación* (Barcelona, Barral Editores, 1974), claims that the most typical, essential characterstic of kitsch is that it confuses ethics and aesthetics. Kitsch is after something beautiful, not something good, so its aim is an aesthetic effect (p.426).

⁵¹*A Biographical Dictionary*, pp.527 – 28.

⁵²*Kiss of the Spider Woman*, translated by Thomas Colchie (London, Arrow Books Ltd., An Arena Book), 1984. (First published in New York by Alfred A. Knopf, 1979).

⁵³*The Spoken Seen*, p.41.

⁵⁴'This comparison was first pointed out by Echavarren, 'Metáforas', p.66.

⁵⁵*El beso de la mujer araña* y el cine', p.105.

⁵⁶'L'Invention de Molina', p.112.

⁵⁷Thomas Szasz, in *Sex: Facts Frauds and Follies* (Oxford, Basil Blackwell 1981; originally published in the United States in 1980), talks of 'the special virtues of the poor, the special spirituality of the Negro, and the special authenticity of the mad', to which list he claims that 'the special sexual sensitivity of the homosexual' has recently been added. Perhaps we could make one more suggestion: the specially deserving nature of the unattractive. Szasz's original reference is to B. Russell, 'The Superior Virtue of the Oppressed', in *Unpopular Essays* (New York, Simon & Schuster, 1959), pp.59 – 64.

⁵⁸'Manuel Puig — O Rio é o verdadeiro paraíso terrestre'.

⁵⁹'Metáforas', p.73.

⁶⁰See George Yudice, '*El beso de la mujer araña* y *Pubis angelical:* entre el placer y el saber', in *Literature and Popular Culture*, pp.43 – 57.

⁶¹Stanley Cavell, *The World Viewed*, enlarged edition (Cambridge, Mass. and London, Harvard University Press, 1979), p.185. First edition: 1971.

⁶²*The Great Mother*, pp.15, 35, 38 and 43.

⁶³Michael Wood, 'The Claims of Mischief', p.43 and Yves Macchi, 'Fonction Narrative', pp.68, 71 and 74.

⁶⁴*La narrativa*, p.385.

[65]See Raúl Silva-Cáceres on this: 'Técnicas de suspensión y alienación en *El beso de la mujer araña*', *Actes du Colloque,* pp.123 – 29.

[66]In fact, Puig admitted in an interview in 1979 that he had invented one of the excerpts: 'All the notes are quotations — except for one', he said. 'I advanced an idea of my own'. Ronald Christ, 'Interview with Manuel Puig', *Christopher Street,* III, 9 (April 1979), 25 – 31.

[67]Charles Rycroft, *Reich* (London, Fontana/Collins, 1971), pp.63, 62 and 69.

[68]Elizabeth Pérez Luna, 'Con Manuel Puig en Nueva York', *Hombre de mundo,* III, 8, 69 – 72 and 104 – 07.

[69]*The World Viewed,* p.83.

[70]*Fear of Freedom,* pp.11 – 12.

[71]Frank McConnell makes this point when discussing the ending of the film *The Graduate.* See *Storytelling and Mythmaking. Images from Film and Literature* (New York and Oxford, Oxford University Press, 1979), p.248.

[72]Erich Fromm, *Greatness and Limitations of Freud's Thought* (London, Jonathan Cape, 1980), p.28. (First published as *Sigmund Freuds Psychoanalyse — Grösse und Greuzen,* 1979).

[73]'Introductory Lectures on Psychoanalysis' (1916 – 17).

[74]See Bruno Bettelheim, *Freud and Man's Soul* (London, Chatto & Windus, The Hogarth Press, 1982), p.109.

[75]Ibid., p.16.

[76]Antoine Vergote, Forward to *Jacques Lacan,* p.xx.

Notes to Chapter VI

[1]Eduardo Mejía (with Elena Urrutia), 'Entre la bendición y la maldición', *La Onda,* 396 (11 January 1981), p.4. As both the title and the date of this article suggest, it deals mainly with *Maldición eterna a quien lea estas páginas,* Puig's sixth book, published in 1980.

[2]I am thinking particularly of Gustavo Pellón's 'Manuel Puig's Contradictory Strategy: Kitsch Paradigm *versus* Paradigmatic Structure in *El beso de la mujer araña* and *Pubis angelical*', George Yudice's '*El beso de la mujer araña y Pubis angelical:* entre el placer y el saber' and, brief but both perceptive and telling, Juan Goytisolo's 'Manuel Puig: una novela política'.

[3]Elisabeth Pérez Luna, 'Con Manuel Puig en Nueva York', p.70.

[4]For example, Danubio Torres Fierro, in '*Pubis angelical* de Manuel Puig', *Vuelta,* 36 (November 1979), p.43.

[5]J.-Michel Quiblier and J.-Pierre Joecker, 'Entretien avec Manuel Puig', *Masques: Revue des homosexualités,* XI (1981), 29 – 32. Quotations: p.31.

[6]S. Leclaire, 'La Réalité du désir', in *Sur la Sexualité humaine* (Centre d'Études Laennec); quoted in Anika Lemaire, *Jacques Lacan,* pp.137 – 38.

[7]See for example Susan Sontag, *Illness as Metaphor* (New York, Farrer, Strauss and Giroux, 1978). A relevant reference in a recent Latin-American novel can be found in Mario Vargas Llosa, *La guerra del fin del mundo* (Barcelona, Seix Barral, 1981): not only has an idealist character published a pamphlet entitled 'Contra la opresión de la enfermedad' ('Against the Tyranny of Illness'), but he also attributes to the revolution that he supports the aim of wresting mankind from the prejudices that surround illness in a class-ridden society.

[8] *'El beso de la mujer araña* y *Pubis angelical:* entre el placer y el saber', p.43.

[9] Richard von Krafft-Ebing, 'Bemerkungen ueber "geschlechtliche Hoerigkeit" und Masochismus', *Jahrbueche fuer Psychiatrie,* X Bd. (1928).

[10] Later, one of W218's sexual partners calls her 'bella' ('beautiful') and 'generosa' ('generous') (p.259).

[11] Jorge Rodríguez Padrón, 'Las mujeres de las novelas de Manuel Puig', *El Día* (21 October 1979). This article was originally published in *El País.*

[12] 'Manuel Puig's Contradictory Strategy', p.191.

[13] Hedy Lamarr, *Ecstasy and Me. My Life as a Woman* (London, W.H. Allen, 1967), pp.19 and 23. It is obvious that she saw herself as exploited even at this stage in her life and career, as she sued her ghost writers for $21 million because of her dissatisfaction with the book.

[14] Later, we shall find that at one point in the third story, the treacherous lover raises his eyebrows after the style of Mephistopheles (p.189).

[15] One example is the 'aromático líquido ambarino' ('aromatic amber-coloured liquid') that is provided for the *Ama*'s delectation. It is 'un líquido delicioso y refrescante, pero sin forma, la copa cuadrada estaba allí para prestársela, y mientras tanto lo aprisionaba' ('a delicious, refreshing liquid, but without form; the square glass was there to grant that and, meanwhile, held it imprisoned') (pp.14–15).

[16] See, among others, Juan-Eduardo Cirlot, *Diccionario de símbolos* (Barcelona, Labor, 1969). One fascinating connection is that the Titans of mythology include Thea, daughter of Heaven and Earth. When the Titans depose Uranus (Coelus), natural order replaces spiritual order. These ferocious giants, belonging to the shadows, the inferior regions, appear more than once in this section in descriptions of décor: at the great Viennese mansion there are grey marble Titans who guard the only exit; one has an expression of suffering and one has not. Neither of them looks at the *Ama* as they support a relief consisting of two women who contemplate a young stallion (p.43).

[17] This is somewhat surprising, since one tends to think of the fluid lines of artists such as Gustav Klimt, and other Secession painters, when considering the period. However, there was a tendency towards geometric regularity in some areas of design, particularly furniture (that of Hoffmann, for example) and architecture.

[18] *La narrativa,* p.445.

[19] Bart L. Lewis, *Pubis angelical:* la mujer codificada', *Revista Iberoamericana,* 123–24 (April–September 1983), 531–40.

[20] We remember that in the main story, during an argument, Ana says to Pozzi: 'Te gusta estar por encima' ('You like to be on top') (p.173). On the subject of the Region of Eternal Ice, although the obvious parallel is Siberia, there may also be a reference here to the concentration camps established in the south of Argentina by Perón in the forties. See, among others, George I. Blanksten, *Perón's Argentina* (Chicago, The University of Chicago Press, 1974. First published 1953), p.56.

[21] See Cirlot, *Diccionario.*

[22] *La narrativa,* p.425.

[23] Another Puig *mise en abyme* as Ana, in her delirium, 'becomes' W218, and W218, in hers, 'becomes' her dying companion.

[24]There are strong connections between Ana's feelings towards her late father, judging him the fount of all wisdom (though slightly dated in his supposed views) and the *Ama*'s father who, if the Freud parallel is borne in mind, could interpret and therefore understand what was in the minds of others. For W218, her computer plays the same role. But they are all unknown quantities and potentially dangerous. Even Ana's father was not all he seemed, she discovers: he had been a Mason and connected with people that the present régime thought of as highly undesirable (pp.103 – 4).

[25]'Manuel Puig's Contradictory Strategy', p.199.

[26]Jeffrey Weeks, *Sexuality and its Discontents* (London, Routledge & Kegan Paul, 1985), pp.112 – 23.

[27]See Cirlot, *Diccionario,* for indications of some of the connotations of this colour. Also, Victor Wolfgang von Hagen, in *The Ancient Sun Kingdoms of the Americas* (St. Albans, Paladin, 1973. First edition: 1962), points out that blue was the colour of sacrifice in Ancient Mexico and mentions the well-known 'Maya blue' (p.148).

[28]In Spanish 'Prince Charming' is *príncipe azul* ('blue prince').

[29]Cirlot, *Diccionario.*

[30]The *Ama* is 'broken' when she loses her virginity while drugged; Ana because she has undergone surgery. All women are taken advantage of, in Ana's view.

[31]Alicia Borinsky, *Ver/Ser visto. Notas para una analítica poética* (Barcelona, Antoni Bosch, 1978), p.62.

[32]It is worth noting that the view first expressed by Karl Heinrich Ulrichs that homosexuals are a woman's soul in a man's body has been forcefully repudiated by the contemporary gay world. Puig is not, of course, interested in homosexuality as such (he sees this as potentially a new site of power, a new orthodoxy), but in 'polymorphous perversity'. He actually uses this Freudian term in the Quibler and Joecker 'Entretien'.

[33]'Manuel Puig: una novela política', p. 63.

[34]*La narrativa,* pp. 475, 449 and 459. Puig's statement comes from *El País* (31 May 1979).

[35]'Manuel Puig: una novela política', p. 63.

[36]Ernesto Sábato, *El otro rostro del peronismo. Carta abierta a Mario Amadeo* (Buenos Aires, 1956), pp.29 – 30.

[37]For a concise history of these years see William F. Sater, *The Southern Cone Nations of Latin America* (Arlington Heights, Illinois, The Forum Press, Inc., 1984).

[38]*El otro rostro,* p. 19.

[39]See, for example, Robert J. Alexander, *Juan Domingo Perón: A History* (Boulder, Colorado, Westview Press, Inc., 1979), p. 129 *et seq.*

[40]In 1973 a surrogate president, Héctor Cámpora, was elected and promptly resigned in order to allow further elections to be held. This time Perón himself took part and won 62 per cent of the vote; his wife, Isabel, was sworn in as vice-president. Perón was just a month short of his seventy-eighth birthday. In June 1974 he died.

[41]ERP stands for *Ejército Revolucionario del Pueblo* (People's Revolutionary Army); the PRT is the *Partido Revolucionario de Trabajadores* (Revolutionary Workers' Party).

[42]When being told the story of *Cat People*, Valentín refuses to identify with the architect hero, presumably because he himself has turned his back on his profession.

[43]Argentina's first dictator, Juan Manuel de Rosas, ruled from 1835 to 1852. Though of a higher social class than other *caudillos*, he was much loved by the *gauchos*. Blanksten, pp.26–27, quotes Rosas on his concern for them and for the lower classes in general.

[44]Carlos Fuentes, *Terra nostra* (Barcelona, Seix Barral, 1975), p. 70. As Alicia Borinsky observes in *Ver/Ser visto*, the ethic of the tango is based on loyalty to where one belongs (p.73). This would seem to make patriotism a strong, if conditioned, Argentine characteristic.

[45]In conversation with the author of this work.

[46]Jorge Panesi, 'Manuel Puig: las relaciones peligrosas', *Revista Iberoamericana*, 125 (October–December 1983), 903–17.

[47]*El otro rostro*, p.57. This very personal view of the situation is fascinating, since it was written in 1956. At that moment Sábato was fearful of the possibility of a new wave of Peronism, and in spite of his understanding only too well the historical reasons for the rise of the movement and his genuine admiration for the people and concern for their welfare, he warns against the neo-Peronist doctrine of seeing the workers as the only sector of society of any importance. This, he says, is not only quantitatively false but also qualitatively harmful, demagogic and dangerous. It is, perhaps, not withot significance that the Plaza de Mayo in Buenos Aires, thinly disguised in the story of W218 in *Pubis angelical*, should have had its name changed to the Plaza del Pueblo ('People's Square', p.265).

[48]Pozzi actually says this; for him, the situation in Argentina is like the conflict between the Arabs and the Israelis and the civil war in Northern Ireland in that 'todos tienen razón' ('everyone is right') (p.123).

[49]The *locas* of *El beso de la mujer araña* — Molina and his friends — were very aware of this. They saw themselves as barren women.

[50]The Region of Eternal Ice provides a fitting alternative if we recall that for Heraclitus ice symbolized the death of the soul.

[51]*Sexuality and its Discontents*, p.188. Weeks is commenting on Michel Foucault (editor), *Herculin Barbin: Being the Recently Discovered Memoirs of a Nineteenth Century French Hermaphrodite* (New York, Pantheon, 1980), which he sees as 'a gentle hymn to what Foucault calls "the happy limbo of a non-identity" hidden behind the ambiguities of outward appearance' (p.187). (Foucault: pp.xiii, viii.)

[52]*Sexuality and its Discontents* p.259.

[53]Raymond Williams, *Towards 2000* (London, Chatto & Windus, 1983), pp.12–15. *Sexuality and its Discontents*, pp.259–60.

[54]*La narrativa*, p.482.

[55]Jacques Lacan, 'Le stade du miroir comme formateur de la fonction du Je' (1937), in *Écrits* (Paris, Éditions du Seuil, 1966). For convenience I quote from the English translation by Alan Sheridan-Smith, published by Tavistock Publications (London, 1977).

[56]*Écrits*, p.196. This is the famous 'desire of the mother', in which the fantasy of the child is completion by means of the mother and that of the mother

completion via her child. The more one reads Lacanian theory, the more convinced one becomes that Puig has consciously and deliberately used it as a framework to this novel. It may even be that the three stories represents Lacan's three categories: the Real (brute existence, Ana), the Symbolic (the *Ama*/Actress), and the Imaginary (W218).

[57] I use the word 'gaze' somewhat reluctantly as it does not seem to me to be the ideal equivalent of the French *regard*. However, this is the way this is always translated in English versions of Lacan's writings.

[58] Elizabeth Wright, *Psychoanalytic Criticism. Theory in Practice*, p.117.

[59] Christian Metz, *Le Signifiant imaginaire. Psychanalyse et cinéma* (Paris, Union Générale d'Éditions, 1977). The spectator may identify with a fictional character or with the actor, according to Metz, but he adds that when (like Ana with Hedy Lamarr) the latter is the case, the film-goer identifies with the actor or actress in the very best of his or her roles, that of the star (pp.67, 93).

[60] *Sexuality and its Discontents*, p.13.

[61] *La Volonté de savoir*, pp.12, 17 – 18 and 123.

[62] *Sexuality and its Discontents*, p.44.

[63] Ana refers to 'all those little tales that help us sometimes' (pp.194 – 95), and Puig himself once commented that the advantage that the submissive woman has is that once she has admitted the existence of 'the superior man', great imaginative adventures become possible. See Quiblier and Joecker, 'Entretien', p.32.

Notes to Chapter VII

[1] *Maldición eterna a quien lea estas páginas* (Barcelona, Seix Barral, 1980). All page references are to this edition.

[2] 'A minha ideia é que se pode fazer uma literatura acessível e profunda ao mesmo tempo' ('My view is that it's possible to create literature that is both accessible and profound'), he said in an interview with Sheila Kaplan in *O Globo* ('Manuel Puig e seu *Maldição eterna*', diálogo de culturas inconciliáveis', 26 October 1983). To Elisabeth Pérez Luna ('Con Manuel Puig'), he said: 'Lo que me parece inmoral es el aburrimiento' ('What strikes me as immoral is being boring'). He was talking about the theatre when he made this assertion, but the judgment applies equally well to his view of his novelistic output.

[3] Elisabeth Pérez Luna, 'Con Manuel Puig', pp.70 and 72.

[4] 'Ei caso Puig', *Quimera*, XXIII (1982), p.31.

[5] Joaquín Marco, 'La peor novela de Manuel Puig: *Maldición eterna a quien lea estas páginas*', *La Vanguardia* (8 January 1981), p.29.

[6] 'Manuel Puig, final de itinerario'.

[7] 'Entre la bendición y la maldición'.

[8] 'El problema fundamental de ambos personajes consiste en romper la soledad en la que se encuentran' ('The basic problem for both protagonists consists of breaking out of the solitude in which they find themselves'), says Joaquín Marco ('La peor novela'). 'Pero el tema de la soledad y de la incomunicación no es nuevo ni en la literatura ni en el arte contemporáneo' ('But the theme of solitude and lack of communication is not new in literature or in

contemporary art'). This seems to me to be a totally valueless statement.

[9]Héctor Anibitarte, '*Maldición eterna a quien lea estas páginas:* carta al hijo', *El Viejo Topo*, No. 53 (February 1981), p.66.

[10]See Christopher Lehmann-Haupt in *The New York Times*, and an unsigned review in *Publishers Weekly*, both referred to in *The New York Review of Books* (15 July 1982). See, too, Ángel Rama, 'El último Puig. El diálogo imposible', in *Unomásuno*, reprinted in *El Universal* (24 January 1982).

[11]There is no indication in the novel that the North American, Larry, speaks any Spanish. Indeed, at one point he says, half-jokingly, that he will ask for more money if he has to give lessons in English (p.10).

[12]Eduardo Mejía, 'Entre la bendición y la maldición', complains on this score, but as Jesús Lázaro so rightly observes, a good novelist is not the one who makes the fewest mistakes, but one who constructs a complex and problematic world in the reader's imagination. See Jesús Lázaro, 'La inquisición sobre la soledad de Manuel Puig', *Quimera* (February 1981).

[13]See the title of the interview with Sheila Kaplan in *O Globo* (note 2).

[14]See Paulo Nogueira, 'Conversas mágicas', *Veja* (14 September 1983), p.110.

[15]Sheila Kaplan, 'Manuel Puig e seu *Maldição eterna*'.

[16]See note 10.

[17]With Gladys and Leo it is a question of the war between the sexes, with the two protagonists representing extreme and complementary positions. In *El beso de la mujer araña* there is an important variation in that the man has raised consciousness on the subject of exploitation, and the 'woman' is in a unique position to understand men: this is potentially a more advanced stage on the road to equilibrium. In *Pubis angelical* there is at least the hope of reaching this when the novel ends. But in all three stories one of the characters dies and the survivor gains little because an essential bond has been dissolved. I do not except Valentín from this interpretation, since by the end of *El beso de la mujer araña* he subconsciously sees Molina and Marta as one and the same person. The variation in *Maldición eterna a quien lea estas páginas*, of course, is that though the *existence* of the father-son relationship is essential for the life cycle, its continuation is not.

[18]Jorge Rodríguez Padrón makes the point in 'Manuel Puig: el diálogo como catarsis', *Diario de Las Palmas* (20 February 1981), p.18, that the relationship between Ramírez and Larry is one made up of 'necesidad y dominio al mismo tiempo' ('need and domination at the same time').

[19]*Enchantment*, p.99. Bettelheim's comment on youthful rebelliousness in general may be relevant where Larry is concerned. He thinks that adolescents' conflict 'is not with the adult world, or society, but really only with their parents' (pp.98–99).

[20]'El diálogo imposible'.

[21]This thesis furnishes a defence against critics who, like Eduardo Mejía ('Entre la bendición y la maldición'), have complained that Puig has failed to give a distinctive voice to the two characters. Although they are strikingly dissimilar in so many ways, the younger man can be seen as a continuation of the older.

[22]Vladimir Propp, *Las raíces históricas del cuento* (Madrid, Fundamentos, 1984), pp.69, 70, 71, 74, 75 and 415.

[23]Elena Urrutia ('Entre la bendición y la maldición') reminds us of the

similarity between these circumstances and those of Molina and Valentín in *El beso de la mujer araña*: 'ambos protagonistas están reducidos a no hablar casi con nadie más que entre sí' ('both protagonists are reduced to talking to virtually no one but each other'). Like all enclosure situtations, the characters are temporarily released from immediate external pressures and can concentrate on themselves. It is as if the outside world no longer existed. In *El beso de la mujer araña* and in *Maldición eterna a quien lea estas páginas* there is an extra factor: unlike, say, Thomas Mann's *The Magic Mountain*, we are dealing with only two people, and this highlights their isolation and mutual dependency. The absence of action and the emphasis on words in this closed world could also represent the monotony of existence.

²⁴'El diálogo imposible'.

²⁵Erich Fromm, *Greatness and Limitations of Freud's Thought*, p.40. The lifelessness indicated by Ramírez' immobility is emphasized when he is described as being depressed after a nervous 'collapse' (p.10).

²⁶'In semantics and modern linguistic analysis, the ''emotive'' meaning of words and statements has become one of the main topics to exercise the minds of those whose writings are found in the professional journals', claimed James Hillman as long ago as 1960. See *Emotion. A Comprehensive Phenomenology of Theories and their Meanings for Therapy* (London, Routledge & Kegan Paul, 1960), p.5.

²⁷*Emotion*, p.188.

²⁸Saturn cut off his father's genitals and threw them into the sea. Then, fearing possible retaliation from his own offspring, he was obliged to devour these at birth. (There is a school of thought that claims that this was actually Cronos, not Saturn: see Richard Cavendish, *The Black Arts* (London, Routledge & Kegan Paul, 1967), p.211. but what is important is that most people connect this deed with Saturn.) Saturn is the ruling planet of Capricornians, is traditionally associated with the concept of freedom, and is also invariably linked with coldness.

²⁹*Enchantment*, p.98.

³⁰This question could be acid sarcasm, with Larry behaving in a disagreeable way. More charitably, he may be humouring Ramírez. However, neither of these explanations invalidates my view of the purpose of the author's technique, especially as he uses it on several occaisons in his writings. There are many more examples of it in the present novel.

³¹*The Black Arts*, p.205.

³²Larry is always hungry, we remember, and Ramírez pays for meals for him (p.57).

³³C. G. Jung, *Psychology and Alchemy*, 2nd edition (London, Routledge & Kegan Paul, 1980), pp.330–31.

³⁴*The Black Arts*, p.221.

³⁵Mircea Eliade, *Mito y realidad*, 3rd edition (Madrid: Guadarrama, 1978), p.95. (Originally published as *Aspects du Mythe*.)

³⁶Sheila Kaplan, 'Manuel Puig e seu *Maldição eterna*'.

³⁷See René Zazzo, *Psychologie et Marxisme. La Vie et l'oeuvre d'Henri Wallon* (Paris, Denoël/Gonthier, 1975), especially Chapter 3: 'Le problème de l'autre dans la psychologie d'Henri Wallon', pp.53–64. In several articles spread over

many years Wallon himself explicitly defined his method as one based on dialectical materialism.

[38] 'Le rôle de *l'autre* dans la conscience du moi', *Journal Égyptien de Psychologie*, II, no.1 (1946), reprinted in *Enfance*, 3–4 (1959), 279–86, and 'Niveaux et fluctuations du moi', *L'Évolution psychiatrique*, I (1956), 389–401, reprinted in *Enfance*, 1–2 (1963), 87–98.

[39] *Psychologie et Marxisme*, pp.62–63. The quotation is taken from Wallon's 'Post-scriptum en réponse à M.Piaget', *Cahiers Internationaux de Sociologie*, X (1951), p.175.

[40] The term 'mental automatism' was coined by Clérambault: *Psychologie et Marxisme*, p.59. The persecution complex has a factual basis for Ramírez, of course.

[41] *Psychologie et Marxisme*, pp.60–61.

[42] This is Zazzo's summing-up: *Psychologie et Marxisme*, p.64.

[43] L. Cazamian, *A History of French Literature* (Oxford University Press, 1960), p.283. First edition, Oxford, Clarendon Press, 1955.

[44] Albert Thibault, *Histoire de la Littérature française de 1789 à nos jours* (Paris, Stock, 1936), p.59.

[45] R.D. Laing, *Knots* (Harmondsworth, Penguin Books Ltd., 1972), p.1.

[46] Paris, the almost archetypal incarnation of eroticism, is usually portrayed wearing a Phrygian cap; its connections with liberty and freedom are illustrated when it is worn by French Revolutionaries. See, *inter alia*, Cirlot, *Diccionario*.

[47] 'Contribution to the Psychology of Love'.

[48] 'Manuel Puig, final de itinerario'.

[49] Joaquín Marco, 'La peor novela de Manuel Puig'.

[50] Molina, too, quotes this in *El beso de la mujer araña*.

[51] *Emotion*, pp.188–89. my italics.

[52] Magda B. Arnold, editor, *The Nature of Emotion* (Harmondsworth, Penguin Books Ltd., 1968), Introduction to Part Three, 'Emotion in Depth Psychology', p.81.

[53] *Freud and Man's Soul*, pp.4, 25, 32, 33 and 35. Bettelheim objects to many features of the standard translation of Freud into English; one of his complaints is that the English word 'instinct' is misleadingly inaccurate. Instinct cannot, he says, apply to human beings (p.104).

[54] The reported last words of the real Edith Cavell, 'Patriotism is not enough', presumably refer to the need for love and altruism in the world.

[55] 'El diálogo imposible'.

[56] Ramírez dreams of seeing the tree when he is with the woman who will never abandon him. It is snowing (p.168). This suggests a subconscious coming-to-awareness of the centrality of the family in human existence: his wife never did abandon him, and the tree, in addition to being phallic and redemptive, is often a symbol of a central point, especially when — as here — it is in a square, the centre of a town. Snow suggests the numinous, and the mystical sublimation of the earth. It is often connected with longed-for escape to happiness in Puig's characters, but its coldness and purity indicate that this is unlikely to be tainted by earthly conditions.

[57] He is also named after Saint Lawrence who, in spite of the popular legend of

the gridiron, is actually thought to have been beheaded.

[58]This vital sentence is missing from the English translation of the novel: *Eternal Curse on the Reader of these Pages* (London, Arrow Books Ltd., An Arena Book, 1982), p.125.

[59]See John McQuarrie, *Existentialism* (Harmondsworth, Penguin Books Ltd., 1976), pp.195, 197, 198, 113, 114 and 115–16. First edition: New York, World Publishing Co., 1972.

[60]Miguel de Unamuno, *Del sentimiento trágico de la vida*, 10th edition (Madrid, Austral, 1952), Chapter Three, 'El hambre de la inmortalidad'. Another relevant passage is found in this same chapter when Unamuno refers to the usual human reaction to the injunction to sacrifice oneself for one's children: 'Y te sacrificas por ellos, porque son tuyos, parte y prolongación de ti, y ellos a su vez se sacrificarán por los suyos, y éstos por los de ellos, y así irá, sin término, un sacrificio estéril de que nadie se aprovecha' ('And you sacrifice yourself for them, because they are yours, a part and prolongation of yourself, and they in their turn will sacrifice themselves for their children, and these will do the same, and it will go on like that ad infinitum, a sterile sacrifice that benefits nobody'). The unavoidable response will be: 'Vine al mundo a hacer mi yo' ('I came into the world to become who I am') (p.43).

[61]See Luis Suñén, 'Amor correspondido y juego sentimental', *El País* (13 June 1982), p.4, who refers to the fact that *Maldición eterna a quien lea estas páginas* has been subject to some critical reservations, 'quizá porque la relación entre el autor y personajes pasaba . . . por un distanciamiento que eximía a aquél do los errores de éstos' ('perhaps because in the relationship between the author and his characters there is a kind of distancing element that exempted him from their mistakes'). Nevertheless, like me, Suñén attributes critical coolness to the fact that the novel goes in new and uncharted directions. Furthermore, on another occasion, Suñén called this 'Puig's best novel, the most solid of his stories': 'Manuel Puig: la imagen es el otro', *El País* (11 January 1981).

[62]I am borrowing David Thomson's words here. See *A Biographical Dictionary*, p.10.

[63]*Enchantment*, p.199.

[64]Joseph Campbell, *The Hero*, pp. 256 and 38.

Notes to Chapter VIII

[1]See Ronald Christ, 'Interview', p.25: 'The description of my aunt was supposed to take one page, but it took almost twenty-five!'

[2]Barcelona, Seix Barral (1982). All quotations will be taken from this edition.

[3]Gustavo Álvarez Gardeazábal, 'La aventura del lenguaje correspondido (O la sangre de amor de Puig)', *El Colombiano* (27 June 1982), in what is admittedly an otherwise favourable review, says that there are some chapters where 'la transcripción se vuelve ininteligible' ('the transcription becomes unintelligible'). He goes on to give an example which is actually far from unintelligible: 'Se quemó toda. El padre pensó que era ya sabía quien que había prendido fuego a la máquina' ('The whole thing was destroyed by fire. My father thought you-know-who had set the machine alight') (*Sangre de amor*

correspondido, p.30).

[4]This comes from Joaquín Marco, 'Manuel Puig reincide en la vulgaridad: *Sangre de amor correspondido', La Vanguardia* (28 April 1982), p.43. This is not the first time that this critic has written harshly about Puig's work. The review ends with a jibe based on the title of the previous novel: 'Maldición eterna a quien haya *escrito* estas páginas' ('An eternal curse on whoever has *written* these pages').

[5]See, for example, Luis Suñén, 'Amor correspondido'; Ricardo Bellveser, 'La última novela de Manuel Puig', *Las Provincias*, 124 (15 April 1982); and Joel Silveira, 'O carioca Puig', *Última Hora* (26 May 1982).

[6]Puig's own words were: 'Em espanhol, o livro é uma coisa diferente, no sentido de que inventei uma linguagem popular que não é o portenho, nem o pampeano ou mexicano: no pior dos casos, apenas viria ser a tentativa frustrada de conseguir um denominador comum da linguagem proletária latinoamericana' ('In Spanish, the book is different, in the sense that I invented a popular way of speaking, not that of Buenos Aires, or the Pampa, or Mexico: at the very worst it could turn out to be an unsuccessful attempt to find a common denominator for proletarian Latin-American speech'). See Bella Josef, 'O romance "carioca" de Manuel Puig. A alegria de viver de um pedreiro, inspiração de *Sangue de Amor Correspondido', O Globo* (16 May 1982). An example of the author's compromise between Spanish and Portuguese is the name of the heroine. In Portuguese it would be Maria da Glória; in Spanish, María de la Gloria.

[7]Joel Silveira, 'O carioca Puig'.

[8]Jorge Rodríguez Padrón, 'Las múltiples voces de la narrativa de Manuel Puig', *Diario de Las Palmas* (11 and 19 June, 1982).

[9]Bellveser, 'La última novela'.

[10]I am thinking in particular of long-winded introductory locutions such as 'o problema é o seguinte' ('the problem is as follows'), to which Josemar is much given.

[11]It is probably true to say that this would not apply to readers familiar with all the novels: as we have already noted, this is a device that the author has used before. For another example of it in *Sangre de amor correspondido*, see pp.136–37.

[12]Nevertheless, there are later indications of some contribution having been made to their upkeep: 'la madre de sus hijos' ('the mother of his children') complains that she is finding it difficult to manage on her income. After all, 'tienen que comer con los cuatro mil que él les da para pensión de las criaturas' ('they have to buy food with the four thousand that he gives her for the children's keep') (p.200). Previously he has claimed that he has more responsibility with his two sons than his own father had in his whole life (p.161).

[13]Elías Miguel Muñoz, '*Sangre de amor correspondido* y el discurso del poder judeocristiano', *Revista Iberoamericana*, 130–31 (January–June 1985), 73–88, p.74.

[14]It is fascinating to note how often the protagonist of fairy stories and folk-tales is the third son. Bettelheim, in *The Uses of Enchantment*, explains this by saying: 'When in a fairy story the child is the third one, the hearer easily identifies with him because within the most basic family constellation the child is third down,

irrespective of whether he is the oldest, middle, or youngest among his siblings' (p.106).

[15] Milagros Sánchez Arnosi, 'Manuel Puig: la búsqueda del lenguaje popular', *Ínsula*, 428–29 (1982), p.14.

[16] Luis Suñén, 'Amor correspondido'.

[17] Milagros Sánchez Arnosi, 'La búsqueda'.

[18] Bella Josef, 'O romance "carioca"'.

[19] Gustavo Álvarez Gardeazábal, "La aventura".

[20] Joaquín Marco, 'Manuel Puig reincide en la vulgaridad'.

[21] Jorge Campos, 'Dos novelas recientes', *Ínsula*, 428–29 (1982), p.18.

[22] Elías Miguel Muñoz, *'Sangre de amor correspondido'*, makes this point, and draws on Ilse Adriana Luraschi, 'Donde se trata de la virginidad, otros milagros y demás razones de amor y sexo en dos textos de Manuel Puig, con todo sistema', *Hispanic Journal*, I, 1 (1979), to illustrate it.

[23] Otto Rank, *Truth and Reality*, translated and edited by Jessie Taft (New York and London, W.W. Norton & Co., 1978), p. 3. The original title is *Wahrheit und Wirklichkeit. Entwurf einer Philosophie des Seelischen* (1929).

[24] Ibid., pp. 57, 58, 59, 337, 42, 52, 53, 62, 66, 68, 89, 92, 39 and 41.

[25] Nathaniel Branden, *The Psychology of Romantic Love* (New York, Bantam Books, 1983), p.81. First published: 1980.

[26] *'Sangre de amor correspondido'*, p.75.

[27] Juliet Mitchell, *Psychoanalysis and Feminism* (Harmondsworth, Penguin Books, 1982) makes this point (p.xviii). First edition: 1974.

[28] *'Sangre de amor correspondido'*.

[29] Kate Millett, *Sexual Politics* (London, Virago Press, 1985), p.52. First edition: 1969.

[30] See Northrop Frye, *The Great Code. The Bible and Literature* (London, Ark Paperbacks, 1982), pp.107 and 154.

[31] See Geoffrey Ashe, *The Virgin* (London, Routledge & Kegan Paul, 1976), p.63. Ashe noted that in the 4th century St. Jerome rebuked Helvidius who had claimed that Mary had other children (p.64).

[32] For example, at one point Maria da Gloria's voice talks about Santísimo: 'el nombre es lindo, un santo que te protege de todos los peligros'. But then she adds, 'Pero no te protege nada' ('the name is lovely, a saint protecting you from all danger. But he doesn't protect you at all') (p.97). There are many other explicit and implicit references, not all of which have been picked up by Muñoz. He does not mention, for instance, that Josemar leaves Cocotá and goes to the Estado de San Pablo (the State of São Paulo), and St. Paul is surely the most anti-feminist of all the apostles.

[33] Women are all treacherous whores and deserve violent treatment, says Josemar (p.198).

[34] There is further evidence of the hero's preoccupation with his irregular status in Astolfo's household in this section: when he is (supposed to be) acclaimed by the public, 'Ahí lo aceptaron como si fuera un hijo de la casa' ('There they accepted him as if he were a son of the house') (p.131).

[35] For example, M. Jouhandeau, quoted by Jean Rousset, *Le Mythe de Don Juan* (Paris, Armand Colin, 1978), p.95.

[36] Ronald Christ, 'Interview'.

[37] Josemar's mother slaughters their goat at one point, and he remembers how delicious the meat was (p.68). But when he himself kills the cow, he refuses to eat the meat (p.34).

[38] Northrop Frye, *The Great Code*, pp. 147–48.

[39] An aspect of female-orientated imagery in the hero is that he recalls how he cooked Maria da Gloria slowly, in a double saucepan (fittingly a *baño María*—Mary-bath—in Spanish) until he abandoned her (p.102).

[40] Milagros Sánchez Arnosi, 'La búsqueda'.

[41] Geoffrey Ashe, *The Virgin*, p.65.

[42] *'Sangre de amor correspondido'*, p.88.

[43] Josemar thinks that discourse will help Maria da Gloria back to sanity (p.12); but he is the one who is saved by it, not her. His 'official' father does not find salvation after his rejection: he gives up living, to all intents and purposes (p.67).

[44] *'Sangre de amor correspondido'*, p.86.

[45] 'Prologue' to Puig's most recent book, two film scripts: *La cara del villano* and *Recuerdo de Tijuana* (Barcelona, Seix Barral, 1985), p.11.

Bibliography

I   Novels by Manuel Puig

La traición de Rita Hayworth (Buenos Aires: Editorial Jorge Álvarez; Colección Narradores Argentinos, 1968).
Seventh edition: Buenos Aires (Editorial Sudamericana), 1974.
First edition in Spain: Barcelona (Seix Barral; Nueva Narrativa Hispánica), 1971.
Second, complete, edition: Barcelona (Seix Barral; Nueva Narrativa Hispánica), 1976.
Boquitas pintadas. Folletín (Buenos Aires: Editorial Sudamericana; Colección 'El Espejo', 1969).
First edition in Spain: Barcelona (Seix Barral; Nueva Narrativa Hispánica), 1972.
The Buenos Aires Affair (Mexico City: Joaquín Mortiz; Nueva Narrativa Hispánica, 1973).
First edition in Spain: Barcelona (Seix Barral; Nueva Narrativa Hispánica), 1977.
El beso de la mujer araña (Barcelona: Seix Barral; Nueva Narrativa Hispánica, 1976).
Pubis angelical (Barcelona: Seix Barral; Nueva Narrativa Hispánica, 1979).
Maldición eterna a quien lea estas páginas (Barcelona: Seix Barral; Nueva Narrativa, 1980).
Sangre de amor correspondido (Barcelona: Seix Barral; Nueva Narrativa Hispánica, 1982) / *Sangue de Amor Correspondido* (Rio de Janeiro: Editora Nova Fronteira, 1982).

II   Plays by Manuel Puig

Bajo un manto de estrellas/El beso de la mujer araña (Barcelona: Seix Barral, 1983).

Bajo un manto de estrellas had its première with the title *Quero* . . . in the Teatro Ipanema, Rio de Janeiro, in 1982.

III Film scripts by Manuel Puig

La cara del villano. Recuerdo de Tijuana (Barcelona: Seix Barral, 1985). Both of these texts are, in a way, new since *Recuerdo de Tijuana* was never made into a film, and the author has dissociated himself from that made by Arturo Ripstein in 1984 with the title *Otro* (originally a short story by Silvina Ocampo), because it bore so little relation to the script that he had written. This he now calls *La cara del villano.*

IV Interviews with Manuel Puig

Anon., 'Entrevista a Manuel Puig', *Zona de carga y descarga*, (7 September 1984), p.10.

Anon., 'Entrevista con Manuel Puig', *Panorama* (30 July 1968).

Anon., 'Manuel Puig: fulgor del folletín', *Panorama* (26 August 1969).

Chamorro, Eduardo, 'Manuel Puig, secuestrado', *Cambio 16* (26 June 1977), p.41.

Christ, Ronald, 'An Interview with Manuel Puig', *Partisan Review*, 44, No. 1 (1977), 52–61.

Christ, Ronald, 'Interview with Manuel Puig', *Christopher Street*, III, 9 (April 1979) 25–31.

Coddou, Marcelo, 'Seis preguntas a Manuel Puig sobre su última novela: *El beso de la mujer araña*', *The American Hispanist*, II, 18 (May 1977), 12–13.

Corbatta, Jorgelina, 'Encuentros con Manuel Puig', *Revista Iberoamericana*, 123–24 (April–September 1983), 591–620.

Díez, Luys A., '*El beso de la mujer araña*: parábola de la represión sexual', *Camp de l'Arpa*, 40 (January 1977), 23–26.

Fossey, Jean-Michel, *Galaxia latinoamericana* (Las Palmas de Gran Canaria: Inventarios Provisionales, 1973), pp.137–52.

García, Gustavo and Andrés de Luna, 'Rock, arañas, nenonas y manuelas. Manuel Puig en Nueva York', *Revista de la Universidad de México*, 33, No.7 (1978), 25–27.

Josef, Bella, 'O Romance "Carioca" de Manuel Puig. A alegria de viver de um pedreiro, inspiração de *Sangue de Amor Correspondido*', *O Globo* (16 May 1982), p.3.

Kaplan, Sheila, 'Manuel Puig e seu *Maldição eterna*, diálogo de culturas inconciliáveis', *O Globo* (26 October 1983).

MacPherson, Don, 'Betraying a Latin Dream', *The Sunday Times* (Colour Supplement) (8 April 1984), 51–52.

Mactas, Mario, 'Yo soy Manuel Puig', *Gente* (16 October 1969), 20–22.

Osorio, M., 'Entrevista con Manuel Puig. "Soy tan macho que las mujeres me parecen maricas" ', *Cuadernos para el diálogo*, 231 (1977), 51–53.

Pereda, Rosa María, 'Exilio solo y fané; Manuel Puig no es profeta en su Buenos Aires querido', *Cambio 16*, (16–23 January 1984), 84–85.

Pérez Luna, Elisabeth, 'Con Manuel Puig en Nueva York', *Hombre de mundo*, III, No.8, 69–72 and 104–07.

Quiblier J.–Michel and J.–Pierre Joecker, 'Entretien avec Manuel Puig', *Masques: Revue des homosexualités* XI (1981), 29–32.

Rodrigues, Teresa Cristina, 'Manuel Puig—O Rio é o verdadeiro paraíso terrestre, sonho de beleza e humanismo', *O Globo* (30 August 1981).

Rodríguez Monegal, Emir, 'El folletín rescatado', *Revista de la Universidad de México*, 27, No.2 (October 1972), 27–35.

Sánchez Arnosi, Milagros, 'Manuel Puig: la búsqueda del lenguaje popular', *Ínsula*, 428–29 (1982), 14.

Schild, Susana, 'Manuel Puig, "Felizmente, o meu desconforto parece ser o de muita gente"', *Jornal do Brasil* (12 September 1983).

Sosnowski, Saúl, 'Manuel Puig. Entrevista', *Hispamérica*, III (May 1973), 69–80.

Torres Fierro, Danubio, 'Conversación con Manuel Puig: la redención de la cursilería', *Eco*, XXVIII/5, No.193 (March 1975), 507–15.

V   Interview with Manuel Puig on video cassette

Roffé, Reina, 'Manuel Puig. Del "kitsch" a Lacan'; text also available, in Reina Roffé (ed.), *Espejo de escritores. Entrevistas con Borges, Cortázar, Fuentes, Goytisolo, Onetti, Puig, Rama, Rulfo, Sánchez, Vargas Llosa* (Hanover, N.H: Ediciones del Norte, 1985).

VI   Statements and discussions

Bouman, Katherine A., 'Manuel Puig at the University of Missouri-Columbia', *The American Hispanist*, II, 17 (April 1977), 11–12.

Puig, Manuel, 'Growing up at the movies; a chronology', *Review 72* (Winter 1971–Spring 1972), 49–51.

Puig, Manuel, Contribution to a Conference on the Novel at the University Center for International Studies, The University of Pittsburgh (April 1984). (Unpublished).

Puig, Manuel and Levine, Suzanne Jill, 'Author and Translator: A Discussion of *Heartbreak Tango*', *Translation*, II, 1–11 (1974), 32–41.

VII   Bibliography

Epple, Juan Armando, 'Bibliografía de Manuel Puig y sobre él', *Inter-American Review of Bibliography*, XXVIII, 165–68. (Goes up to 1977 only.)

VIII   Criticism: articles, reviews, books

Almeida, Amylton de, 'Em português, Puig fala do povo e Roberto Carlos', *Gazeta* (7 May 1982).

Alsina, Jean, *'El beso de la mujer araña* de Manuel Puig como relato. Algunas sugerencias', in *Organizaciones textuales* (q.v.), pp.279–85.

Álvarez Gardeazábal, Gustavo, 'La aventura del lenguaje correspondido (o la sangre de amor de Puig)', *El Colombiano* (27 June 1982).

Anabitarte, Héctor, *'Maldición eterna a quien lea estas páginas:* carta al hijo', *El Viejo Topo*, 53 (February 1981).

Andreu, Alicia G., 'El folletín: de Galdós a Manuel Puig', *Revista*

Iberoamericana, 123–24 (April–September 1983), 541–46.

Anon., *'Sangre de amor correspondido', Última Hora* (17 April 1982).

Anon., 'Characters', *Review 74* (Winter 1974), 84–85.

Armas Marcelo, J.J., 'De la Corte', *La Vanguardia* (4 May 1982).

Bacarisse, Pamela, 'The First Four Novels of Manuel Puig: Parts of a Whole?' *Ibero-Amerikanisches Archiv,* N.F., Jg 4, H4 (1978), 253–63.

Bellveser, Ricardo, 'La última novela de Manuel Puig', *Las Provincias* (15 April 1981).

Bianchi, Soledad, 'Discurso e historia en *La traición de Rita Hayworth',* in *Actes du Colloque sur l'Oeuvre de Puig et Vargas Llosa, Avril 1982* (q.v.), pp. 93–100.

Borinsky, Alicia, 'Castración y lujos', *Revista Iberoamericana,* 90 (1975), 29–45.

— — *Ver/Ser visto. Notas para una analítica poética* (Barcelona: Antoni Bosch, 1978).

Brooks, Valerie, 'Movie Dreams in Argentina', *Newsweek* (7 May 1979).

Bueno Chávez, Raúl, 'Sobre la enunciación narrativa: de la teoría a la crítica y viceversa (a propósito de la novelística de M. Puig)', *Hispamérica,* XXXII (1982).

Camozzi, Rolando, 'Literatura oral'. *El beso de la mujer araña', Reseña,* 104 (April 1977), 14–15.

Campos, Jorge, 'Dos novelas recientes', *Ínsula,* 428–29 (1982), p.18.

Campos, René Alberto, 'El juego de espejos: la textura cinemática en *La traición de Rita Hayworth* de Manuel Puig', unpublished Ph.D. dissertation, State University of New York at Stony Brook (1982).

— — 'Las "películas de mujeres" y *La traición de Rita Hayworth',* in *Literature and Popular Culture,* ed. Rose S. Minc (q.v.), pp.59–67.

Carranza, José María, 'Sobre Manuel Puig, *La traición de Rita Hayworth', Revista Iberoamericana,* 38 (1972).

Carvalho, Joaquim de Montezuma de, 'Manuel Puig em Lisboa', *Minas Gerais. Suplemento Literário,* No. 17 (November 1973), p.11.

Catelli, Nora, 'El caso Puig', *Quimera,* 23 (1982), 30–25.

Coddou, Marcelo, 'Complejidad estructural de *El beso de la mujer araña,* de Manuel Puig', *Inti,* VII (Spring 1978), 15–27.

Christ, Ronald, 'Fact and Fiction', *Review 73* (Fall 1973), 49–54.

Corbatta, Jorgelina, 'Mito personal y mitos colectivos en las novelas de Manuel Puig', unpublished Ph.D. dissertation, University of Pittsburgh (1983).

Costa, Caio Túlio, 'O Brasileiro Simplório de Puig', *Folha de São Paulo* (16 May 1982), p.65.

Coussat, André, 'Le plus beau tango du monde', *L'Humanité* (2 August 1972).

Débax, Michelle, 'Autorepresentación y autoreferencialidad en un texto narrativo: *El beso de la mujer araña* de Manuel Puig', in *Organizaciones textuales* (q.v.), pp.287–94.

Débax, Michelle, Milagros Ezquerro and Michèle Ramond, 'La marginalité des personnages et ses effets sur le discours dans *El beso de la mujer araña* de Manuel Puig', *Imprévue* (1980–81), 91–111.

Díez, Luys A., '*El beso de la mujer araña*: parábola de la represión sexual', *Camp de l'Arpa,* 40 (January 1977), 23–26.

Echavarren, Roberto, 'La superficie de lectura de *The Buenos Aires Affair*', *Espiral/Revista*, 3 (1977), 147–74.

— — '*El beso de la mujer araña* y las metáforas del sujeto', *Revista Iberoamericana*, 102–3 (1978), 65–75.

Epple, Juan Armando, '*The Buenos Aires Affair* y la estructura de la novela policíaca', *Revista de Literaturas Hispánicas*, X (1976), 19–56.

Esplugas, Celia Catalina, 'Female Sexual Encounters in Works by Sherwood Anderson and Manuel Puig and Existential Themes and Literary Techniques in Sherwood Anderson's and Manuel Puig's Works', unpublished Ph.D. dissertation, University of Toledo (1981).

Ezquerro, Milagros, *Que raconter c'est apprendre à mourir* (Toulouse-Le-Mirail: Institut d'Études Hispaniques et Hispano-Américaines, Université de Toulouse-Le-Mirail, 1981).

— — 'Le fonctionnement sémiologique des personnages dans *Bajo un manto de estrellas* de Manuel Puig', *Caravelle*, XL (1983).

— — 'Norme et transgression dans *El beso de la mujer araña*, in *Actes du Colloque sur l'Oeuvre de Puig et Vargas Llosa*, Avril 1982 (q.v.), pp.143–46.

— — 'La organización narrativa: el relato y el diálogo', in *Organizaciones textuales* (q.v.), pp.295–99. See also under Débax.

Fiorillo, Marília Pacheco, 'Um romance fora do lugar', *IstoÉ* (2 June 1982), p.18.

Foster, D.W., 'Manuel Puig and the Uses of Nostalgia', *Latin American Literary Review*, I (1972), 79–81.

— — 'Manuel Puig', in *Modern Latin American Literature*, II, eds. D.W. Foster and Virginia Ramos (New York: Frederick Ungar Publishing Co., 1975), pp. 190–96.

— — *Currents in the Contemporary Argentine Novel* (Columbia: The University of Missouri Press, 1975), pp.144–48.

Galán, Diego, '*Boquitas pintadas*', *Triunfo*, 756 (23 July 1977). (Review of the film.)

Gallagher, D.P., *Modern Latin American Literature* (Oxford University Press, 1973), pp.186–88.

Galvão, João Cândido, 'Pedreiro do Rio', *Veja* (19 May 1982), p.153.

García, Franklin, 'Distintas formas de montaje en la novelística hispano-americana contemporánea', *Revista Canadiense de Estudios Hispánicos*, III, No.1 (1978), 1–25.

García Ramos, Juan Manuel, '*Pubis angelical* o de la imposibilidad del discurso', *Liminar*, III (September–October 1979), p.19.

— — 'Manuel Puig, final de itinerario', *El País* (8 August 1982).

— — *La narrativa de Manuel Puig (Por una crítica en libertad)*. (La Laguna: Secretariado de Publicaciones de la Universidad de La Laguna, 1982).

Gimferrer, Pere, 'Aproximaciones a Manuel Puig', *Plural*, V, 9, 57 (June 1976), 21–25. Reprinted in *Radicalidades* (Barcelona: Antoni Bosch, 1978), pp.84–97.

Girón, Socorro, 'Tango, técnica y lenguaje en *Boquitas pintadas*', *Ceiba*, IX-X (July–December 1976, January–June 1977), 5–27.

Golluscio de Montoya, Eva, 'Director y procesado: elementos pseudo dramáticos en *El beso de la mujer araña*, in *Actes du Colloque sur l'Oeuvre de Puig et*

Vargas Llosa, Avril 1982 (q.v.), pp. 147–52.

González Uriarte, Walter, El beso de la mujer araña y el cine', in *Actes du Colloque sur l'Oeuvre de Puig et Vargas Llosa, Avril 1982* (q.v.), pp.101–5.

Goytisolo, Juan, 'Manuel Puig: una novela política', *El Viejo Topo* (December 1979), 63–64.

Gramuglio, María Teresa, 'El discreto encanto de Manuel Puig', *Punto de vista*, III (1980), p.8.

Hazera, Lydia H., 'Narrative Technique in Manuel Puig's *Boquitas pintadas*', *Latin American Literary Review*, II, No.3 (Fall–Winter 1973), 45–53.

Josef, Bella, 'Manuel Puig: Renovação pela linguagem', *O Estado de São Paulo* (27 June 1971), p.1. Also in Spanish, in *Literatura de la emancipación hispanoamericana y otros ensayos* (Memoria del XX Congreso del Instituto de Literatura Iberoamericana, Lima: Universidad de San Marcos, 1972), pp.287–89.

— — 'Reflexión al nivel de la enunciación', *Nueva Narrativa Hispanoamericana*, IV (1974), 111–16.

Kerr, Lucille, 'The Fiction of Popular Design and Desire: Manuel Puig's *Boquitas pintadas*', *Modern Language Notes*, 97 (1982), 411–21.

Lázaro, Jesús, 'La inquisición sobre la soledad de Manuel Puig', *Quimera* (February 1981), 43–46.

Le Bigot, Claude, 'Fantasme, mythe et parole dans *El beso de la mujer araña*', *Les Langues Néo-Latines*, 75, No.3 (1981), 25–56. Reprinted in part as 'Mito órfico y lectura mítica de *El beso de la mujer araña* de Manuel Puig', *Nueva Estafeta*, 45–46 (August–September 1982), 67–70.

Lewis, Bart L., '*Pubis angelical*: la mujer codificada', *Revista Iberoamericana* 123–24 (April–September 1983), 531–40.

Libertella, Héctor, *Nueva escritura en Latinoamérica* (Caracas: Monte Ávila, 1977), pp.86–89.

Lindstrom, Naomi, 'The Problem of Pop Culture in the Novels of Manuel 'Puig', *The American Hispanist* (November–December 1978), 28–31.

Linenberg, Raquel, 'Léxico argentino en *El beso de la mujer araña* y algunos apuntes más', *Les Langues Néo-Latines*, 76, No.1 (1982), 49–66.

Londres, Maria Cecília Garcia, '*Boquinhas Pintadas*: o direito e avesso do mito', *Tempo Brasileiro*, 40 (1975), 29–34.

Luchting, Wolfgang A., 'Betrayed by Education: Manuel Puig's *La traición de Rita Hayworth*', *Proceedings of the Pacific Northwest Conference on Foreign Languages*, 28, No.1 (1977), 134–37.

Ludmer, Iris Josefina, '*Boquitas pintadas*: siete recorridos', *Actual* (January–December 1971), 3–21.

Luraschi, Ilse Adriana, 'Donde se trata de la virginidad, otros milagros y demás razones de amor y sexo en dos textos de Manuel Puig, con todo sistema', *Hispanic Journal*, I, 1 (1979).

MacAdam, Alfred J., 'Las crónicas de Manuel Puig', *Cuadernos Hispanoamericanos*, 274 (April 1973), 84–107. Published in English as 'Manuel Puig's Chronicles of Provincial Life', *Revista Hispánica Moderna*, 36 (1970–71), 50–65. There is a modified version of this article in the author's *Modern Latin American Narratives. The Dreams of Reason*, called 'Things as they are' (The University of Chicago Press, 1977), pp.91–101.

McCracken, E., 'Manuel Puig's *Heartbreak Tango*: Women and Mass Culture', *Latin American Literary Review*, 18 (1980–81), 27–36.

Macchi, Yves, 'Fonction narrative des notes infrapaginales dans *El beso de la mujer araña* de Manuel Puig', *Les Langues Néo-Latines*, 76 (1982), 67–81.

Magnarelli, Sharon, 'Manuel Puig's *La traición de Rita Hayworth*: Betrayed by the Cross-Stitch', in *The Lost Rib. Female Characters in the Spanish-American Novel* (London and Toronto: Associated University Presses, 1985), pp.117–46.

Maillard, Lucien, '*La Trahison de Rita Hayworth* — l'enfance déflorée de Manuel Puig', *Combat* (26 June 1969).

Maldonado, Armando, 'Manuel Puig: The aesthetics of cinematic and psychological fiction', unpublished Ph.D. dissertation, University of Oklahoma (1977).

Marco, Joaquín, 'La peor novela de Manuel Puig: *Maldición eterna a quien lea estas páginas*', *La Vanguardia* (8 January 1981).

— — 'Manuel Puig reincide en la vulgaridad: *Sangre de amor correspondido*', *La Vanguardia* (28 April 1982.)

Masiello, Francine R., 'Jail House Flicks: Projections by Manuel Puig', *Symposium*, XXXII, No.1 (Spring 1978), 15–24.

Madeiros, Benício, 'O Novo Romance do Carioca Manuel Puig', *IstoÉ* (January 1981).

Mejía, Eduardo (with Urrutia, q.v.), 'Entre la bendición y la maldición', *La Onda* (11 January 1981), p.4.

Merrim, Stephanie, 'For a New (Psychological) Novel in the Works of Manuel Puig', *Novel: A Forum on Fiction*, 17, 2 (Winter 1984), 141–57.

Mimoso-Ruiz, Duarte, 'Aspects des "média" dans *El beso de la mujer araña* et *La tía Julia y el escribidor*', *Les Langues Néo-Latines*, 76 (1982), 29–47.

Minard, Evelyne, '*La traición de Rita Hayworth:* violence et mort dans l'Argentine de Manuel Puig', *Caravelle*, 39, 75–80.

Minc, Rose S. (ed.), *Literature and Popular Culture in the Hispanic World* (Gaithersburg: Hispamérica and Montclair State College, 1981).

Miranda, Julio E., 'Manuel Puig: la explosión del lenguaje', *Zona Franca*, I (1978), 51–54.

Mitchell, Phyllis, 'The Reel against the Real: Cinema in the Novels of Guillermo Cabrera Infante and Manuel Puig', *Latin American Literary Review*, VI, 2 (1978), 22–29.

Molho, Maurice, 'Tango de la madre arana', in *Actes du Colloque sur l'Oeuvre de Puig et Vargas Llosa, Avril 1982* (q.v.), pp. 161–68.

Morales, Miguel Ángel, 'The Puig affair', *Revista de la Universidad de México*, 33, No. 7 (1978), 22–24.

Morello-Frosch, Marta, '*La traición de Rita Hayworth,* o el nuevo arte de narrar películas', *Sin Nombre*, IV, No. 1 (1970), 77–82. In English as 'The New Art of Narrating Films', *Review 72* (Winter 1971–Spring 1972), 52–55.

— — 'Manuel Puig: *La traición de Rita Hayworth* y *Boquitas pintadas*', in *Narradores hispanoamericanos de hoy* (Chapel Hill, 1973).

— — 'La sexualidad opresiva en las obras de Manuel Puig', *Nueva Narrativa Hispanoamericana*, V, (1975), 151–58.

— — 'Usos y abusos de la cultura popular: *Pubis angelical* de Manuel Puig', in

Literature and Popular Culture, ed. Rose S. Minc (q.v.), pp.31–42.

Muñoz, Elías Miguel, 'El discurso de la sexualidad en Manuel Puig', unpublished Ph.D. dissertation, University of California at Irvine (1984).

—— 'Sangre de amor correspondido y el discurso del poder judeocristiano', *Revista Iberoamericana*, 130–31 (January–June 1985), 73–88.

Nogueira, Paulo, 'Conversas Mágicas', *Veja* (14 September 1983), 109–110.

Nolla, Olga, 'The Buenos Aires Affair', *Zona carga y descarga*, I, No. 6 (September–December 1973), 28–29.

Obregón, Osvaldo, 'El beso de la mujer araña: la adaptación teatral de Manuel Puig', in *Actes du Colloque sur l'Oeuvre de Puig et Vargas Llosa, Avril 1982* (q.v.), pp.115–21.

Ordóñez de Parra, Montserrat, 'Tres tristes tigres y La traición de Rita Hayworth: teoría y práctica del discurso narrativo', *Eco,* XXVIII/5, No. 173 (March 1975), 516–29.

—— 'Fragmentation and Narrative Levels in Manuel Puig's *Boquitas pintadas:* Computer-assisted Analysis of an Experimental Novel', unpublished Ph.D. dissertation, University of Wisconsin, Madison (1976).

—— 'El computador como instrumento de investigación: una concordancia de *Boquitas pintadas* de Manuel Puig', in *Los escritores hispanoamericanos frente a sus críticos* (International Colloquium, Toulouse, March 10–12 1982; Toulouse-Le-Mirail: Travaux de l'Université de Toulouse-Le-Mirail, 1983), pp.87–105.

Oviedo, José Miguel, 'La doble exposición de Manuel Puig', *Eco,* XXXI/6, No. 192 (October 1977), 607–26.

Panesi, Jorge, 'Manuel Puig: las relaciones peligrosas', *Revista Iberoamericana*, 125 (October–December 1983), 903–17.

Pellón, Gustavo, 'Manuel Puig's Contradictory Strategy: Kitsch Paradigm *versus* Paradigmatic Structure in *El beso de la mujer araña* and *Pubis angelical*', *Symposium*, XXXVII (1983), 186–201.

Perrin, Annie and Françoise Zmantar Pez, 'La telaraña modelo de organización textual en *El beso de la mujer araña* de Manuel Puig. Elementos para una hifología del texto', in *Organizaciones textuales* (q.v.), pp.263–69.

Piglia, Ricardo, 'Clase media: cuerpo y destino (Una lectura de *La traición de Rita Hayworth* de Manuel Puig)', *Nueva Novela Latinoamericana*, II, ed. J. Lafforgue (Buenos Aires: Editorial Paidós, 1972), pp.350–62.

Pontes, Mário, 'Um diálogo extenuante', *Jornal do Brasil* (12 September 1983).

Rama, Ángel, 'El último Puig. La máxima ambigüedad', *El Universal* (31 January 1982). Also in *Unomásuno*, called 'El diálogo imposible'.

Ramond, Michèle, 'La femme ombilicale (Quelques réflexions sur la *Femme araignée* à partir de l'image de couverture)', in *Actes du Colloque sur l'Oeuvre de Puig et Vargas Llosa, Avril 1982* (q.v.), pp.155–59. See also under Débax.

Reedy, Daniel R., 'Del beso de la mujer araña a la tía Julia: estructura y distancia interior', *Revista Iberoamericana*, 116–17 (July–December 1981), 109–16.

Rodríguez-Luis, J., 'Boquitas pintadas ¿folletín unanimista?' *Sin Nombre,* V, No. 1 (1974), 50–56.

Rodríguez Monegal, Emir, 'A Literary Myth Exploded', *Review 72* (Winter 1971–Spring 1972), p.64.

—— 'La traición de Rita Hayworth: una tarea de desmitificación', in *Narradores de esta América*, II (Buenos Aires: Editorial Alfa Argentina, 1974), pp.365–80.

—— 'Los sueños de Evita: a propósito de la última novela de Manuel Puig', in *Narradores de esta América*, II (Buenos Aires: Editorial Alfa Argentina, 1974), pp.381–93.

Rodríguez Padrón, Jorge, 'Manuel Puig y la capacidad expresiva de la lengua popular', *Cuadernos Hispanoamericanos*, 245 (1970), 490–97.

—— 'Las mujeres de la novelas de Manuel Puig', *El Día* (21 October 1979). Also in *El País*.

—— 'Manuel Puig: el diálogo como catarsis', Nos. 1 and 2, *Diario de Las Palmas* (20 February 1981 and 3 March 1981).

—— 'Las múltiples voces de la narrativa de Manuel Puig', Nos. 1 and 2, *Diario de Las Palmas* (11 June 1982 and 19 June 1982).

Rodríguez Rivero, Manuel, 'Besos y panfletos', *Cuadernos para el diálogo,* 205 (April 1977), p.56.

Ruffinelli, Jorge, 'Manuel Puig: el arte y el artificio', *Marcha*, XXXIV, No.1646 (8 June 1973), p. 31. Reprinted in *Crítica en Marcha* (Mexico City: Premia, 1979), pp.192–95.

Safir, Margery A., 'Mitología: otro nivel de metalenguaje en *Boquitas pintadas*', *Revista Iberoamericana*, 90 (1975), 47–58.

Salado, Ana, '*Sangre de amor correspondido*, de Manuel Puig', *Hoja del lunes* (12 April 1982).

San José, Antonio, 'Un narrador llamado Manuel Puig', *Región* (3 February 1981).

Sánchez, Alfonso, 'El gran Torre Nilsson no está ausente en *Boquitas pintadas*', *Informaciones* (19 September 1974).

Sánchez Arnosi, Milagros, '*Bajo un manto de estrellas*', *Ínsula*, 452–53 (1984), p.15.

Sarduy, Severo, '*Boquitas pintadas*; parodia e injerto', *Sur*, 321 (November–December 1969), 71–77.

—— 'Notas a las notas a las notas . . . a propósito de Manuel Puig', *Revista Iberoamericana*, 37 (July–December 1971), 555–67.

Sarlo, Beatriz, 'Cortázar, Sábato, Puig: ¿parodia o reportaje?' *Los Libros*, 36 (July–August 1974), 32–33.

Sarris, Andrew, 'Rerunning Puig and Cabrera Infante', *Review 73* (Fall 1973), 46–48.

Sarrochi, Augusto C., 'Sobre el narrador de *La traición de Rita Hayworth*', *Signos*, IX–X (1973–74), 95–104.

Schmucler, Héctor, 'Los silencios significativos', *Los Libros*, IV (1969).

Shaw, Donald L., *Nueva Narrativa Hispanoamericana* (Madrid: Cátedra, 1981), pp.197–201.

Silva-Cáceres, Raúl, 'Técnicas de suspensión y alienación en *El beso de la mujer araña*', in *Actes du Colloque sur l'Oeuvre de Puig et Vargas Llosa, Avril 1982* (q.v.), pp.123–30.

Silveira, Joel, 'O Carioca Puig', *Ultima Hora* (26 May 1982).

Solotorevsky, Myrna, 'El cliché en *Pubis angelical* y *Boquitas pintadas*: desgaste y creatividad', *Hispamérica*, XIII, No.38 (1984), 3–18.

Southward, David R., 'Betrayed by Manuel Puig: Reader Deception and

Anti-climax in his Novels', *Latin American Literary Review*, IV, 9 (Fall–Winter 1976), 22–28.

Suñén, Luis, 'Manuel Puig: la imagen es el otro', *El País* (11 January 1981).

—— 'Amor correspondido y juego sentimental', *El País* (13 June 1982).

Thiebaut, Guy, *'El beso de la mujer araña*, novela comprometida', in *Actes du Colloque sur l'Oeuvre de Puig et Vargas Llosa, Avril 1982* (q.v.), pp.131–42.

Tittler, Jonathan, *Narrative Irony in the Contemporary Spanish-American Novel* (Ithaca: Cornell University Press, 1983), pp.78–100.

—— 'Order, Chaos and Re-order: The Novels of Manuel Puig', *Kentucky Romance Quarterly*, II (1983).

Torres Fierro, Danubio, *'Pubis angelical* de Manuel Puig', *Vuelta*, 36 (November 1979), 42–44.

Trejo, Mario, 'Enigma para directores', *Cambio 16*, 612 (22 August 1983), p.96.

Triviños, Gilberto, 'La destrucción del verosímil folletinesco en *Boquitas pintadas*', *Texto Crítico*, IX (1976), 117–30. Also in *Acta Literaria*, I (Universidad de Concepción, 1975), pp.113–47.

Urrutia, Elena (with Mejía, q.v.) 'Entre la bendición y la maldición', *La Onda* (11 January 1981), p.4.

Vanderlynden, Anne-Marie, 'Hacia una semiología de los discursos referidos en *El beso de la mujer araña*', in *Organizaciones textuales* (q.v.), pp. 271–77.

Various, *Organizaciones textuales (Textos hispánicos)*, Actas del III Simposio del Séminaire d'Études Littéraires de l'Université de Toulouse-Le-Mirail, Toulouse, May 1980 (Toulouse: Publications de l'Université de Toulouse-Le-Mirail, Travaux de l'Université No.XVI, 1981). Section B: *'El beso de la mujer araña* de Manuel Puig. La especificidad de una organización narrativa', pp. 261–99. See also under Alsina, Débax, Ezquerro, Perrin and Vanderlynden.

Various, *Actes du Colloque sur l'Oeuvre de Puig et Vargas Llosa, Avril 1982* (Fontenay-aux-Roses: les Cahiers de Fontenay, No. 26.27, 1982), pp.93–168. See also under Bianchi, Ezquerro, Golluscio de Montoya, González Uriarte, Molho, Obregón, Ramond, Silva-Cáceres, Thiebaut and Vich-Campos.

Vich-Campos, Maryse, 'L'invention de Molina (à propos du film *Cat People* dans *El beso de la mujer araña*, de Manuel Puig)', *Actes du Colloque sur l'Oeuvre de Puig et Vargas Llosa, Avril 1982* (q.v.), pp.107–13.

Weiss, Judith, 'Dynamic Correlations in *Heartbreak Tango*', *Latin American Literary Review*, III, No.5 (Fall–Winter 1974), 137–41.

Wood, Michael, 'The Claims of Mischief', *The New York Review of Books* (24 January 1980), 43–47.

Worley, Joan Yvonne, 'Film into Fiction: Thomas Pynchon and Manuel Puig', unpublished Ph.D. dissertation, Ohio University (1983),

Wyers (Weber), Frances, 'Manuel Puig at the Movies', *Hispanic Review*, 49, 2 (1981), 163–81.

Yakir, Dan, *"O Beijo da Mulher Aranha*. Atores e Produtores Americanos Filmam a Obra de Manuel Puig', *Jornal do Brasil* (13 March 1984).

Yudice, George, *'El beso de la mujer araña* y *Pubis angelical:* entre el placer y el saber', in *Literature and Popular Culture*, ed. Rose S. Minc (q.v.), pp.43–57.

Zmantar Pez, Françoise, see under Perrin.

IX   General

Adler, Alfred, *Social Interest: A Challenge to Mankind*, trans. John Linton and Richard Vaughan (London: Faber & Faber, 1938).

Alexander, Robert J., *The Perón Era* (New York: Russell & Russell, 1965). First published: 1951.

—— *Juan Domingo Perón: A History* (Boulder, Colorado: Westview Press, 1979).

Allen, Rupert C., *Psyche and Symbol in the Theater of Federico García Lorca* (Austin: The University of Texas Press, 1974).

Alter, Robert, 'Mimesis and the Motive for Fiction', *Tri-Quarterly*, 42 (1978), p.247.

Amorós, Andrés, *Sociología de una novela rosa* (Madrid: Taurus, 1968).

—— *Subliteraturas* (Barcelona: Ariel, 1974).

Appleyard, Bryan, 'A risky stand against the ironic mode', *The Times* (14 February 1984), p.17.

Arnaud, Noël, Francis Lacassin and Jean Portel, *Entretiens sur la Paralittérature. Colloque de Cerisy-la-Salle* (Paris: Éditions Plon, 1970).

Arnold, Magda B. (ed.), *The Nature of Emotion* (Harmondsworth: Penguin Books Ltd., 1968).

Ashe, Geoffrey, *The Virgin* (London: Routledge & Kegan Paul, 1976).

Avellaneda, Andrés Óscar, 'El tema del peronismo en la narrativa argentina', unpublished Ph.D. dissertation, University of Illinois at Urbana-Champaign, (1973).

Bacarisse, Pamela, *A Alma Amortalhada. Mário de Sá-Carneiro's Use of Metaphor and Image* (London: Tamesis, 1984).

Bacarisse, Salvador (ed.), *Contemporary Latin American Fiction* (Edinburgh: Scottish Academic Press, 1980).

Bakhtin, Mikhail, *Rabelais and his World*, trans. Helene Iswolsky (Cambridge, Mass: The MIT Press, 1968).

—— *Problems of Dostoevsky's Poetics*, trans. Caryl Emerson (Manchester University Press, 1984).

Bellemin-Noël, Jean, *Psychanalyse et Littérature* (Paris: Presses Universitaires de France, 1978).

Bettelheim, Bruno, *The Uses of Enchantment. The Meaning and Importance of Fairy Tales* (London: Thames & Hudson, 1976).

—— *Freud and Man's Soul* (London: Chatto & Windus, 1983).

Blanksten, George I., *Perón's Argentina* (The University of Chicago Press, Midway Reprint, 1974). First published: 1953.

Bold, Alan (ed.), *The Sexual Dimension in Literature* (London: Vision and Barnes & Noble, 1982).

Booth, Mark, *Camp* (London: Quartet Books, 1983).

Booth, Wayne, *A Rhetoric of Irony* (Chicago: The University of Chicago Press, 1974).

Branden, Nathaniel, *The Psychology of Romantic Love* (New York: Bantam Books, 1983). First published: 1980.

Broch, Hermann, 'Algunas consideraciones acerca del problema del *kitsch*', and 'El kitsch', in *Poesía e investigación* (Barcelona: Barral Editores, 1974), pp.367–83 and 424–32.

Campbell, Joseph, *The Hero with a Thousand Faces* (Princeton University Press, Bollingen Series XVII, 1973). First published: 1949.

Cantón, Darío, *El mundo de los tangos de Gardel* (Buenos Aires: Instituto Torcuato Di Tella, Centro de Investigaciones Sociales, 1969).

Cavell, Stanley, *The World Viewed* (Cambridge, Mass. and London: Harvard University Press, enlarged edition, 1979). First published: 1971.

Cavendish, Richard, *The Black Arts* (London: Routledge & Kegan Paul, 1967).

Cazamian, L., *A History of French Literature* (Oxford University Press, 1960). First published: 1955.

Cirlot, Juan-Eduardo, *Diccionario de símbolos* (Barcelona: Labor, 1969).

Collins, Richard, 'The Film', in *Discrimination and Popular Culture*, ed. Denys Thompson (q.v.).

Cornejo, Carlos Alberto, 'Sin límites fuera de Chile', *Ercilla* (31 May 1967), p.62.

Deleuze, Gilles, *Masochismo e Sadismo* (Milan: Iota Libri, 1973).

Dellepiane, Ángela, 'Diez años de novela argentina', *Problemas de literatura*, I, No. 1 (1972), 57–74.

Denevi, Marco, *Rosaura a las diez* (1955) (Buenos Aires: Corregidor, 1980).

Duarte de Perón, Evita, *La razón de mi vida* (1953).

Eliade, Mircea, *Mito y realidad*, 3rd edition (Madrid: Guadarrama, 1978).

Enzensberger, Hans Magnus, *The Consciousness Industry. On Literature, Politics and the Media* (New York: Seabury, 1974).

Erens, Patricia (ed.), *Sexual Stratagems. The World of Women in Film* (New York: Horizon Press, 1979).

Fell, John L., *Film and the Narrative Tradition* (Norman: The University of Oklahoma Press, 1974).

Fiedler, Leslie A., *What was Literature? Class Culture and Mass Society* (New York: Simon & Schuster, 1984). First published: 1982.

Flora, Cornelia Butler and Flora, Jan L., 'The *fotonovela* as a cultural domination', *Latin American Perspectives*, 16, V, No. 1, 'Culture in the Age of Mass Media' (Winter 1978), 134–50.

Foucault, Michel, *Les Mots et les choses* (Paris: Gallimard, 1966).

—— *La Volonté de savoir (Histoire de la Sexualité, I)* (Paris: Gallimard, 1976).

Freud, Sigmund, *The Standard Edition of the Complete Psychological Works of Sigmund Freud*, trans. and ed. by James Strachey in collaboration with Anna Freud (London: The Hogarth Press and the Institute of Psycho-analysis, 1974).

Fromm, Erich, *The Fear of Freedom* (London: Routledge & Kegan Paul, 1961). First published: 1942.

—— *The Art of Loving* (New York: Harper & Row, Perennial Library, 1974). First published: 1956.

—— *Greatness and Limitations of Freud's Thought* (London: Jonathan Cape, 1980). First published as *Sigmund Freuds Psychanalyse — Grösse und Greuzen* (1979).

Frye, Northrop, *The Great Code. The Bible and Literature* (London: Routledge & Kegan Paul, 1983). First published: 1982.

García Ramos, Juan Manuel, 'Vargas Llosa y el "kitsch"', *Camp de l'Arpa*, 55–56 (October 1978), 73–75.

Gaskell, G.A., *Dictionary of All Scriptures and Myths* (New York: The Julian Press Inc., 1960).

Goffman, Erving, *Gender Advertisements* (New York: Harper & Row, 1979). Originally in *Studies in the Anthropology of Visual Communication*, III, No.2 (Fall 1976).

Graves, Robert, *The White Goddess* (London: Faber & Faber, 1961).

Hagen, Wolfgang von, *The Ancient Sun Kingdoms of the Americas* (St. Albans: Paladin, 1973). First published: 1962.

Haskell, Molly, *From Reverence to Rape. The Treatment of Women in the Movies* (Harmondsworth: Penguin Books Ltd., 1974).

Hillman, James, *Emotion. A Comprehensive Phenomenology of Theories and their Meanings for Therapy* (London: Routledge & Kegan Paul. 1960).

Howe, Irving, 'Notes on Mass Culture', *Politics*, 5 (Spring 1949), 120–23.

Hutcheon, Linda, *Formalism and the Freudian Aesthetic: The Example of Charles Mauron* (Cambridge University Press, 1984).

Isherwood, Christopher, *The World in the Evening* (London: Methuen, 1954).

Jacobs, Joseph (ed.), *More English Fairy Tales* (New York: Schocken Books, 1968).

Jankélevitch, Vladimir, *L'Ironie* (Paris: Flammarion, 1964).

Jung, Carl Gustav, *Psychology of the Unconscious. A Study of the Transformation and Symbolisms of the Libido* (1917) (London: Routledge & Kegan Paul, 1951).

—— *Alchemical Studies*, trans. R.F.C. Hull (New York: Bollingen Foundation, 1967).

—— *Psychology and Alchemy*, 2nd edition (London: Routledge & Kegan Paul, 1980).

Kael, Pauline, 'The Current Cinema: Dreamers', *The New Yorker* (21 December 1981), 122–33.

Kaputschenko, Ludmila, 'El tango: máxima expresión de un pueblo', in *Literature and Popular Culture*, ed. Rose S. Minc (q.v.).

Keppler, C.F., *The Literature of the Second Self* (Tucson: The University of Arizona Press, 1972).

Kracauer, Siegfried, *Theory of Film. The Redemption of Physical Reality* (Oxford University Press, 1960).

Krafft-Ebing, Richard von, 'Bemerkungen ueber "geschlechtliche Hoerigkeit" und 'Masochismus', *Jahrbueche fuer Psychiatrie*, X Bd. (1892).

Kuhn, Annette, *Women's Pictures. Feminism and Cinema* (London: Routledge & Kegan Paul, 1982).

—— *The Power of the Image. Essays on Representation and Sexuality* (London: Routledge & Kegan Paul, 1985).

Lacan, Jacques, 'La signification du phallus', in *Écrits*, II (Paris: Éditions du Seuil, 1971).

—— *The Four Fundamental Concepts of Psycho-Analysis*, trans. Alan Sheridan (Harmondsworth: Penguin Books Ltd., 1979). First published: 1973.

Laing, R.D., *Knots* (Harmondsworth: Penguin Books Ltd., 1972).

Lemarr, Hedy, *Ecstasy and Me. My Life as a Woman* (London: W.H. Allen, 1967).

Laplanche, Jean and Pontalis, Jean-Bertrand, *Diccionario de psicoanálisis* (Barcelona: Labor, 1974). Originally *Vocabulaire de la Psychanalyse*, 2nd, revised edition, Paris: Presses Universitaires de France (1968).

Leclaire, S., 'La Réalité du désir', in *Sur la Sexualité humaine* (Centre d'Études Laennec).

Lemaire, Anika, *Jacques Lacan*, trans. David Macey (London: Routledge & Kegan Paul, 1982). First published: 1970.

Libertella, Héctor, 'Algo sobre la novísima literatura argentina', *Hispamérica*, II, No.6 (1974), 13–19.

McConnell, Frank D., *The Spoken Seen: Film and the Romantic Imagination* (Baltimore: The Johns Hopkins University Press, 1975).

— — *Storytelling and Mythmaking. Images from Film and Literature* (New York: Oxford University Press, 1979).

McCracken, Ellen, 'Vargas Llosa's *La tía Julia y el escribidor:* The New Novel and the Mass Media', *Ideologies and Literature*, III (1980), 54–69.

McQuarrie, John, *Existentialism* (Harmondsworth: Penguin Books Ltd., 1976). First published: 1972.

Madariaga, Salvador de, *Guía del lector del "Quijote"* (Mexico City: Editorial Hermés, 1953).

Mattelart, Armand, 'The Nature of Communications Practice in a Dependent Society', *Latin American Perspectives,* 16, V, No. 1, 'Culture in the Age of Mass Media' (Winter 1978), 13–34.

Mercier Vega, Louis, *Autopsia de Perón. Balance del peronismo* (Barcelona: Tusquets, 1975). Originally *Autopsie de Peron. Bilan du péronisme* (Gembloux: J. Duculot, 1974).

Metz, Christian, *Le Signifiant imaginaire. Psychanalyse et cinéma* (Paris: Union Générale d'Éditions, 1977).

Mieli, Mario, *Elementos de crítica homosexual* (Barcelona: Anagrama, 1979). Originally *Elementi di critica omosessuale* (Turin: Giulio Einaudi Editore, 1977).

Millett, Kate, *Sexual Politics* (London: Virago Press, 1985). First edition: 1974.

Mitchell, Juliet, *Psychoanalysis and Feminism* (Harmondsworth: Penguin Books Ltd., 1982). First published: 1974.

Moi, Toril, *Sexual/Textual Politics: Feminist Literary Theory* (London and New York: Methuen, New Accents, 1985).

Muecke, D.C., *Irony* (London: Methuen, 1970).

Naipaul, V.S., *The Return of Eva Perón, with the Killings in Trinidad* (Harmondsworth: Penguin Books Ltd., 1981), esp. pp.150–51.

Neumann, Erich, *The Great Mother,* trans. Ralph Manheim, 2nd ed.(Princeton University Press, 1963). First published: 1955.

Orwell, 'Good Bad Books' (1945), in *The Collected Essays. Journalism and Letters of George Orwell*, Vol. IV (London: Secker & Warburg, 1968).

Paz, Octavio, *Conjunciones y disyunciones* (Mexico City: Joaquín Mortiz, 1969).

Prieto, Ramón, *Treinta años de vida argentina, 1945–1975* (Buenos Aires: Editorial Sudamericana, 1977).

Propp, Vladimir, *Morfología del cuento*, trans. Lourdes Ortiz (Madrid: Editorial Fundamentos, 1985). First published: 1928.

— — *Las raíces históricas del cuento*, trans. José Martín Arancibia (Madrid: Editorial Fundamentos, 1984). First published: 1946.

Radin, Paul, *The Trickster: A Study in American Indian Mythology* (New York: Philosophical Library, 1956).

Ramos, Jorge Abelardo, *La era del peronismo 1943–1976*, 8th edition (Buenos Aires: Ediciones del Mar Dulce, 1981).

Rank, Otto, *The Myth of the Birth of the Hero* (1909), trans. F. Robbins and S.E. Gelife (New York, 1952).

—— *Don Juan et Le Double. Études Psychanalytiques* (1922 and 1914), trans. S. Lautman (Paris: Petite Bibliothèque Payot, s.d.).

—— *Art and Artist*, trans. Charles Francis Atkinson (New York: Alfred A. Knopf Inc., 1943).

—— *Truth and Reality. The Central Statement of Rank's Ideas* (1929), trans. Jessie Taft (New York: W.W. Norton and Co., 1978).

Rascovsky, Arnaldo, *La cara oculta del cine. Cine a la luz del psicoanálisis* (Buenos Aires: Schapire, 1975).

Rivera, Jorge B., *El folletín y la novela popular* (Buenos Aires: Centro Editor de América Latina, 1971).

Rodríguez Sánchez, Margarita, *Gravitación política de Perón (1955/1973)* (Mexico City: Editorial Extemporáneos, 1979).

Rose, H.J., *A Handbook of Greek Mythology* (London: Methuen, 1928).

Rosen, Marjorie, *Popcorn Venus: Women, Movies and the American Dream* (New York: Coward, McCann & Geoghegan, 1973).

Rousset, Jean, *Le Mythe de Don Juan* (Paris: Armand Colin, 1978).

Rudwin, Maximilian, *The Devil in Legend and Literature* (La Salle, Illinois: The Open Court Publishing Co., 1973). First published: 1931.

Russell, B., 'The Superior Virtue of the Oppressed', in *Unpopular Essays* (New York: Simon & Schuster, 1959), pp.59–64.

Rycroft, Charles, *Reich* (London: Fontana/Collins, 1971).

Sábato, Ernesto, *El otro rostro del peronismo. Carta abierta a Mario Amadeo* (Buenos Aires, 1956).

—— *Tango. Discusión y clave* (Buenos Aires: Losada, 1963).

Sánchez, Luis Rafael, 'Apuntación mínima de lo soez', in *Literature and Popular Culture*, ed. Rose S. Minc (q.v.), pp.9–14.

Sater, William F., *The Southern Cone Nations of Latin America* (Arlington Heights, Illinois: The Forum Press, 1984).

Schenk, H.G., *The Mind of the European Romantics* (Oxford University Press, 1979).

Schiminovich, Flora H., 'El juego narcisista y ficcional en *Sangre de amor correspondido*', *Discurso literario,* I, 2 (Spring 1984), 295–301.

Schwartz, Kessel, 'Homosexuality as a Theme in Representative Contemporary Spanish American Novels', *Kentucky Romance Quarterly,* 22 (1975), 247–57.

Sebreli, Juan José, *Eva Perón ¿aventurera o militante?* (Buenos Aires: Siglo XXI, 1966).

Serrano Poncela, Segundo, *Literatura y subliteratura* (Caracas: Universidad Central de Venezuela, 1966).

Sontag, Susan, *Illness as Metaphor* (New York: Farrer, Strauss and Giroux, 1978).

—— *A Susan Sontag Reader* (Harmondsworth: Penguin Books Ltd., 1983), esp.

'Notes on "Camp"', pp.105–19, and 'The Pornographic Imagination', pp. 205–33.

Stafford-Clark, David, *What Freud Really Said* (Harmondsworth: Penguin Books Ltd., 1967). First published: 1965.

Storr, Anthony, *Sexual Deviation* (Harmondsworth: Penguin Books Ltd., 1964).

Swan, Helena, *Girls' Christian Names* (Rutland, Vermont: Charles E. Tuttle, 1973).

Szasz, Thomas, *Sex: Facts, Frauds and Follies* (Oxford: Basil Blackwell, 1981). First published: 1980.

Thibault, Albert, *Histoire de la Littérature française de 1789 à nos jours* (Paris: Stock, 1936).

Thomson, David, *A Biographical Dictionary of the Cinema* (London: Secker & Warburg, 1975).

Thompson, Denys (ed.), *Discrimination and Popular Culture*, 2nd ed. (Harmondsworth: Penguin Books Ltd., 1973).

Trilling, Lionel, *The Liberal Imagination* (London: Heinemann, Mercury Books, 1961), esp. 'Art and Neurosis', pp.160–80. First published: 1950.

Tunstall, Jeremy, *The Media are American* (New York: Columbia University Press, 1977).

Tyler, Parker, *The Hollywood Hallucination* (1944) (New York: Garland Publishing Inc., 1982).

—— *Magic and Myth of the Movies* (1947) (London: Secker & Warburg, 1971).

Ulla, Noemí, *Tango, rebelión y nostalgia* (Buenos Aires: Editorial Jorge Álvarez, 1967).

Viñas, David, 'Después de Cortázar: historia e interiorización', *Actual Narrativa Latinoamericana* (Havana: Casa de las Américas, 1970), pp. 149–87.

—— *Grotesco, inmigración fracaso* (Buenos Aires: Corregidor, 1973)

Wallon, Henri, 'Post-scriptum en réponse à M. Piaget', *Cahiers Internationaux de Sociologie*, X (1951).

Warner, Marina, *Alone of All her Sex. The Myth and the Cult of the Virgin Mary* (London: Weidenfeld & Nicholson, 1976).

—— *Monuments and Maidens. The Allegory of the Female Form* (London: Weidenfeld & Nicholson, 1985).

Weeks, Jeffrey, *Sexuality and its Discontents* (London: Routledge & Kegan Paul, 1985).

Williams, Raymond, *Towards 2000* (London: Chatto & Windus, 1983).

Wood, Michael, *America in the Movies* (London: Secker & Warburg, 1975).

Wright, Elizabeth, *Psychoanalytic Criticism. Theory in Practice* (London and New York: Methuen, New Accents, 1984).

Ynduráin, Francisco, *Galdós entre la novela y el folletín* (Madrid: Taurus, 1970).

Zazzo, René, *Psychologie et Marxisme. La Vie et l'œuvre d'Henri Wallon* (Paris: Denoël/Gonthier, 1975).

Index